MAY

CHRIST

LIFT

THEE UP

MAY CHRIST LIFT THEE UP

TALKS FROM THE 1998
WOMEN'S CONFERENCE
SPONSORED BY BRIGHAM YOUNG
UNIVERSITY AND
THE RELIEF SOCIETY

DESERET BOOK COMPANY
SALT LAKE CITY, UTAH

Library of Congress Cataloging-in-Publication Data
  Women's Conference (1998 : Brigham Young University)
    May Christ lift thee up : selections from the 1998 Women's
  Conference.
      p.   cm.
    "Sponsored by Brigham Young University and the Relief Society."
    ISBN 1-57345-522-9
    1. Mormon women—Religious life—Congresses.   I. Brigham Young
  University.   II. Relief Society (Church of Jesus Christ of Latter-day
  Saints)   III. Title.
  BX8641.W73   1998
  248.8'43'088283—dc21   99-11518
                                                                              CIP

Printed in the United States of America
10   9   8   7   6   5   4   3   2   1

Contents

Becoming Righteous Leaders

Preface

The thirteenth in the series, this volume represents the prayers, insights, and living and learning of participants in the 1998 Women's Conference, sponsored jointly by Brigham Young University and the Relief Society of The Church of Jesus Christ of Latter-day Saints. The presenters were originally assigned their topics, but these sisters and brothers quickly made them their own. They allowed the conference theme, from Moroni 9:25, to guide and challenge them, with the result that all who listened were indeed lifted. For this book, the presenters worked with talented editors Dawn Hall Anderson, Dlora Hall Dalton, Susette Fletcher Green, Jennifer Adams, and Suzanne Brady, who have shared their desire to extend the reach of the conference by changing the medium from the spoken to the written word. The result is a labor of love.

As chair of the planning committee—an exceptional group of faithful, creative women who represent Brigham Young University, the Relief Society, and the community—I am grateful to each one who has contributed to this volume. We dreamed and planned the broad strokes of the conference, and the authors and editors filled in the intricate details to make this publication reflect not only the best of their thinking but also the spiritual lessons they learned along the way.

Our wish is that whether you attended the conference in person or are experiencing its spirit through the following selections, you will be buoyed up and sustained by these messages of hope, humanity, endurance, and faith.

Kathy D. Pullins
Chair, 1998 Women's Conference

"May Christ Lift Thee Up"

VIRGINIA H. PEARCE

"My son, be faithful in Christ; and may not the things which I have written grieve thee, to weigh thee down unto death; but may Christ lift thee up, and may his sufferings and death, and the showing his body unto our fathers, and his mercy and long-suffering, and the hope of his glory and of eternal life, rest in your mind forever" (Moroni 9:25).

I hope you won't mind if we delay talking about that verse for a while. I'd like to take you around the neighborhood, through some friendly streets and alleys, and then finally in the back door, where we'll meet up once again with Mormon and Moroni.

For our first detour, let me take you back three or four years ago to a spring morning. I was driving to work down South Temple Street in Salt Lake City. The sun was shining; the world seemed fresh and alive; there were daffodils everywhere and lots of that vibrant new green that we see only in the early spring. I was feeling good. It was one of those days when everything seemed to be right in my world. You know the kind of day. I was overwhelmed with love for my husband—he seemed particularly handsome and good; my children seemed like they were going to make it in the world. And they were nice people, too. We were all in good health; in fact, at that moment I felt extraordinarily healthy and strong. I thought about all of the wonderful people—friends, neighbors, associates at work—who made my world so good. My thoughts went to the day ahead. Yes, it was going to be a good one. There was work ahead that I felt I could do—work that was satisfying and interesting and that

Virginia H. Pearce, former first counselor in the Young Women General Presidency, received a master's degree in social work from the University of Utah. She and her husband, Dr. James R. Pearce, are the parents of six and the grandparents of seven.

might even make a difference. I'm telling you, the cheerfulness in my car was almost edible!

Yet even as I was reviewing how great my life was, part of me was looking on saying, *What's going on here? None of the hard data in your life has changed that much, and yet everything seems wonderfully better this morning than it was last week!* My analytical nature surfaced: *Maybe the biorhythms are peaking; perhaps there has been a sudden change in serotonin levels; maybe I created extra endorphins on my morning walk.* Anyway, even as I looked for ways to explain it (I didn't really care how it happened), the daffodils were catching the sun, and I was happy. Arriving at the office a little early that morning—isn't that what you would do on a practically perfect day?—I even had time to leaf through my scriptures.

Now, let me interrupt this happy picture and take you to a different scene. This is one a friend described to me. On this particular morning she lay in a psychiatric hospital at the bottom point of a terrible battle with an emotional illness. The war had exhausted her. She lay there thinking that she no longer knew herself. All of the talents, characteristics, and abilities she had developed over her life seemed to have fled. The things she had done in the past no longer brought meaning. Her husband, children, parents, and friends were in tatters. Prayer, scriptures, blessings—nothing seemed to help. She said the image that came to her so forcefully that morning was of a tree stump, cut off at ground level, all of the living branches gone, a maimed and broken thing.

I have been thinking of my daffodil day—and also of that tree stump. Is there a symbol, or a sign, or an idea that is so fundamental to life that it would speak to both of those days?

The ankh is a symbol common in Egyptian art. It is simple and beautiful. The ankh is called the sign of life, the symbol of life, or sometimes the key of life. We know little about its meaning anciently until the period of the Coptic Christians, when we begin to see it take more of the form and meaning of the cross.

I have told you that on that spring morning I reached for my scriptures, still thinking of my incredible sense of well-being, and started paging through the Topical Guide, stopping on the word *cheer*. As I read through the sentence stubs, I was surprised by a pattern:

"Be of good cheer: it is I" (Mark 6:50).

"Be of good cheer, little children" (D&C 61:36).

"Be of good cheer, for I will lead you along" (D&C 78:18).

"Be of good cheer; I have overcome the world" (John 16:33).

That touched a chord. Everything about my morning became an expression of gratitude to the Savior: the spring morning spoke of him, eternal ties and family relationships spoke of him, my health, strength, work—all found meaning because of him.

Now to my friend in the hospital. She said, "My mind wasn't working right, and so I was unable to get the daily reassurance that you depend on to feel good. But even without that normal reassurance, as I saw the image of the stump, I was aware of the roots. Somehow, I knew that I still had roots and that there would be growth again someday. I knew that the time would come when I would look back and see this impaired time almost like Rip Van Winkle. I knew my mind wasn't working right. But even as I knew that, I could feel those roots alive— somewhere very, very deep underground."

"Lift up your head and be of good cheer" (3 Nephi 1:13).

"Be of good cheer, and do not fear, for I the Lord am with you" (D&C 68:6).

Jesus Christ. Our sign of life, our key to life in all of its majestic and meaningful simplicity, is Jesus Christ. He fits every door, every life experience, every death experience that any mortal can possibly encounter. He is the undergirding of the daffodil days, the root which teams with the hope of life, even when it has been pruned to the ground. He stands as the fountain in ancient times as well as today. He is our key to life. He is the light and the life.

If he is the key, how can we most simply express that key in terms of us, in terms of what we feel and think and do? Again, the simplicity of his life showed us the way. He said, "This is the gospel which I have given unto you—that I came into the world *to do the will of my Father*" (3 Nephi 27:13; emphasis added).

If I could borrow a simple phrase—not even a complete sentence, but just the heart of a sentence—to express the key of life in practical everyday language for us, I would use this phrase, written by Alice T. Clark in her article on humility in the *Encyclopedia of Mormonism*: to "joyfully, voluntarily, and quietly submit one's whole life to the Lord's will."[1]

This phrase seems to me so basic. Like the ankh, it is beautiful in its clean and simple design. It cannot be spoken without a deep and complete faith in Christ and his doctrine. And the speaking of it weds that faith to its partner, agency. When we gathered in that council in heaven, before the foundation of this world, and heard the plan in all of its simple beauty, we understood about our need for faith as well as the importance of our Father's gift to us: agency. And we understood about the central and saving role of our Elder Brother. I'm sure it seemed wonderful in its simplicity to us then, just as it does now.

Everything since that premortal experience persuades and calls for us to exercise faith in Christ, using our agency to choose him and his ways.

Scriptural . . . synonyms give rich and deep meaning to this phrase: "spiritually . . . born of God" (Alma 5:14).

"To take upon them [his] name . . . , and always remember him" (D&C 20:77).

To "love God with all your might, mind and strength" (Moroni 10:32).

"An eye single to the glory of God" (D&C 4:5).

"That . . . we shall be like him" (Moroni 7:48).

To offer "a broken heart and a contrite spirit" (2 Nephi 2:7).

I love the picture of the charming little girl on the Mary Engelbreit greeting card, her heart in outstretched hands and the caption reading "Here!"[2]

If, in fact, we do choose to submit our whole lives joyfully, voluntarily, and quietly to the Lord's will, what are some things that will follow? What will some of the immediate and natural outcomes be?

We will live our covenants, because living them is a happy choice. Covenants are not restrictive burdens; they are offerings joyfully made. We will strive to live covenants within that glorious cycle of repentance and growth. "I delight to do thy will, O my God: yea, thy law is within my heart" (Psalm 40:8).

Let me tell you about my friend Pat Pinegar, Primary General President. One day we were in a meeting together. There was a long and belabored discussion about sexual morality, particularly concerning young people. We were discussing their vulnerability and the tragic results of sin, but most of all we were talking about how to convince them to obey the law of chastity. Why would they want to remain chaste, against the flow of the world and their natural desires? There were many voices, lots of ideas, and then Sister Pinegar said, "I don't understand all of this. It seems so simple. Why don't we teach them to obey just because they love Heavenly Father?"

Stops you short, doesn't it?

4

There was an extended silence in the meeting. Sister Pinegar is one who constantly strives to submit her whole life to God's will. Certainly a life lived with that motivation would be a covenant-keeping life—and a much simpler life.

Another implication: *Our accountability to God will be clearer, and our scrambling to meet the expectations of everyone else will be muted.* That seems to bring sweet relief, doesn't it? One of the difficult things about life can be all of the conflicting expectations of others. Everyone needs help; everyone has an idea of who we should be and what we should do. What if we have submitted our life to God's will? Then we receive direction from him and answer to him. Not that we won't accommodate and help others. Of course we will be doing that constantly. He has told us that we are to help and serve one another, but how, where, when, etc., will be answered in the peaceful corners of our hearts—between him and us.

Sister Marjorie Hinckley recently said: "We each do the best we can. My best may not be as good as your best, but it's my best. The fact is that we know when we are doing our best and when we are not. If we are not . . . it leaves us with a gnawing hunger and frustration. But when we do our level best, we experience peace."[3]

Yes, when we have joyfully, voluntarily, and quietly submitted our whole lives to the Lord's will, we will not have the burden of judging ourselves or others by an outward checklist. We can never judge the inward righteousness of another. What if someone looking at my friend in the psychiatric ward condemned her for failing to do her church work, for failing to adequately care for her family, for contributing so little to her neighborhood? What if we condemned her, not knowing that in a very real and heart-wrenching way, she was doing her best by waiting upon the Lord's will and that her holding onto the image of a root that will send forth shoots again—that simple thought—was a heroic expression of faith and agency?

Think about the Relief Society sister who seems energetically and consistently to stretch the hours of the day to serve family, church, and community. Loaves of bread, enthusiasm, and perfect visiting teaching records pour out of her front door. But we can't judge her, either. Are these things expressions of her faith and choice to align her will with the Lord's? They may be—or they may not be. Elder Dallin H. Oaks taught us about the different motivations for service. He said there are

"selfish and self-centered . . . reasons for service" that are "unworthy of Saints." There are "those who serve out of fear of punishment or out of a sense of duty." "Although [these] undoubtedly qualify for the blessings of heaven, there are still higher reasons for service."[4] Elder Oaks then taught us that the highest reason for service is out of a pure love of Christ.

Paul taught the same lesson about service: "Not with eyeservice, as menpleasers; but as the servants of Christ, doing the will of God from the heart; with good will doing service, as to the Lord, and not to men" (Ephesians 6:6–7).

What a relief! We don't have to judge ourselves or another against an incredibly long list. We are plainly and simply accountable to the Lord and to ourselves. President Gordon B. Hinckley expressed this accountability in a recent general conference address: "The work in which we are engaged is their work [meaning the Father and the Son], and we are their servants, who are answerable to them." In another talk he reminded us that it doesn't matter what others think of us: "How we regard ourselves is what is important."[5]

This accountability frees us each night, using the words of President Brigham Young, to "review the acts of the day, repent of our sins, . . . and say our prayers; then we can lie down and sleep in peace until the morning, arise with gratitude to God, commence the labors of another day, and strive to live the whole day to God and nobody else."[6]

Which brings us to the next implication: *We will view our daily, temporal tasks and duties differently—as offerings, not as repetitive or meaningless drudgery.* It seems that every task I do—be it visiting teaching, carpooling, solving problems in the workplace, changing diapers, writing memos, making arrangements on the telephone—becomes ennobled if I do it in the spirit of an offering to God. Throughout the ages, humankind has been confused about what giving one's life to God really means—what it looks like. Some have thought it means renouncing physical comfort—wearing scratchy clothes and sleeping on hard floors. Others have thought it means drawing away from earning a living or handling the things of the world, retreating from people and entangling relationships—particularly intimate family ones that require so much thought and care.

One of the startling and happy truths of the Restoration is the truth about the relationship between the temporal and the spiritual. President

Brigham Young said: "If I am in the line of my duty, I am doing the will of God, whether I am preaching; praying, laboring with my hands for an honorable support; whether I am in the field, mechanic's shop, or following mercantile business, or wherever duty calls, I am serving God as much in one place as another. . . . In the mind of God there is no such a thing as dividing spiritual from temporal . . . , for they are one in the Lord."[7]

Something about our mortal life says that we cannot just give our lives to God in our hearts and then withdraw from daily living. Our temporal tasks become an expression of and a builder of our commitment to him.

Elder Henry B. Eyring illustrates this point with a story about his father, also named Henry Eyring. I will use Elder Eyring's words, because they carry the heart and meaning so beautifully:

"[My father] once told [this story] to me with the intention of chuckling at himself. . . . To appreciate this story, you have to realize that it occurred when he was nearly eighty and had bone cancer. He had bone cancer so badly in his hips that he could hardly move. The pain was great. . . .

"An assignment was given to weed a field of onions, so Dad [as the high councilor in charge of the stake farm] assigned himself [as well as others] to go work on the farm."[8]

When others who were with Brother Eyring that day told his son about it, they said that his father's pain was terrible. Brother Eyring couldn't kneel because of his hips and went painstakingly up and down the rows, pulling himself along on his stomach—smiling, laughing, and talking as they all worked together in the field of onions.

Quoting Elder Eyring again: "Now, this is the joke Dad told me on himself afterward. He said . . . after all the work was finished and the onions were all weeded, someone said to him, 'Henry, good heavens! You didn't pull those weeds, did you? Those weeds were sprayed two days ago, and they were going to die anyway.'

"Dad just roared. He thought that was the funniest thing. . . . He had worked through the day in the wrong weeds. They had been sprayed and would have died anyway. . . .

"I asked him, 'Dad, how could you make a joke out of that? How could you take it so pleasantly?' He said something to me that I will never forget. . . . He said, 'Hal, I wasn't there for the weeds.'"

And then Elder Eyring turns to us and speaks: "Now, you'll be in an onion patch much of your life. So will I. It will be hard to see the powers of heaven magnifying us or our efforts. It may even be hard to see our work being of any value at all. And sometimes our work won't go well.

"But you didn't come for the weeds. You came for the Savior."[9]

Do you hear our simple key? "Joyfully, voluntarily, quietly . . . "

The next implication of our simple key is this: *We will live nobly, on a higher plane, because we will constantly think above our own individual needs.*

Sometimes it is easier to recognize a lack of nobility than it is to recognize nobility. For that reason I will tell you of my less-than-noble conduct one afternoon. I was in a neighborhood store, waiting for my turn and chatting with a neighbor in line next to me. Somehow the name of a mutual acquaintance came up—actually someone we both like very much but who is quite eccentric. My neighbor told a funny story about her; that reminded me of another funny story; she topped that one . . . Pretty soon we were laughing uproariously. Out of the corner of my eye I saw the clerk listening to us. It startled me into a recognition of what I was doing. I should have stopped. I didn't. But as I finished my transaction and walked to the car, I was overwhelmed with my smallness. They weren't mean or slandering stories, but I would have been ashamed if the subject of our stories had overheard us. I was so uncomfortable that I had to return later and apologize to the clerk as well as express my shame to my neighbor. Most of all, I had to let the Lord know that I knew that kind of behavior was wrong and I needed forgiveness. Nobility is a correlate of devotion to the Lord.

Justice Potter Stewart is an associate justice of the Supreme Court. He defined ethics in the following way: "Knowing the difference between what you have a right to do, and what is the right thing to do."[10]

That's a good one to think about, even memorize. "Knowing the difference between what you have a right to do, and what is the right thing to do." Quite often we have a right to lash out, to retaliate and to punish. But is it the right thing to do?

Nobility suggests that even when we receive injury, we refuse to seek petty revenge. We may seek to right a wrong, but revenge is another story. We desire to rise above our side of the story, to absorb pain and choose not to pass it on. Isn't that what the Savior did?

Next point: *We will never be truly victimized by our failures, adverse circumstances, or the bad choices of other people. Equally important, we will not be victimized by success.* Now, how could that be?

Even though our performance is uneven and awkward, there is something that we can count on as we come to Him in humility and submissiveness. It is that every event, every task that we are a party to, can be made to benefit our souls. That is a stunning thought, isn't it? Given the natural way, there are so many things that we do or that we are victims of that could hurt our souls. Only God, through the intervention of his Son, can change, in a miraculous way we don't understand, how things will affect us.

"Pray always, and not faint; that ye must not perform any thing unto the Lord save in the first place ye shall pray unto the Father in the name of Christ, that he will consecrate thy performance unto thee, that thy performance may be for the welfare of thy soul" (2 Nephi 32:9).

The Savior can turn negative things to our good. Rather than bitterness, when we turn to him, we can forgive. Then, our own suffering can help us develop the capacity to withhold judgment and to reach out compassionately to others who suffer.

Turning to the Savior can also protect us against our successes. We see every day evidence of how success can result in destroying a person's soul. The media holds up lives ruined by success. What if, on a daffodil day, we really, really think that all of the good things in our lives are there because we are simply so smart, so talented, so effective that everything we enjoy comes as a direct result of our work and brains?

Do you see my point? Pride and egotism injure a soul as surely as do the bitterness and pain of affliction and failure. Success is an affliction to the soul unless it is recognized for what it is—God's working in our lives. With success, as well as adversity, we pray that our performance will be consecrated for the welfare of our souls. And he will do that, because each prayer we offer will somehow be an expression that we are joyfully, voluntarily, and quietly desiring to give our lives to him. Then desperate days refine us rather than destroy us. And daffodil days become days of worship and gratitude rather than days of pride and boasting.

Another dimension: *We will live with the security that our real needs will be met and that we will be fully able to do our part in meeting the real needs of others.*

Not long ago our youngest child and only son—in a suit, missionary nametag on his lapel—waved as he disappeared into the plane that would drop him off in the Chile Santiago North Mission—only another hemisphere away! You know this story. I went home with that big hole in my stomach and went about my life, trying not to think of him every single minute. Well, about nine days had passed, and I was beginning to check on the mailbox more than once a day. On Thursday morning came a telephone call. A gentle man with a Spanish accent introduced himself. He said that his wife had been in sacrament meeting in Santiago the Sunday before, and our son, who had been assigned to their ward, was asked to introduce himself and bear his testimony. After the meeting she had offered to deliver a letter from him to his family, because she was leaving for general conference in Salt Lake City the following week.

You can imagine that I wasted no time in driving to the hotel to meet these good people. How do I describe that little exchange? I have just told you that you can't always judge who the people are who have joyfully, voluntarily, and quietly given their lives to the Lord. Well, I could tell with these two. The conversation between Sister Jaramillo and me was in two different languages—her husband translated as we spoke a few words. She told me that her youngest son was in the Missionary Training Center on his way to Phoenix. She told me that she had met my son and that he was a very humble missionary. And then she reached out to me and spoke gentle Spanish words. Her husband followed: "My wife is telling you that she will take good care of your son." That took two Kleenexes to wipe up. Actually, it took all I had to prevent myself from making gasping noises as she handed me the letter. I told her that I wouldn't be in Phoenix to take care of her son but that I would pray for him.

I walked out of that hotel lobby with such a feeling of peace and comfort.

What do I really expect she could or should do for James? Stop by his apartment once a week, write him notes, cheer him up with periodic pep talks, bake cookies? No. Not at all. In fact, I doubt that she will need to do anything. Then why should I feel so good? The security I feel is rooted in her devotion to the Lord's will, because that means that if my son does have some real need, the Lord will know of it and Sister Jaramillo is at least one person in that city who would unhesitatingly respond when prompted by the Lord.

I cannot tell you the security and gratitude I feel for each of you who kneels and offers herself to the Lord. You are the ones whom he will direct to teach my grandchildren, who answer the needs of my married children, who invite my missionary daughter to dinner, whom carry letters home to an anxious mother, who work respectfully beside my husband. You don't need to do everything all of the time for every member of my family. But I know that if you have given yourself to do the Lord's will, you will do the right thing at the right time.

I love you.

Another implication as we use this simple key: *We will be assured success.*

This is a personal metaphor, but it helps me understand the power of guaranteed success. I hate to shop. Did I say that strongly enough? I *hate* to shop. I have very little skill and so have very limited success. And besides, I don't have good feet. Anyway, one day one of my daughters and I were shopping. She needed a particular piece of clothing for a particular occasion that would make her look close to spectacular. All this for a reasonable amount of money. Is that the worst formula? We started out in the morning full of energy and hope. But by early afternoon, we were dragging in and out of the dressing rooms. Her hair was full of static, my feet hurt, we were hungry, and we were getting grouchy. And then we had a startling idea. If we knew, absolutely guaranteed *knew*, that at the end of the afternoon we would have found the perfect dress, would it make any difference to how we felt now? We inventoried—the hair, the feet, the hunger, the discouragement—and we said unhesitatingly yes! We could easily go another three hours, *if* we knew there was unequivocal success ahead. And so we simply told ourselves that we were going to find the outfit—and, I am amazed to tell you, it worked! We were laughing and talking again instead of whining and dragging.

Could it be the same with life? Do we get exhausted because we quit believing that success is assured? You know, it is! In the sooner and later context, it might not be sooner, but it will *for sure* be later.

"Thy God shall stand by thee forever and ever" (D&C 122:4). "And the world passeth away and the lust thereof: but he that doeth the will of God abideth forever" (1 John 2:17). "He that endureth in faith and doeth my will, the same shall overcome, and shall receive an inheritance upon the earth when the day of transfiguration shall come" (D&C 63:20).

There must be dozens more implications, but I will only mention one more: *We will expect to have to make this choice many, many times.* Our ongoing responsibility is to keep offering ourselves and everything that we have and are to Him—to work actively but to cease judging each task with our mortal measurements. This is the great paradox of the gospel: In the total giving away, we receive total abundance, the only total security available. When we submit voluntarily and joyfully, far from being passive victims, we become victors, because we have accepted a partnership with an all-powerful and all-loving Being.

We aren't in the onion patch for the weeds. We are here for him. We are here with him.

Now I've worn you out. Surely we must be at the back door. Let's walk through it and sit in the living room for a last moment with Moroni 9:25. Mormon writes his final letter (at least the last one we have) to his son Moroni. He describes the "horrible scene" (v. 20), the "depravity of my people" (v. 18), who are "without order and without mercy" (v. 18), "strong in their perversion" (v. 19), "brutal, sparing none" (v. 19). "But behold, my son, I recommend thee unto God, and I trust in Christ that thou wilt be saved" (v. 22); and then our verse:

"My son, be faithful in Christ; and may not the things which I have written grieve thee, to weigh thee down unto death; but may Christ lift thee up, and may his sufferings and death, and the showing his body unto our fathers, and his mercy and long-suffering, and the hope of his glory and of eternal life, rest in your mind forever" (v. 25).

It doesn't matter what time we live in: the time of Mormon (A.D. 421), the 1950s (doesn't everyone talk about what a good time that was?), or this very day. It doesn't matter whether we are talking about a difficult individual environment or a sin-filled culture. The only thing that provides real lifting—lifting beyond mortality and all of its chaos and troubles, beyond our own weaknesses and sins and changing fortunes, beyond our own pain and suffering and success—the only real lifting comes through our Savior and Redeemer, Jesus Christ.

Daffodils do bring gladness. Healthy, happy children cause our hearts to sing. Balanced brain chemistry and physical health maximize our enjoyment of this world. Rides in convertibles, picnics in a pine-scented forest, shelter during the cold storms of winter—these are delights I wouldn't want to have missed. Economic security lightens our load of worry. Attentive husbands and the warmth of good friends bring contentment. Accomplishment, a job well done, music, art, an exquisitely written piece of literature—yes, there are so many things that lift in happy ways, but if some of these, if all of these, were to evaporate, to be snatched away from us, cut off at ground level, we could still count on Christ: the one who did only the will of his Father, the co-creator of all that is good, the one who knows every soul—the sick, the oppressed, the gifted, the gorgeous, the abused, the charismatic, the brilliant, as well as the bumbling and stumbling soul who can't seem to make anything work. Yes, you and me. He knows us. He not only knows us but loves us so much that the focus of his mortal and heavenly life is us. His simple key is a statement about us: "This is my work and my glory—to bring to pass the immortality and eternal life of man" (Moses 1:39). He suffered himself to be lifted up upon the cross that we might be lifted up, back to our Father, clothed with immortality and eternal life. And our part is easy, as simple in design as the Egyptian ankh. In faith, each of us takes the only thing we really have—our agency—and offers it back to him joyfully, voluntarily, and quietly.

NOTES

1. *Encyclopedia of Mormonism*, ed. Daniel H. Ludlow, 4 vols. (New York: Macmillan, 1992), 2:663; verb tense changed.
2. Used by permission.
3. As quoted in *Church News*, 18 April 1998.
4. Dallin H. Oaks, *Ensign*, November 1984, 14.
5. Gordon B. Hinckley, *Ensign*, May 1998, 71, 4.
6. *Brigham Young*, Teachings of Presidents of the Church Series (Salt Lake City: The Church of Jesus Christ of Latter-day Saints, 1997), 25.
7. *Brigham Young*, 22.
8. Henry B. Eyring, *To Draw Closer to God* (Salt Lake City: Deseret Book, 1997), 101.
9. Eyring, *To Draw Closer to God*, 101–2.
10. As quoted in Rex E. Lee, "Honesty and Integrity," address delivered at Brigham Young University, Provo, Utah, 5 September 1995.

Meditation and Mediation: Finding and Offering the Savior's Peace

KATHY D. PULLINS

Meditation and *mediation*, two words distinguished only by a *T*. When I first began thinking about those two terms, I immediately sensed a strong connection between them. My thinking and research led me to spend quite a bit of time exploring them as separate concepts and exercises. Then I looked for linkage between the two, only to discover that the connection is almost as close as their spelling. Quite simply, we meditate to draw closer to our Heavenly Father; we are able to do so because of the mediation of our Redeemer between us and the Father. Then, when we have gathered peace and inspiration from that process, we commit ourselves to follow the Savior's example. That can lead us, when we observe conflict, to offer to mediate and thus offer peace to others.

So, how do we become such a conduit for peace? How do we effectively meditate, and what skills do we need to develop in order to mediate when given the opportunity? First, let's consider the quest for meditation that taps these divine resources.

Obviously, the turbulence and discontent of mortality does not offer peace. In recent years, the two days of Women's Conference have come to represent to me a refuge from the distraction and distortion of the

Kathy D. Pullins, chair of the 1998 Brigham Young University–Relief Society Women's Conference, is the assistant dean of the J. Reuben Clark Law School at BYU. She is a trained mediator and teaches alternative dispute resolution. She and her husband, Gary Pullins, are the parents of four sons. An avid baseball fan, she is also interested in step aerobics and gardening.

world. I leave here with a more peaceful soul. Consider the words of Moroni 9:25: "May Christ lift thee up, and may . . . the hope of his glory and of eternal life, rest in your mind forever." Focus for a moment on the last five words of that verse: "rest in your mind forever." I think that the verb *rest* is used to convey more than a mere "settling in" or "finding of place." It speaks of peace and acceptance of Christ's mission. Mormon writes his precious son, Moroni, a heartfelt letter in which he acknowledges the sin-laden, "past-feeling" world they live in. Yet, even against this tortured backdrop, Mormon admonishes his son to be faithful, believing, and strong. He wishes for Moroni (and for each of us as we read his words and are taught) meaningful understanding of the Savior's atoning sacrifice. This understanding allows peace to rest within us despite external turmoil. It's the type of rest mentioned in Doctrine and Covenants 43:34—"Let the solemnities of eternity rest upon your minds"—that Mormon wishes for each of us. And, at times, we must rest and not be anxious as the Lord's timing unfolds; for in Psalm 37:7, David urges us to "rest in the Lord, and wait patiently for him."

In today's self-help literature, the soul is a popular topic. Best-sellers instruct us in how to care for our souls, how to discover peace and the sacred in our everyday lives. Meditation can be defined as such an exercise of the soul. But in the context of the gospel, the definition is expanded and deepened: 2 Nephi 4:15 instructs us that one of the things that delights our souls is the study of the scriptures. In addition, President Brigham Young stressed that our "first and foremost duty [is] seeking unto the Lord our God until we open the path of communication from heaven to earth—from God to our own souls."[1]

Meditation is that communication that accesses peace. It is that soul-searching, reflecting, pondering contemplation that President James E. Faust encouraged at the general Young Women's meeting in March 1998 when he urged those beautiful young daughters of God to "hold your soul very still, and listen to the whisperings of the Holy Spirit. Follow the noble, intuitive feelings planted deep within your souls by Deity in the previous world."[2]

Are you concerned with the comparison of our lives of perpetual motion to stillness? I am. What do I need to learn about stillness and its relationship to establishing a loving, replenishing relationship with our Father in Heaven? The scriptures hold the answers as they also urge us to practice stillness. Psalm 46:10 and Doctrine and Covenants 101:16

command us to "be still, and know that I am God." The kind of stillness that invites the Spirit to instruct us is one of quiet repose and focus. President David O. McKay has defined meditation as "the language of the soul." He points to our weekly recommitment to our baptismal covenants as we partake of the sacrament and speak our daily private prayers as times of meditation when we feel the "yearnings of the soul to reach out to feel the presence of God."[3] Similarly, Elder Franklin D. Richards concludes that meditation includes thinking, planning, analyzing, praying, and fasting.[4]

I am comforted by these definitions, because, like many other things I've learned in the gospel, I had supposed that meditation was a finished state; but the yearnings President McKay and Elder Richards describe sound more like a process, an ongoing effort. When we seek to feel the presence of God, we are not often able to leave behind our responsibilities to climb to a mountaintop and breathe in the quiet of wooded silence or spend a day at a deserted beach on an outcropping of rock, meditating and communing with God. This may not yet be our season for stillness and aloneness; so, in our need now, we must search for soulful peace and discover it en route—we must order our meditation "to go." Until we have the time and the setting to shut out the world's interference and renew and refresh, how can we be still—at least momentarily—and gather peace? What can allow us—if only for an instant—to meditate, to recharge our souls?

I have two pictures I see nearly every day on my beaten path that inspire such meditation in me. One is a photograph I took some years ago on my first trip back East. It was a beautiful summer day, and as I followed the path down from Thomas Jefferson's beloved Monticello, I came around a bend and was suddenly overcome by the beauty of the scene just in front of me. Standing amid the lush greenness, dappled by summer sunlight, I was struck by beauty and a Sacred Grove kind of reverence. My soul was captivated by the scene, and I knew I needed to "be still" as the scriptures direct; I could almost hear the Lakota tribal saying admonish me: "The trail is beautiful. Be still." I wanted to capture those feelings, to carry them with me from that place and access them when my heart and mind were unfocused and in need of peace. When I remembered I had my camera with me, I decided to take a couple of pictures. I am not an expert photographer—I'm known in our family for being spatially inept. When I point the camera at a scene, somehow I manage to get the focal point, usually a group of people, off-center while I preserve for posterity the blank wall above their heads. As a result, I had little confidence that, once developed, the pictures would communicate any part of what the actual experience had meant to me. Surprisingly and blessedly, the picture did turn out, and every time I look at it, it speaks peace and replenishment to my soul.

Another reminder of the source of true peace in this life is a picture of the Savior by Gary Kapp that hangs above the stairs in our home. If I lift my eyes as I race down from my bedroom towards the front door, I see this portrayal of my Redeemer, the bearer of truth and light to a darkening world. In an instant, this picture can remind me of his intercession for me with my Father. It also instructs me about why I seek peace—not merely to achieve some inner level of being but that I might be a better servant, that I might offer peace as my Savior did and does.

What triggers our meditation, our own process of gathering peace as we move quickly through our day? One friend described the replenishment he feels while he is sculpting. When his hands are productively engaged in this familiar activity, his mind is left to meditate, to reflect and recommit to true principles. Another dear friend who has children who range from early elementary school to mission age told me, "The closest thing I practice to meditation happens when I'm in the car alone, usually on the way to pick someone up or to deliver someone somewhere else. I can have relative quiet and must sit still in my seat. Often, I utter a prayer as I drive, and I can feel a real connection to my Heavenly Father." Because this friend has, on many occasions, brought calmness and perspective to my troubled soul, I know she finds peace even on the go or she wouldn't have it to offer to me.

That brings me to the reason we meditate to seek peace: so we can be instruments in the Lord's hands in giving peace to our sisters and brothers. Thomas à Kempis, a German author of religious texts who lived in the late fourteenth and early fifteenth centuries, taught that we cannot offer what we do not have; thus, we must keep peace within ourselves before we can give it to others. When our hearts are aching and wounded by anger, where do we find solace and wholeness for our souls? Privately, lovingly, the peace comes from our Savior and Friend.[5]

Similarly, in John 14:27, the Savior offers peace that will soothe our troubled, fearful hearts; and two chapters later, in 16:33, he speaks of his peace in contrast to the tribulation of the world: "These things I have spoken unto you, that in me ye might have peace. In the world ye shall have tribulation: but be of good cheer; I have overcome the world."

The Savior knows our times, and he knows our hearts. He also understands the effect that such unrest can have upon our souls, and he offers perspective that allows us to find joy even amidst the tribulation. As we meditate, we seek inspiration; and the Holy Ghost seeks to convey the Savior's empathy and love. In our world filled with noise and motion, the Spirit will not shout to get our attention; we must allow its whisperings to get through to us. And what will the Spirit instruct us to do? To love and serve one another.

Thus, the reason the Lord urges us to draw near unto him through prayer and meditation is so we can speak and act in his name. He encourages us to strive for unity of purpose with Heavenly Father through him, to be "one in me as I am one in the Father, as the Father is one in me, that we may be one" (D&C 35:2). What we must seek to do, then, is to take the peace, the connection with the divine, the understanding that we have of Heavenly Father's love for us because of our Savior's atoning and mediating acts; and, in an unbroken line, extend that love and accompanying peace to others.

President Merrill J. Bateman commented not long ago that meditation and mediation are one and the same to the Lord. His comment reminded me of Doctrine and Covenants 59:23: "But learn that he who doeth the works of righteousness shall receive his reward, even peace in this world, and eternal life in the world to come." Our service, if offered in righteousness, with "love unfeigned" (2 Corinthians 6:6), becomes a kind of meditation in that it draws us closer to God and replenishes the peace within our souls.

Service offers a way to bring peaceful resolution to the inevitable conflicts in our lives and the lives of others. The Beatitudes affirm that "blessed are the peacemakers: for they shall be called the children of God" (Matthew 5:9). In a general conference session in 1930, Elder Hyrum G. Smith urged all members of the Church to increase their efforts toward peacemaking. "We should all be peacemakers, every one of us, first with ourselves, in our homes, and then with our neighbors. I bespeak for you, my brethren and sisters, a further degree of energy and diligence in the preparation for peace in our own homes and in our own hearts."[6]

What is mediation, and what are the skills of a mediator, a peacemaker, who is seeking to follow the Savior's example? How do we acquire and hone these skills and then effectively apply them in our spheres of influence?

Mediation can be defined globally, academically, or by context. In a broad sense, it is a win-win solution, the opportunity to be creative and to promote the healing of relationships in conflict. In the world of legal education, mediation is classified as one of the alternatives to mainstream dispute resolution or, in other words, litigation. It is a process for resolving disputes outside the courtroom that uses the presence and skills of a neutral third party to create a safe environment, to help the parties identify and discuss their needs and interests, and to facilitate the creation of possible solutions that serve well all who are affected.

In addition, mediation is a family member bringing together two cousins who have quarreled and have been avoiding one another and encouraging them to truly listen to each other. It is the sixth-grader who sees a problem at recess and gets a warring group of fourth-graders cooperating on the playground again. It is the elderly woman who cares enough about her neighbors to risk a few moments of discomfort to get them talking to each other about how they will get on with life after a dispute between their children.

Although the process may not be formally labeled "mediation," we are all involved in facilitating and healing. When I think of my toughest mediations, I recall one that occurred before I had read any theory on mediation or received the skills training to mediate. The parties were my husband, an avid baseball fan and coach, and our oldest son, who was about seven years old at the time. Gary had always assumed that his sons—due to both genetics and environment (and brainwashing)—would love the game of baseball as much as he always had. When, after one year of T-ball, Travis announced to his dad and me that he'd really rather be part of a children's performing group, I could see we had a clash of interests and expectations. They needed a mediator, and I happened to be the closest (and only) one available. Through a few "perspective" comments, I was able to facilitate their truly listening to and even empathizing with each other. They took it from there, because their relationship was more important than the opinions they held in conflict. I'm happy to report that, lo these many years later, Travis continues to prefer dancing to double plays (although he's an avid supporter of his dad's and brothers' teams), and Gary has actually learned to appreciate the performing arts.

Jim Holbrook, a friend who is an experienced mediator, has commented on this focus on relationships and the effect that conflict can have upon them. He says, "Resolution is healing. When you are in conflict, the world is out of kilter, you are miles apart, and you cannot help each other reassemble the known universe. Achieving resolution helps you restore your balance, mend your relationship, get what you both need, and make you whole again."

When our world spins out of orbit, we more fully appreciate the need for healing. That description of the loss of our bearings can apply to disputes in many contexts, whether they be business, government, neighborhood, or family; it is definitely true of our closest interpersonal relationships. The scriptures admonish us to "come now, and let us reason together" (Isaiah 1:18), to avoid contention and strife; however, rather than instructing us *never* to disagree with another person (which is humanly impossible), I feel this instruction and warning are advising us about the constructive tone and prospective focus that the resolving of these disagreements should have. To help others keep the process kind and forward-looking, we can ask a simple, essential question: "What would the Savior do in this instance?" The answer always includes a personal dedication to study both the divine model through prayer and the scriptures as well as the topic through research and experience. Thus we must invoke meditation—study, prayer, and pondering—*and* apply effort to become a conduit for peace, to mediate.

Over the past ten years, I've had the opportunity, in both formal and informal settings, to assist people in conflict. As I have observed them setting aside their pride, applying newly learned skills, and looking to a better future, I have glimpsed a tiny portion of the joy and satisfaction that the Savior must feel as he observes our progress toward peace.

As sisters and brothers in the gospel, we should work alongside one another in our homes and our wards and branches in a way that promotes mutual growth and progress. These same principles of promoting peace should also be applied beyond those circles to our neighborhoods and communities. When we encounter conflict and the potential destruction of relationships, we must be prepared to offer healing assistance through mediation.

Learning to be a good mediator involves the pursuit of both an art and a science. The art of it may involve some natural talent combined with humility that permits us to see people and their problems in an objective, constructive light. The science part of this effort requires study and practice that cultivate the following skills: impartiality, listening, understanding, questioning, reframing, raising doubts, making suggestions, directing the process, patience.

Impartiality involves resisting the urge to judge, remaining balanced and objective, and extending fairness and courtesy to all parties. If one or more parties feel that you are favoring one side, they will assume that they will not be dealt with evenly and will not invest themselves in the process.

Listening, really listening, to someone's story, is one of the most exhausting and most important exercises you'll ever engage in. Demonstrate empathy and make reflective statements that show you really understand what is being said.

Understanding seeks to know the personalities and backgrounds of the parties as well as the facts of the immediate conflict while showing concern for the feelings of those involved.

Questioning allows discovery by the mediator and the parties and should, therefore, be open ended and inclusive. Seek advice from the parties on a regular basis.

Reframing removes strong, emotional, or value-laden phrases and words and paraphrases the communication in neutral or positive language. For example, if a child says of his older brother, "Jared hates me and treats me like a baby! Whenever his friends are around, he doesn't know I'm alive!" your reframed comment could be, "You're feeling left out when Jared has his friends over to play." Working from this statement, the speaker would feel heard and his older brother could be pulled into joint problem-solving about how to deal with this situation in the future.

Raising doubts invites parties to move from the positions they're stuck in to examine their underlying interests. It also allows them to move to a place where they can begin to understand the interests of the other party.

Making suggestions primes the pump and invites the parties to engage in some creative brainstorming. As they do, they are more able to discover mutual interests and begin to collaborate on some possible solutions.

Directing the process sets a hopeful, positive tone and permits the parties to feel the security of an orderly, fair structure. It keeps the discussion focused on the problems rather than on the people and moving forward productively.

Patience is that genuine, unwavering confidence in the parties' ability to craft a fair solution. It provides a foundation that permits the parties to resolve their own conflict.

The New Testament is filled with instances of Jesus' masterfully using these skills to bring peace and instruction to his followers. In one instance, captured in the eighth chapter of John, he demonstrates his mastery of understanding, patience, raising doubts and reframing. Jesus fully understood the motivation of the scribes and Pharisees who brought the accused woman to him, and he knew the law that dictated her punishment. Drawing on the dusty ground as they badgered him, Jesus patiently endured their questioning of him and their reciting of Mosaic law. When he at last responded to their question of whether the woman should be stoned, he did so with a masterful reframing in verse 7: "He that is without sin among you, let him first cast a stone at her." After the accusers, forced to look in the dark corners of their own hearts, had dispersed, the Savior, in verse 10, gently questioned the woman, "Where are those thine accusers?" He had used these mediation skills to defuse a volatile conflict and invite learning and growth in those present at the time and in those of us reading these words so many centuries later.

Thus, as we seek to be instruments of peace, to establish a connection with our Heavenly Father through the atonement of Jesus Christ through meditation, this internal exercise must have external evidence. That is the reason for such soul searching and pondering, and it constitutes true worship. As we become peacemakers, our lives can become a form of prayer, of demonstrated devotion.

To help me remember how I can take inspiration, knowledge, and skills and put them into action by extending peace to others, the *T* that distinguishes the word *meditate* from the word *mediate* has become symbolic to me of the bridge between these two concepts. Five words that begin with a *T* serve as continual reminders to me to transfer the peace I find into efforts to assist others who seek it.

1. *Thanks* for all of our blessings from God should be expressed continually and openly. As we, through our meditation, become assured of Heavenly Father's awareness of us and his desire for our well-being that prompted him to offer his only Son to atone for our sins, we are filled

with gratitude and a desire to return that thanks. How can we offer thanksgiving to our Father and our Savior? By loving and serving one another. We are reminded in Mosiah 2:17 that when we serve our fellow beings, we serve our God. Offering peace to those who are troubled and weighed down by contention in their lives is a particular act of love and service.

We are all part of a great and eternal family, and we are charged—individually and collectively—with the opportunity and blessing of returning to our heavenly home. Last year, the six of us in our family could feel the pace of our individual lives accelerating with college, missions, callings, and work. As a result, we felt a need to have something specific to remind us of the eternal truths of the gospel that connect us. The result, after trial, error, editing, and much discussion, was a family mission statement. As I reread it recently, I was impressed that its application extends beyond our immediate family to our sisters and brothers everywhere. It reads, "We strive to show our unfailing love for and commitment to one another through an attitude of appreciation, honest communication, and selfless service that we may find laughter in each day of this life and be worthy in the next to return to our Heavenly Father together."

2. *Trust* in the inspiration and instruction you receive through the Spirit. As Psalm 37:3 exhorts, "Trust in the Lord, and do good." Follow his example, and bring your motivation and actions in line with his. Allow the Spirit to direct you in acquiring knowledge and skills that bring peace to those around you. Surrender yourself completely to the Savior's work; ask that his will be done, and mean it. Then, create an atmosphere that permits others—even those weighed down by conflict in their lives—to trust you to assist them in working through their problems and learning essential, even eternal, lessons from the process.

3. *Teachability,* or humility, is essential in the quest for peace. It permits a vulnerability, an open heart that invites change and growth both in ourselves and others. When Enos offered his lengthy, mighty prayer unto the Lord, he did so with complete humility. That humility caused him to turn from his guilt, to believe that his faith had made him whole, and to immediately begin to pray for the welfare of his brethren. Like Enos, we can earnestly seek, through prayer, to understand how to assist others. Frequently, when parties come to discuss their differences, they each have their own firm, predetermined plan for reaching their goals;

however, as a mediator, you can assist them in coming up with a third option, a better one, for meeting the needs and interests of both sides. When we are teachable, when we help others set aside pride that blocks out apology and selfishness that shuts down learning, our minds are enlightened, and we experience growth and can foster it in others.

4. *Temple* learning keeps our sights lifted and our souls renewed. When peace eludes us, when we are burdened and discouraged and, therefore, unable to serve others effectively, the experience of worshiping in the house of the Lord can right our thinking and allow truth and light to filter through; we cannot restrain them in that sacred place. One of the important truths we learn in the temple is the eternal connection between receiving enlightenment and offering service. The sacrifice spoken of in Mark 8:35—"For whosoever will save his life shall lose it; but whosoever shall lose his life for my sake and the gospel's, the same shall save it"—teaches us the divine irony that as we lose ourselves in service, we find the substance of our own souls.

Such is the mutual fulfillment, I've come to realize, that is the message of Mosiah 18:8–10: "And now, as ye are desirous to come into the fold of God, and to be called his people, and are willing to bear one another's burdens, that they may be light; yea, and are willing to mourn with those that mourn; yea, and comfort those that stand in need of comfort . . . " Since I joined the Church in Texas some twenty-plus years ago, that has been my favorite passage of scripture. As I was taught the truths of the gospel by two dedicated, earnest sister missionaries, I felt a kinship with those good people who were lined up at the Waters of Mormon to be baptized by the prophet Alma. I was transported back in time to experience with them their joy and their commitment to "bear one another's burdens." I viewed this as a one-way act, a demonstration of the depth of my belief and acceptance of gospel principles. I must be "strong" and lift the heavy load of a "weaker" brother or sister.

Not many years later, I needed to revisit the meaning I had attached to these scriptures. I am an only child, and when I was young, I chose to mow lawns for extra money rather than baby-sit. As a result, my understanding of the skills and patience required to care for children was just this side of nonexistent: I knew how to change a grass catcher but not a baby. And marriage came earlier in life for me than I had planned. Soon, as the mother of four active, inquisitive sons, I frequently felt overwhelmed. From that vantage point, the verses in Mosiah spoke to me differently. Because I was now frequently in need of perspective and lifting from others rather than being the one offering the lightening, I viewed the words of the scripture to mean that we, as brothers and sisters, take turns with the burden bearing. At times, I am in need, and you are able to lift part of my burden as we journey together; soon, our experiences will be reversed, and I can shoulder a portion of your load.

Lately, I've decided that the service Alma is instructing these new members of the Church to render goes even beyond such reciprocity. I have been struck by the mutually beneficial experience that true service, the kind worthy to be called charity, truly is. In our baptismal covenant, in which we promise to serve one another, we are committing ourselves beyond merely helping someone we see as weak or offering tools to fix someone else's problems. We must offer ourselves to serve with a purity born of following Christ's example. As Rachel Ramen Spring has said, fixing and helping may often be the work of the ego, but service is the work of the soul. Thus, Mosiah 18:8–10 is about serving and giving and, through this very same act, receiving blessings because we are following the Lord's way. That mutual service is the process by which we can simultaneously receive and offer equilibrium and peace.

5. *Truth*, wherever it is discovered, is embraced by the gospel of Jesus Christ. As the Savior revealed to Thomas in John 14:6: "I am the way, the truth, and the life: no man cometh unto the Father, but by me." His role as mediator between us and our Father in Heaven is enlivened by truth. As we seek to work past the deceptions, lies, and, most treacherous of all, half-truths that the adversary continually assaults us with, and assist our brothers and sisters to do the same, we must stay focused on eternal truths. Truth is our beacon and our homing device. It offers us security and peace when things seem to shift around us. As we embrace it, we claim our heritage as daughters and sons of God.

Elder Franklin D. Richards spoke in a general conference address in 1974 about why the Lord pronounces peacemakers to be "blessed": "The blessed part of being a peacemaker is that those who are peacemakers and who live the gospel principles receive a testimony borne of the Holy Ghost. They enjoy the peace that surpasseth all understanding, relief from inner tensions, joy and happiness, contentment, growth and development."[7] Such blessings are wonderful by-products of having our hearts and minds dedicated to mediating the conflicts of those around us.

If we seek to be instruments of peace in the Lord's hands, if we plead as David did in Psalm 19:14, "Let the words of my mouth, and the meditation of my heart, be acceptable in thy sight, O Lord, my strength, and my redeemer," he will make us fit for his service. When we yearn for understanding and inspiration, when our minds and hearts race and our souls reach out, our Heavenly Father truly "reaches [our] reaching."[8] What we currently have is substance enough if we will be still, submit, and be pliable. He will shape our hearts and refine our minds so that we can be pure instruments of peace in his hands. Then, as we are assured in Psalm 23:3, the Lord will restore our souls and lead us in the paths of righteousness for his name's sake. I pray that we may offer our whole souls, without a single hesitation or reservation, to the building of his peaceful kingdom.

NOTES

1. Brigham Young, *Discourses of Brigham Young*, sel. John A. Widtsoe (Salt Lake City: Deseret Book, 1954), 41.
2. James E. Faust, *Ensign*, May 1998, 97.
3. David O. McKay, Conference Report, April 1946, 113, 115.
4. Franklin D. Richards, Conference Report, October 1964, 76.
5. See *Hymns of The Church of Jesus Christ of Latter-day Saints* (Salt Lake City: The Church of Jesus Christ of Latter-day Saints, 1985), no. 129.
6. Hyrum G. Smith, Conference Report, October 1930, 111.
7. Franklin D. Richards, Conference Report, October 1974, 154.
8. *Hymns*, no. 129.

"I Can Do All Things through Christ"

VIRGINIA U. JENSEN

A few years ago a young boy was lost in a cave for several days. Searchers spent frantic hours trying to find him in the total blackness of the cave. Finally, he was found and brought to safety. It was learned that he had gotten separated from those with lights and had wedged himself into a crevice—not seeing anything or knowing which way to go. I tried to imagine what it would be like to be in total darkness. How terrifying and disorienting it would be!

This life experience we are all having can get pretty dark at times. I have been by the side of my elderly mother as she laid her husband of fifty years (my father) to rest and wondered how she could go on without him. I have been with my sister as she suffered the sudden, unexpected death of her eight-year-old son—her firstborn—and wondered, *How could this happen to such a lovely, lively boy?* I have listened to the pain of a woman who wanted desperately to be a mother and yet did not get the wish of her heart. I know single women who want to be married and have a family, and year after year find no realization of this desire. As I have visited with women all over the world, I have learned that no one is immune to sorrow and suffering of all kinds. In fact, I have come to realize that challenges and adversity, as Joseph Smith taught, are "at the core of saintliness" and are an integral part of God's plan for us.[1] When Joseph Smith was in Liberty Jail, he cried to the Lord for comfort, and

---

Virginia U. Jensen serves as first counselor in the Relief Society General Presidency. A homemaker, she and her husband, J. Rees Jensen, are the parents of four children and the grandparents of six. She has served in numerous volunteer and Church service missionary assignments and enjoys gardening, grandchildren, and family activities.

the Lord gave it to him, saying, "If the very jaws of hell shall gape open the mouth wide after thee, know thou, my son, that all these things shall give thee experience, and shall be for thy good" (D&C 122:7).

There is a lot of the "natural man" attitude in me, and there are times when I have thought, *This certainly does not feel like it's for my good.* Then I think of other women and what they have done. I think of Eve, for example. Her calling was to be the "mother of all living" (Genesis 3:20). A rather daunting task, don't you think? I have only four children, and yet there have been times when I have felt like "the mother of all living." And it's not as if she had a handbook to rely on! Yet she was steadfast and true, pushing on despite hardship and heartbreak. And in the end she "blessed the name of God" and "was glad, saying: Were it not for our transgression we never should have had seed, and never should have known good and evil, and the joy of our redemption, and the eternal life which God giveth unto all the obedient" (Moses 5:11–12).

I think also of Noah's wife, whose name is not recorded for us. Sometimes we forget that she must have stood by him during all the years of preaching and building, and I cannot even begin to imagine what housekeeping was like on the ark. And then, when they were once again on dry ground, she and her family began all over again. She, too, was a faithful daughter of God who endured and overcame by faith.

Surely all of us are moved by the fortitude and faithfulness of the women of the Restoration, whose calling it was to lay the foundations of the Church in the latter days. Many of them repeatedly sacrificed their homes in Kirtland, in Missouri, in Nauvoo, and elsewhere. They packed up their households and began again and again, with more than mortal courage.

Faithful women in every age have learned, "I can do all things through Christ which strengtheneth me" (Philippians 4:13).

In my backyard is an extensive rock garden with huge rocks. My grandchildren love to climb those rocks. For them, it is like mountain climbing because the rocks are so big and they are so small. One day five-year-old Will was scrambling up and down with relative ease, but his younger brother, James Patrick, who was only two at the time, was having a great deal of difficulty. The rocks were very large compared to his little two-year-old body. Now, James Patrick is a determined young man and was not about to give up, but he was making no progress, and his hands were getting scratched and beginning to bleed from his attempts. His knees got banged every time he slid back down a rock.

His wise and watchful mother was surveying the scene from the kitchen window. As she saw his frustration about to overtake him, she stepped outside and said, "You can do it, James Patrick. Keep trying. You can do it. I know you can." Spurred on by her words of encouragement, he gritted his teeth, made one more attempt, and got himself to the top. His mother went back into the house, and James Patrick played at the top of the yard for a while, where I was pulling weeds. When he decided he'd had enough and started to climb down, I heard him quietly whisper to himself as his foot started to slip, "I can do it. I can do it."

We live in a world filled with rocks of all sizes. It was created that way by divine design, as a proving ground for our faith and a vital step in our eternal progression. One of the great tasks of our mortal life is to learn that, through the grace and mercy of Jesus Christ, we can climb every rock, or overcome every challenge, that we encounter.

Some of the rocks in our lives are self-chosen. For example, most mothers would admit that their children can be both their greatest blessing and their greatest trial. Many of the things mothers slog through daily—fixing meals, doing laundry, running the perpetual carpool, helping with homework, sitting up late at night with sick babies or heartsick teenagers—are natural outgrowths of the choice to have children. It's not always convenient to be a mom, and it's certainly not always easy. Yet we would make that choice again if we were starting from scratch, rocky though it may be at times. Sometimes it helps to remind ourselves that we really wanted those children.

I remember when I was wheeled out of the delivery room after giving birth to my first child. I had two thoughts. The first was *Did anyone get the license number of the truck that just hit me?* The second was *Wow, my mother did this for me*. Suddenly I had an incredible increase in appreciation and love for my mother, and I realized I had a tremendous debt to repay her in love, respect, devotion, and service.

The same idea of self-chosen challenges applies to single women. I know many who have chosen professions that are rewarding, but I don't know one whose job is problem free. Climbing over rocks is part of the mortal experience.

Another mortal reality is that we will encounter in our earthly sojourn some climbs that we would not have chosen for ourselves, over rocks that leave our hands and knees scraped and bleeding. That will happen even to faithful, tithe-paying, temple-attending, scripture-reading, Homemaking-meeting-supporting, 100-percent-visiting-teaching Latter-day Saint women. In the words of Carlfred Broderick, "The gospel of Jesus Christ is not insurance against pain. It is [a] resource in [the] event of pain."[2]

My friend Chris Stevens, a beautiful young mother of six who lost her beloved husband to cancer two years ago, knows something of the resources available to those who trust in the Lord. "Never forget that the Lord sees the big picture," she writes. "Never, ever doubt how intricately the Lord can be involved in your life if you allow him. He knows exactly when and where to place the next piece in the puzzle of life to best complete the picture." Chris goes on to bear testimony of the Lord's loving, guiding hand in putting together puzzle pieces that made it possible for her young children to go on without their father. Here is one of the many faith-promoting incidents she relates:

"In the fall, just three weeks before his death, one of Robert's colleagues at work called to tell me of his concern and love for him. They all wanted to do something for Robert to help relieve his mind of concerns for his family. They had learned that we were in a new home that did not have any landscaping, and they wanted to put in our front yard. A couple of days later this same man called back to report that the response had been so good they would also be doing the side yard. The next day he called to say, 'Be ready for a lot of people to show up Saturday. We have enough sod coming to do your whole yard.' On Saturday, about seventy-five of Robert's coworkers and family members showed up ready to work. When they left three hours later our whole yard was sodded, tulip bulbs had been planted, a new lawn mower and weed eater had been put together, and there was money left over for trees."

Chris continues: "On Sunday, October 29, our oldest child, Ryan, had his missionary farewell. Two days later, as Robert lay dying, his boss came to our home to hand deliver a letter from the president of the company. He hand delivered the letter so that it would arrive before Robert passed on. The company had voted to forgo a Christmas party and had placed the money that would have been spent on that party in an account for us. The balance in the account was $10,000. The tremendous burden of the cost of the funeral was lifted off my shoulders with this unbelievably generous gift."

Chris closes her letter: "No, I don't doubt the love of my Father in Heaven. I don't doubt what part he can play in our lives. He may bless us through other people, but he is the director. Bitterness and doubt have no place in trials when we know that all experiences are for our good in the eternal perspective."[3]

It's safe to say that none of us would choose to scale the rock that Chris faced, that of losing a husband or other loved ones. Yet sometimes such rocks surface in our paths, and we have no choice but to find a way over. Chris's letter displays a great deal of faith and hope.

Elder Neal A. Maxwell has said: "Daily hope is vital, since the 'winter quarters' of our lives are not immediately adjacent to our promised land. An arduous trek still awaits, but hope spurs weary disciples on. Jesus waits with open arms to receive those who finally overcome by faith and hope. His welcome will consist not of a brief, loving pat, but, instead, being clasped in the arms of Jesus."[4]

I love to work in my garden and plant things and then watch them blossom into something wonderful. I have learned that one must get to know one's garden in order to have success in cultivating it. There is a spot where for years I planted one thing after another without much success. When, over time, I came to understand the subtleties of that spot—how long the sun shone on it each day, when it fell into shade, how much water could be expected there, and the characteristics of the soil—then I was able to select plants that could flourish there.

There is another Garden we must come to understand in order to experience the fullness of its import in our lives. We must all come to realize in a profound way what Jesus did for us in the Garden of Gethsemane and on Calvary's hill.

Consider the account preserved for us of Christ's last hours on earth. In Matthew 26 we read of how he approached Gethsemane with his disciples, "and he took with him Peter and the two sons of Zebedee, and began to be sorrowful and very heavy. Then saith he unto them, My soul is exceeding sorrowful, even unto death: tarry ye here, and watch with me" (Matthew 26:37–38). What do you suppose it means to be "sorrowful . . . unto death?" Perhaps there are those listening today who have felt that same kind of soul-crushing sorrow. Try to imagine the weight of that sorrow, and notice that even Christ, who obviously had a strong and loving relationship with his Father in Heaven, sought additional strength from his earthly friends. Jesus pleads, "Tarry ye here, and watch with me." Has there ever been a time in your life when you have said to someone, "Don't leave me; stay with me"? We crave a loved one's presence when a spiritual night falls.

The scripture continues, "And he went a little further, and fell on his face, and prayed." Now, this is not the peaceful, contemplative prayer we often see in the paintings: Christ "fell on his face." "And [then Jesus] prayed, saying, O my Father, if it be possible, let this cup pass from me: nevertheless not as I will, but as thou wilt" (Matthew 26:39). The Savior clearly knows what it is like to come up against a rock that seems too hard to climb. And, as in all things, his response is the perfect example for our own response to trials: "Not as I will, but as thou wilt." Almost two thousand years later, the Lord described the pain of that experience: "Behold, I, God, have suffered these things for all, that they might not suffer if they would repent; but if they would not repent they must suffer even as I; which suffering caused myself . . . to tremble because of pain, and to bleed at every pore, and to suffer both body and spirit" (D&C 19:16–18).

Sometimes when we come up against adversity, it helps us just to know someone else understands what we are going through.

In the book of Alma in the Book of Mormon, chapter 7, we read of Christ and his mission on earth. Verse 11 tells us, "And he shall go forth, suffering pains and afflictions and temptations of every kind; and this that the word might be fulfilled which saith he will take upon him the pains and the sicknesses of his people."

Verse 12: "And he will take upon him death, that he may loose the bands of death which bind his people; and he will take upon him their infirmities, that his bowels may be filled with mercy, according to the flesh, that he may know according to the flesh how to succor his people according to their infirmities."

When we tremble, when we bleed, when we suffer, either in body or in spirit, he understands. None is better qualified to see us through our mortal trials than he who "descended below all things" (D&C 88:6). If we truly understand what happened in the Garden of Gethsemane, we will have confidence in his sure promise found in Hebrews 13:5: "I will never leave thee, nor forsake thee."

Just as my little grandson's mother did not immediately rush out and lift him up over the rocks, so our Savior does not remove our trials from us, though he clearly could. We are promised our trials will not be more than we can handle, but they cannot be less if we are to fulfill the measure of our creation.

President Spencer W. Kimball, who experienced so many severe trials in his life, said: "I am positive in my mind that the Lord has planned our destiny. Sometime we will fully understand. And when we see back from the vantage point of the future, we shall be satisfied with many of the happenings of this life that are so difficult for us to comprehend."[5]

The landscape of Southern Utah is filled with spectacular reminders of the refining nature of trials. In Arches National Park, harsh elements—wind, ice, and rain—have penetrated cracks in stone and dissolved the weaker materials, leaving the stronger materials to create structures so magnificent that people travel from all over the world to see them.

Similarly, the hardships we encounter in our life are the very tools the Lord uses, like a master sculptor, to shape us into the divine creations we are destined to become.

C. S. Lewis said, "God who foresaw your tribulation has specially armed you to get through it, not without pain, but without stain."[6]

President Howard W. Hunter said: "Every generation since time began has had things to overcome and problems to work out. Furthermore, every individual person has a set of challenges which sometimes seem to be earmarked for him individually. We understood that in our premortal existence.

"When these experiences humble, refine, and teach us, they make us better people, more grateful, loving, and considerate of other people in their own times of difficulty.

"Even in the most severe of times, problems and prophecies were never intended to do anything but bless the righteous and help those who are less righteous move toward repentance."[7]

In Romans 5:8 we read, "God commendeth his love toward us, in that, while we were yet sinners, Christ died for us." Think of the tremendous trust he shows in us. He trusted us that his anguish in the Garden of Gethsemane and his sacrifice on Calvary's hill would not have been in vain.

Sometimes our earthly vision is limited. It is difficult for us to understand fully Christ's promise. In 1 Corinthians 13:12 we read, "For now we see through a glass, darkly; but then face to face: now I know in part; but then shall I know even as also I am known." When we come face to face with our Savior, we will understand every rock in our mortal path, why they were placed there, and how they helped sculpt us. Then we will more fully understand the Atonement and we will thank him—oh, how we will thank him—for his sacrifice on our behalf. We will also gain perspective and realize that the actual size of our rocks was much smaller than it appeared to be when we faced them.

My grandson Peter once held a small pebble in front of his eye as he looked into the evening sky and said to his father, "Look, Dad, this rock is as big as the moon!" Like Peter's pebble, trials often block our vision and seem "as big as the moon." With eternal perspective, we see each trial only as a tiny piece of a beautiful mosaic made up of a variety of earthly experiences.

When Moses complained to the Lord that he was slow of speech and therefore ill-equipped to lead the children of Israel, God replied, "Who hath made man's mouth? . . . have not I the Lord?" (Exodus 4:11). In similar tone, the Lord comforted Moroni's fear of inadequacy in writing the record of his people by reminding him that "I give unto men weakness that they may be humble; and my grace is sufficient for all men that humble themselves before me; for if they humble themselves before me, and have faith in me, then will I make weak things become strong unto them" (Ether 12:27). The Savior trod the rockiest ground of all, the path of Calvary. Having experienced mortality, he is "acquainted with grief" (Isaiah 53:3) and asks only our meek petition for his rescuing arm.

When it seems we cannot climb any further, and we slide to the bottom of the rocks with banged and bloodied knees, he whispers, "You can do it!" And he knows that we can, because his grace is the enabling power that makes all things possible.

As Bruce Hafen explains in his book *The Broken Heart:* "The Savior's victory can compensate not only for our sins but also for our inadequacies; not only for our deliberate mistakes but also for our sins committed in ignorance, our errors of judgment, and our unavoidable imperfections. Our ultimate aspiration is more than being forgiven of sin—we seek to become holy, endowed affirmatively with *Christlike* attributes, at one with him, like him. Divine grace is the only source that can finally fulfill that aspiration, after all we can do."[8] His words echo Nephi's testimony, "We know that it is by grace that we are saved, after all we can do"

(2 Nephi 25:23). These words give us the proper perspective on the interweaving of grace and agency: we must do what we can, knowing that the Lord will make up what must surely be a huge deficit.

When Jesus lived on the earth he taught using uncomplicated words and stories that all could understand, knowing that open hearts would receive the full impact of his message (Matthew 13:3–16). His sermons and parables provide elegantly simple instructions that we might compare to a mountain climber's tools: They are compact, multipurpose, and applicable to any number of possible situations. We can distill from the New Testament a selection of these tools to carry in our spiritual backpack as we hike the steep and rocky, as well as the smooth, trails of our earthly excursion. Here are a few I have chosen, though Christ's teachings afford a wealth of others.

The first tool I recommend: *Seek God's peace*. The world teaches us to seek peace in possessions, wealth, and physical comforts and pleasures. As Paul wrote to the Corinthians, "The wisdom of this world is foolishness with God" (1 Corinthians 3:19). God's peace transcends worldly peace, for it is not based on conditions that are subject to change unexpectedly. As Christ consoled his disciples prior to his crucifixion, "Peace I leave with you, my peace I give unto you: not as the world giveth, give I unto you. Let not your heart be troubled, neither let it be afraid" (John 14:27).

President Joseph F. Smith describes the difference between the Lord's peace and that of the world: "There is no such thing as physical rest in the Church of Jesus Christ. Reference is made to the spiritual rest and peace which are born from a settled conviction of the truth in the minds of men. We may thus enter into the rest of the Lord today, by coming to an understanding of the truths of the gospel." He further writes that those who seek peace "will not find satisfaction in the doctrines of Men. Let them seek for it in the written word of God; let them pray to him in their secret chambers, where no human ear can hear, and in their closets petition for light; let them obey the doctrines of Jesus. . . . This course will bring peace to their souls, joy to their hearts, and a settled conviction which no change can disturb."[9]

Another tool: *Trust in the Lord*. Christ has traversed the route we are now climbing and knows where the obstacles lie. Brigham Young taught departing missionaries "that he who goes forth in the name of the Lord, trusting in him with all his heart, will never want for wisdom."[10]

How completely our unnamed sister in the New Testament exhibited her trust when more than wisdom was wanting. Having suffered illness for twelve years, depleted in her physical strength and worldly goods, she said, "If I may touch but his clothes, I shall be whole" (Mark 5:28). Jesus, not seeing her but feeling her use of his power, sought her in the throng: "Daughter, thy faith hath made thee whole; go in peace" (Mark 5:34). By remembering and trusting the Divine One who wishes to shape us in his image, we gain courage to overcome the obstacles we encounter in life and receive the promise of exaltation described in Alma 36:3: "Whosoever shall put their trust in God shall be supported in their trials, and their troubles, and their afflictions, and shall be lifted up at the last day."

The next tool: *Forgive an enemy*. Forgiveness is a cleansing act that softens our heart and frees us from the past, allowing us to focus on the present—the only time in which we can take action. Grudges we carry are additional weight that slows us as we climb, an unnecessary burden we must shed if we are to progress. Knowing this, Christ instructed that if someone should "trespass against thee seven times in a day, and seven times in a day turn again to thee, saying, I repent; thou shalt forgive him" (Luke 17:4). The apostles were as challenged by the difficulty of this simple admonition as we are. "Lord," they responded, "increase our faith" (Luke 17:5). Joseph Smith taught us to "ever keep in exercise the principle of mercy, and be ready to forgive our brother on first intimations of repentance . . . ; and should we even forgive our brother, or even our enemy, before he repent or ask forgiveness, our Heavenly Father would be equally as merciful unto us."[11]

Another tool: *Give thanks*. Give thanks for God's gifts to you. Do you recall the story of the ten lepers who called to Jesus as he passed through their village, pleading, "Master, have mercy on us"? (Luke 17:13). Jesus did have mercy upon them, and he caused them to be healed. "And one of them, when he saw that he was healed, turned back . . . and fell down on his face at his feet, giving him thanks. . . . And Jesus answering said, Were there not ten cleansed? but where are the nine?" (Luke 17:15–17). No matter how bleak the landscape of our lives may periodically appear, grateful eyes can find a spot of beauty somewhere. Searching for the beauty in our lives, finding it, and giving sincere thanks are an invigorating and refreshing exercise for the soul.

The last tool I recommend: *Feed his lambs*. When the risen Christ sat with his disciples on the shore of the Sea of Tiberias, he asked Peter if he loved him. The response was quick and heartfelt: "Yea, Lord; thou knowest that I love thee." Jesus responded, "Feed my lambs" (John 21:15).

He gave that injunction to Peter three times: "Feed my lambs. . . . Feed my sheep. . . . Feed my sheep" (John 21:15–17). We may sometimes feel burdened and overwhelmed by the multitude of duties jostling for our attention. We feel pressure to keep up with standards real and imagined, external and self-imposed. But remember that the gospel in its purest form consists of the simple teachings of one wearing tattered clothes and having bare feet, speaking without pretense and in gentle tones the loving message of his Father: Trust in me. Love one another. Forgive him. Go in peace. Feed my lambs. These are simple tools he has provided us to help us find our way back to him.

Toward the close of his ministry, the apostle Paul said, "I have fought a good fight, I have finished my course, I have kept the faith: henceforth there is laid up for me a crown of righteousness, which the Lord, the righteous judge, shall give me at that day: and not to me only, but unto all them also that love his appearing" (2 Timothy 4:7–8). Notice that he says nothing about winning the fight or the race, only about completing it honorably. In fact, he implies that all the contestants can be winners, that a crown is laid up "not to [him] only" but to all who look forward to the coming of Christ. Indeed, "the race is not to the swift, nor the battle to the strong" (Ecclesiastes 9:11), but "unto him that endureth to the end will [the Lord] give eternal life" (3 Nephi 15:9). We don't have to be fast, we don't have to show great prowess, but we do have to keep climbing. You can do it!

In his book *Believing Christ*, Stephen E. Robinson tells us: "In making the gospel covenant, we become part of a team whose captain and quarterback is Jesus Christ, a cosmic Heisman Trophy winner who throws nothing but touchdowns. If we are on his team, we will go undefeated." But we have "to be on *his* team, not [our] own and not somebody else's." Brother Robinson says further, "When we become one with Jesus Christ, spiritually we form a partnership with a joint account, and his assets and our liabilities flow into each other."[12]

In her book *The Story of My Life*, Helen Keller relates snatches of memories of the illness that took her sight and hearing when she was nineteen months old and dim recollections of how the world looked and sounded. She writes: "Gradually I got used to the silence and darkness that surrounded me and forgot that it had ever been different, until she came, my teacher, who was to set my spirit free. During the first nineteen months of my life I had caught glimpses of broad, green fields, a luminous sky, trees and flowers which the darkness that followed could not wholly blot out. If we have once seen, 'the day is ours, and what the day has shown.'"[13]

We have once seen. Every now and then the Spirit whispers to us of remembered light. We are not lost in a black cave. We know the source of all light! If we could truly recall for a few moments some dim memory of our premortal existence, we would do anything to assure our return to the Father who sent us here. If we could thrust aside the veil and get an inkling of who we were before we came to earth, we would be that much closer to knowing ourselves as Christ knows us.

Remember little James Patrick and his mother? Just as he repeated to himself over and over, "I can do it," we need to trust the Lord when he promises that we can overcome our mortal trials. "God is faithful," Paul reminds us, "who will not suffer you to be tempted above that ye are able; but will with the temptation also make a way to escape, that ye may be able to bear it" (1 Corinthians 10:13). Like the child's mother who recognized his ability to climb the rocks if he would just keep trying, the Lord knows each one of us individually and personally. He knows what we can bear. He knows what strengths we have; and, even though many of us foolishly try to hide them, he knows our weaknesses as well. He would not ask us to climb any rock without preparing a way for us to accomplish it (see 1 Nephi 3:7). He knows that we can succeed, because he has already paid the price that covers all the conditions of mortality, including the rocks.

I love this year's conference theme: "May Christ lift thee up, and may his sufferings and death, and the showing his body unto our fathers, and his mercy and long-suffering, and the hope of his glory and of eternal life, rest in your mind forever" (Moroni 9:25). We've talked about Christ's "sufferings and death." We need to remember that none of the rest of what has been said here has any meaning in the absence of that infinite and eternal atonement.

Bruce Hafen writes: "The Atonement . . . makes possible the infusion of spiritual endowments that actually change and purify our nature, moving us toward that state of holiness or completeness we call eternal life or Godlike life. At that ultimate stage we will exhibit divine characteristics not just because we think we should but because that is the way we are."[14] Hence we have hope of his glory and of eternal life, not because we have finally climbed high enough all by ourselves but because we have "come unto Christ, and [become] perfected in him" (Moroni 10:32).

The next phrase of the conference theme is a more obscure one. What does Christ's "showing his body unto our fathers" have to do with our hope of eternal life? To fully understand the import of this passage, we can turn to 3 Nephi 11, which details the Savior's appearance to the Nephites following his resurrection. After he had introduced himself as "Jesus Christ, whom the prophets testified shall come into the world," he invited the people to "arise and come forth unto me, that ye may thrust your hands into my side, and also that ye may feel the prints of the nails in my hands and in my feet, that ye may know that I am the God of Israel, and the God of the whole earth, and have been slain for the sins of the world.

"And it came to pass that the multitude went forth, and thrust their hands into his side, and did feel the prints of the nails in his hands and in his feet; and this they did do, going forth one by one until they had all gone forth, and did see with their eyes and did feel with their hands, and did know of a surety and did bear record, that it was he, of whom it was written by the prophets, that should come" (3 Nephi 11:10, 14–15).

Then he called for one of those faithful prophets, Nephi, who was among the multitude, to come forward, and in one of the tenderest scenes imaginable, "Nephi arose and went forth, and bowed himself before the Lord and did kiss his feet" (3 Nephi 11:19).

There are many lessons in those few verses of scripture. First, we learn from Christ's own testimony that he is the God not just of the Israelites but of every one of the children of earth. We understand that he was slain as a sacrifice for our sins and that the body he took up out of the grave was the same one that had been laid down, with the prints of the nails and the sword still evident as a witness of his identity. This is one chief element of our hope of eternity: the indisputable reality of his own resurrection.

Picture the multitude—a "great multitude," we read in verse 1 of the chapter—going forth to feel the nail prints and to thrust their hands into his side. They didn't just send a representative up to the front to do that for them. Every one of them, one by one, filed past and experienced this solemn ritual. It would have taken many hours. Can you imagine the patience and love of our Savior to submit to such a thing? I can envision him looking lovingly into the eyes of each person who came forth, saying a few kind words to heal each soul and ignite the flame of testimony in every heart. Can there be any question of his concern for us as individuals? Can we suppose that "borrowed light" would ever be enough for us, when he took such great pains to be sure that every single person there could bear a personal witness?

Finally, think about Nephi for a minute. This was the faithful prophet whose ministry had begun more than thirty years earlier, when the lives of the faithful were threatened unless the signs of Christ's birth were given. He had been with them through that crisis, through the terrible and frightening era of the Gadiantons, and through the subsequent deterioration of the Church due to pride. He had borne powerful testimony and cried repentance to a generation steeped in abomination, raising his brother from the dead and performing many other mighty miracles, which only made the wicked people angrier. For more than thirty years he had remained faithful to the cause to which he had been called.

Picture him now among the multitude. The Lord whom he had served all these long, persecution-filled years had finally come, as he had promised. Can you imagine the feelings of Nephi's heart when the Savior called him by name and invited him to come forward? Was there any question in his mind that Jesus Christ knew him personally and recognized the work he had done?

I testify that our Savior's knowledge of you is no less personal. He knows the sacrifices you have made and are making. He recognizes the efforts you make to keep a Primary class in order, to teach a two-year-old to pray, to help out at the cannery so that his children will be fed, to get a concept through to a Sunday School class full of teenagers. He knows how you've worked and the discipline required to be worthy to attend his temple. Won't all those efforts seem worth it when one day he calls you to come before him?

His knowledge of you goes beyond a catalog of your deeds. He knows you individually and completely. He understands your darkest hours when things seem as black as a cave with no light. He understands when you are feeling unworthy or forgotten or depressed or desperate or alone. He constantly and gently invites you to open up those dark recesses of

40

your heart to him that he may fill them with his light. You can't shock him. You can't surprise him. He won't turn away from you in disgust, shaking his head and saying, "Oh, this is worse than I thought. There's nothing I can do here." When he healed the sick, he often forgave their sins as well. His healing extends to the crippled heart just as surely as to the crippled leg.

All this we learn because of "the showing his body unto our fathers." How grateful I am for the Book of Mormon, which preserves for us this miraculous account. May "his mercy and long-suffering, and the hope of his glory and of eternal life, rest in [our minds] forever" (Moroni 9:25). May we feel the peace, his peace, that comes from a true knowledge of our Lord and his atoning sacrifice. May we be lifted up in him, that we may lift each other over all the rocks we encounter in the paths of our mortality. May we never forget that we "can do all things through Christ which strengtheneth" us.

NOTES

1. Truman G. Madsen, *Joseph Smith the Prophet* (Salt Lake City: Bookcraft, 1989), 76.
2. Carlfred Broderick, *My Parents Married on a Dare* (Salt Lake City: Deseret Book, 1996), 123.
3. Chris Stevens to Virginia U. Jensen; used by permission.
4. Neal A. Maxwell, *Ensign*, November 1994, 36.
5. Spencer W. Kimball, *Faith Precedes the Miracle* (Salt Lake City: Deseret Book, 1969), 105.
6. C. S. Lewis, *Letters of C. S. Lewis*, ed. W. H. Lewis (New York: Harcourt Brace Jovanovich, 1966), 219.
7. Howard W. Hunter, *New Era*, January 1994, 6.
8. Bruce C. Hafen, *The Broken Heart* (Salt Lake City: Deseret Book, 1989), 20.
9. Joseph F. Smith, *Gospel Doctrine* (Salt Lake City: Deseret Book, 1939), 126.
10. Brigham Young, *Discourses of Brigham Young*, sel. John A. Widtsoe (Salt Lake City: Deseret Book, 1954), 323.
11. Joseph Smith, *Teachings of the Prophet Joseph Smith*, sel. Joseph Fielding Smith (Salt Lake City: Deseret Book, 1938), 155.
12. Stephen E. Robinson, *Believing Christ* (Salt Lake City: Deseret Book, 1992), 29, 25.
13. Helen Keller, *The Story of My Life* (Garden City, N.Y.: Doubleday, 1954).
14. Hafen, *Broken Heart*, 18.

Life-Giving and Life-Changing Relationships

WENDY L. WATSON

Many of us have a passion for making a difference in the relationships in which we're involved. We would like those relationships to be more vibrant, more life giving, and more life changing for us. We may even wish they were a little less guilt inducing.

In Moroni 8:4, Mormon wrote to his son Moroni, grieving about the state of the Nephites: "They have lost their love one towards another." He also lamented the anger that had caught hold of their hearts. I work with women and their families who have lost, or believe they have lost, their love for each other. Their love is now gone. Some even believe they never found it in the first place.

A popular song asks, "What's love got to do with it?" Yet a prophet proclaims that "love is the answer." President Gordon B. Hinckley stated, "There are good families everywhere. But there are too many who are in trouble. This is a malady with a cure. The prescription is simple and wonderfully effective. It is love."[1]

When I ask myself, "What is the biggest difference between a life-giving relationship and a life-grieving relationship?" the answer is love. Yet some say that love really is not enough. And it's true: Love is not enough when it is feigned or forced or demanded or commanded. Love is not enough when it is really lust. Love is not enough when it is really guilt or control. But love is always enough and will always be enough

Wendy L. Watson holds a Ph.D. in family therapy and gerontology from the University of Calgary in Calgary, Alberta, Canada. She is a professor in the marriage and family therapy graduate programs at Brigham Young University and served as chair-elect for the 1998 BYU–Relief Society Women's Conference.

and to spare when it is really love. In fact, it is our only "prescription," as our prophet has said, for life-giving and life-changing relationships.

President Hinckley also said, "Love is of the very essence of life. . . . I am one who believes that love, like faith, is a gift of God."[2] We have been told that we should seek after the gifts of the Spirit. If love is a gift of the Spirit, then we need to pray for it. Are we praying for love? Are we praying to love? Are we praying to love as the Savior loves? Do we pray, "Help me to love my husband. Help me to see all that is good about him. Help me to see him even as the Savior sees him"?

If love is a gift from God, then it follows that love could not be present where the Spirit could not be. If we are breaking commandments, don't call it love. It cannot be. Love invites the Spirit, and the Spirit invites love.

The reality of love and relationships comes as we interact with others and our environment. The adversary tries to give us his lens of love, sometimes through the media and in a most deadly fashion through pornography. President Hinckley has warned about pornography: "Stay away from pornography! Avoid it as you would a terrible disease. It is a consuming disease. It is addictive."[3]

Pornography will change your view of love. People involved with pornography bring the adversary's view of love into their marriages. And that view of love is deadly to marriage. When you are introduced to love through the adversary's lens, which is designed to destroy you, you learn to lust, not to love. Even initial sweet feelings of love turn quickly into lust. To get rid of those feelings, you will have to pray for a purification by the Spirit, and your prayers will need to be relentless, because the lustful feelings will be. One day you will wake up in deep grief and realize, "I could have experienced pure love, undefiled love, love that goes way beyond anything this world dreams of and certainly way beyond anything that the TV and movies portray." A young man, not long ago, grieved in my office, realizing that he had missed the opportunity to really love his wife. For years, pornography held him tightly in its grip. He could not distinguish love from lust. Sadly, his wife had died just a few months before.

True love, pure love, "suffereth long, and is kind, and envieth not, and is not puffed up, seeketh not her own, is not easily provoked, thinketh no evil, and rejoiceth not in iniquity but rejoiceth in the truth, beareth all things, believeth all things, hopeth all things, endureth all things" (Moroni 7:45).

What difference does love make? When love is present, it changes everything. Eyes change, hearts change, cells change, souls change in the presence of love. One of our hymns speaks to this truth as well, saying, "There is beauty all around when there's love at home."[4] The operative word is "when." When love is not at home, beauty, either in yourself or others, can be very elusive. Robert L. Millet, dean of Religious Education at Brigham Young University, has said: "Charity is a fruit of the Spirit, something given to us by a gracious Lord. It empowers us to love and lift and lighten burdens more than any other single thing in this life."[5] If that is true, if love can empower us to "love and lift and lighten burdens more than any other single thing in this life," wouldn't you be willing to do anything to increase your charity, the pure love of Christ? Let me share some experiences that show the power of love—love that can literally be life giving and life changing.

The Chilean biologist Humberto Maturana says that love is the basic emotion for health and healing. "The only thing that I know is that love is a fundamental emotion in human beings." I love to hear a biologist teaching that truth. He further proposes that "most human diseases, most human suffering, arise from interference with these fundamental emotions."[6] That's quite a statement. Our diseases and suffering come from a lack of love? He defines love as the ability to open space for the existence of another or acceptance of another living beside us in daily living."[7] What a wonderful definition.

Whenever I offer that idea to couples, to families, to siblings, they understand it. I ask them, "If you want to increase by just 10 percent your love for your husband, for your son, according to this definition, what would you change?" At that point, family members become brilliant. They consider this concept, and a thousand ideas come to their minds.

Love is a biological dynamic with deep roots. As Latter-day Saint women, we would add that love is a spiritual dynamic with eons of premortal development. The power of love to change biology is legendary, built into folklore, country and western songs, everyday experience, and even research. Medalie and Goldbourt surveyed ten thousand men with heart disease. They found a 50 percent reduction in the frequency of chest pain in men who perceived that their wives were supportive and loving.[8] Amazing! John Gottman, renowned for his research into marital interaction, found that women in ailing or failing marriages experienced increased infectious illnesses when their husbands showed a pattern of stone-walling and withdrawing from marital conflict. So, it makes women sick when their husbands either pretend not to notice conflict or withdraw from conflict. Gottman also found that as marital interaction deteriorated, the increasing distance, isolation, and loneliness had a negative effect on the husband's health as well.[9]

In my own clinical work with families, I am amazed at how physical symptoms and emotional symptoms actually diminish or disappear when family conflict is reduced and powerful, loving emotions return. Passion for living together makes wonderful things happen in families. I believe that illness often appears to strike out of the blue because we cannot see or know all that may have led up to its appearance. If we were able to peer into one another's organs or cells, we could monitor the effects of our relationships.

Even our conversations do not go unnoticed by our cells. Have you had a conversation and felt lighter, better? On the other hand, has a conversation ever given you a headache? Of course, disease can just happen, but do you think our organs or cells malfunction when the emotional dynamics in our relationships are disturbed? Could a change in our biology be observed if we were able to "open space for the existence of another," if we were really able to love? And if someone really loved us, what changes might we see in our cells?

One family sought help to resolve long-standing marital conflict and resentment. The couple reported a marital separation and several previous unsatisfactory experiences with marital counseling. The young wife was suffering with terminal cancer and wanted to resolve the marital issues with her husband before she died. We wondered if she would feel free to die after resolving her emotional conflict. How should we pace the therapy—ethically? If the couple resolved things quickly, would she die quickly? When we asked the couple what one question they would most like answered in our work together, the wife's answer summarized her dilemma well: "Why did a relationship that started out so precious become so very destructive?"

We saw this couple three times over three weeks. By the third session, they were reporting less conflict and increased ability to show caring and love to each other. The wife commented, "I feel like these past few weeks have been very special; he's made a much bigger effort to listen." The wife died shortly after the third session. Did her husband's words heal her and set her free? The husband told us a month later that his wife had died peacefully, that they had been able to forgive each other and begin to write a new story of their relationship.

What do the scriptures say about creating life-giving relationships and life-changing relationships? Of all the how-to instruction books on relationships, the scriptures are by far the best. In 1 Nephi, we find stories about the struggles and successes in various relationships: marital, parental, sibling, in-laws, out-laws. Moroni gives us many tender examples of father-son connections reaching out for support and strength. I wanted to see what I could distill out of just one section of the Book of Mormon, the best book on relationships. I chose 3 Nephi and prayerfully studied a few chapters. There I found ten principles, true principles, that undergird life-changing, life-giving relationships.

Principle 1: A small voice penetrates positively, or, there's nothing small about a small voice. "It was not a harsh voice, neither was it a loud voice," says 3 Nephi 11:3, but "it did pierce them . . . to the center." Have you ever heard a loved one say, "I am so sorry," "I love you," "I need you," "I want to help you"? Those words came in the volume and tone of a small voice. That volume and tone add to the intensity of the message.

These days my dad's voice is a small one. He's on dialysis three times a week. He has survived cancer for the past nine years without treatment. He is our miracle man. He has a small voice these days, but his voice is like the sound of a trump to my heart when I phone him in Canada. His small voice does indeed pierce me to my very soul and cause my heart to burn when he says, "You are such a comfort to me" or "I'm so proud of you. I love you."

Indeed, a soft voice penetrates positively. Conversely, we need to avoid harsh or loud voices. Our words stick in the walls of our homes. They also stick in our cells. We need to be very careful what we say but also watch the tone and volume of our voices. Embedded in a harsh or loud voice is usually a command, a demand, a stance of "I'm right and you're wrong." Harsh, loud voices grieve life, grieve the Spirit, and shrink your spirit.

Principle 2: Repetition is good. The small voice in 3 Nephi came three times. I love to think about that. Three times the voice came, "and the people understood it not," until the third repetition. Because we are always changing, the words we hear the second time are falling on new ears. Think about the temple. Think about repetition. Think about how we continually hear or see things in a whole new way because of intervening experiences that change us. We can never say, "I've already read the Book of Mormon." Every time we read it, it's new. Saying "I love you" in word, in deed, never gets old. Hearing "I love you" never gets old. Hearing "I am so sorry" never gets old. Repetition is good.

It took the Nephites three times before they understood. I wonder how differently you might experience interactions with your children if you believed that it was not a personal affront if your child did not respond to you the first time. Try it the second time; try it the third time. Three is a good number, a wonderful number that may build our relationships.

Principle 3: Commendations are vital to life-giving, life-changing relationships. Listen to this phrase: "Behold my Beloved Son, in whom I am well pleased" (3 Nephi 11:7). In that one statement, God the Father does three things: he establishes his relationship publicly with his son; he expresses love for his son; and he commends his son. Do we need to establish relationships with loved ones in the presence of others? I often ask couples, "Do you feel more like a couple when you're by yourself or when you're with other people?" They tell me that part of becoming a couple involves being with others. Witnesses are important to relationships.

Thinking back to the Father's introduction of his beloved Son, I wonder if your relationship with your child would change if every time you introduced your child to someone, you indicated your love of and pleasure with that child. Wouldn't those words breathe life into him or her, into yourself, and into your relationship? Imagine what would happen to cells and souls, hearts and minds, if every time you introduced your husband you indicated that you loved him, that you were well pleased with him. Commend your loved ones publicly. The best-kept secret in many families is the strengths that mothers see in their children and spouses. The reverse is also true. If you were to discover that your child thought you were "cool" and your husband thought you were "more than he had ever hoped for" and he "would marry you all over just as you are today," what difference would it make in the way you show love for them?

A woman came to my office the other day and said, "Well, I always try to tell my children that I love my husband." I said, "Do you tell them with about as much enthusiasm as you just now told me? If you did, it's a well-kept secret!" We figured out that she really needed to go home and fall in love with her husband all over again—or, as Truman Madsen has said, rise in love.[10] One of the very best things you can do for your children is not just to love their father but to fall/rise in love with their father and let your husband and children know.

Principle 4: Be persistent in letting someone know that you want to be close to him or her. In 3 Nephi 9:13–22, the Lord persistently offers to help us: "Return unto me" (v. 13); "I [will] heal you" (v. 13); "Come unto me" (v. 14). Are we really entreating in our invitations for others to come closer to us? Are we repetitious in our invitations to others? Are we persistent in sending the message "I want to have a relationship with you"?

Principle 5: Receive and rejoice in the gifts that are offered. "How oft I would have gathered you," the Savior says over and over (3 Nephi 10:5–6). The Savior is willing to help us. Far too often, however, we reject his gift of helping and healing: "And ye would not" (v. 5). Do we deepen the Savior's wounds—the very wounds that would heal us—with our nonreceptivity?

Have you ever offered a gift, or an offering of love, and been rejected? Do you know the feeling of being wounded because your gift of love was rejected? Have you unwittingly rejected or neglected someone and his or her gift of love?

Principle 6: Do not negate someone's concerns, expressions of love, or commendations. When you negate what someone says, you really negate the person. It's like putting a big slash through them.

The Lord never does that. All through 3 Nephi, for example, the Lord makes it clear that he has come to hear—to heal your suffering and pain (see also Alma 7:11–14). If you want someone to talk to who really understands, then talk to the "fully comprehending Savior," as Elder Neal A. Maxwell has termed Jesus Christ.[11] Talk to the Lord; he really has been there. He really does understand. He will never negate your longings or your love. And if we want to love as the Savior loves, we must not negate the concerns or love expressed by others.

Principle 7: Make time for one-on-one experiences that include touch. Third Nephi 11:15 tells us that one by one the people "thrust their hands into his side, and did feel the prints of the nails in his hands and in his feet." Their relationship with the Savior, their coming unto him, included touching him.

There is something about pure, loving touch that elevates and deepens our experiences with each other. We can strengthen others emotionally and physically through touch. Some people say that we each need eight hugs a day to keep our immune system healthy. What is a loving, comfortable way for you to show your affection to others?

Principle 8: Be responsive when others need to be with you, need more time with you. In 3 Nephi 17, when the Savior was ready to leave the people, he realized that they needed him to stay. He said, in effect, "I perceive that you don't want me to go, so I'll stay." Do our relationships suffer because we are so busy managing our time? Can you imagine what would happen if your husband knew you changed your plans in order to be with him a little longer? What would happen if you said to your daughter, "It seems like you're not ready for me to go, so I'll stay"? Changing plans to give our loved ones our time is a powerful message of love.

Principle 9. Put anger away. Contention is not of God. Learn to disagree without being disagreeable. Don't let anger rule your life. That's just one of the many keys offered in the relationship manual of the Beatitudes (see 3 Nephi 12).

How does anger arise in relationships? Maturana, the Chilean biologist, defines emotional violence as "holding an idea to be true, such that another's idea is wrong and must change."[12] The "and must change" part brings about the violence. Disagreeing with others should not cause problems. You offer your idea; they offer theirs; we're all happy. But when you say, "You have to change your view," emotional violence kicks in. In family therapy, each family member inevitably views problems differently. For instance, the husband says, "This is a picture of a clown." And the wife says, "You've gotta be kidding. This is a picture of the whole circus." Each spouse is passionately committed to his or her own view. Each is certain that he or she is right and the other is wrong. Has the sin of certainty crept into your life, keeping you from having life-changing, life-giving relationships?

Principle 10: Forgive and apologize. Listen to 3 Nephi 12:23–24: "Therefore, if ye shall come unto me, or shall desire to come unto me, and rememberest that thy brother hath aught against thee—go thy way unto thy brother, and first be reconciled to thy brother, and then come unto me with full purpose of heart, and I will receive you." Withholding apologies and forgiveness prevents us from coming closer to the Savior and to others. I love and admire the man who sat in my office and humbly said, "I am willing to do whatever it takes to help my wife heal." It has meant apologizing to others with his wife present. Apologies initially seemed humiliating to him, but they actually healed and strengthened both marriage partners. At one point, I asked the wife how many of the one hundred bricks in the walls built between them would come down with just one apology. Twenty bricks, she said. To knit our hearts together, we need to acknowledge our wrongdoing and apologize in the presence of people who matter.

I believe that as we apply these ten principles, we will be increasingly immersed in life-giving, life-changing relationships. Then we will arise as the women we really are. There is an amazing connection between arising and coming unto the Savior. "Arise and come forth unto me," the Savior says (3 Nephi 11:14). *Arise* is a very sacred word in the temple. Think of that and listen again to what the Savior says: "Arise and come forth unto me." We will never be all that we can be, never be able to arise as the women we really are, until we come unto the Savior. Then we will hear him say, "Arise, and put on your beautiful garments."

Life-giving, life-changing relationships are created as we come unto the Savior. Even the sweet experiences of life, if not grounded in the Savior, are as cotton candy, sweet for a moment and then gone.

I can think of at least two kinds of relationships that have helped me draw closer to the Savior. An obvious kind is relationships based on obedience; such relationships naturally lead and draw us to the Lord. But I have learned that disappointing relationships can also draw us nearer to the Savior, if we will let them. When we feel that no one understands us, that there is no one we can trust, that we need someone who will always be there, we can turn to the Lord, even in our despair, in our disappointment, and also later in our gratitude. We can turn to him when we are afraid or when we anticipate change.

If you're thinking, "Well, I don't need to worry about love because there is no one in my life to love or who loves me," that thought should turn you even more to the Savior, the ultimate source of love. In the midst of one of the most emotionally painful experiences of my life, I remember realizing that I didn't have to feel alone if I had the Savior close by. How could I feel lonely if I would do my part to have him as my companion? It doesn't mean I don't slip some days—some overwhelming, too-much-to-do, can't-see-any-light-at-the-end-of-the-tunnel kind of days—but I can snap myself out of it when I remember and make efforts to move closer to the Savior.

President Howard W. Hunter gave us a wonderful message about loving the Lord completely: "He loves the Lord with all his heart who loves nothing in comparison [to] him and nothing but in reference to Him."[13] As we increase our interactions with the Savior, as we really draw close to him, he will become an increasing reality in our lives. And as we seek to understand the power of the Atonement, that it can be applied to our sins, our deficiencies, our pains, our frustrations, it can be the greatest reality in our lives. As we attach ourselves to the Savior, we will increase our interaction with him and increase our feelings for him.

The Savior entreats us to "come unto him." He wants us close to him, he wants us to have increasingly repeated interactions with him, to really get to know him. A sociological principle states, "Increased interaction leads to increased sentiment." Thus, increased interactions with the Lord lead to increased feelings for him, which lead us to want more interactions with him. And according to the biological principle of structural coupling, increased interactions with the Savior lead us increasingly to become like him. I love that concept. I have always loved the concept of structural coupling. But I was stunned when I started to wrap my mind around it and see how it relates to our becoming more like the Savior. Because the Savior never changes, the changes that occur through our interactions with the Savior will all be in us. And as we change, our capacity to show love, to express love, to enter into life-changing and life-giving relationships will be our absolute reward.

NOTES

1. Gordon B. Hinckley, *Ensign*, November 1997, 69.
2. Gordon B. Hinckley, *Ensign*, March 1984, 3.
3. Gordon B. Hinckley, *Teachings of Gordon B. Hinckley* (Salt Lake City: Deseret Book, 1997), 463.
4. *Hymns of The Church of Jesus Christ of Latter-day Saints* (Salt Lake City: The Church of Jesus Christ of Latter-day Saints, 1985), no. 294.
5. Robert L. Millet, *Alive in Christ* (Salt Lake City: Deseret Book, 1997), 62.
6. Humberto R. Maturana, *Telephone Conversation: The Calgary-Chile Coupling* (unpublished transcript; Calgary, Canada: University of Calgary, 1988), 9.
7. Humberto Maturana and Francisco Varela, *The Tree of Knowledge: Biological Roots of Human Understanding* (Boston: Shambhala Press, 1988).
8. J. Medalie and V. Goldbourt, "Angina Predictors among Ten Thousand Men: II.

Psychosocial and Other Risk Factors as Evidenced by a Multivariate Analysis of a Five-Year Incidence Study," *American Journal of Medicine* 60 (1976): 910–21.

9. John Gottman, *What Predicts Divorce? The Relationship between Marital Processes and Marital Outcomes* (Hillsdale, N. J.: Erlbaum, 1994).

10. See Truman G. Madsen, *Four Essays on Love* (Salt Lake City: Bookcraft, 1971), 30.

11. See, for instance, Neal A. Maxwell, *Men and Women of Christ* (Salt Lake City: Bookcraft, 1991), 67.

12. Maturana and Varela, *Tree of Knowledge*, 246–47.

13. Hunter, *Teachings of Howard W. Hunter*, 1.

After All We Can Do:
The Meaning of Grace
in Our Lives

ROBERT L. MILLET

The matter of the grace of God, as mediated through Jesus the Christ, has for the last fifteen years seemed to "occupy my mind, and press itself upon my feelings" (D&C 128:1). I have not desired to become a crusader or to be a part of some new theological craze in the Church but have sought with real intent to better understand what it means to trust in and rely "upon the merits, and mercy, and grace of the Holy Messiah" (2 Nephi 2:8).

IN CONTEXT

I have felt for some time that the concept of the grace of Jesus Christ deserves more of our attention as Latter-day Saints, especially as it is such a central doctrine in the Book of Mormon and the New Testament. Perhaps some of us have been hesitant to perceive the truthfulness and eternal relevance of this doctrine because it brings us face to face with our own limitations. Perhaps we shy away from it because we sense that we may have to alter our present way of viewing things. Whatever the cause, it just may be that we have not enjoyed the quiet, pervasive power that comes to those who acknowledge their weakness and turn to him who has all power. I believe, however, that there is wisdom in presenting this doctrinal message in context, in the way it is presented in

Robert L. Millet is dean of Religious Education and professor of ancient scripture at Brigham Young University. He serves as president of the BYU Fourteenth Stake. He and his wife, Shauna Sizemore Millet, are the parents of six children and the grandparents of one.

scripture—the context of the Atonement. That is to say, grace is not a doctrine that stands alone; it is inextricably tied to several others and therefore makes sense and brings peace only when seen in that context.

Latter-day Saints have often criticized those who stress salvation by grace alone, and we have often been criticized for a type of works-righteousness. The gospel is, in fact, a covenant—a two-way promise. The Lord agrees to do for us what we could never do for ourselves—forgive our sins, lift our burdens, renew our souls and re-create our nature, raise us from the dead and qualify us for glory hereafter. At the same time, we promise to do what we *can* do: receive the ordinances of salvation, love and serve one another (Mosiah 18:8–10), and do all in our power to put off the "natural man" and deny ourselves of ungodliness (Mosiah 3:19; Moroni 10:32). We must do more than offer a verbal expression of faith in the Lord, more than confess with the lips that we have received Christ into our hearts. The scriptures of the Restoration add perspective and balance to the majestic teachings of the apostle Paul on the matter of salvation by grace. We know without question that the power to save us, to change us, to renew our souls is in Christ. True faith, however, always manifests itself in faithfulness. Good works evidence our faith, our desire to remain in covenant with Christ. But these good works, though necessary, are not sufficient.

Too often we view grace as that increment of goodness, that final gift of God that will make up the difference and thereby boost us into the celestial kingdom, "after all we can do" (2 Nephi 25:23). To be sure, we will need a full measure of divine assistance to become celestial material. But the grace of God, through Jesus Christ our Lord, is available to us every hour of every day of our lives. "True grace," as one non–Latter-day Saint writer has suggested, "is more than just a giant freebie, opening the door to heaven in the sweet by and by, but leaving us to wallow in sin in the bitter here and now. Grace is God presently at work in our lives."[1] The grace of God is a precious gift, a power enabling us to face life with quiet courage, to do things we could never do on our own. The Great Physician does more than forgive sins. He ministers relief to the disconsolate, comfort to the bereaved, confidence to those who wrestle with infirmities and feelings of inadequacy, strength and peace to those who have been battered and scarred by the ironies of this life (Isaiah 61:1–2; Alma 7:11–13).

Few things would be more sinister than encouraging lip service to

God but discouraging obedience and faithful discipleship. On the other hand, surely nothing could be more offensive to God than a smug self-assurance that comes from trusting in one's own works or relying upon one's own strength. Understanding this sacred principle—the relationship between the grace of an infinite being and the works of finite man—is not easy, but it is immensely rewarding.

WHO'S IN CONTROL?

I cannot speak for the Church. I am, however, an expert on my own feelings. I have come to know firsthand some of the despondency and guilt associated with falling short of my goals, of trying to do it all, of striving to make myself perfect. The apostle Paul seems to have been addressing a similar problem in his day. He wrote: "Brethren, my heart's desire and prayer to God for Israel is, that they might be saved. For I bear them record that they have a zeal of God, but not according to knowledge. For they being ignorant of God's righteousness, and going about to establish their own righteousness, have not submitted themselves unto the righteousness of God. For Christ is the end of the law for righteousness to every one that believeth" (Romans 10:1–4).

I have been associated with many wonderful, caring people who struggle often with feelings of inadequacy, who hope against hope that one day—in some distant age in the future—in spite of their frailty in this sphere, they might qualify to feel comfortable where gods and angels are. Since it is true that the gospel of Jesus Christ is intended to liberate us, to ease and lighten our burdens, to bring that comfort and rest found in no other way, why do some of us struggle at times? Why do we find ourselves simply going through the motions, doing our duty in the Church but finding little fulfillment and enjoyment in it? Why do we carry our religion as a burden rather than a joy?

I suspect that many Latter-day Saints will agree to the same faulty orientation I find occasionally in myself. My greatest frustrations seem to come as a result of my efforts to "handle it" myself or, in other words, my failure to trust in and rely on the Lord. Maybe our culture contributes to our dilemma; maybe it's the constant chant of "You can do anything you put your mind to" or "You have unlimited possibilities and potential" that tends to focus our attention away from the powers of the divine toward our abilities, our merits, and our contributions. Our problems cannot be solved by humanity alone, no matter how impressive our accomplishments. The programs of society will not fill the soul's yearning for solace. In fact, we almost need to work at cross purposes to social trends, to attune our ears to a quiet voice that beckons us amidst the loud babble of competing voices. That quiet voice pleads with us simply to come unto Christ. The answer to individual hurt and personal pain cannot be found in congressional decisions, in personnel management, or in louder cries of victimization. Solace comes in and through Jesus Christ. The most pertinent crusade in which the Christian is involved is the quest for personal peace, for purity of heart, all of which come from Christ through the ordinances of the priesthood and by the power of the Holy Ghost. The scriptures teach plainly and persuasively that coming unto Christ entails a moment of decision, a poignant point in our progression wherein we realize that man-made solutions are in reality "broken cisterns, that can hold no water" (Jeremiah 2:13) and that only through yoking ourselves to the Master may we rid ourselves of the burdens of Babylon.

Few things in this life are exactly as they seem. We live in a time, for example, when we hear constantly the importance of being in control, in charge, in power. We must have access to and management over all variables. We operate by plans and formulae and procedures, surrounded by lists and tables and charts. A harsh reality facing those acclimated to and successful in this fallen world is that spiritual things cannot be programmed. We cannot require or demand or shape spiritual experience. The Spirit is in control, not us. The Lord through his Spirit works his marvelous wonders in his own time, in his own way, and according to his own will and purposes. To enter the realm of divine experience, therefore, is to enter a realm where we are not in complete control. We can seek to be worthy, strive to be in a position to be blessed, plead and pray for divine intervention, but we do not force the hand of the Almighty.

Though such matters as self-reliance and self-confidence may prove valuable in some of life's dealings, the reciprocal principles of submission, surrender, and having an eye single to the glory of God are essential if we are to acquire that enabling power described in scripture as the saving grace of Jesus Christ. It is as if the Lord inquires of us: "Do you want to possess all things such that all things are subject unto you?" We of course respond in the affirmative. He then says: "Good. Then submit to me. Yield your heart unto me." The Lord asks further: "Do you want to have victory over all things?" We nod. He follows up: "Then surrender to me. Unconditionally." Odd, isn't it? We incorporate the powers of divinity only through acknowledging our own inabilities, accepting our limitations, and realizing our weaknesses. We open ourselves to infinite strength only through accepting our finite condition. We, in time, gain control through being willing to relinquish control.

I am haunted by the words of Paul in his second epistle to the Corinthians. Paul was required to spend a significant amount of time defending his apostolic calling. Having been a zealous Pharisee and even a persecutor of the Christians before his conversion and not having been one of the original witnesses of the resurrection of Christ, he felt the need to testify to his detractors that his call had indeed come from God. In doing so with the Corinthian Saints, he described some marvelous spiritual experiences the Lord had given to him. "And lest I should be exalted above measure," Paul hastened to add, "through the abundance of the revelations, there was given to me a thorn in the flesh, the messenger of Satan to buffet me, lest I should be exalted above measure. For this thing I besought the Lord thrice, that it might depart from me. And [the Lord] said unto me, My grace is sufficient for thee: for my strength is made perfect in weakness." Paul then remarked: "Most gladly therefore will I rather glory in my infirmities, . . . in reproaches, in necessities, in persecutions, in distresses for Christ's sake: for when I am weak, then am I strong" (2 Corinthians 12:7–10).

No one really knows what his "thorn in the flesh" was. Was it a lingering sickness, perhaps malaria, so common in Galatia? Was it a memory of his past, a hellish reminder of who he had once been? Was it an evil spirit that dogged his steps and wearied him in his ministry? Perhaps one day we'll know. Whatever it was, however, it forced Paul to his knees in humility. His impotence in the face of this particular challenge was ever before him. I rather think that when Paul states that he "besought the Lord thrice" for the removal of the thorn that he is not describing merely three prayers but instead three seasons of prayer, extended periods of wrestling and laboring in the Spirit for a specific blessing that never came. Indeed, as he suggests, another kind of blessing came—a closeness, a sensitivity, an acquaintance with Deity, a sanctified strength that came through pain and suffering. Up against the wall of faith, shorn of self-assurance and naked in his extremity and his frightening finitude, a mere mortal received that enabling power we know as the grace of Christ. As the Savior explained to Moroni, when we acknowledge and confess our weakness—not just our specific weaknesses, our individual sins, but our weakness, our mortal limitations—and submit ourselves unto him, we transform weakness into strength (Ether 12:27).

As Jacob, son of Lehi, affirmed: "Wherefore, we search the prophets, and we have many revelations and the spirit of prophecy; and having all these witnesses we obtain a hope, and our faith becometh unshaken, insomuch that we truly can command in the name of Jesus and the very trees obey us, or the mountains, or the waves of the sea." Now note these words: "Nevertheless, the Lord God showeth us our weakness that we may know that it is by his grace, and his great condescensions unto the children of men, that we have power to do these things" (Jacob 4:6–7).

Too much of my own frustration over the years has come as a result of my refusal to let go and thus let God. Something—I suppose it is the natural man, the prideful self that automatically asserts its own agenda—drives me to want to do it myself. Oh, I believe in God, to be sure—that he loves me, that he sent his Son to earth to help me. All too often, however, my actions have betrayed my limited orientation, my vision of Christ as a type of spiritual advisor, a sort of celestial cheerleader who stands on the sidelines and whispers encouragement but not the Lord God Omnipotent who came to earth to make men and women into new creatures by empowering them to do what they could never do for themselves.

In an eagerness to draw closer to Christ, some Church members seem to have begun to cross a sacred line and go beyond that reverential barrier that must be observed by true followers of the Christ. They speak of Jesus as though he were their next-door neighbor, their buddy or chum, their pal. This is not the way to intimacy with the Savior. Oddly enough, strangely enough, it is not through humanizing Jesus, through trying to make him one of the boys, that we draw closer to him and incorporate his saving powers. It is, rather, through recognizing his godhood, his divinity, his unspeakable power. In short, the more I sense his greatness, his infinity, his capacity to transform the human soul, and my utter helplessness without him, the more I come unto him. Remember, it is through recognizing our own nothingness and weakness that we derive strength (Mosiah 2:20–21; 4:11–12; Moses 1:10).

Sometimes we speak of Jesus as our Elder Brother. He is, of course, our elder brother in that he was the firstborn spirit child of God in the premortal existence. But it interests me that the Book of Mormon prophets never speak of Jehovah as our Elder Brother. Rather, he is the Almighty God, the Eternal Judge, the Holy One of Israel, the Holy Messiah, the Everlasting Father, the Father of heaven and of earth, the God of nature, the Supreme Being, the Keeper of the gate, the King of heaven, and the Lord God Omnipotent. Elder M. Russell Ballard recently explained: "We occasionally hear some members refer to Jesus as our Elder Brother, which is a true concept based on our understanding of the premortal life with our Father in Heaven. But like many points of gospel doctrine, that simple truth doesn't go far enough in terms of describing the Savior's role in our present lives and His great position as a member of the Godhead. Thus, some non-LDS Christians are uncomfortable with what they perceive as a secondary role for Christ in our theology. They feel that we view Jesus as a spiritual peer. They believe that we view Christ as an implementor, if you will, for God but that we don't view Him as God to us and to all mankind, which, of course, is counter to biblical testimony about Christ's divinity. Let me help us understand, with clarity and testimony, our belief about Jesus Christ. We declare He is the King of Kings, Lord of Lords, the Creator, the Savior, the Captain of our Salvation, the Bright and Morning Star. He has taught us that He is in all things, above all things, through all things and round about all things, that He is Alpha and Omega, the Lord of the Universe, the first and the last relative to our salvation, and that His name is above every name and is in fact the only name under heaven by which we can be saved.

" . . . [W]e can understand why some Latter-day Saints have tended to focus on Christ's Sonship as opposed to His Godhood. As members of earthly families, we can relate to Him as a child, as a Son, and as a Brother because we know how that feels. We can personalize that relationship because we ourselves are children, sons and daughters, brothers and sisters. For some it may be more difficult to relate to Him as a God. And so in an attempt to draw closer to Christ and to cultivate warm and personal feelings toward Him, some tend to humanize Him, sometimes at the expense of acknowledging His Divinity. So let us be very clear on this point: it is true that Jesus was our Elder Brother in the premortal life, but we believe that in this life it is crucial that we become 'born again' as His sons and daughters in the gospel covenant."[2]

Too many of my efforts and, unfortunately, too many of my prayers have been bent on succeeding—according to my own predetermined plan. Instead of opening myself to divine direction and incorporating the powers of heaven, I wanted to be able to look back on life and sing with gusto, "I did it my way!" Too little time was spent in sacred submission; on too few occasions did I say the words (and mean it!), "Thy will be done, O Lord, and not mine." Instead of praying to know my limits, to know when my offering was acceptable, I prayed for more drive and more willpower. I have since come to believe that "fallen man is not simply an imperfect creature who needs improvement: he is a rebel who must lay down his arms."[3] The saving and ironic truth is this: as we submit, we come to know his will. As we surrender, we come to gain his power. As we yield our hearts unto God, our affections and our feelings are sanctified by his grace. As President Ezra Taft Benson has taught, once we turn our lives over to the Lord, we discover that he can do far more with us than we could ever do with ourselves.[4]

It is one thing to say to God, "Thy will be done," and another thing to entirely mean it. It takes moral courage and spiritual foresight to mean it. It takes divine aid. As a part of the dedicatory prayer of the Kirtland Temple, the Prophet Joseph Smith implored: "Help thy servants to say, *with thy grace assisting them:* Thy will be done, O Lord, and not ours" (D&C 109:44; emphasis added). It is true that praying "Thy will be done" may entail submitting to difficult or challenging circumstances ahead. C. S. Lewis provides a slightly different approach to this scripture: "'Thy will *be done.'* But a great deal of it is to be done by God's creatures; including me. The petition, then, is not merely that I may patiently suffer God's will but also that I may vigorously do it. I must be an agent as well as a patient. I am asking that I may be enabled to do it. . . .

"Taken this way, I find the words have a more regular daily application. For there isn't always—or we don't always have reason to suspect that there is—some great affliction looming in the near future, but there are always duties to be done; usually, for me, neglected duties to be caught up with. 'Thy will be *done*—by me—now' brings one back to brass tacks." Further, Lewis explains that "Thy will be done" may also imply a readiness on our part to receive and experience new and unanticipated blessings. "I know it sounds fantastic," he adds, "but think it over. It seems to me that we often, almost sulkily, reject the good that God offers us because, at that moment, we expected some other good."[5]

60

"Thy will be done" thus represents our petition that the Almighty work his wonders through us, that he soften our hearts to new ideas, new avenues of understanding, and open us to new paths and new doors of opportunity when it is best for us to move in another direction.

IN WHOM DO I TRUST?

There is a passage in the Book of Mormon that can be rather frightening. Jacob explained: "And [Christ] commandeth all men that they must repent, and be baptized in his name, having perfect faith in the Holy One of Israel, or they cannot be saved in the kingdom of God" (2 Nephi 9:23). Perfect faith. *Perfect* faith! Who do you know that has perfect faith, at least as we gauge perfection? I suggest that Jacob is here driving at a point that we are prone to miss—those who have perfect faith in the Holy One of Israel are those who have learned to trust in him completely, to trust in his purposes, as well as his timetable. To come out of the world is to realize that we cannot place our trust in the world. "To come out of the world," President Stephen L Richards observed, "one must forsake the philosophy of the world, and to come into Zion one must adopt the philosophy of Zion. In my own thinking," he continued, "I have reduced the process to a simple formula: Forsake the philosophy of self-sufficiency, which is the philosophy of the world, and adopt the philosophy of faith, which is the philosophy of Christ. Substitute faith for self-assurance."[6]

If I trust completely (or perfectly) in Christ, then how much do I trust in myself? Answer: None. My works are necessary. My reception of the ordinances, the performance of my duties in the Church, acts of service and kindness—these are a part of my Christian covenantal obligation. They are the things I strive to do. But let us come face to face with the reality that there are not enough loaves of bread, enough home or visiting teaching appointments, enough meetings—believe it or not!—or enough encouraging notes to assure my exaltation. My good works are necessary, but they are not sufficient. I cannot work myself into celestial glory, and I cannot guarantee myself a place among the sanctified through my own unaided efforts. Therefore, even though my own merits are essential to salvation, they alone will not take me where I need to go. Rather, it is by and through the merits of Christ. This transcendent truth should create, not feelings of futility, but feelings of deep humility.

"Suppose we have the scriptures," Elder Bruce R. McConkie explained, "the gospel, the priesthood, the Church, the ordinances, the organization, even the keys of the kingdom—everything that now is, down to the last jot and tittle—and yet there is no atonement of Christ. What then? Can we be saved? Will all our good works save us? Will we be rewarded for all our righteousness?

"Most assuredly we will not. We are not saved by works alone, no matter how good; we are saved because God sent his Son to shed his blood in Gethsemane and on Calvary that all through him might ransomed be. We are saved by the blood of Christ (Acts 20:28; 1 Cor. 6:20).

"To paraphrase Abinadi [see Mosiah 13:28], 'Salvation doth not come by the Church alone; and were it not for the atonement, given by the grace of God as a free gift, all men must unavoidably perish, and this notwithstanding the Church and all that appertains to it.'"[7] Or, as Elder Dallin H. Oaks observed: "Man unquestionably has impressive powers and can bring to pass great things by tireless efforts and indomitable will. But after all our obedience and good works, we cannot be saved from the effect of our sins without the grace extended by the atonement of Jesus Christ."[8]

Lehi addressed his son Jacob with these words: "Wherefore, I know that thou art redeemed." Why was he redeemed? Because he was such an obedient son? Because he had followed the direction of his elder brother? Because he was sensitive and submissive and faithful? We know that he was all of those. But note Lehi's words: "Wherefore, I know that thou art redeemed, because of the righteousness of thy Redeemer" (2 Nephi 2:3). Jacob was bound for glory because of the goodness of Jesus! But didn't Jacob's goodness matter? Of course it did. Jacob's carefulness to live according to the commandments evidenced his commitment to the Lord and his desire to keep his part of the covenant. But as noble a son as Jacob was, he could never save himself. As a modern revelation attests, Christ pleads our cause before the Father on the basis of his own suffering and death and perfection (D&C 45:3–5). Imperfect people can be redeemed only by a perfect Being.

Nephi encouraged his readers to rely "wholly upon the merits of him who is mighty to save" (2 Nephi 31:19). Aaron explained that "since man had fallen he could not merit anything of himself; but the suffering and death of Christ atone for their sins, through faith and repentance" (Alma 22:14). Moroni added that the Saints of God rely "alone upon the merits of Christ, who [is] the author and the finisher of [our] faith" (Moroni 6:4). We are indeed saved by merits—the merits of our

Redeemer. The debate has raged for far too long over whether we are saved by grace or by works, a squabble originating in early Christianity into which too many of the Latter-day Saints have been drawn. It is a silly argument, an unnecessary struggle, one that has generated much more heat than light. It is, in fact, the wrong question. The real questions—the ones that get to the heart of the matter—are these: In whom do I trust? On whom do I rely? Truly, as someone has suggested, the word *grace* is an acronym for a glorious concept: "God's Riches At Christ's Expense."[9]

My confidence in God is essential. My confidence in myself is incidental, inextricably tied to my trust in God. As Bruce Hafen has observed: "When we place our confidence in God rather than in ourselves, our need for self-esteem takes care of itself—not because of our manipulation of successful experiences but because our fundamental attitude allows us access to the only trustworthy source for knowing that the course of life we pursue is known to and accepted by God. It is not just the mistake-free, no-fault life that pleases God. He has deliberately placed us in a sphere where the most sharply focused purpose is to learn from our experience and to grow in both our desires and our understanding to be like him. Obviously that includes the greatest effort and integrity we can muster as we seek to do his will. But the heart of it all is not *self*-confidence. It is confidence in *him*, and in his power to make us into creatures far beyond the reach of what our goal-setting and goal-achieving can ultimately accomplish in the process of becoming as he is."[10]

There is, then, a life in Christ, a new life in Christ that we cannot know or experience unless we yield to and appropriate his transforming powers and stop trying to do everything ourselves. In the spiritual realm, there is nothing weak about trusting, nothing passive about reliance. In one sense, as C. S. Lewis observed, "The road back to God is a road of moral effort, of trying harder and harder. But in another sense it is not trying that is ever going to bring us home. All this trying leads up to the vital moment at which you turn to God and say, 'You must do this; I can't.'" Such submission, Lewis adds, represents a significant change in our nature, "the change from being confident about our own efforts to the state in which we despair of doing anything for ourselves and leave it to God. "I know the words 'leave it to God' can be misunderstood," Lewis continues. "The sense in which a Christian leaves it to God is that he puts all his trust in Christ: trusts that Christ will somehow share with him the perfect human obedience which He carried out from His birth to His crucifixion: that Christ will make the man [or woman] more like Himself and, in a sense, make good his [or her] deficiencies."[11] In a word, I am incomplete or partial, whereas Christ is whole or complete. As I come unto Christ by covenant, we (Christ and I) are complete. I am unfinished, whereas Christ is finished. Through "relying alone" upon the merits of the Author and Finisher of my faith (Moroni 6:4; compare Hebrews 12:2), I become finished or fully formed. I am so very imperfect, while Christ is perfect. Together we are perfect. Truly, as the apostle Paul taught, we "are complete in him, [who] is the head of all principality and power" (Colossians 2:10). Those who come unto Christ become perfect *in him* (see Moroni 10:32). Those who inherit the celestial kingdom are just men and just women who have been "made perfect through Jesus the mediator of the new covenant, who wrought out this perfect atonement through the shedding of his own blood" (D&C 76:69).

GRACEFUL LIVING

Knowing as we do that we are saved by grace, after all we can do (2 Nephi 25:23), how shall we then live? What does it mean to live by grace? Consider the following simple points:

It is unhealthy, inappropriate, and spiritually counterproductive to compare ourselves with others, whether in terms of perks or crosses. None of us knows what goes on in the hidden parts of another's life, either the successes or the failures. We are told by the Savior to judge righteous judgment (JST Matthew 7:1); that includes a warning against judging ourselves too harshly as a result of what we think we know about others. Always remember that the Lord can do extraordinary things with very ordinary people, if they will let him. President Joseph F. Smith explained that "to do well those things which God ordained to be the common lot of all mankind, is the truest greatness."[12]

Jesus warned about being unduly anxious or concerned about having enough food or clothing for the future (see 3 Nephi 13:25). That is good counsel about life in general; the disciples would do well to stop worrying and fretting so much about making the cut. The more we learn to trust the Lord and rely upon his merits and mercy, the less anxious we become about life here and hereafter. "Thus if you have really handed yourself over to Him," C. S. Lewis wisely remarked, "it must follow that you are trying to obey Him. But trying in a new way, a less worried way."[13]

The work of spiritual transformation is only partly our work. We will become holy people as we do our best to keep our covenants and then, as Moses said, "Stand still, and see the salvation of the Lord" (Exodus 14:13). C. S. Lewis taught that God "will make the feeblest and filthiest of us into a god or goddess, a dazzling, radiant, immortal creature, pulsating all through with such energy and joy and wisdom and love as we cannot now imagine, a bright stainless mirror which reflects back to God perfectly (though, of course, on a smaller scale) His own boundless power and delight and goodness. The process will be long and in parts very painful; but that is what we are in for. Nothing less. He meant what He said."[14]

The Lord God loves us and desires to save us with an everlasting salvation. There is no quota on the number of saved beings, no bell curve to determine our final standing in the royal gradebooks. We can make it. God knows that and desires for each one of us to know it as well. Lucifer would prefer, of course, that we think otherwise. Whereas the ultimate blessings of salvation do not come until the next life, there is a sense in which people in this life may enjoy the assurance of salvation and the peace that accompanies that knowledge (D&C 59:23).

True faith in Christ produces hope in Christ—not worldly wishing but expectation, anticipation, assurance. As the apostle Paul wrote, the Holy Spirit provides the "earnest of our inheritance," the promise or evidence that we are on course, in covenant, and thus in line for full salvation in the world to come (Ephesians 1:13–14; 2 Corinthians 1:21–22; 5:5). That is, the Spirit of God operating in our lives is like the Lord's "earnest money" on us—his sweet certification that he seriously intends to save us with an everlasting salvation. Thus if we are striving to cultivate the gift of the Holy Ghost, we are living in what might be called a "saved" condition.

Too many of us wrestle with feelings of inadequacy, struggle with hopelessness, and in general are much too anxious about our standing before God. It is important to keep the ultimate goal of exaltation ever before us, but it seems so much more profitable to focus on fundamentals and on the here and now—staying in covenant, being dependable and true to our promises, cultivating the gift of the Holy Ghost.

President Brigham Young taught that "our work is a work of the present. The salvation we are seeking is for the present, and, sought correctly, it can be obtained, and be continually enjoyed. If it continues to-day, it is upon the same principle that it will continue to-morrow, the next day, the next week, or the next year, and, we might say, the next eternity."[15]

BALANCE

The principle of grace has been a part of the restored gospel since the beginning. It has been an integral part of the lives of those Latter-day Saints whose trust in the Lord is greater than their trust in other things. Living by grace is a way of life, an understanding, a perspective that comes to us as we come unto Him who embodies peace and rest. Perhaps it is the complexity of life in a modern world that drives many of us to our knees more frequently and causes us to search the scriptures with an earnestness born of pressing need. We sense more than ever the need to do our duty, to attend to our family and Church responsibilities, all as a part of keeping our covenant with Christ. That is, we come to know the value and necessity of good works. Those works, motivated by his Spirit, are evidence of our covenant. But we also seek for that balance, that critical and elusive balance in life that allows us to do our best without browbeating ourselves because of all we cannot do at the moment.

I know the Lord wants us to succeed. Discouragement and despondency are not of the Lord. They are of Lucifer. The arch-deceiver would have us lose our balance, lose track of what matters most in life, and labor to exhaustion in secondary causes. We cannot do everything we are asked to do, at least not in a few weeks or months. There is great virtue in praying that the Lord will reveal to us our limits, let us know when enough is enough, when doubling or tripling our efforts will in reality be spiritually counterproductive.

Because we are human—because we are weak and mortal and tired—we will probably never reach the point in this life when we have done "all we can do." Too many of us misread 2 Nephi 25:23 and conclude that the Lord can assist us only *after,* meaning following the time that we have done "all we can do." That is incorrect; he can and does help us all along the way. I think Nephi is trying to emphasize that no matter how much we do, it simply will not be enough to guarantee salvation without Christ's intervention. Restating Nephi, "Above and beyond all we can do, it is by the grace of Christ that we are saved." And what is true of our ultimate salvation is true of our daily salvation, the

66

redemption of our personality and our passions, our walk and talk. Above and beyond all efforts at self-control, behavior modification, or reducing our sins to manageable categories, "everything which really needs to be done in our souls can be done only by God."[16]

There is yet another way to look at 2 Nephi 25:23. After the conversion of thousands of Lamanites by the sons of Mosiah, the brother of Lamoni, named Anti-Nephi-Lehi, counseled with his people, those who had covenanted not to take up weapons against their brethren in war. He first expressed to his people his gratitude for the goodness of God—for sending the Spirit, softening the hearts of the Lamanites, opening doors of communication between the Nephites and the Lamanites, and convincing the people of their sins. He continued: "And I also thank my God, yea, my great God, that he hath granted unto us that we might repent of these things, and also that he hath forgiven us of those our many sins and murders which we have committed, and taken away the guilt from our hearts, through the merits of his Son.

"And now behold, my brethren, since it has been all that we could do, (as we were the most lost of all mankind) to repent of all our sins and the many murders which we have committed, and to get God to take them away from our hearts, for it was all we could do to repent sufficiently before God that he would take away our stain—

"Now, my best beloved brethren, since God hath taken away our stains, and our swords have become bright, then let us stain our swords no more with the blood of our brethren" (Alma 24:10–12).

There is a very real sense in which "all we can do" is come before the Lord in reverent humility, confess our weakness, and plead for his forgiveness, for his mercy and grace. It occurred to me recently that life is repentance, that progression and improvement and growth and maturity and refinement are all forms of repentance, and that the God-fearing live in a constant state of repentance. This truth means not that we should live in a constant state of fear or frustration or anxiety but rather that we have desires for holiness and purity, longings to feel quiet confidence before God. Indeed, King Benjamin taught that those who regularly and consistently acknowledge the greatness of God and their own nothingness without Him retain a remission of sins from day to day (Mosiah 4:11–12).

Pushing ourselves beyond what is appropriate is, in a strange sort of way, acknowledging a fear that we must do the job ourselves if we expect it to get done. Of course, we must do our duty in the Church; the works of righteousness are also necessary. What seems so very unnecessary is the type of pharisaical extremism and the subsequent negative feelings that too often characterize the efforts of some Church members. I have a conviction that God is unquestionably aware of us. He loves you, and he loves me. This I know. He certainly wants us to improve, but he definitely does not want us to spend our days languishing in guilt. I reaffirm that the gospel of Jesus Christ is intended to liberate us, to lift and lighten our burdens. If it is not doing that in our personal lives, then perhaps our approach and understanding, our orientation—not necessarily the quantity of work to be done—may need some adjustment. Balance. Balance. That is the key. I have come to sense the need to balance a type of "divine discontent"—a healthy longing to improve—with what Nephi called a "perfect brightness of hope" (2 Nephi 31:20)—the Spirit-given assurance that in and through Jesus Christ we are going to make it.

CONCLUSION

I am very much aware that many have been subjected to much pain and distress, to abuse, to neglect, to the agonies of wanting more than anything to live a normal life and to feel normal feelings but who seem unable to do so. I would say, first of all, that each of us, no matter who we are, wrestle with something. It may be our weight or height or complexion or baldness or I.Q. Perhaps it's a trial that passes in time, like a phase. Perhaps it's the torture of watching helplessly as loved ones choose unwisely and thereby close doors of opportunity for themselves and foreclose future privileges. Or we may suffer a terrible trauma when someone we love deals a blow that strikes at the center of all we hold dear and value about ourselves.

I bear my witness that the day is coming when all the wrongs, the awful wrongs of this life, will be righted. I bear witness that the God of justice will attend to all evil. And I certify that those things that are beyond our power to control will be corrected, either here or hereafter. Many of us may come to experience the lifting, liberating powers of the Atonement in this life; all our losses will be made up before we pass from this sphere of existence. Some of us may wrestle all our days with our traumas, but He will surely fix the time of our release. When a person passes through the veil of death, all those impediments and challenges and crosses that were beyond his or her power to control—abuse, neglect, immoral environment, weighty traditions—will be torn away

like a film, and perfect peace will prevail in our hearts. "Some frustrations," Elder Boyd K. Packer taught, "we must endure without really
solving the problem. Some things that ought to be put in order are not
put in order because we cannot control them. Things we cannot solve,
we must survive."[17]

Our Lord and Master seems to ask of us the impossible—to forgive
those who have hurt us so dreadfully. As Bruce and Marie Hafen have
observed, "It seems fair to ask why the victims of abuse should be
required to do *anything* to deserve the Lord's vast healing powers in such
a case. Because abuse victims suffer so many of the same symptoms of
guilt and estrangement from God as do willful transgressors, the irony
that they should need to forgive those who have wronged them is almost
overpowering.

"Still, there lurks between the lines of the scriptures on forgiveness a
message of transcendent meaning—not only about abuse victims but
about all of us, and about all of the Atonement."

The Hafens continue, "What are we doing when we are willing to
absorb a terrible trauma of the spirit, caused not by our own doing but
by one who claimed to love us—and we absorb the trauma even to help
the sinner? That picture somehow has a familiar look—we've seen all
this before. Of course, because this picture depicts the sacrifice of Jesus
Christ: he took upon himself undeserved and unbearable burdens,
heaped upon him by people who often said, and often believed, that
they loved him. And he assumed that load not for any need of his, but
only to help them.

"So to forgive—not just for abuse victims, but for each of us—is to be
a Christ figure, a transitional point in the war between good and evil,
stopping the current of evil by absorbing it in every pore, thereby protecting the innocent next generation and helping to enable the repentance and healing of those whose failures sent the jolts into our own
systems."[18]

I know of the power that is in Christ, power not only to create the
worlds and divide the seas but also to still the storms of the human heart,
to right life's wrongs, to ease and eventually even remove the pain of
scarred and beaten souls. There is no bitterness, no anger, no fear, no
jealousy, no feelings of inadequacy that cannot be healed by the Great
Physician. He is the Balm of Gilead. He is the One sent by the Father
to "bind up the brokenhearted, to proclaim liberty to the captives, and

the opening of the prison to them that are bound" (Isaiah 61:1). True followers of Christ learn to trust in him more, in the arm of flesh less. They learn to rely on him more, on human solutions less. They learn to surrender their burdens to him more. They learn to work to their limits and then be willing to seek that grace of enabling power that will make up the difference, that sacred power that makes all the difference!

As Moroni has instructed us on the last page of the Book of Mormon, when we come unto Christ and seek, all through our lives, to deny ourselves of ungodliness and give ourselves without let or hindrance to God, "then is his grace sufficient for you, that by his grace ye may be perfect in Christ"—whole, complete, fully formed: "and if by the grace of God ye are perfect in Christ, ye can in nowise deny the power of God" (Moroni 10:32). In other words, those who completely surrender and submit to the Almighty cannot deny—block, stop, or prevent—the power of God from coming into their lives. In short, to come unto the Savior is to come to life, to awaken to an entirely new realm. Because of who Christ our Lord is and what he has done, there is no obstacle to peace and joy here or hereafter too great to face or overcome. Because of him, our minds can be at peace. Our souls may rest.

NOTES

1. John F. MacArthur Jr., *Faith Works: The Gospel according to the Apostles* (Dallas: Word Publishing, 1993), 32.
2. M. Russell Ballard, "Building Bridges of Understanding," address delivered to the Logan, Utah, Institute of Religion, 17 February 1998, typescript, 6–7.
3. C. S. Lewis, *Mere Christianity* (New York: Simon & Schuster, 1996), 59.
4. See *Teachings of Ezra Taft Benson* (Salt Lake City: Bookcraft, 1988), 361.
5. C. S. Lewis, *Letters to Malcolm: Chiefly on Prayer* (New York: Harcourt Brace & Company, 1992), 25–26; emphasis in original.
6. Stephen L Richards, *Where Is Wisdom?* (Salt Lake City: Deseret Book, 1955), 419.
7. Bruce R. McConkie, "What Think Ye of Salvation by Grace?" devotional address, Brigham Young University, Provo, Utah, 10 January 1984; in *Doctrines of the Restoration*, ed. Mark L. McConkie (Salt Lake City: Bookcraft, 1989), 76.
8. Dallin H. Oaks, Conference Report, October 1988, 78.
9. MacArthur, *Faith Works*, 57.
10. Bruce C. Hafen, *The Broken Heart: Applying the Atonement to Life's Experiences* (Salt Lake City: Deseret Book, 1989), 120; emphasis in original.
11. Lewis, *Mere Christianity*, 129–30.
12. Joseph F. Smith, *Gospel Doctrine* (Salt Lake City: Deseret Book, 1971), 285.
13. Lewis, *Mere Christianity*, 131.
14. Lewis, *Mere Christianity*, 176.

15. Brigham Young, *Journal of Discourses*, 26 vols. (London: Latter-day Saints' Book Depot, 1854–86), 1:131; see also 8:124–25.
16. Lewis, *Mere Christianity*, 166.
17. Boyd K. Packer, Conference Report, October 1987, 20.
18. Bruce C. Hafen and Marie K. Hafen, *The Belonging Heart: The Atonement and Relationships with God and Family* (Salt Lake City: Deseret Book, 1994), 122–23.

Relief Society, the Possible Dream

MARY ELLEN SMOOT

In 1605, Spanish novelist Cervantes wrote his masterpiece about an idealist named Don Quixote. You know the story. It later became the Broadway musical *Man of La Mancha*. Don Quixote believed in the power of vision, of seeing the good in every individual and lifting others to greater heights. He helped many to believe in themselves by teaching them to dream—to dream the impossible dream. I would like to visit with you instead about dreaming the possible dream. Good dreams, firmly grounded in the gospel of Jesus Christ, lift and inspire.

When I was a young mother, we were living in an apartment with two small children. My husband was finishing his schooling at the university, working full time, and serving in the bishopric. Because of two years' military service, we had already moved five times, both in and out of the state, and we had been married only three years. So, as you might imagine, I was thrilled at the idea of settling into a home of our own. It was an exciting day when we moved into that little home. I thought I was at the end of my troubles—but I did not realize which end.

For twenty-five years we lived in that home, and our family grew from two to seven children. From the beginning, the home presented great challenges. We had to dig a well for water, and the water we got from it was so full of iron that it often tasted as bad as it looked. Even though we purchased better pumps and found solutions to our continuing water problems, we had a steady stream of leaks, floods, and repairs while living

Mary Ellen Wood Smoot began her service as Relief Society General President in April 1997. She loves family history and research and has written several histories of parents, grandparents, and their local community. She served with her husband, Stanley M. Smoot, when he was called as a mission president in Ohio, and they later served together as directors of Church Hosting. They are the parents of seven children and the grandparents of forty-five.

there. If you turned on the cold water in the kitchen while the shower was in use, the person was drenched in hot water, causing a loud yelp. And when I turned on the water to wash a batch of clothes, I had to watch closely to turn the fill cycle twice just to get enough water to wash the clothes. If I mastered that feat, I almost never could get enough water into the rinse cycle to wash out the soap.

This water system became the bane of my life. At times I felt trapped in what seemed an impossible situation. Do you think I dreamed about a better way? Of course I did. My father gave me some sage advice: "When you feel you have reached the end of your rope, tie a knot and hang on!" Sometimes I pleaded with my husband to move. But we both knew that was not the answer. For one thing, we couldn't afford it.

Once when my husband was out of town, my neighbor and I moved the washer and dryer to the garage, wallpapered the utility room, bought a love seat, rocker, lamp, and table, and made a sitting room. Then, for a period of time, I took all of our dirty clothes to the laundromat once a week. I would bring the clean and folded clothes home, place them in the children's drawers and closets, and feel better about my home.

We learned to live with our water problems, however annoying they became. Our children developed patience and long-suffering—and so did their mother. For the sake of my family, I determined to stop whining and make the best of our situation. And I did.

I came to the realization that the pluses were better than the minuses. We really had a happy life in that small home. Our children could work at their grandfather's dairy, ride horses, build forts, feed baby calves, and pick fruit from the orchard.

When we sold that home some twenty-five years later, I was thrilled with the new home we built: it had an excellent water system in it. My impossible dream had finally become a reality, but I now cherished the lessons learned. We had learned to live with some rather unfavorable circumstances that had actually helped us to achieve our more important dream of being a happy and united family.

As we work to realize our dreams, greater possibilities will unfold for us—and for those we love and serve. Throughout the scriptures, the Savior shares this truth in its full and most correct sense. He teaches us to do more than just dream. And he makes it clear that only "with God all things are possible" (Matthew 19:26). The Lord shows us the way; he is "the way" to make our dreams come true. With him, impossible dreams can become possible, even realities.

Let me illustrate with the story of Enoch. He built a city called Zion, in which the people were "of one heart and one mind, and dwelt in righteousness" (Moses 7:18). Building Zion must have seemed like an impossible dream even to Enoch at first. But as Enoch and his people worked toward their righteous goal, the Lord blessed them.

Establishing Zion not only is possible but is our charge as Latter-day Saints. It will not happen overnight, but each of us can be inspired by the way Enoch overcame challenges and became all that our Father in Heaven wanted him to be.

As members of Relief Society, we help each other. We unitedly seek for purity of heart. We strive to become all that our Heavenly Father wants us to be—individually and collectively.

The Prophet Joseph Smith reminded the first members of the Relief Society about our divine purpose: "This organization is not only for the purpose of administering to the sick and afflicted, the poor and the needy, but it is to save souls. If ye are pure in all things nothing on earth or heaven can hinder the angels from associating with you."[1]

As individuals and as a Society, we are here to save souls. As each of us does the Lord's work in our own sphere of influence, the Lord's great work of the latter day will be accomplished. We are here to usher this Society into the next century, to join hands with sisters across the globe, and to lead each other into life eternal.

In a recent general conference President Boyd K. Packer spoke of our essential role as Relief Society sisters: "However much priesthood power and authority the men may possess—however much wisdom and experience they may accumulate—the safety of the family, the integrity of the doctrine, the ordinances, the covenants, indeed the future of the Church, rests equally upon the women. The defenses of the home and family are greatly reinforced when the wife and mother and daughters belong to Relief Society."[2]

The time has come for the members of Relief Society to realize fully the magnitude of its mission and to represent the Lord and his leaders to the women of the world. The time has come to raise our heads and fly the banner of righteousness. Devote yourself to Relief Society. Or, as President Packer admonished, "Do not allow yourselves to be organized under another banner which cannot, in truth, fulfill your needs."[3] As a devoted Relief Society sister, you will see miracles happen in your own lives—and in the lives of those you serve. Under its banner, impossible dreams can come true.

Using Enoch's experience as a model, I'd like to suggest four steps toward realizing our righteous dreams as daughters of God—as wives, mothers, and Relief Society sisters.

Learn the ways of God. In Moses 6:21 we read about Enoch's upbringing. His father, Jared, "taught [his sons and daughters] in all the ways of God."

We too must learn the ways of God. For Enoch and for each of us, learning gospel truths and living them is essential to all else. We begin with ourselves and then we strengthen our families. We always start in our own hearts and homes. By creating loving relationships with our husbands and children, they see and feel the difference from the ways of the world.

Prophets throughout the ages have counseled us to read, study, ponder, and pray—and to set the proper example of love and service to others. If we develop and then live our testimony, the kingdom of God will flourish and grow.

Every sister must find her Sacred Grove—whether it's a quiet place in the bedroom or a private spot in the yard. Go to the Lord with the desires of your heart and ask for strength and direction. If you feel you are short on faith and hope, start by asking for even the "desire to believe" (Alma 32:27). And then put to the test the process outlined in Alma 32. Plant a seed of faith in your heart. You will be blessed with answers. You will not be disappointed. For every principle you pray about and live, you will be assured of its truth, and your heart will swell with love, peace, and joy. The principle will become "delicious" unto you (Alma 32:28).

Being fully taught in the ways of God also means we must make and keep necessary ordinances and sacred covenants. Elder Boyd K. Packer has said: "Ordinances and covenants become our credentials for admission into [God's] presence. To worthily receive them is the quest of a lifetime. To keep them thereafter is the challenge of mortality."[4]

The completeness of the gospel of Jesus Christ is beautiful. It is a restoration rather than a reformation. You cannot find all that we have anywhere else because we have a fulness of truth. It will not fail us, if we live it. What makes the gospel of Jesus Christ unique? Through the teachings of the gospel of Jesus Christ, we learn the following:

1. We were spirit children of our Father in Heaven.

2. We lived with him before we came to this earth.

3. There was a Grand Council in Heaven, and we chose to follow his plan, which included receiving a mortal body and being sent to this earth to be tested—to prove ourselves worthy to live with him throughout eternity.

4. The priesthood of God has been restored to the earth, and through the priesthood we may be baptized by immersion as planned by the Savior.

5. We can be together forever as a family if we live worthily and receive the saving ordinances.

6. We can also assist in the completion of the vicarious ordinance work for our ancestors through genealogy and temple work.

Let me share the story of one sister's conversion. About thirty-five years ago, a young girl of ten was introduced to the gospel when the missionaries started meeting with her family in Uruguay. She listened carefully and knew what she was hearing was true. She chose to be baptized, even though no one else in her family joined the Church.

That young girl prayed, studied the scriptures, and remained faithful through many years. Her faith in Jesus Christ carried her along. She weathered the challenges that come to someone so young and so alone in her beliefs because she continued to search the scriptures and to ponder and pray about them. She learned the ways of God, even though she had not been taught them by her parents. The Spirit of the Holy Ghost rested upon her and guided her. She received her education, filled a mission, and became a valiant instrument in the Lord's kingdom.

She eventually moved close to a temple and completed the temple work for thousands of her deceased family members. She will truly be a savior on Mount Zion and be praised throughout eternity for her strength, courage, and determination.

Neither this faithful sister nor I would say the way is easy. But as President Howard W. Hunter explains, the Lord would have us press forward with a perfect brightness of hope. President Hunter said: "This faith and hope of which I speak is not a Pollyanna-like approach to significant personal and public problems. I don't believe we can wake up in the morning and simply by drawing a big 'happy face' on the chalkboard believe that is going to take care of the world's difficulties. But if our faith and hope are anchored in Christ, in his teachings, commandments, and promises, then we are able to count on something truly remarkable, genuinely miraculous."[5]

For Enoch, and for each of us, the promise is sure: "Ask, and it shall be given you; seek, and ye shall find; knock, and it shall be opened unto you" (Matthew 7:7). It really will. The Lord told Enoch, and each of us in turn, how to achieve what some might consider the impossible. We begin by learning the ways of God and then teaching our children and those we love and serve. As we do, our dreams will take a more celestial shape. The Spirit of the Lord not only will help us design worthy dreams but will guide us in our efforts to realize them.

Ask, "Why me?" Enoch's story begins in much the same way any of ours would. He was faced with a challenge, given him of the Lord, and—at first—he doubted his ability to meet it.

What challenges are you facing in your life? Now think of yourself in the place of Enoch. "[Enoch] heard a voice from heaven, saying: Enoch, my son, prophesy unto this people, and say unto them—Repent, for thus saith the Lord: I am angry with this people, and my fierce anger is kindled against them; for their hearts have waxed hard, and their ears are dull of hearing, and their eyes cannot see afar off" (Moses 6:27).

Much like the people in Enoch's time, our vision can so easily become clouded by worldly concerns and cares so that our "eyes cannot see afar off" (Moses 6:27). And when we are surrounded by hearts that "have waxed hard" (v. 27)—hearts that would tell us not to believe, not to dream—how do we keep our hearts soft and strong? How do we go forward with faith?

Even Enoch had a moment of asking, "Why me?" "And when Enoch had heard [the Lord's] words, he bowed himself to the earth, before the Lord, and spake . . . : Why is it that I have found favor in thy sight, and am but a lad, and all the people hate me; for I am slow of speech; wherefore am I thy servant?" (Moses 6:31–32). At first, Enoch could think only of his weaknesses. He was slow of speech, unpopular, and "but a lad" (Moses 6:31). But the Lord saw greatness in him.

President Gordon B. Hinckley wrote: "I believe that I am a child of God, endowed with a divine birthright. I believe that there is something of divinity within me and within each of you. I believe that we have a godly inheritance and that it is our responsibility, our obligation, and our opportunity to cultivate and nurture the very best of these qualities within us."[6]

When a reporter asked Helen Keller, who was blind and deaf from infancy, what could be worse than being blind, she responded, "Having eyes to see . . . and no vision."[7]

Like you and me, Enoch may not have caught in an instant the vision of what one person can do. We don't create a Zion society, people, or family overnight. But as we become pure in heart, as we not only dream the dream but also strive to live the reality, we will be blessed with strength and vision beyond our own.

Enoch lived in a very wicked world. He did not welcome the responsibility of calling the people to repentance. It must have seemed like an overwhelming challenge.

I will never forget when one challenge, in the form of a calling, was given to me. My husband and I had been serving as directors of Church Hosting for four years. We loved this calling and expected to remain in it for at least one more year.

On 25 March 1997, my husband and I left the First Presidency's office after introducing them to a dignitary from Russia whom we were hosting. This was not an unusual interaction. But receiving a call to return and meet with President Hinckley again, shortly after returning to our Public Affairs office, was unusual.

President Hinckley greeted us and visited warmly with my husband for a time. Then he sat back in his chair and said, "I would like to call Mary Ellen Smoot as the new general Relief Society president."

I could hardly breathe. I will never forget the first words out of my mouth. I said to a prophet of the Lord, "Are you sure?"

Much like Enoch, I was deeply humbled by this calling. I, too, felt slow of speech and inadequate. But I have taken great comfort in the fact that if we humble ourselves before the Lord and have faith in him, he will "make weak things become strong" (Ether 12:27). If we are willing to do our part, our Father in Heaven will make us equal to anything he calls us to do.

Have you ever wanted to ask, "Why me?" in your calling as a mother, a teacher, or a Relief Society leader? I suggest that you do ask, "Why me?" And this is the second step toward realizing impossible dreams. Yes, ask, "Why me?" Not with a quiver of doubt but, instead, with all the faith you can muster, humbly ask the Lord what he would have you do and why you are uniquely suited to serve. Ask yourself questions like these: "What can I contribute?" "Why was I chosen to be the mother of these children?" "What can I do to strengthen the sisters in my ward?" and so forth. We each have purpose and reason for being. Every sister has a thread to weave in the tapestry of time. Discover your thread and begin to weave.

We are living in a trying time, to be sure. We see evil all around us. But do you suppose the call that came to Enoch could be for each of us who knows the gospel of Jesus Christ and yet still wastes time complaining? Are we going to allow Satan to win? We can't afford to settle back in our easy chairs and say, "What can I do? I'm just one person."

Instead, we can say, "I am one person. And 'I can do all things through Christ which strengtheneth me'" (Philippians 4:13). How the faith of one person can make a difference if we forget ourselves and go to work!

One sister knelt in prayer and asked her Heavenly Father to help her have vision for her life. She wanted his help in defining a worthy dream, and so she humbly and fervently prayed, "How can I be of service? What would thou have me do?" And she received an answer in her heart. She felt that her calling on earth was to raise a righteous family.

This sister magnified her calling as a wife and mother and met the challenge of rearing a large family. Challenges do come our way as we teach our Father in Heaven's Saturday's Warriors. In moments of frustration or doubt, she was able to recall the peace she felt for the direction she had taken. Because she knew that her calling came from the Lord, because she had sincerely and faithfully asked, "Why me?" she became equal to the task.

Upon such faith great families have been built. Upon such faith our Relief Society was established. At the celebration of the fortieth anniversary of the Relief Society, Sarah M. Kimball detailed how the organization came about. Eliza R. Snow wrote a constitution for the women to begin an organization to assist those who were building the temple. The Prophet Joseph Smith read her constitution and said that it was one of the best he had ever read. And then he declared: "This is not what the sisters want, there is something better for them. I have desired to organize the sisters in the order of the priesthood. I now have the key by which I can do it."[8]

The Prophet had vision for what this Society was to become. Not only would it be one of the largest organizations of women in the world but it would also be the only one organized "in the order of the priesthood." The purpose and mission of Relief Society extends beyond the year 2000 or the year 2002. Relief Society reaches into the eternities. What can you and I do to bring it out of obscurity? Why were we called to be Relief Society sisters in the latter day?

Choose ye this day to serve the Lord God. Let's look back at the conditions in Enoch's time and see how similar they were to our own. The Lord said of the people of Enoch: "Ever since the day that I created them, have they gone astray, and have denied me, and have sought their own counsels in the dark; . . . and have not kept the commandments, which I gave unto their father, Adam" (Moses 6:28).

And yet, what did the Lord tell Enoch? "Go forth and do as I have commanded thee, and no man shall pierce thee. Open thy mouth, and it shall be filled, and I will give thee utterance, for all flesh is in my hands, and I will do as seemeth me good. Say unto this people: Choose ye this day, to serve the Lord God who made you" (Moses 6:32–33).

The third step I would suggest to you in realizing your dreams is just that: "Choose ye this day, to serve the Lord God who made you." Right now, renew your commitment. Choose this day to serve the Lord, and the windows of heaven will open for you.

Remember the new home my husband and I built after twenty-five years of living in that small home with water problems? Let me tell you the rest of the story. Shortly after we moved into our dream home, my husband and I were called to preside over the Ohio Columbus Mission.

The most difficult part about leaving home, however, had little to do with my leaving my lovely new home with its glorious water system. I was concerned about transplanting my thirteen-year-old son and leaving one of my married daughters who had just given birth to her fourth child, a son named Ben, who had been born with Crouzzons Syndrome, which created severe health problems.

I wanted to be there for her in her time of need. I wanted to be the attentive mother and grandmother I knew I should be, but I also wanted to serve the Lord.

And so I had to choose. I had to choose whether to answer a calling from the Lord or to stay at home and serve my family at a time when my help was really needed. At that point in my life, I knew that when the Lord calls, you go. But it still was not easy to say good-bye to my family.

What I came to realize, though, was that through my choosing to serve the Lord in the mission field, my family was truly blessed. The Relief Society rallied around my daughter. Our new ward in Ohio welcomed my teenage son. And with the perspective of many years, I can see how that single decision to serve the Lord blessed my family in ways that I would not have realized had I remained at home. But still, it took a leap of faith.

When we choose to serve the Lord, we choose to submit our will to his and to respond to the promptings of the Spirit. We start asking, "How can I be of service?" and "What would the Lord have me do?" By humbly and faithfully submitting our will to God, the once "impossible" dream ultimately becomes a living reality.

How could I have known that after arriving in Ohio our teenage son would find friends who were nationally ranked wrestling stars and coaches with an incredible wrestling program? He later became a state and national champion and then a coach of the junior high school that my daughter's son Ben would attend.

Ben, over the years, faced his health problems with faith and humility. Through obedience, he grew in testimony and confidence. Ben, under the skilled, experienced coaching of his uncle, won the regional championship as a seventh grader and was honored as outstanding wrestler of the tournament by all the coaches. My daughter and I stood and wept as the final buzzer of the championship match sounded, declaring Ben regional champion. I knew that the Lord had answered my prayers of many years ago.

Choice is essential to our Heavenly Father's plan for happiness. Happiness cannot be forced upon us; it comes as we make righteous choices. Joseph Smith explained: "I teach the people correct principles, and they govern themselves."[9] Using correct principles to govern ourselves is the challenge of mortality.

Think of all the good and important choices you have already made. You chose to come to this earth. That choice alone speaks of your faithfulness. At baptism, you chose to take the name of Christ upon you. In the temple, you chose to make sacred covenants. As your Relief Society leaders, we believe in your ability to make good choices. We trust you to make correct decisions that will bring you lasting joy and peace.

In our world today, we have more choices than ever before and a lot of tough decisions to make. It can be difficult to sort through it all—

especially for those who must live with the unfavorable consequences of another's bad choice. But no matter what our status in life, no matter what choices were made in the past, we can choose to be on the Lord's side now. We may need to redesign some of our dreams, we may need to renew some of our covenants, but we can choose the Lord's plan for happiness today.

David Gelernter, the professor at Yale University whose life was nearly taken by the explosive package sent to him from the Unabomber, commends women such as you. Mr. Gelernter writes:

"Back in 1940 you could never tell why housewives did what they did, whether it was devotion or just momentum. But today you know exactly why homemakers do it: out of love. Some of their families can easily forgo the second income, some cannot; but every one of them could improve her standing in society by taking a job. So today you can see these stubborn women for what they are, the moral backbone of the country. A country with this kind of backbone can't be such a terrible place and is probably capable of weathering anything, in the end."[10] He goes on to say that nobody loves a child as does his or her own parent. And I wholeheartedly agree. Children are given to us as gifts from God; how we choose to rear them is our gift to him.

All of us who love, lead, and guide God's children know the depth of that commitment and the meaning of that gift. Mothers don't get sick days, time off, or overtime compensation. Their reward is of a heavenly kind. I salute you for your efforts to make righteous choices and to be where the Lord would have you be.

To "choose ye this day, to serve the Lord" (Moses 6:33) is to commit faithfully to be where the Lord would have you be, whether that is at home with your family, on a mission in a foreign land, in the temple serving your ancestors, or in the home of the afflicted.

Walk with me. A great promise was given to Enoch, and to each of us in turn, if we will do as the Lord commands: "Behold my Spirit is upon you, wherefore all thy words will I justify; and the mountains shall flee before you, and the rivers shall turn from their course; and thou shalt abide in me, and I in you; therefore walk with me" (Moses 6:34).

What a magnificent blessing! What more could we dream of than abiding in the Lord and walking with him? And that is the fourth and final suggestion I offer for realizing your dreams: walk with the Lord.

Faithful people have walked with God all through the ages. King

Benjamin taught his people what it is like to walk with Him: "And ye will not have a mind to injure one another, but to live peaceably, and to render to every man according to that which is his due" (Mosiah 4:13).

Zion is born of such purity of heart. Dreams are turned into realities with such peaceable and godly living. And that's what Relief Society is all about. As sisters in Zion, we help each other and our families to walk with God and return to our heavenly home.

As sisters we are united with the Brethren of the Church, and they have confidence in us. The Lord is allowing us to move the work forward in a rapid manner that will bless each of our lives. We must unite in Relief Society as never before. Listen to the prophets and follow their words. Brigham Young explained that "a perfect oneness will save a people." And, he continued, "The religion of heaven unites the hearts of the people and makes them one."[11] We become one as we turn our backs on sin, selfishness, materialism, and self-indulgence. We become one as we look to God and give our lives to him.

In the early days of the Church, Relief Society president Bathsheba Smith taught how the greatness of the Relief Society is found in the pure hearts of its individual members. She encouraged the sisters to set aside petty grievances and unite in spirit and deed that they might bring to pass the great mission of this organization. On the occasion of the fiftieth birthday of Relief Society, she said, "Let us take renewed courage and be more united and earnest in this great work, and if anyone has ill feelings towards another, banish them and make this a Jubilee in very deed."[12]

Unity in our Relief Society, unity in our homes, unity in our hearts, is born of banishing ill feelings and taking renewed courage to be more earnest in our endeavors. As sisters in Zion, we can be nothing less than unified.

John Winthrop said of his band of Pilgrims in 1630, and we could say of ourselves and this Relief Society: "We shall be a city upon a hill. The eyes of all people are upon us, so that if we shall deal falsely with our God in this work we have undertaken, and so cause Him to withdraw His presence [and] help from us, we shall be made a story and a byword through the world."[13]

We will be a light to the world—but only to the degree that we are living the principles of the gospel of Jesus Christ and making them an integral part of our everyday lives. May we look to Christ to lift us up at a time when we truly can be a light to the world; when, in the coming years, we really will be "a city upon a hill."

Who will be prepared for the Lord's tremendous promises to those who hearken unto his words and receive his Spirit to guide and direct them? Who will dream what the world thinks is impossible but what the Lord, through his prophets, assures us is possible? Faithful women everywhere.

Does the Lord need each of us to walk with him? Does this world cry out for someone with a clear, clarion call to obedience, truth, and righteous living? Yes!

Everyone wants to find answers that will make the difference in this monumental time in history when we will soon enter the new millennial year. As Relief Society sisters, we can help all of God's children to see that answers are found where they always have been: in scriptures, in prophets' teachings, and in obedience to them.

Enoch was not especially looking forward to what the Lord called him to do. But as we read in Moses 7, Enoch was obedient. He taught and led the people in righteousness. The city of Zion was established, miracles occurred, and Enoch foresaw the coming of the Son of Man, his atoning sacrifice, and the return of Zion.

Ultimately, Enoch and his people did walk with God, and "he dwelt in the midst of Zion; and it came to pass that Zion was not, for God received it up into his own bosom; and from thence went forth the saying, ZION IS FLED" (Moses 7:69).

The people of Enoch walked with God because they walked together and bolstered one another. God did not ask them—or any of us—to walk only with him. He expects us to walk also with each other. Only as we are there to love and serve our family members, our ward members, and our neighbors can he work miracles in our lives. When the bishop calls us to serve, do we ask, "Are you sure?" When our children need extra love and attention, do we respond, "Not now"? Or do we offer a silent prayer and plead for strength, wisdom, and vision beyond our own?

At some time in our lives, each of us will go through a personal Garden of Gethsemane. And each day we have an opportunity to prepare ourselves to go through this period of life by strengthening ourselves spiritually and making righteous decisions.

Several years ago President Hinckley told about a divorced mother of seven children who felt that all of her dreams had been shattered. Not only was she afraid to dream anymore but she felt she faced a mountain of impossibilities. As she returned to her home late one night, she looked at her house and saw that all of the lights were still on. Her children, ages five through sixteen, were waiting for her. "I could hear echoes of my children as I walked out the door . . . : 'Mom, what are we going to have for dinner?' 'Can you take me to the library?' 'I have to get some poster paper tonight.' Tired and weary, I looked at that house and saw the light on in each of the rooms. I thought of all of those children who were home waiting for me to come and meet their needs. My burdens felt very heavy on my shoulders.

"I remember looking through tears toward the sky, and I said, 'Oh, my Father, I just can't do it tonight. I'm too tired. I can't face it. I can't go home and take care of all those children alone. Could I just come to You and stay with You for just one night? I'll come back in the morning.'"

And then she felt the peace of God. In her heart, she heard the answer: "No, little one, you can't come to me now. You would never wish to come back. But I can come to you."[14]

And he will. The promise is sure: "Draw near unto me and I will draw near unto you" (D&C 88:63).

No matter our circumstances, we can dream. And dreams can and will become possible for us as we learn the ways of the Lord, seek his guidance, and choose to serve him. He will walk with us. As individual sisters and as a Relief Society, let us have a vision of where we want to be and build inner strength to get there. Like Enoch, we can have the Spirit of the Lord with us each day as we strive to do his will and make impossible dreams come true.

Like the man of La Mancha and my grandson Ben, may we dream dreams and walk with God, who will assist us in making those dreams become realities as we look to the millennial year and beyond.

NOTES

1. Minutes of Female Relief Society of Nauvoo, 9 June 1842, Archives of The Church of Jesus Christ of Latter-day Saints, Salt Lake City, Utah, 1:63.
2. Boyd K. Packer, *Ensign,* May 1998, 73.
3. Packer, *Ensign,* May 1998, 73.
4. Boyd K. Packer, *Ensign,* May 1987, 24.
5. Howard W. Hunter, *That We Might Have Joy* (Salt Lake City: Deseret Book, 1994), 95.
6. Gordon B. Hinckley, *Ensign,* August 1992, 2–7.

7. As quoted in *May Peace Be with You: Messages from "The Spoken Word"* (Salt Lake City: Deseret Book, 1994), 5.

8. Minutes of the Relief Society, 1:30.

9. Quoted by John Taylor, *Journal of Discourses*, 26 vols. (London: Latter-day Saints' Book Depot, 1854–86), 10:57–58.

10. David Gelernter, *Drawing Life: Surviving the Unabomber* (New York: Simon and Schuster, 1997), 115.

11. Brigham Young, *Discourses of Brigham Young*, sel. John A. Widtsoe (Salt Lake City: Deseret Book, 1954), 282, 285.

12. Bathsheba W. Smith, *Woman's Exponent* 20 (1 April 1892): 139.

13. John Winthrop, *A Model of Christian Charity* (1630).

14. Gordon B. Hinckley, *Ensign*, May 1991, 73.

To Nurture and Be Nurtured: The Friendships of Eliza R. Snow

JILL MULVAY DERR

When Eliza R. Snow was twenty-six years old, she published in the *Ohio Star* a poem entitled "Friendship." Living at home with her parents and siblings in Mantua, Ohio, the town where she had grown up, Eliza had already published six poems in local newspapers. Her 1830 poem described friendship as the "Softest chain that binds our spirits" and concluded with the plea: "When I see life's light retreating, / May it hover round me still."[1] The young woman may not have imagined how her remarkable life would unfold over the next half century, but she hoped friendship would be part of it. And her hopes were realized. Eliza R. Snow, that monumental figure among nineteenth-century Mormon women, was distinct but not detached. Across a lifetime, she nurtured and was nurtured by a multitude of friends. Women who have felt the power of such bonds, as I have in my own life, will recognize the significance of those sweet social ties in Eliza's life.

Cataloguing the public accomplishments of Eliza R. Snow is not a simple task. A gifted thinker and writer, she published seven books, wrote dozens of articles, and penned more than four hundred poems, including the hymns for which she is widely remembered. She exercised the spiritual gifts of tongues, healing, and prophecy and ministered to her sisters in the ordinances of the temple. As general president of the Relief Society from 1866 to 1887, she also essentially presided over the

Jill Mulvay Derr, an associate professor of Church history and research historian with the Joseph Fielding Smith Institute for Latter-day Saint History at Brigham Young University, is writing a biography of Eliza R. Snow. She and her husband, C. Brooklyn Derr, are the parents of four children.

work of the young women's Retrenchment or Mutual Improvement Association and the Primary Association, which she had helped to organize. She addressed hundreds of stake and local meetings during her twenty-year presidency, and her sisters devotedly recorded reams of her inspiring words. The unique place granted her by nineteenth-century Latter-day Saints is evident in the *Juvenile Instructor*'s admonition to Primary teachers in 1890 to cultivate in Mormon children "a reverence for the Prophet Joseph Smith, Sister Eliza R. Snow, and the Holy Priesthood."[2] Though it has been more than a century since her death, we are still trying to grasp her importance to Latter-day Saint women and the Church as a whole.

Yet, however deeply we respect such extraordinary achievements, and perhaps precisely because we respect them, we want somehow to know the woman herself. Examining significant relationships in the life of Eliza Snow tells us a great deal about her. She was affectionately devoted to her family, particularly to her older sister Leonora and her younger brother Lorenzo, the only two members of her family to remain active Latter-day Saints and move west to Utah. She was a plural wife of Joseph Smith and later of Brigham Young but remained childless. And she had many friends, a small handful of whom can be discussed here.

In April 1835, after five years of study and reflection, Eliza Snow requested baptism and became a Latter-day Saint. Within four months she had written her first hymn for the Saints, "Praise Ye the Lord."[3] This and a second hymn, "The Glorious Day Is Rolling On," may well have been composed at the request of Emma Smith, who included both hymns in her *Collection of Sacred Hymns, for the Church of the Latter Day Saints*, published at Kirtland in 1835.[4] Sometime between 1831, when Eliza first met Joseph Smith, and 1836, when she first boarded at Joseph and Emma's home in Kirtland, Eliza Snow and Emma Smith became friends. Similarities and circumstances drew them together. Both were born in 1804, Eliza in Massachusetts and Emma in Pennsylvania. Each was an attractive and intelligent woman. Emma had a beautiful voice and loved to sing. Since her childhood, Eliza had written verses to the measure of popular tunes. The two women thus shared a love of music and song.

The extent to which Emma and Eliza ever became true "soul mates" is not clear. But their deep regard for one another is evident. Eliza was invited to board in Joseph and Emma's home in Kirtland while she taught school, first in spring 1836 and again starting in January 1837. The Smith children were among her students.

Following the Missouri persecutions and the move of the Saints to Nauvoo, Illinois, the friendship between Eliza and Emma deepened. In June 1841, after the arrest of Joseph Smith by Missouri officials on trumped-up charges of treason, Eliza wrote a poem to console Emma. Eliza's poetry is a significant source of information regarding her friendships. In many instances, her poems are the only extant record of her reaction to an event or relationship. Eliza prefaced this poem of thirty-eight lines—seventeen rhymed couplets—with the note: "respectfully inscribed to Mrs. Emma Smith." The lines reveal Eliza's respect for Emma and provide insight into the character of Mormonism's First Lady from someone who knew her well.

> I saw her in the throng, that met to pray
> For her companion—torn from her away,
> And from the church; thro' the device of those,
> Who in Missouri, vow'd to be our foes!
> I gazed a moment, then I turn'd aside,
> The agitation of my soul to hide;
> And asked the Lord, to send a quick relief
> To her, who ever wept o'er others' grief—
> To her, whose presence heav'nly lustre shed—
> Who cloth'd the naked, and the hungry fed.
> Ah! why should deep, intense anxiety,
> Pervade a breast where sensibility
> Like hers resides? Oh! why should trouble roll
> Its restless waves across her spotless soul?
> Ah! why should sorrow's bitterness corrode
> A heart that is sweet innocence' abode?
> Why should suspense, with racking torture bind
> The impulse of her noble, virtuous mind?

The poet concluded that Emma, who was "Beloved of God and every faithful saint," would see her absent husband restored to her side through the blessings of the merciful "God on high."[5]

Nine months after this poem was written, on 17 March 1842, the Female Relief Society of Nauvoo was organized with Emma Smith as president and Eliza Snow as secretary. Four months later, in July 1842,

responding to further legal action against Joseph Smith, the two women
and Amanda Barnes Smith traveled together to Quincy to personally
present to Governor Thomas Carlin petitions from the Relief Society
for the Prophet's protection. The next month, in August 1842, Emma
invited Eliza to again live in the Smith household. Eliza remained with
Joseph and Emma until February 1843. She was not alone, of course, in
being welcomed to reside in the Smith home: Emma's hospitality was
legendary. For six months, during the winter of 1842–43, Eliza seems to
have felt part of the family. She waited with Emma for news when
Joseph went into hiding to avoid the Missouri officials pressing for his
arrest in October 1842. He left reluctantly, after nursing Emma through
a week of severe sickness. "President Smith," Eliza wrote, having
received news of the Prophet's safe arrival at the home of a friend,

> Sir, for your consolation permit me to tell
> That your Emma is *better*—she soon will be *well*;
> Mrs. Durfee stands by her, night & day like a friend
> And is prompt every call—every wish to attend;
> Then pray for your Emma, but indulge not a fear
> For the God of our forefathers, smiles on us here.[6]

This poem conveys a sense of warm household intimacy as well as shared
feeling and purpose.

Ironically, it was Eliza's intimate connection to the Smith family that
eventually created a breach between Emma and Eliza. Eliza became a
plural wife of Joseph Smith in June 1842, two months before Emma
invited her to move into the Smith household. Exactly when Emma
became aware of their marriage is not clear. In an oft-told story, repeated
in many versions, a jealous Emma, upon seeing Eliza and Joseph
embrace, hit Eliza with a broom or pushed her down the stairs or forced
her out of the house into the cold. There are no extant contempor-
aneous accounts of such an event, and Eliza herself never mentioned any
such incident. But the persistence of the story and the terse entry in
Eliza's journal in February 1843—"Took board and had my lodging
removed to the residence of br. J. Holmes"—suggest the possibility of
some kind of conflict.[7] Even so, Eliza's diary entries following that date
include references to conversations with Emma and four months after
the martyrdom, upon the birth of Joseph and Emma's son David Hyrum,
Eliza composed a consolatory poem for the mother and son.[8] The women

may well have made their peace. Yet, the suspension of the Relief Society, in part because Emma was using that forum to teach the sisters to oppose plural marriage, and Emma's estrangement from the Twelve as matters of property were settled and plural marriage continued after Joseph's death, gradually distanced Emma from those who followed Brigham Young and ultimately alienated her from the Saints who came West, including Eliza Snow.[9]

Circumstances and shared experiences can bring friends together, and a different set of circumstances can pull friends apart. Was the distance that grew between them difficult for Emma and Eliza? Extant sources do not answer that question. We have only Eliza's later affirmation that she "once dearly loved 'Sister Emma.'"[10] And we see reflected in Eliza's presidency of the Relief Society precedents Emma had established during her presidency: commitment to lift the poor and weary, to seek to influence government policies that affect women and the Church, and to maintain a forum where women address one another honestly. Emulation is the highest mark of respect.

Eliza left her much-loved "City of Joseph" in February 1846 to journey westward with the Saints, traveling with the family of Hannah and Stephen Markham. She left behind in Illinois her mother Rosetta and her sister Amanda, whom she would never see again.[11] Her sister Leonora and her brother Lorenzo traveled west in different companies than she. Hungry for caring relationships, Eliza cherished friends at hand during the long trek west. Their kindnesses meant a great deal to her. Shortly after she arrived in Winter Quarters, she became miserably sick with chills and fever which lasted "nearly 40 days." In her diary, after remarking on her suffering, she noted: "I had the satisfacion of experiencing kindness from many of my friends, which is indelibly inscrib'd upon my memory: Particularly Cornelia C.L.—Sis. Whitney—Sis. Kimball, Sis. Young, Sis. Lott, Sis. Holmes, & Sis. Taylor. Without whose attentions I must have suffer'd much more, as I was the last in the fam. taken sick & nobody able to wait on or administer to me as I needed."[12] This sweet acknowledgment of kindness is something that all of us do either consciously or unconsciously, but it is significant that Eliza took time to leave in writing a lasting witness of the kindness of her friends.

Eliza traveled from Winter Quarters to the Salt Lake Valley with the family of Robert and Hannah Pierce. Their daughter Margarett had become a widow at age twenty-two, after just seven months of marriage to Morris Whitesides. Like Eliza, Margarett had been sealed to Brigham Young before the Saints left Nauvoo. She was nineteen years younger than Eliza, but the two sister-wives became close. Again, bits of poetry provide a glimpse of their relationship. On 16 October 1847, Margarett presented Eliza with sixteen lines, beginning:

> I love thee; and I'll ne'er forget
> The time we've spent together
> Thro' many toilsome scenes of wet
> And storms of windy weather.

The next day, in response, Eliza addressed twenty lines to Margarett, including these:

> I love thee with the tenderness
> That sister spirits love—
> I love thee, for thy loveliness
> Is like to theirs above.
>
> . . . .
>
> I love thee for the kindness show'd
> To me in feeble health,
> When journeying on a tedious road—
> I prize it more than wealth.[13]

Eliza and Margarett frequently had occasion to renew the special bond between them since they were both part of Brigham Young's household. In 1875, Margarett Young's only child, Brigham Morris Young, married Eliza's niece, Celestia Armeda Snow, further strengthening the connection between the two women. Thus Eliza and Margarett, who first became dear to each other as companions on their journey westward, kept in close touch and maintained an affectionate bond. Eliza resided in Brigham Young's family home in Utah for nearly forty years, forming attachments to her sister-wives in the Lion House much like the ties she had earlier shared with her own three sisters. Long-remembered and often mentioned in women's histories,[14] Eliza's abiding and complementary friendship with Zina D. H. Young, with whom she worked so closely in Relief Society, epitomizes the strong relationships that tied women together within Brigham Young's extended family.

Although Eliza enjoyed solitude—which as a woman without children she seems to have had plenty of—she rejoiced in association and loved having a kindred spirit to really talk to. Along the trail she composed a poem to a Mrs. Eleanor Bringhurst celebrating the affinity the two women felt:

> . . . when I think
> Of thee, a thrill of near affinity
> O'erspreads my senses & I truly feel
> Within my bosom a strong kindred tie
> As tho' we'd been associated in
> Existence, ere we condescended to
> Our present state of being. Lady, yes.
> When our small understandings shall expand
> And with the recollection of the past
> Some knowledge of the future be inspir'd
> We'll find a thousand kindred ties that form
> Amalgamation's wreath, & which are twin'd
> And intertwin'd, combining & combin'd
> Connecting noble spirits here & there
> O'er all the face of earth—from earth to heav'n
> And still extending . . . on from world to world
> Unto creation's undefin'd extent.[15]

Immediate recognition of a soul mate and the sense of perhaps having known a sister in the premortal world was as important, and sometimes more important, to Eliza than common circumstances or shared experiences. Certainly, her closest and most enduring relationships had spiritual and intellectual components. Eliza's friendship with Sarah M. Kimball, so intertwined with their commitment to work on behalf of women, spanned nearly half a century. The two women probably became friends in Nauvoo when Sarah was a young bride and Eliza a middle-aged schoolteacher. Sarah Melissa Granger had recently married Hiram Kimball, a wealthy non-Mormon Nauvoo merchant who was later baptized. In the spring of 1842, Sarah invited a group of sisters, including her seamstress, Margaret Cook, to form a ladies' society to sew shirts for workmen on the Nauvoo Temple. Sarah approached Eliza and asked her to write a constitution for that little organization, which con-stitution Eliza showed to Joseph Smith. He praised it but, promising "something better," invited the sisters to come and be organized "under the priesthood after the pattern of the priesthood."[16] The Female Relief Society of Nauvoo was organized 17 March 1842 with both Sarah and Eliza present. In later years, both women frequently spoke of the impor-tance of that occasion.

But dozens of other connections and commonalities strengthened this friendship. Sarah did not travel with Eliza on the trail because she remained with her husband and children in Nauvoo for several years before moving to Utah. On the other hand, she is a prominent figure in Eliza's trail diaries. Eliza and the Markham family, with whom she was traveling, stopped at the home of Hiram and Sarah Kimball on their way out of the city. A few days later, Eliza wrote to Sarah and then continued to write her every three or four weeks during the trek. Eliza received from Sarah ("SMK" in her diary) letters that always delighted her.

Sarah was a very thoughtful friend. She knew Eliza was a skilled seam-stress who hired out to make clothing and caps. Eliza had learned sewing and stitchery in her youth and throughout her life she did very fine needlework (some of which is on display at the Daughters of Utah Pioneers Museum in Salt Lake City). On 14 April 1846, Eliza noted in her diary that David Markham, "brought me a package this eve. which prov'd to be another token from S.M. Kimball, a roll of neat *gimp*," a kind of silk thread, "yet I had to regret that the envelop contain'd only her *signature* & her *love*."[17] But five days later, Eliza had "the treat of a letter from S.M. Kimball" and promptly responded.[18] About a year later, on 22 April 1847, she noted in her diary that two of her friends: "brought me a present from S.M.K. of dress pins, stockings, hooks & eyes & sewing silk. O God bless her for this I pray thee."[19] It is wonderful when we can somehow figure out what to give one another and enlarge one another by our thoughtful exchanges, anticipating what might bring comfort or joy or pleasure.

Delayed in Nauvoo by business concerns, the Kimballs did not travel to Utah until 1851. In fact, when they arrived, Sarah remembered, her husband "was financially much embarrassed and broken in health." Sarah would later say that she had traveled in "all levels of society"; she knew what it meant to be rich and she knew what it meant to be poor.[20] We have no documents to suggest how Eliza Snow might have helped the friend who had given so generously to her, only poems she penned in Sarah's autograph book in 1852 and 1853. The second begins:

> Sarah! I love you—I have lov'd you long
> With love that can't be utter'd in a song—
> That will not perish with life's hopes and fears,
> But lives and strengthens with increasing years.[21]

Of course, with increasing years, these women became even more closely connected. At the end of 1866, Brigham Young called Eliza to help bishops reorganize Relief Societies in all the local wards. Sarah Kimball became president of the Salt Lake City Fifteenth Ward Relief Society, which served as a model for many other local societies, and prospered "beyond that of any branch in Zion." Either Eliza and Sarah worked together directly or they consulted one another in effecting and extending the basic organizational pattern they had learned in Nauvoo. Their combined talents were critical to the flowering of women's participation and sisterhood that distinguished the work of Latter-day Saint women from 1867 to 1887, the last two decades of Eliza's life. In an array of impressive activities difficult to match in any era, ward societies like Sarah's built halls and granaries of their own, engaged in home manufacture, addressed women's health concerns, and supported sisters in receiving professional medical training, in addition to caring for the poor. Eliza essentially served as Relief Society general president during all of this period, though she was not formally called to that position until 1880, when she invited her dear friend Sarah to be general secretary.[22]

Eliza was such a daunting public figure that it is easy to minimize the facets of her character that shone brightly in the private arenas and gave texture to her life and her leadership. As we have seen, she was quick to express affection and appreciation. She loved sharing "heart unto heart and mind to mind," and she possessed a quick and charming wit.

I am particularly fond of a poem Eliza composed for her friend Leonora Cannon Taylor. Originally from the Isle of Man in England, Leonora had been baptized in 1836 in Canada, about one year after Eliza's baptism. The aunt of George Q. Cannon and the wife of John Taylor, Leonora has been described by B. H. Roberts as "refined both by nature and education, gentle and lady like in manner, intelligent, gifted with rare conversational powers, and, withal, beautiful in person as in mind."[23] She was also a gifted gardener, one of the first pioneers to grow flowers, vegetables, and fruit trees in the Salt Lake Valley. If Eliza and Leonora conversed upon politics, world history, art and literature, the scriptures and theology, they also found time to celebrate less ethereal matters. In the midst of the second harvest in the Salt Lake Valley in September 1848, Eliza wrote these lines, "To Mrs. Leonora Taylor":

> A deep love in our nature for nature's own self
> Is a trait unassum'd by the counterfeit elf:
> 'Tis a fountain's free gush that proceeds from the heart
> By simplicity prompted, untinctur'd by art.
>
> With flow'rs from your garden, my toilet is grac'd,
> Their unstudied selection does honor to taste.
> They're a compliment too, to your patience & toil
> And their growth is a proof of our newly tried soil.
>
> They truly are lovely—I gaze on them oft—
> Their fragrance is sweet, their expression is soft;
> They have goodness, grace, beauty, and dignity too;
> With *all these combining*, they represent *you*.
>
> Dear Lady, I'm thankful indeed for the flow'rs,
> They afford me *amusement* in my lonely hours;
> But for *med'cine*, there's nothing more welcome to me,
> Of the "vain things of earth," than *the bundle of Tea*.
>
> You were sly as a smuggler: I chanc'd to espy
> *Something hidden*, just when you were bidding "good bye":
> I might have expos'd it with thanks, but you know,
> Good manners prevented.
> Eliza R. Snow[24]

Few lines in the voluminous corpus of Eliza Snow's poems are as gracious and delightfully witty and familiar as these. Like good photographs, they capture revealing moments. We can almost see the flowers, Eliza's smile as she retrieves the hidden bundle, Leonora's smile upon reading the thank-you poem. This sweet and harmonious combination of head, hand, and heart suggests the richness of a multifaceted relationship.

A number of women who immigrated from the British Isles were among Eliza's closest associates, including sister poet Hannah Tapfield King and trusted Relief Society co-worker Elizabeth Anderson Howard. Another was Martha Spence Heywood. Martha Spence, schoolteacher, seamstress, and hatmaker, immigrated to the United States from Ireland. She was an intelligent and articulate woman who affiliated for a time with the Millerites, an American religious sect. In fact, she was a preacher among the Millerites before she became acquainted with the Latter-day Saints, traveled west, and eventually became a plural wife of Joseph Heywood. Martha arrived in Utah in 1850, and her honest and perceptive journal, covering the years 1850 to 1856, has been edited by Juanita Brooks and published under the title, *Not by Bread Alone*.[25]

Martha loved to spend time by herself. She called her moments of meditation "enjoying my mind." But her inclination for solitude was counterbalanced by an appreciation for good companionship. In August 1850, as she journeyed west, Martha reflected in her diary: "How much would I not give at times to see some choice spirits to mingle with as I was wont to do in past times."[26] On 27 October 1850, just two weeks after she arrived in the Salt Lake Valley, she noted in her diary: "I made a call on sister Eliza Snow and was so pleased with her that I was persuaded to remain the afternoon."[27] In the year that followed, Martha was actively involved in an elocution society, which presented exhibitions and staged plays in Salt Lake City. She was also employed by Brigham Young to make hats and, in that capacity, visited his household. But her diary does not mention Eliza Snow again until 1856. By then Martha had left Salt Lake City to help her husband Joseph settle Salt Creek (Nephi), had borne two children, and had returned to Salt Lake City. She came back without her second child, a two-year-old daughter, who died at Salt Creek in March 1856. Eliza composed a short consolatory poem for Martha the next month.[28]

Clearly, however, the two women had maintained some contact across the years because Eliza wrote a poem in Martha's autograph album in 1853. Their lives intersected again in Salt Lake City in the spring of 1856, when Martha was invited to attend the Polysophical Society established by Eliza's brother Lorenzo Snow. The Polysophical Society was a sort of study group in which men and women shared essays or poems to entertain and uplift one another. Eliza and Martha were both contributors.

The poems Eliza presented to the Polysophical Society in 1856 reflect her unwavering loyalty to the Church and its leaders, her grasp of Latter-day Saint theology, and her concern with woman's place in Mormon belief and culture. I surmise that Eliza and Martha, and other friends, talked at length about the role of women and the peculiar difficulties of Latter-day Saint women in the 1850s. These sisters had to contend with a barrage of criticism from opponents outraged by the 1852 public announcement that Latter-day Saints were practicing plural marriage at the same time that many of them, like Martha Heywood, were themselves in the throes of adjusting to the challenges of plural marriage.

In addition, Church leaders' admonitions to women during this period were unusually harsh. As converts arrived in Utah, President Brigham Young, Heber C. Kimball, and other leaders were intent on establishing order and emphasizing the hierarchy of priesthood government in burgeoning towns and settlements. They sometimes employed rhetoric that was unsettling or even offensive to women. "Women are made to be led, and counselled, and directed," proclaimed Heber C. Kimball in 1857.[29] Martha Spence Heywood ordinarily commented with enthusiasm on President Young's sermons. In March 1856, for example, she noted that "his remarks were of thrilling interest to me" and "my feelings were that I could not have missed hearing that sermon for all I had ever heard before. The subject of equality was splendidly handled by him as also that of love or the social affection. I was fairly drunk with enjoyment."[30] On the other hand, the next month, Martha prayerfully struggled to be able to accept harder words from President Young, namely, as she recorded in her diary, "that a woman be she ever so smart, she cannot know more than her husband if he magnifies his Priesthood. That God never in any age of the world endowed woman with knowledge above the man."[31]

Eliza's poems for this period likewise raise concerns about woman's worth, capacity, and destiny. Who am I as a woman? What is my position temporally, spiritually, eternally? The poems are subtle, sometimes painfully understated. Honoring human priesthood leaders as an integral part of divine priesthood order and ordinances, she doggedly refrained from questioning their authority or pronouncements. Troubled but not truculent, Eliza and friends like Martha examined their hurts in light of the restored truth they cherished and gradually gained for themselves a clearer sense of their divine origin and purpose.

In 1853 Eliza wrote a poem in Martha's autograph album of which I am very fond. The poem speaks of "figures incog."—"*incog.*" being short-hand for *incognito*. We might find ourselves in various positions here on the earth, Eliza seems to say, but we really don't know exactly who we were in the premortal existence and to what extent our being in a certain situation or having a certain calling in the Church reflects who we are eternally. The clothes we wear, our wealth or poverty, prominence or obscurity, tell us little of who we really are. These are external features only, while that which is of greatest worth is internal.

Martha Spence Heywood was an exceedingly plain woman, and Joseph Heywood's first wife was known for her beauty. Knowing that fact gives this bit of poetry just that much more punch. Eliza wrote in Martha's album, "To Mrs. Haywood":

> Like the figures *incog.*, in a masquerade scene,
> Are some spirits now dwelling on earth;
> And we judge of them only by actions and mien,
> Unappriz'd of all relative worth.
>
> In the transforming mask of mortality clad,
> Kings and princes and peasants appear;
> All forgetting whatever acquaintance they had
> In existence preceding this here.
>
> When the *past* shall develop, the *future* unfold,
> When the *present* its sequel shall tell—
> When unmask'd we shall know, be beheld, and behold;
> O how blest, if *incog. we've done well.*[32]

Discovering Eliza's friendship with Hannah Gould Perkins has been a delight to me, perhaps because Hannah is an obscure rather than a prominent woman. She seems to have been a special friend of Eliza. She, too, was born in England and was intelligent and well educated. She was a temple worker and worked with Eliza in the Endowment House in Salt Lake City, where temple ordinances were performed previous to the completion of the St. George, Logan, and Manti Temples. I have not yet determined when the two women became acquainted, but they knew one another well in 1861, when Hannah and her husband, William Perkins, were called by Brigham Young to go south with the first large group sent to settle St. George. Few documents exist to tell us about

Hannah Perkins: one poem from Eliza to Hannah, one letter from Eliza to Hannah, and a short diary kept by Hannah.

From October through December 1861, as she and her husband traveled south with the settlers moving to St. George, Hannah kept a diary. Five days after they left, she wrote: "I walked a good deal and thought much of those loved one's left behind but still my feelings are, push ahead, push ahead." The eleventh day out, she noted: "It has been long up hill work all day thought of Sister Snow in the house of the Lord. She prayed doubtless for me, for my heart hung closely to her." Two days later, Hannah wrote: "Another Sabbath out, thought all day of the Saints in the city and tho' they have the teachings of the Prophets, I am not left alone for surely I have the inward Moniter, which is beyond all price."[33]

On December 13, two weeks before the group entered St. George, they assembled in a meeting at which Erastus Snow, the head of the company, presided. This five-hour meeting was significant to Hannah. She recorded that Erastus Snow "Spoke—prayed with power—as soon as he began to pray in the opening of the meeting I had a vision of Sister Snow. She stood so near to me that I could have touched her. She looked *so good*. I felt all day as if I had been visiting with her—when the view closed I considered the thing and wondered how it could be, then I remembered it was Friday & at that time she was in the House of the Lord and possibly she was thinking of me and probably she was praying for me and that her spirit was allowed to visit me. How such things are whether it can be so or not I am not able to say. At all events I feel that I have had a visit."[34]

The letter Eliza wrote to Hannah nine months later conveys a similar sense of connectedness:

"Sunday mor. Oct. 12, 1862.

"My Dear Sister Hannah,

"I have preceded the family at breakfast that I may enjoy a morning solo with my dear friend. Conference is over, which has given a most powerful impulse to the kingdom of God upon the earth. I am sure that you and dear sis. Lizzie participated freely in the holy and cheering influence of the spirit which pervaded the assemblies of the saints in this City during the Conference. If you did not, it was not because your sis. Eliza did not pray earnestly to that effect. . . .

"Sister Goddard spent the first sunday noon with me after her return, and I almost felt that you were here, but *not quite*. With me, there is no one on the earth that can fill your place, but dear Hannah Gould Perkins. My brother said he shook hands with you and regretted he could not have gone to your home. He says St. George will be a splendid place, also I think all speak highly of it. . . .

"I daily think of the very hard work you are all doing—I know you never could perform it if you did not live near to the Lord so that you draw strength and support from Him. How many prayers ascend in your behalf!"[35]

Providing a bit more detail about Hannah in St. George is the record of another diarist. Elizabeth Kane, wife of that highly regarded friend of the Mormons Thomas Kane, visited St. George with her husband in 1872 and wrote an account of their visit to the Perkins home. The room was very small, but, Elizabeth wrote: "It was in the neatest order. There was a clean damask table cover on the old dressing table, a clean valance to the shelf above, and clean white covers on the various boxes that served as furniture. . . . Close to the chimney stood the tiniest cooking stove I ever saw: with room for two pots only."[36] Hannah, like Eliza, had no children. Eliza, like Hannah, lived in a tiny room, Eliza's in the Lion House. In 1866, nearly five years after Hannah left Salt Lake City, Eliza wrote a poem to "Sister Hannah Perkins" expressing how much she missed her friend. It is another of my favorite Eliza poems, partly because we so rarely hear Eliza Snow speak personally about people.

> I miss thee, my Sister—I miss thee at home
> In my own little room where I lov'd thee to come
> I miss thee at meeting—I miss thy dear smile
> And I miss thy warm grip as I pass thro' the aisle.[37]

We can see, at least in the sources that we have for this relationship, that these sisters cared for each other deeply and each prayed for the other constantly. Their friendship epitomized the admonition in Doctrine and Covenants 108:7, which we might read: "Therefore, strengthen your [sisters] in all your conversation, in all your prayers, in all your exhortations, and in all your doings." Eliza and Hannah offered one another spiritual nourishment.

There existed between Hannah and Eliza a palpable closeness. We can feel the "warm grip" that united the women, much as we can feel Eliza's delight at Leonora Taylor's thoughtful flowers or the cheering silk thread sent by Sarah Kimball. But not all relationships bind "heart to heart and mind to mind." Distance is as much a factor in some friendships as closeness is in others. As Eliza got older and her public duties consumed more of her time, she seems to have become less emotionally spontaneous and accessible. Sometimes her reserve separated her from those who had not already come to know her in informal family and friendship circles. Emmeline B. Wells was about twenty-four years younger than Eliza, obviously young enough to be her daughter. Though both women took an interest in literature and politics and both were writers, Emmeline's early personal history could not have been more different from Eliza's. Emmeline was married at age fifteen, but her husband disappeared a few months after the young couple moved to Nauvoo. Their infant son died and Emmeline, alone without family, became a plural wife of Newel K. Whitney. After his death in 1850, she married Daniel H. Wells. Through the 1850s and 60s, Emmeline's life was centered on her five daughters. In the late 1860s, she became engaged in Relief Society work in Salt Lake City's Thirteenth Ward and soon began writing for the *Woman's Exponent*, the semiofficial newspaper published by Latter-day Saint women (1872–1914). In 1877 Emmeline became editor of the *Exponent* and served in that capacity until it was replaced by the *Relief Society Magazine* in 1914. In 1910 she succeeded Eliza's successors, Zina D. H. Young and Bathsheba W. Smith, as general president of the Relief Society.

Some forty volumes of Emmeline's diaries are extant, and they provide a slightly different perspective on Eliza, the point of view of a close associate in Relief Society work. Emmeline served as Eliza's corresponding secretary and often as her traveling companion on frequent visits to the Relief Societies and young women's and children's associations of various wards and stakes. During one such visit, in July 1878, Emmeline expressed in her diary her hurt at not being able to talk with Eliza about her deepest feelings. Three months before the visit, on 8 April 1878, Emmeline had suffered the devastating loss of her dear twenty-four-year-old daughter Em. Emmeline wrote:

"[July, 1878] Wednesday 10.

"This morning went with Aunt Eliza R. Snow to attend the Conference at Farmington and had as pleasant a time as possible when one's heart is broken, I cannot say much to Aunt Eliza she does not think I ought to giveway to emotions not in the least."[38]

Indeed, Eliza's reputation for controlling her emotions has outlived the memory of many of her other character traits. Certainly, she was a woman who kept a stiff upper lip and could be more inclined to teach than to nurse, more apt to instruct than to empathize. Discipline was a survival skill that had carried Eliza through her own difficult times. Her capacity to set personal considerations aside in order to press forward in launching the important work of the Relief Society and the Young Ladies' work, so new to women in the 1860s and 70s, might be deemed weakness by some and strength by others. The very visit reported by Emmeline with such sadness included the conversation between Eliza R. Snow and Aurelia Spencer Rogers that resulted a few weeks later in the organization of the first Primary Association in Farmington, Utah, in August 1878 and launched the new movement to organize Primaries throughout the Church.

Emmeline and Eliza were both passionate women. Emmeline regularly confided to her diary over the years, and though Eliza's diary record is much shorter, it too is filled with emotional confidences. We all feel frustration in not being able to read another's feelings, particularly if the other is someone we genuinely like.

In March 1887, as Eliza endured one of several sick spells during the last year of her life, Emmeline wrote of her continuing disappointment in communicating with Eliza:

"This is a fine warm day Aunt Eliza is much worse and no prospect of her being better soon. I have been in to see her but it is really no satisfaction. She has no strength to talk. . . . I have offered to write letters for her or to [do] all in my power in other ways, but she has required nothing of me. Whether she is a real friend or only one who does for her own sake, I cannot determine."[39]

Emmeline's comment is of great interest to me for what it says about her, about Eliza, and about relationships between women. Sometimes in a relationship, we are not sure what is happening. We are trying our best, yet we are unsure whether or not we are meeting a need. We do not know if by talking about a subject we are prying where we should not be prying, or if by evading a subject we are ignoring issues that someone needs to discuss. Obviously, Eliza did not have the answers, nor did Emmeline. Sometimes, as close as we try to get, painful distances remain.

Emmeline had great respect and love for Eliza. She recorded with pleasure many conversations and travels with Eliza and noted with concern her daily visits during Eliza's final illness. In later years Emmeline spoke and wrote reverently of all that Eliza had given her and how much she had done for the women of the Church. Perhaps her own subsequent years of experience helped Emmeline shorten the perceived distances that once had troubled her. In 1910, some twenty-three years after Eliza's death, Emmeline composed a tribute for a celebration in Eliza's honor. "Here she taught us life's great lessons," Emmeline wrote,

> From the fount above obtaining;
> As we trod life's paths together,
> Always righteousness maintaining—
> With that wondrous gift of power,
> Her true heritage and dower.

"Zion's daughters down the ages," Emmeline affirmed, "Will her messages be telling."[40]

Emmeline herself would echo those messages far into the twentieth century. Whatever personal frustration she experienced, she learned from Eliza R. Snow the importance of women standing together as sisters and friends to nurture and fortify one another and unitedly accomplish works far beyond the capacity of any individual woman. Thus, Eliza R. Snow's monumental achievements were not hers alone. The women who traveled with her, talked and wrote to her, prayed for her, and bore with her significantly strengthened her capacities as friend, teacher, and leader. All of us have people around us who build us up, who inform and expand our thought, strengthen and enlarge our souls.

Eliza praised the blessing of Relief Society in bringing women "together, like coals of fire, imparting warmth and life to one another."[41] She delivered hundreds of sermons to Relief Society sisters, one of which will serve as a fitting conclusion here. It reflects not only Eliza's thought regarding women's capacities, but her cherished friendships with individual women who nurtured and enlightened her. These remarks are taken from her address to Relief Society sisters in Lehi, Utah, in October 1869.

"While sitting here, I have been looking upon the faces of my sisters and can see the form of deity there and I have been reflecting on the great work we have to perform, even in helping in the salvation of the living and the dead.

"The Lord has organized these [Relief] Societies that we may gain knowledge and practice in an organized capacity and learn to respect our labors and one another and give honor where honor is due. We want to be ladies in very deed, not according to the term of the word as the world judges, but fit companions of the Gods and Holy Ones. In an organized capacity we can assist each other in not only doing good but in refining ourselves and whether few or many come forward and help to prosecute this great work, they will be those that will fill honorable positions in the Kingdom of God. We should not act from feeling but from principle and seek to understand the workings of the Spirit of God, for it is not trouble, grief, and sadness that it bringeth, but peace, joy, and satisfaction. We have got to cooperate not only with our husbands but with God so that we may become Saviors upon Mount Zion, for it is one thing to be a savior and another to be saved, one thing to be a queen and govern and control and another to be a subject and be governed. Women should be women and not babies that need petting and correction all the time. I know we like to be appreciated, but if we do not get all the appreciation which we think is our due, what matters? We know the Lord's laid high responsibility upon us, and there is not a wish or desire that the Lord has implanted in our hearts in righteousness but will be realized, and the greatest good we can do to ourselves and each other is to refine and cultivate ourselves in everything that is good and ennobling to qualify us for those responsibilities."[42]

The women who nurtured Eliza R. Snow helped her refine and cultivate everything good and ennobling, and she in turn blessed and enriched their lives. I pray we might likewise seek to nurture one another and be nurtured.

Notes

The author gratefully acknowledges Jennifer Jacob and Rebekah Rogers for assisting with research for this article.

1. "Friendship," (Ravenna) *Ohio Star*, 12 May 1830.
2. "Review of Primary Associations, and Instructions," *Juvenile Instructor* 25 (15 November 1890): 685.
3. "Praise Ye the Lord," *Messenger and Advocate* 1 (August 1835): 176. Also in *A Collection of Sacred Hymns, for the Church of the Latter Day Saints*, selected by Emma Smith (Kirtland, Ohio: F. G. Williams & co., 1835), 92–93.
4. In a revelation given to her husband, the Prophet Joseph Smith, Emma had been instructed "to make a selection of sacred hymns" for the Church (D&C 25:11).
5. The full preface to the untitled poem reads: "The following lines were written during the late arrest of Pres. Joseph Smith, which was instigated through the untiring malice of Missouri persecution; and are respectfully inscribed to Mrs. EMMA SMITH;

BY MISS ELIZA R. SNOW." *Times and Seasons* 2 (15 June 1841): 452–53. The arrest of Joseph Smith and his release following a hearing are described in Joseph Smith, *History of The Church of Jesus Christ of Latter-day Saints*, ed. B. H. Roberts, 2d ed. rev., 7 vols. (Salt Lake City: The Church of Jesus Christ of Latter-day Saints, 1932–51), 4:364–71.

6. Eliza R. Snow, Nauvoo Journal and Notebook, 12 October 1842, in Maureen Ursenbach Beecher, ed., *The Personal Writings of Eliza Roxcy Snow* (Salt Lake City: University of Utah Press, 1995), 58; also in Eliza R. Snow, *Poems, Religious, Historical, and Political*, 2 vols. (Liverpool: F. D. Richards, 1856; Salt Lake City: LDS Printing and Publishing Establishment, 1877), 1:133.

7. See Maureen Ursenbach Beecher, Linda King Newell, and Valeen Tippetts Avery, "Emma and Eliza and the Stairs," *BYU Studies* 22 (Winter 1982): 87–96.

8. Eliza R. Snow, "Lines written on the birth of the infant son of Mrs. Emma, widow of the late General Joseph Smith," *Times and Seasons* 5 (15 December 1844): 735; Snow, *Poems* 1:168–69.

9. The suspension of Relief Society meetings is discussed in Jill Mulvay Derr, Janath Russell Cannon, and Maureen Ursenbach Beecher, *Women of Covenant: The Story of Relief Society* (Salt Lake City: Deseret Book, 1992), 59–64.

10. "Letter on Plural Marriage," *Woman's Exponent* 8 (1 November 1879): 85, signed "Eliza R. Snow, A wife of Joseph Smith the Prophet."

11. Rosetta Leonora Pettibone Snow died at Walnut Grove, Knox County, Illinois, 12 October 1846. Percy Amanda Snow McConoughey died at Henry, Illinois, 27/28 August 1848. Beecher, *Personal Writings of Eliza Roxcy Snow*, 232.

12. Eliza R. Snow, Trail Diary, February 1846 to May 1847, undated entry following 29 August 1846, in Beecher, *Personal Writings of Eliza Roxcy Snow*, 143–44; spelling not standardized.

13. Snow, Trail Diary, June 1847 to September 1849, 16 and 17 October 1847, in Beecher, *Personal Writings of Eliza Roxcy Snow*, 207–8.

14. See, for instance, *Women of Covenant*, 121–27; Susa Young Gates, *History of the Young Ladies' Mutual Improvement Association* (Salt Lake City: General Board of Y.L.M.I.A., 1911), 21.

15. Snow, Trail Diary, June 1847 to September 1849, 19 March 1848, in Beecher, *Personal Writings of Eliza Roxcy Snow*, 221–22.

16. *Woman's Exponent* 12 (1 September 1883): 51; see also Derr, Cannon, and Beecher, *Women of Covenant*, 26–27, 41, 446.

17. Snow, Trail Diary, February 1846 to May 1847, 14 April 1846, in Beecher, *Personal Writings of Eliza Roxcy Snow*, 128.

18. Snow, Trail Diary, February 1846 to May 1847, 19 April 1846, in Beecher, *Personal Writings of Eliza Roxcy Snow*, 129.

19. Snow, Trail Diary, February 1846 to May 1847, 22 April 1847, in Beecher, *Personal Writings of Eliza Roxcy Snow*, 166.

20. An introduction to the life of Sarah M. Kimball is Jill C. Mulvay [Derr], "The Liberal Shall Be Blessed: Sarah M. Kimball," *Utah Historical Quarterly* 44 (Summer 1976): 205–21.

21. Eliza R. Snow to Mrs. Sarah M. Kimball, Sarah M. Kimball autograph book, dated 4

April 1853, holograph, Archives of The Church of Jesus Christ of Latter-day Saints, Salt Lake City; published in Snow, *Poems*, 1:58.

22. The indefatigable labors of Eliza R. Snow and Sarah M. Kimball are discussed in Derr, Cannon, and Beecher, *Women of Covenant*, 83–126.

23. B. H. Roberts, A *Comprehensive History of the Church of Jesus Christ of Latter-day Saints*, 6 vols. (Salt Lake City: The Church of Jesus Christ of Latter-day Saints, 1930), 5:256–57.

24. Eliza R. Snow, "To Mrs. Leonora Taylor," 7 September 1848, holograph, John Taylor Collection, Archives of The Church of Jesus Christ of Latter-day Saints, Salt Lake City.

25. *Not by Bread Alone: The Journal of Martha Spence Heywood, 1850–56*, ed. Juanita Brooks (Salt Lake City: Utah State Historical Society, 1978).

26. Heywood Diary, 31 August 1850, in Brooks, *Not by Bread Alone*, 21. See also Maureen Ursenbach [Beecher], "Three Women and the Life of the Mind," *Utah Historical Quarterly* 43 (Winter 1975): 26–40; reprinted in Maureen Ursenbach Beecher, *Eliza and Her Sisters* (Salt Lake City: Aspen Books, 1991), 109–28.

27. Heywood Diary, 27 October 1850, in Brooks, *Not by Bread Alone*, 35.

28. E. R. Snow, "To Mrs. Martha Spence Heywood," poem dated 14 April 1856, holograph, Archives of The Church of Jesus Christ of Latter-day Saints, Salt Lake City.

29. Heber C. Kimball, in *Journal of Discourses*, 26 vols. (London: Latter-day Saints' Book Depot, 1854–86), 5:29, 12 July 1857.

30. Heywood Diary, 30 March 1856, in Brooks, *Not by Bread Alone*, 120.

31. Heywood Diary, 27 April 1856, in Brooks, *Not by Bread Alone*, 122.

32. "To Mrs. Haywood," 27 May 1853, MS, Album of Mrs. Martha S. Heywood, 27 May 1853, holograph, Archives of The Church of Jesus Christ of Latter-day Saints, Salt Lake City; published in Snow, *Poems*, 1:99.

33. Journal of Hannah Gould Perkins, 29 October 1861 to 26 December 1861, holograph, Archives of The Church of Jesus Christ of Latter-day Saints, Salt Lake City, 3, 8, and 10 November 1861.

34. Journal of Hannah Gould Perkins, 13 December 1861; spelling not standardized.

35. Eliza R. Snow to Hannah Gould Perkins, 12 October 1862, holograph, Archives of The Church of Jesus Christ of Latter-day Saints, Salt Lake City.

36. *A Gentile Account of Life in Utah's Dixie, 1872–73: Elizabeth Kane's St. George Journal* (Salt Lake City: University of Utah, 1995), 163.

37. Eliza R. Snow, Nauvoo Journal and Notebook, poem dated 7 November 1866, holograph, Archives of The Church of Jesus Christ of Latter-day Saints, Salt Lake City.

38. Diary of Emmeline B. Wells, 10 July 1878, typescript, Joseph Fielding Smith Institute for Latter-day Saint History, Brigham Young University, Provo, Utah; holograph, Archives and Manuscripts, Harold B. Lee Library, Brigham Young University. The author appreciates Carol Cornwall Madsen, who is working on a biography of Wells, for bringing this entry to her attention.

39. Diary of Emmeline B. Wells, 29 March 1887.

40. "Quest and Message, E. R. Snow's Anniversary," in Emmeline B. Wells, *Musings and Memories*, 2d ed. rev. (Salt Lake City: Deseret News, 1915), 324–26.

41. Minutes of Quarterly Conference of the Relief Society of Utah Stake, 31 August 1883, "Utah Stake," *Woman's Exponent* 12 (15 October 1883): 78.

42. Lehi Ward, Utah Stake, Relief Society Minutes, 1868–1879, 27 October 1869, Archives of The Church of Jesus Christ of Latter-day Saints, Salt Lake City; spelling and punctuation standardized.

Old Testament Sisters and Divine Instruction

CAROLYN GREEN OWEN

Jewish midrash is an age-old, rabbinical way of explaining a Bible story by telling more story—which is far more entertaining than looking up facts in a Bible dictionary. One rabbi describes midrash as a palimpsest, "a text written over another text. . . . between the lines . . . betwixt each word, around each letter."[1] Midrash attempts to supply the rest of the story—the "whole truth"—from between the lines.

One intriguing midrash is about Sarah the Matriarch. It claims that Abraham never knew how beautiful Sarah was because she always modestly wore a veil. Do you believe that? Well, the rabbis believed it—and apparently the Lord believed it, too. Otherwise, why would he have had to point out to Abraham, "Behold, Sarai, thy wife, is a very fair woman to look upon"? (Abraham 2:22). According to the midrash, as Sarah was crossing a river on their way to Egypt, her veil became disarranged and fell aside, revealing her face. Abraham glimpsed it at last, not directly but reflected in the water, and he was dazzled—and afraid for his life. Here is what happened: "Abraham put her in a crate and nailed it up so no one might see her beauty. When he got to the Egyptian border, the customs officials told him, 'Pay duty.'

"Abraham said, 'Fine. I'll pay.'

"They asked, 'Are you carrying clothing?'

"He said, 'I'll pay for clothing.'

Carolyn Green Owen has worked as a writer, an editor, and a teacher of college writing and is completing her master's degree in literary biblical criticism from Brigham Young University. She has taught the Gospel Doctrine class in Sunday School and edited the ward newsletter. She and her husband, Earl Francis Owen, are the parents of four daughters.

"They asked, 'Are you carrying gold?'

"He said, 'I'll pay for gold.'

"They asked, 'Are you carrying silks?'

"He said, 'I'll pay for silks.'

"They said, 'Are you carrying jewels?'

"He said, 'I'll pay for jewels.'

"They said, 'It isn't possible! Open the crate and we'll have a look at what's inside.'

"When Abraham pried open the crate, all of Egypt glowed from her radiance."[2]

Much new midrash is being written today by people who believe they can clarify the brief Old Testament stories by retelling them with more detail. Their aim is to reconsider details that they believe earlier writers and commentators have suppressed, thus recovering for contemporary readers "what *really* happens in the Bible." The result is a purportedly restored text, full of guilty "little secrets" but a "rollicking good read."[3] One author introduces his collection of retold stories like this: "The stories you are about to read are some of the most violent and sexually explicit in all of Western literature. They are tales of human passion in all of its infinite variety: adultery, seduction, incest, rape, mutilation, assassination, torture, sacrifice, and murder. And yet every one of these stories is drawn directly from the pages of the Holy Bible."[4]

When this author adds that "the Bible describes and even seems to encourage a range of human conduct that goes far beyond what is permitted in the Ten Commandments,"[5] it seems clear that he has misunderstood the essential nature of his material—what is really *really* happening in the Bible. One does not have to read many retold stories to recognize that all of the vulgarity in these "neglected and forbidden tales" is in the language of the reteller.

Many of these stories are about biblical women, who often do not fare as well in the contemporary retellings as the beautiful Sarah did in the rabbinic midrash. Critics talk now about Sarah cruelly expelling Hagar; Rebekah deceiving Isaac, conspiring with one son against another; Rachel stealing the teraphim; Tamar seducing Judah; Rahab entertaining the Israelite spies.[6] The stories have become disarranged, like Sarah's veil, but what we glimpse underneath is not attractive. The implication, in this new midrash, is that the wives of the patriarchs were reputable women of Abrahamic descent who nevertheless chose to break the rules;[7] the other women were simply clever survivors.

Truly, these women of another age and culture often appear complicated and mysterious. Their motives are not transparent; they might be anyone's guess. Yet, in all the official—and often ingenious—guessing, a crucial element of their daily walk is being regularly overlooked: the almost certain fact that many biblical women were in faithful communication with the Lord. In their diverse circumstances, they turned to the Lord—appealing for, receiving, and accepting divine instruction. This factor can transform the interpretation of their stories.

But how does anyone know for certain that these divine communications took place? That is just the point: "anyone" may or may not know. But we may legitimately expect a unique affection between Latter-day Saint sisters and these Old Testament women. As Latter-day Saints living in covenant families—in other words, as modern Israel—we subscribe to the same essential religion as did Sarah, Rebekah, Rachel, and other faithful women in ancient Israel. We "have," or "belong to," the same religious faith. As we read scripture, this powerful affinity may provide helpful clues to meaning and truth. It is possible, even probable, that our religious experience is in many ways analogous to that of these ancient sisters—the ADS, or "Ancient-day Saints." Tentatively, we can know interesting things about Rebekah, for example, because of this analogue. Her responses to adversity and adventure may significantly parallel our own. At the very least, they might help us to write better midrash.

ABIGAIL'S PROPHECIES

To see what interpretive difference this sisterly understanding might make, let's consider the story of Abigail, first the wife of Nabal and later the wife of David. At this point, David is a fugitive at the bottom of his fortunes, hiding himself and six hundred men from King Saul (see 1 Samuel 25). While camped in Calebite pasture lands, they extend their protection to the herdsmen of a nearby wealthy sheep rancher, Nabal of Carmel; but when David asks Nabal for provisions in return, Nabal insults him, refusing to give him even bread and water. When David hears of it, he and four hundred of his men strap on their swords. David swears an oath to exterminate Nabal's household before morning.

A concerned servant reports to Nabal's wife, Abigail. A quick thinker, she hastily does what any Relief Society sister would do—she goes to David's relief. She packs up a large food train and delivers it her-self. She also delivers a brief, courteous speech, suggesting that the Lord has already persuaded David to go home. Surely he will go now. But not empty-handed—here is food. David is astonished but impressed, and the situation is defused.

Meanwhile, Abigail's husband, Nabal, is feasting at home, unaware of the drama playing out around him. Because he is "very drunk," Abigail does not "tell him anything, either a little or a lot, until the light of morning" (v. 36).[8] When he hears, "his heart die[s] with him" and he becomes "like a stone" (v. 37). Ten days later the Lord "strikes" Nabal in some undisclosed manner, and he dies. Sometime after that, David sends messengers to negotiate with Abigail. They stand there with their hands in their pockets and say, "David sent us to you to take you to him for a wife" (v. 40). Again, she "hastes." She rises, collects her five maids, rides after David's proxies, and becomes his wife—all in verse 42. So you know that the Deuteronomist is speaking and not a Hollywood screen-writer, I should add that "David also took Ahinoam of Jezreel, and the two of them became his wives" (v. 43).

That is the outline of the story for readers on the run. To understand the story in more depth, we need to hear Abigail's speech. What does she say to turn David around—but not so finally that he will not come back and marry her? To begin with, she is terribly sorry. She tumbles off her donkey to apologize: "And Abigail saw David and she hurried and she got down from upon the donkey and she fell before David upon her face and she bowed herself down to the ground and she fell at his feet and she said . . ." (vv. 23–24). Addressing David as "my lord," she says and does all the right things. First, she absorbs David's humiliation by humbling herself. Second, she attempts to draw David's attention away from her husband's rude behavior ("Please, my lord, do not pay atten-tion to this reckless man," v. 25). She calls his attention to herself. According to one possible translation of verse 24, she kneels on the ground in front of four hundred angry men with swords and volunteers to take the punishment ("Upon me, my lord, be the punishment"). Third, she takes the blame for the lack of hospitality from her house. She did not see David's servants who asked for food. Had they come to her, they would not have been turned away, Nabal would not have been involved, and charity would never have failed. Finally, she presents

David with a large consignment of food. It is overpayment—more than he requested. What can he say?

This first part of the speech is direct, politic, and effective. Food speaks to hungry men, and David might have then gone home, if Abigail had not kept talking. But Abigail continues, and the remainder of her speech is hard to explain. First, she audaciously tells David that the Lord himself has restrained him from taking revenge (v. 26). Then she boldly begins to prophesy. She praises David's fortitude: he has tirelessly fought "the battles of the Lord" for Israel; at the same time, he has not avenged himself against Nabal and, in particular, has not shed blood without cause (vv. 26, 28, 31). Because of his valor, she promises, certain rewards will follow: first, the Lord will establish David as a ruler over Israel and the head of a lasting dynasty (vv. 28, 30); and second, the Lord will preserve David from physical and spiritual harm and will personally vanquish his enemies (v. 29). Abigail thus reveals what David has longed to hear. But how can she presume to know God's will for David? How can she be certain that Saul will not surprise David tomorrow? How can she frankly promise David the favor of the Lord? How does she know that the Lord will legitimate her promise?

Two years ago I sat with other students in a literature seminar and considered the question of Abigail's puzzling behavior. Why would a reputedly prudent woman make such outrageous promises? We sat at a long, polished table with our chins in our hands, baffled. The tendency of scholars was to spotlight "her shrewd common sense, and her cunning way with words."[9] They speculated that Abigail was simply a clever, calculating, and rhetorically talented woman, who knew what to say to get what she wanted—power, in the form of a royal husband and the queenship of Israel. Perhaps she knew the future because she was plotting it herself—after she poisoned Nabal, she would snare David. She was "the perfect partner for this headstrong man."[10] In sum, she "sense[d] the drift of history" and "[rode] the crest of the providential wave into personal success"[11] as a sort of "opportunistic surfer."[12]

That sounded to me like unrestricted creative midrash—imaginative embroidery. Unlike classical midrash, it seemed to ignore certain irrepressible clues in the text of the story. For example, the narrator has carefully established Abigail as a woman of prudent understanding, a type of the righteous in Israel—just the sort of woman who would receive divine communication. The narrator identifies her through her words and actions with the capable wife ("virtuous woman") of Proverbs 31, just as he identifies her husband Nabal with the proverbial fool.[13] Together they form a deliberately contrasted pair: spiritual maturity on the one hand; spiritual ignorance or inexperience on the other. Expectations are set up, the story plays out, and each one earns the appropriate reward. But what happens to the polarity if both poles are negative—if Abigail emerges as cunning as Nabal is churlish? A carefully crafted biblical message is frustrated—or replaced. I wanted to hear the message, so I sat with my chin in my hand and began to reread.

I came to verse 26, where Abigail swears an oath to David that all his enemies and everyone who intends him harm will "be as Nabal." Now because I had already read the story, I knew that Nabal was going to die. So being "as Nabal" might mean being "dead as a doornail." But Abigail has not read the story; she is living it. At this moment, all Abigail knows is that Nabal is at home eating, drinking, and being merry with his friends, unaware that tomorrow, in verse 37, he will begin to die. I asked myself, *Could Abigail know otherwise?* I read on to the last line of Abigail's speech, where she says to David, "And the Lord will do well for my lord [meaning David], and you will remember your handmaid [meaning herself—Abigail]" (v. 31)—and I thought, *She knows!* But how could she know the end of the story? Again, here she is speaking in verse 31, and David will not even propose until verse 40. Although she is described as "beautiful of face or form" (*yephat toar,* v. 3), there is no sign as yet that David is any more observant of beauty than Abraham was.

In the end, the ADS-LDS connection suggested an answer. I remembered a similar experience I had had two years before. Admittedly, a household massacre was not imminent, but I was in a harsh predicament. It was critical that I behave with all the evenness of the calmest moment of my life. Without Abigail's talent for prudence, I wanted to rage, to cry. When I found myself finally alone for a moment, I offered a short prayer. Because I was ashamed of my own part in creating the problem, I admitted to the Lord that I knew he could not be proud of me. But because I relied on his help and had no wish to blame him for my difficulty or accuse him of abandoning me, I also told him, "Heavenly Father, I still love *you.*"

From the moment I said those words, I sensed that someone was with me. I began to receive immediate, judicious help. I knew exactly what to say and do and how to compose my feelings. I understood how to read my circumstances—to see things as they really were—and how to respond to them acceptably. I knew something unusual had happened when I was suddenly capable of almost preternatural tact! In the end I was able to negotiate a painful situation without tears or resentment, and what might have been a ruinous misadventure modulated into a consummate learning experience.

My mind returned to Abigail's afternoon, and I thought, *I know what she is doing.* I did not see myself as an Abigail—the archetypal righteous woman living in her faith. I am not married to a Nabal. But I did see Abigail and myself as two sisters involved in the same religious enterprise and sharing the same covenant relationship with God. Given our commonalities, I could guess how she might respond to her situation and what might happen when she did. I was ready to write my own midrash. Here it is:

When Nabal's servant dropped the calamity into Abigail's apron, did she "think to pray"? I believe that she did and that God answered, endowing her with inspired intelligence to interpret her situation, to comprehend her role in it, and to take prompt, effective action. After her prayer, the Holy Spirit may have inspired several realizations: that the Lord was prepared to deliver her and her household from destruction, that the Lord would deal personally with Nabal, that she must personally intervene to carry the word of the Lord to David, and that her obedience would be rewarded. In addition, she might have received practical intelligence to teach her specifically what she must do from moment to moment—how to comport herself, manage her emotions, speak compellingly—to avert disaster. From this revelatory moment, I envision Abigail as a woman acting under instructions, following meticulously the program of inspiration that guides her, checking each thought and action with the Spirit for approval. She was willing to curb her own reactions and initiatives in favor of an attitude of listening. One can hear her anticipating Nephi: "I will *not* put my trust in the arm of flesh" (2 Nephi 4:34; emphasis added).

How was Abigail able not only to subdue her "enemy" with a few words—spontaneously preventing catastrophe and delivering her household—but also to receive his blessing and eventually an invitation to join his household? Critics answer that she was an ambitious adventuress and an experienced mediator. One critic claims Bible stories are

115

constantly reminding us that "biblical history is not always shaped by the hand of God. Rather, the destiny of the Israelites is more often served by willful men and women who act on their own initiative and impulse, often in daring and even shocking ways."[14] What this critic sees and admires is Abigail's effective language and action, which he interprets as self-determined. What he does not see, or acknowledge, is the divine inspiration behind her prophetic words and daring action. Every Relief Society sister knows that in Israel, ancient or modern, it is God who delivers, not the plausible "arm of flesh." Abigail does not single-handedly rescue her household but cooperates with the Lord as a means to bring about a small, but privately important, domestic miracle. We do not see the Lord in this story; we do not hear his still, small voice. But because of what we do see and hear—cross-referenced with our own contemporary experience—we might believe we are watching his agent.

RAHAB AND THE ISRAELITE SPIES

But one single piece of evidence does not prove a theory. Is there another example of an unrecorded but highly probable divine manifestation to an Old Testament sister, a personal revelation that accounts well for her unexpected behavior?

It seems likely that Rahab, a Canaanite woman living in Jericho at the time of the Israelite conquest (see Joshua 2:1–24), was similarly inspired, though the details of her encounter with the Lord are not in the text. The biblical record of Rahab begins when Joshua sends two spies to reconnoiter the city of Jericho before the Israelite attack. In the course of their mission, they come to the house of Rahab, a prostitute, who lives in or on the city wall—symbolically on the border between Israel and Canaan. Apparently they intend to lodge there for the night, but they are discovered and reported to the king. The king directly sends his men to Rahab, demanding the spies. According to Near Eastern scholars, such "female innkeepers" as Rahab were subject to "royal regulation": "Recognized as sources of information valuable to the king, the women were required to report and even arrest suspicious visitors."[15] But Rahab has made no arrests; in fact, she has hidden the two spies under a pile of flax on her roof. Risking execution, she then innocently deflects the searchers' questions: "The men came to me, but I did not know where they came from" (v. 4); and she misleads them: "I do not know where the men went. But pursue them quickly and you may overtake them!" (v. 5). The king's men depart on a wild-goose chase all the way to the fords of the Jordan River, and the city gates are shut behind them.

Returning to the roof, Rahab asks the spies for a reciprocal favor: "Swear to me in the Lord . . . you will let live my father and my mother and my brothers and my sisters and all which is theirs and save our lives from death" (vv. 12, 13). Joshua's men bind themselves with a covenant promise and, warning her not to betray their secret, give her specific instructions for protecting her family during the coming invasion. Rahab then lowers the spies by a rope from the window to a point outside the city wall, and they return safely to their camp. Subsequently, when the walls of Jericho come down, Joshua spares Rahab's family, who live with the Israelites from that time on (Joshua 6:25).

Some Bible critics find this incident amusing. "The story," they say, "is, at first glance, something of an embarrassment. Why should . . . the account of God's wondrous saving acts in settling the nation in its land, . . . begin precisely at the house of a harlot?"[16] One implies that the spies were not "simply looking for a nice hotel."[17] Rahab is described both as "the original hooker with a heart of gold"[18] and as a "small-time harlot . . . with a calculating mind."[19] Some suspect that Rahab herself notified the king about the Israelite spies, hoping to create leverage that she could use to bargain with the spies for her safety.[20] As one critic observes, "Survival, for a woman, is indeed a complicated matter."[21]

May I suggest that at least some of the complications imagined by critics are exotic and probably unnecessary? As with Abigail, the chief clue to Rahab's true nature is in her speech. Listen to what she tells the spies: "*I know that the Lord has given to you the land* and that the fear of you has fallen upon us and that all [the inhabitants] of the land have melted away before your faces. For we heard that the Lord dried up the waters of the Red Sea . . . when you came out of Egypt. . . . And we heard and our hearts melted. . . . *For the Lord your God, he [is] God,* in the heavens above and upon the earth below" (Joshua 2:9–11; emphasis added).

One cynic, commenting on this passage, infers that Rahab is "clearly aware of that which is worthwhile for her to know" in dealing with Israelite men.[22] Another critic claims that "the authors *place* on the lips of Rahab a profession of faith in Yahweh, the living God."[23] But her words do not sound like calculations at the bargaining table; neither do we need to speculate that they are added propaganda. The consistency

117

and integrity of the story itself are best served by taking Rahab's remarks at face value—as genuine testimony.

How is it, then, that a Canaanite woman has come to know the living God? In answer we might ask ourselves, How does a latter-day woman come to know "the only true God"? What makes a contemporary woman decide to admit the Lord into the house of her soul, to allow him to step in with his candle and inspect each corner, making recommendations for improvement? Would that familiar process be different for Rahab? Could some profound dissatisfaction with her life have led to some equally profound searching and then repentant, divinely directed changes in her life? One critic announces Rahab's harlotry with the claim that "she is one known to be conducting . . . a house [of prostitution]."[24] But all that is known for certain is that Rahab *has been* at some point a prostitute. She has that reputation, and her name carries that epithet; but the narrator never states or implies that the house that the spies visit is currently a brothel. Could Rahab be a woman who has gratefully gone her way, sinning no more; and the Lord does not condemn her but instead has fully forgiven her, promising to deliver her and her family from the curse that is on their land?

This reading suggests that Rahab knew in advance that the spies were coming. Every citizen of Jericho knew that the notorious Israelites from Egypt were now at the border, preparing for war—that part of her speech to the spies did not require inspiration. But then, if she had in fact learned to trust the Lord God of Israel, in a time of impending invasion and grave danger almost certainly she would have prayed. Following her prayer, the Holy Spirit might have communicated to her several impressions: that the Lord had given the land to the Israelites to be their "promised land," that the Lord was prepared to deliver her and her family from the coming destruction, that the Lord would personally intervene with Joshua in her behalf, that she must personally intervene to assist the Israelites, and that her righteous obedience would be rewarded. In addition, she might have received, then or later, practical intelligence to teach her specifically what she must do—where to hide the spies, how to answer the king's men, how to pronounce her testimony, how to appeal for her family's safety. When the spies arrived at her house that night, watched and pursued, Rahab may have been, like Abigail, a woman acting under instructions, cooperating intelligently with the Holy Spirit that guided her.

Advance knowledge may have been more generally distributed; specifically, evidence suggests that the spies may have been following inspired instructions of their own. Here on the very doorstep of Canaan they find themselves confronted with a convert, a Gentile who nevertheless knows the God of Israel. What should they do? Never would they swear to exclude Rahab from the *herem* (the ban or devotion to destruction) without divine authorization, yet they do take her oath. And not only do the spies swear deliverance but they also give her elaborate instructions for protecting her family. They tell her to tie a scarlet "thread" in her window, and then, on the day of the battle, whoever is with her in her house will be safe. Under no circumstances should they come out into the street during the fighting, or their lives will be forfeit. Rahab and her family are, in effect, to sit inside her house in the wall, marked by a red thread, while the destroying angel rages outside. What is the sudden source of inspiration for these surprising but not exactly arbitrary initiatives? Considering that the Lord does not destroy the righteous but keeps faith with his faithful, is it possible that the "spies" were sent—knowingly or not—simply to collect Rahab and her household, the faithful in Canaan, first giving her the chance to try her new faith in a risky adventure and be thus "gathered" to Israel? Her rescue is flagrantly symbolic of the first Passover not long ago in Egypt. The red signal that had protected the Israelite families there will now protect Rahab and her kin.

As with Abigail, Rahab's reliance on the Lord and her courage in behalf of her family do not shrink in the face of accusing men. In obedience to the intelligence that is her gift, she passes the test of faith, it is counted as righteousness, and she is adopted into Israel. Hundreds of years in the future, James the bishop of Jerusalem will use her as an example of faith, properly accompanied by works, in his famous epistle: "[W]as not Rahab the prostitute also justified by works when she welcomed the messengers and sent them out by another road? For just as the body without the spirit is dead, so faith without works is also dead" (James 2:25–26, NRSV).[25]

The apostle Paul will mention her as an example of justification by faith in his letter to the Hebrews: "By faith the people passed through the Red Sea as if it were dry land. . . . By faith the walls of Jericho fell after they had been encircled for seven days. By faith Rahab the prostitute did not perish with those who were disobedient, because she received the spies in peace" (Hebrews 11:29–31, NRSV). Note that the same faith that parted the sea and toppled the walls—the faith that precedes and then works miracles—also saved Rahab's life.

Besides becoming a New Testament heroine, what reward did Rahab obtain? Initially, through her faith, she and her family alone in Jericho obtained life. When Joshua came to Jericho with the army of Israel, "they devoted to destruction everything in the city, both man and woman, youth and elder, ox and sheep and donkey, to the mouth of the sword. . . . And the city they burned with fire, and everything in it. . . . But Rahab the prostitute and the house of her father and everything that belonged to it Joshua let live" (Joshua 6:21, 24–25). From this point the rewards multiply through generations. Modern readers like to find an epilogue appended to a good story; this one has several auspicious variations. Unlike Abigail, Rahab does not marry the future king, but one talmudic tradition claims that "Rahab married Joshua and became the progenitor of at least eight prophets including Jeremiah."[26] According to another tradition, "she became the wife of Salmon, who could have been one of the spies."[27] And thus it happens that in the Gospel of Matthew, in the "account of the genealogy of Jesus the Messiah" (Matthew 1:1, NRSV), we are informed that "Salmon [was] the father of Boaz by Rahab, and Boaz the father of Obed by Ruth, and Obed the father of Jesse, and Jesse the father of King David" (Matthew 1:5–6, NRSV). According to this tradition, then, Rahab "became the great-great-grandmother of David, through whose line is traced the Christ."[28]

MOTHERS IN ISRAEL

These are the stories of Abigail and Rahab, two remote and even suspicious characters. They did unexpected and unexplained things, and for this critics have judged them to be "deceivers" and "tricksters." But the eye of shared sisterhood reads them differently. To a latter-day sister, it may appear that faith in the service of family—in the sense of domestic household as well as posterity—is the chief commonality between the two women. It is said that in ancient Israelite society "the first duty of a wife is to uphold the rights and the honor of her husband's household to ensure its survival. . . . [W]hen her household is attacked, . . . it is the duty of the woman to uphold its honor, even at the expense of her own honor or personal safety."[29] That is precisely what our two Old Testament women were doing. It is what "provident homemakers" do now. These are basic and enduring responsibilities. To help meet them, faithful latter-day women have effective spiritual tools—prayer and trust in God's fidelity. Would an ancient-day homemaker, no less faithful and provident, not have had these tools? Would she not have used them? Should this element not be considered when we interpret her story?

Recently I read a scholarly article about "mothers in Israel" in which the author explains that she chose to write about the biblical mother in part "because of her ordinariness—mothers are not major characters."[30] She notes that "the stories of the patriarchs and matriarchs in Genesis 12–50 are stories about a promise, the threefold promise to Abraham."[31] In this scenario, the role of the patriarch is to inherit the promise and the role of the matriarch is "obviously, to bear the children of the promise."[32] It was ever thus. Ho hum. But then, reading more closely, the author discovers an unexpected paradox: "Whereas the important events in Israelite tradition are experienced by men, they are often set in motion and determined by women."[33] In fact, "the matriarchs act at strategic points that move the plot, and thus the promise, in the proper direction toward its fulfillment."[34] In sum—beginning with Eve, it would seem—women's actions have had "important consequences . . . for the divine plan."[35] And since they do, it would be strange indeed if these actions were not guided by divine inspiration.

The article, in fact, concludes with an inductive definition of the role of mothers in Israel that sounds like an abstract of the stories of Abigail and Rahab: "A mother in Israel is one who brings liberation from oppression, provides protection, and ensures the well-being and security of her people."[36] These are her divinely ordained responsibilities—whether she is at the head of an army[37] or at the foot of her family. A Latter-day Saint woman does not have to read it in the text to know that divine help is always available to do what is divinely ordained.

INTERPRETING SCRIPTURE

Let me share two comments from Bible scholars about how to interpret scripture in which the attitude of the scholar is unusually clear:

"One cannot read an ancient literary artifact from a long-dead culture, written in an ancient semitic tongue . . . without some degree of historical grounding."[38]

"The reader of any biblical text . . . becomes obligated, at least minimally, to become acquainted with the history surrounding the text. Inevitably, this means becoming a student of the ancient world, the ancient Near East in the case of the OT [Old Testament], and the

Hellenistic-Roman world in the case of the NT [New Testament]. It also involves familiarity with the ancient languages in which the books were written: Hebrew, Aramaic, and Greek."[39]

When we read these and similar ultimatums, we may feel that the scholars are saying to us, "Watch what we do, my dears—but don't try this at home." As an apprentice literary biblical critic, I have studied classical Hebrew and New Testament Greek. I continue to survey the recommended historical grounding—and the political, social, cultural, literary, and religious grounding as well. Such information has greatly increased my appreciation for scripture and my pleasure in reading it—though not necessarily my chances for salvation. I do not, of course, despise either my education or sound scholarly advice. But to a community of Latter-day Saint sisters, I want to offer a different testimony.

Even if we do not regularly read the *Biblia Hebraica Stuttgartensia*, even if we have never read a single issue of *Vetus Testamentum*, still, as Latter-day Saint women, we have superior tools for getting at the "whole truth" that is "between the lines" of scripture. We have sainthood, we have empathetic sisterhood—and we have something more. Here is an axiom: books are best understood if they are read by the same spirit with which they were written. Original scripture was written by the spirit and power of the Holy Ghost and may be correctly interpreted by that same Spirit. The scholar is right, of course—the Bible is an old book. Joseph Smith said, "I thank God that I have got this old book. . . . but I have got the *oldest* book in my heart, even the gift of the Holy Ghost."[40] Whatever our intellect or education might be, this Spirit is our singular advantage. May the Lord bless us as we read scripture in its company.

NOTES

1. Burton L. Visotzky, *Reading the Book: Making the Bible a Timeless Text* (New York: Schocken Books, 1996), vii.
2. Visotzky, *Reading the Book*, 59–60.
3. Jonathan Kirsch, *The Harlot by the Side of the Road: Forbidden Tales of the Bible* (New York: Ballantine Books, 1997), 1, 9, 14.
4. Kirsch, *Harlot by the Side of the Road*, 1.
5. Kirsch, *Harlot by the Side of the Road*, 2.
6. These judgments often come up incidentally, as if self-evident. See, for example, Kathleen Norris's remark, "The telling of Rebekah's acts of subversion, in which she deceives her husband, betrays her eldest son, and makes an accomplice of her beloved youngest, is a sublime example of narrative skill," from "The Story of Rebekah as a Mother," in David Rosenberg, *Genesis, As It Is Written: Contemporary Writers on Our First Stories* (New York: Harper, 1996), 164–65.

7. See, for example, Clarence Major's comment, "Rebekah of Genesis is a good person who breaks the rules," from "The Story of Rebekah," in Rosenberg, *Genesis*, 158. See also Kathleen Norris's observation that the House of Israel with its twelve tribes "has all come about because Rebekah, who was supposed to be 'safe' as a kinswoman of Abraham, has broken the rules," from "The Story of Rebekah as a Mother," in Rosenberg, *Genesis*, 168.

8. All quotations from the Old Testament in this chapter are the author's own translation. New Testament texts are taken from *The HarperCollins Study Bible: New Revised Standard Version* (New York: HarperCollins, 1993), indicated as NRSV.

9. Walter Brueggemann, *First and Second Samuel. Interpretation: A Bible Commentary for Teaching and Preaching* (Louisville, Ky.: John Knox Press, 1990), 176.

10. Brueggemann, *First and Second Samuel*, 181.

11. Jon D. Levenson, "1 Samuel 25 as Literature and as History," *Catholic Biblical Quarterly* 40 (1978): 20. Levenson's article has functioned as the basal reading of this chapter in contemporary biblical criticism.

12. Alice Bach, "The Pleasure of Her Text," *Union Seminary Quarterly Review* 43 (1989):47. Bach disagrees with this characterization of Abigail.

13. The Hebrew word *nabal* means "fool"—particularly an arrogant, irreligious, and even immoral fool. In this story, Nabal's name is the key to his complete profile.

14. Kirsch, *Harlot by the Side of the Road*, 141.

15. James R. Baker, *Women's Rights in Old Testament Times* (Salt Lake City: Signature Books, 1992), 73.

16. Yair Zakovitch, "Humor and Theology or the Successful Failure of Israelite Intelligence: A Literary-Folkloric Approach to Joshua 2," in *Text and Tradition: The Hebrew Bible and Folklore*, ed. Susan Niditch (Atlanta: Scholars Press, 1990), 76.

17. Zakovitch, "Humor and Theology," 82.

18. Kirsch, *Harlot by the Side of the Road*, 141.

19. Zakovitch, "Humor and Theology," 90.

20. See Zakovitch, "Humor and Theology," 85.

21. Danna Nolan Fewell, "Introduction: Writing, Reading, and Relating," in *Reading between Texts: Intertextuality and the Hebrew Bible*, ed. Danna Nolan Fewell (Louisville, Ky.: Westminister/John Knox Press, 1992), 16.

22. Zakovitch, "Humor and Theology," 89.

23. Judette A. Gallares, *Images of Faith: Spirituality of Women in the Old Testament* (Maryknoll, N.Y.: Orbis Books, 1992), 44; emphasis added.

24. Gallares, *Images of Faith*, 36.

25. Note that James refers to the two Israelite men as "messengers" rather than "spies," prompting a reader to ask who "sent" them to Rahab and what the "message" was. Perhaps their spy detail would be better described as a deliberate rescue mission. Note, too, that James says the messengers were sent home by "another road." Both variations suggest that James had sources of information other than the existing Old Testament account and a different understanding of what happened.

26. Baker, *Women's Rights*, 75.

27. Gallares, *Images of Faith*, 43.

28. Gallares, *Images of Faith*, 43.

29. Victor H. Matthews, "Female Voices: Upholding the Honor of the Household," *Biblical Theology Bulletin* 24 (1994): 8.

30. J. Cheryl Exum, "'Mother in Israel': A Familiar Story Reconsidered," *Feminist Interpretation of the Bible*, ed. Letty M. Russell (Philadelphia: Westminister Press, 1985), 74.

31. Exum, "Mother," 75.

32. Exum, "Mother," 75.

33. Exum, "Mother," 74.

34. Exum, "Mother," 76.

35. Exum, "Mother," 82.

36. Exum, "Mother," 85.

37. The term "mother in Israel" first appears in scripture in the "Song of Deborah," a prophetess and judge who was at the head of the army of Israel (see Judges 5:7). Indeed, Barak, the commander, would not go to battle without her. She was married to Lappidoth (see Judges 4:4), but we do not know whether she had children. In any case, we do not see her in the domestic role of mother but as a protector of the realm. The only other designated "mother in Israel" was a wise woman in the city of Abel of Beth-maacah, one of the "peaceful and faithful of Israel," who saves her city from Joab's attack (see 2 Samuel 20:14–22).

38. K. L. Noll, *The Faces of David,* Journal for the Study of the Old Testament Supplement Series 242 (Sheffield, Eng.: Sheffield Academic Press, 1997), 12–13.

39. Carl R. Holladay, "Contemporary Methods of Reading the Bible," *The New Interpreter's Bible,* 12 vols. (Nashville, Tenn.: Abingdon Press, 1994), 1:129.

40. Alma P. Burton, comp., *Discourses of the Prophet Joseph Smith,* 3d ed. (Salt Lake City: Deseret Book, 1965), 265; emphasis added. The comment is from Joseph Smith's King Follet Discourse, given Sunday, 7 April 1844; see also Joseph Smith, *History of The Church of Jesus Christ of Latter-day Saints*, ed. B. H. Roberts, 2d ed. rev., 7 vols. (Salt Lake City: The Church of Jesus Christ of Latter-day Saints, 1932–51), 6:308.

The Ripple Effect:
Building Zion Communities

JULENE BUTLER

Building Zion can be like tossing a pebble into a pond. Just as ripples work their way outward from one pebble, growing ever larger, so a Zion community can begin with one person working within a family—that first small circle, then gradually moving outward, expanding into broader groups, spreading the principles of godhood through larger circles of people and communities.

What do I mean by "communities"? A community can be a geographic cluster of people, such as a city or town or perhaps a ward or neighborhood. But it is not limited to such groups. Webster's definition specifies groups organized around a "unifying trait."[1] A community might be a local bird-watching group, a political party, the people we work with, or fans of a basketball team during the playoffs. A circle of friends might qualify as a community.

Our Church leaders often note that our homes are laboratories in which we may learn and practice gospel principles.[2] Each community in which we participate is a broader circle for practicing the principles we first experience in the family setting. Those communities offer us opportunities to observe the consequences of good and bad behaviors.

Think for a moment of examples of Zion in the scriptures. The city of Enoch was an entire city of people whose every desire was to live righteously. We are told: "Enoch and *all his people* walked with God, and

Julene Butler is assistant university librarian for public services at Brigham Young University's Harold B. Lee Library. She serves as Relief Society president in her ward.

125

he dwelt in the midst of Zion; and it came to pass that Zion was not, for God received it up into his own bosom" (Moses 7:69; emphasis added).

Fourth Nephi gives us another example of a Zion community. These people had seen Christ when he visited the American continent, had felt his loving influence, and were motivated to be one and to teach their children and their children's children to live together in love and righteousness.

Notice that both these examples of Zion consist of large groups of people, communities of Saints; they were Zion societies. Hugh Nibley suggests that Zion, by its very definition, cannot exist in isolation. We cannot "have all things in common" or "be of one heart and one mind" in isolation from our brothers and sisters, our neighbors and friends.[3]

We need others in order to thrive. In fact, we need them simply to survive. Primitive tribes understood this truth, especially as it related to their physical survival. They came together for protection and nourishment. The same is true in a spiritual sense. If we are to thrive spiritually, or simply survive spiritually, we need each other. We can make only so much spiritual progress in isolation from one another, and then our progress stops.

Over the years, I have heard many women comment that they learned gospel principles most deeply through their roles as wife or mother. They are speaking from their hearts, and I know they are bearing witness to the truth. The sacrifice and selflessness required in those relationships require women to reach deep within their souls. Some seem to suggest, however, that it is only in the context of marriage and family that we can prepare for godhood, and the implication is that a person who lives alone somehow misses the chance to learn those same lessons. I believe very differently. Let me tell you why.

I have two sisters, whom I love dearly. Patsy is the mother of five; Paula, the mother of nine. Each has supported her husband through years of Church activity. Their daily routines over the years have been very different from mine. But on many, many occasions, as we've talked to each other about our latest struggles and discoveries, I have realized that we are on the same path. My experiences are teaching me the same lessons they are learning. Our experiences occur in different settings, but my soul is being stretched to much the same extent as theirs.

A loving Heavenly Father gives each of us the opportunities we need to reach godhood. So when I say that we cannot survive spiritually if we are alone or that we can progress only to a certain point in isolation from each other, I speak more of a condition of the heart than of the nature of our life's circumstances.

Now, back to the idea of isolation. To punish criminals, we remove them from the community, locking them behind bars. Prisoners of war describe the horrors of one especially severe type of punishment: prolonged solitary confinement. Psychologists maintain that extended periods of solitary confinement can lead to severe psychological damage.

One of Satan's strongest tools is to isolate us from each other, to turn our thoughts away from those around us and, in so doing, prevent us from reaching out to others and finding strength through unity. Satan does not want Zion to flourish, and he knows he can stop it most easily by attacking its roots, by dividing righteous people from one another.

Think back on your life for a moment. Have you ever felt alone, deeply alone? I have at times in my life. I am a single woman confined to a wheelchair, who lives alone (by choice!) some distance from immediate family. At one time I honestly felt that if I were to slip in the shower or become ill, none of my neighbors would realize it for weeks. I believed they would never miss me or wonder what had become of me. (That is certainly not true now, and I don't believe it was true then, but at that time, I felt very isolated.)

When I look back on that time of my life, I realize that I was suffering in other ways, too. My physical health was poor. I was on an emotional roller coaster. I thought mostly of myself and my own troubles, I couldn't (or wouldn't) look outward, and I had no desire to serve those around me. I wasn't even aware that people around me had needs that I might have filled. I felt alone, and self-pity and negative behavior reinforced that alone-ness. If I were to characterize myself at that period of my life, I'd say I was very immature—emotionally and spiritually.

I find it interesting that the New Testament word that is translated as "perfect" in scripture, such as "Be ye therefore perfect," may be more correctly translated as "finished" or "complete" (Matthew 5:48, note b). We are here on earth to learn and grow. The process of maturing, of becoming spiritually complete, is a lifelong process.

I had an amusing experience years ago one summer when I needed help with my yard. Yardwork is a little tough from a wheelchair! A good friend who shared my home at the time usually took care of things outdoors, but that summer she wasn't well and couldn't tackle the weeds and other details. I didn't want to ask family or friends for help because I didn't want her to think I was being critical. I fretted and stewed and decided that the only answer was for someone to offer their help, so I prayed intensely that someone would notice our situation. A few days later, my visiting teacher came. We had a pleasant visit. As she stood on our porch saying good-bye, she noticed the yard problem. "Hmmm," she said, "it looks like you're having trouble keeping up with your yard work. But that's okay; none of us mind."

I laughed to myself and silently shared the joke with Heavenly Father. After all, I had prayed that someone would notice. My prayers had been answered, very literally. I learned from that experience to pray in specifics but also to be willing to ask for help when I need it. Perhaps more importantly, I realized that if we are to be a Zion people, we must not only keep our eyes open and notice the needs of those around us but also keep our hearts open—and be one, reaching out and doing for others what they are unable to do for themselves.

In Relief Society a few weeks ago, our teacher spoke of her "kind of naughty" children who are now teens and young adults. She told us how she longs for them to change their lifestyle and how she continues to do all she can to help them get back on the path. She is a counselor in a high school, where she has many opportunities to work with young people who are also "kind of naughty." That day in Relief Society she said, "I've come to realize that as I work with these students at school, I can love them the way I hope other people will love my children." That sounds like Zion behavior to me—lifting and blessing others, reaching out to help when we see a need, praying that others will do the same when they notice our needs.

We're given specific information about a Zion society in the Book of Mormon: "And it came to pass that there was no contention in the land, because of the love of God which did dwell in the hearts of the people. And there were no envyings, nor strifes, nor tumults, nor whoredoms, nor lyings, nor murders, nor any manner of lasciviousness; and surely there could not be a happier people among all the people who had been created by the hand of God. There were no robbers, nor murderers, neither were there Lamanites, nor any manner of -ites; but they were *in one*, the children of Christ, and heirs to the kingdom of God" (4 Nephi 1:15–17; emphasis added).

I have always loved the phrase: "nor any manner of -ites." Imagine a classless society with no "haves" and "have-nots," no divisions among the people. The Savior teaches love and unity. But Satan works to divide and separate us. He introduces contention within our wards, neighborhoods, and families. He whispers things like "How can I talk to her? She doesn't speak English well enough" or "I don't like to visit teach her. Her house is always a mess!" or "Oh them! They never go to church. I can't let my kids play with their kids." I have a friend who seldom goes to church. She attends when her grandchildren are baptized, when they sing in the Primary sacrament meeting program, when they leave for their missions, and again when they return. But other Sundays she's at home or at work. She once told me that only one person in her ward treats her "like a real person." Whatever their reason for not drawing her in, whatever her reason for not reaching out to them, she and her ward are not yet "in one."

How do we improve? How do we reach the point where we truly are one? The scriptures hold the answer. "There was no contention in the land, because of the love of God which did dwell in the hearts of the people" (4 Nephi 1:15).

In a recent general conference, Elder Henry B. Eyring said that through a "unity of [our] faith in Jesus Christ" we will receive the help we need to change our natures and become one. "It is our surrender to the authority of Jesus Christ which will allow us to be bound as families, as a Church, and as the children of our Heavenly Father," he taught. "The Spirit of God never generates contention. . . . It unifies souls."[4]

With the love of God in our hearts, we are able to see the beauty and goodness within each person we meet, no matter where they stand in relation to perfection (or maturity or completeness). Often that beauty is not readily evident.

I think of the first time I went into Manhattan alone. I drove in from my New Jersey home to attend some meetings at New York University. I had carefully planned my day. I called ahead to get the number of the bus that ran from Port Authority to lower Manhattan. When I asked about the return trip, I was told to get back on the same bus, which would then go down to Battery Park, make a loop, and head back uptown. But after lunch, when I went to the bus stop, several buses with my number drove right past me. Finally one stopped and the driver said, "Lady, we're not going to load you and your wheelchair onto this bus just to unload you in two blocks where this line ends!" I asked him how to get uptown from there, and he told me I had to head west six blocks to catch the uptown bus. Then he drove away.

I had been in the city often enough with friends to know that only some streets had curb ramps. Very often my friends had to help me up a curb when we crossed a street. But I couldn't panic for long. I really had only one choice, so I headed west. Approaching the first intersection, I could see through the crowds that there was a down curb-cut I could use. But I couldn't yet see across the street to the other side. The light changed. I started across and halfway there discovered there was no ramp ahead. I glanced cautiously from side to side at the crowd walking across the street with me, trying to decide if I dared ask anyone for help. Before I could ask anyone, a man stepped up, said, "Let me help you," and then boosted me up the curb. He was the last person I would have considered asking. The same thing happened every time I needed help; and often the least likely looking individuals were the first to offer help.

I think of 1 Samuel 16:7: "The Lord seeth not as man seeth; for man looketh on the outward appearance, but the Lord looketh on the heart." The Lord looks on the heart; we need to learn to do the same. As we let the love of God into our hearts, the Spirit will teach us how.

To paraphrase Elder Eyring, we can learn to be one by using our similarities to help us understand one another and our differences to complement each other. Each of us has unique gifts and abilities that will help build up Zion, help us be one.[5]

Let me illustrate with one more personal example. My good friend Linda is blind. When I lived in New Jersey, she and I often ran errands together. We were quite a pair: a blind woman, her guide dog on the harness, and a woman in a motorized wheelchair. I had more fun than Linda did because I could see people's reactions to us. We always got a reaction. Some people smiled and said hello. Others pretended there was nothing unusual about us. Still others stared openly. When we shopped together, we became very good at using our individual abilities to benefit each other. We made a great team! Getting items from the top shelf had always been a problem for me. Linda could reach what I couldn't. (She's not very tall, but she has a higher reach than I do!) I would direct her ("a little bit to the right, now up . . . oops, too far—there!"). Linda and I learned the importance of each person sharing her unique strengths.

Though we do not currently live the united order, we are expected to live the law of consecration. We are to consecrate our time, our means, and our talents to building up Zion. We are each given different types and amounts of talent and time and material goods. And we covenant to consecrate what we have.

Hugh Nibley teaches that the express purpose of the law of consecration is to build up Zion. Contrary to what some believe, says Nibley, "we do not wait until Zion is here to observe it; it is rather the means of bringing us nearer to Zion." In other words, we help create Zion by becoming a Zion people as we consecrate our energies and possessions and abilities.[6]

If we are to build Zion, we must move beyond ourselves and even beyond our families. We must allow our influence to ripple out into the communities that we belong to (our ward, our neighborhood, our friends) and practice Zion principles in these wider circles. We must look for each others' strengths and work in concert, one with another. We must wear off the rough edges of selfishness that form when we isolate ourselves. May we each find our unique gifts and talents, nurture them, and enlarge our desire and ability to consecrate those gifts to building up the kingdom of God. As we do, ripples of righteousness will flow outward, and Zion will begin to flourish.

NOTES

1. Merriam Webster's Collegiate Dictionary, 10th ed., s.v. "community."
2. See, for a recent instance, Dale E. Miller, Ensign, May 1998, 29–31.
3. Hugh Nibley, Approaching Zion, vol. 9 of The Collected Works of Hugh Nibley, ed. Don E. Norton (Salt Lake City: Deseret Book and Foundation for Ancient Research and Mormon Studies, 1989), 394.
4. Henry B. Eyring, Ensign, May 1998, 68, 67.
5. Eyring, Ensign, May 1998, 68.
6. Nibley, Approaching Zion, 390.

Susceptible to Blessings

PATSY URE DARBY

In the Grassmarket Square in Edinburgh, Scotland, a poor farmer from Fenwick was to be hanged. His name was John Paton. He would be the last martyr hanged for the cause of the "Coventeers," or Covenanters, Scottish Presbyterians who had struggled for 150 years to defend their right to pray and receive guidance from God directly instead of through the clergy. This was in opposition both to Anglican teachings and to those of Puritans under Oliver Cromwell. But the Covenanters were bound by covenant to defend their right to worship. Most paid with their lives during a period of savage persecution known as the "killing time."

On 9 May 1684, John Paton stood on the scaffold to bear his final witness of Jesus Christ. Handing his Bible to his wife, Janet, he shared aloud the testimony he had written in the flyleaf of that sacred work. He claimed no special status as a martyr for his beliefs: I "have no righteousness of my own; all is Jesus Christ's and his alone." He closed his statement with a prayer for the welfare of his wife and children: "Now I leave my poor sympathizing wife and six small children upon the Almighty Father, Son, and Holy Ghost, who hath promised to be 'a Father to the fatherless and a husband to the widow . . . [']; be thou all in all unto them, O Lord. Now the blessing of God, and my poor blessing, be with them. And my suit to Thee is, that thou wouldst give them thy salvation. And now farewell wife and children; farewell all friends and relations; farewell all worldly enjoyments; farewell sweet Scriptures, preaching, praying, reading, singing, and all other duties. Welcome,

Patsy Ure Darby, an avid gardener, cook, and genealogist, has been involved in genealogical research since she was sixteen. The single mother of seven and grandmother of eight, she serves in her ward Relief Society presidency.

Father, Son, and Holy Spirit. I desire to commit my soul to thee in well-doing,—Lord, receive my spirit."[1]

And he was hanged.

Can you see why I love this man, my eighth great-grandfather? Learning his story, I feel I have found not only a friend but a sacred obligation.

As I have searched out my ancestors through the years, I have always wondered about their stories. When I see on a parish death record that four children in one family died within a few months of each other and then the father died, I wondered about my ancestor, the wife and mother. Her suffering must have been intense. How did she cope, what did she think, how did she survive economically? Did she know that she could pray for help and comfort? I long to know more about her. As I have researched along family lines, I have become almost obsessed with piecing together these stories.

A scripture well known to many Latter-day Saints is Malachi 4:5–6: "Behold, I will send you Elijah the prophet before the coming of the great and dreadful day of the Lord: and he shall turn the heart of the fathers to the children, and the heart of the children to their fathers, lest I come and smite the earth with a curse." The Prophet Joseph Smith told us that "the word *turn* here should be translated *bind*, or seal."[2] The verse would then read: "And he shall bind and seal the heart of the fathers to the children, and the heart of the children to their fathers."

Elder Boyd K. Packer says: "The spirit of Elijah spoken of by the Prophet . . . is something very real. When a member of the Church comes under its influence, it is a powerful, compelling force which motivates him with a desire to be attending to genealogical and temple work. It leaves him anxious over the well-being of his forebears. When that spirit comes, somehow we desire to know more about those forebears—we desire to *know* them."[3]

For several years, I searched and compiled genealogical information on my father's side of the family, specifically in Scotland. I loved the research process and the excitement of discovery. Then I started to put my mother's genealogical information in my computer. Her father had homesteaded in Canada, and she had not met his large family, who remained in Missouri. As a new LDS convert, Mother had corresponded with many of her Missouri cousins. She had saved many of the letters she received and often the carbon copies of the letters she had written.

These letters preserved fragmentary but tantalizing facts and stories about Mother's family.

I couldn't quit thinking about these people. Information was skimpy on some of the women's lines, and I knew that if I didn't get started, I might never be able to get their stories. Too much time would have passed. So I searched, researched, and sought to know them.

I can hardly wait, someday and in some other realm, to meet Ella May Biggs—the sixth of my great-grandparents' fourteen children. Ella May was fifteen when my grandfather—her brother—was born. Though I never heard Granddad mention any of his brothers or sisters, I have gleaned a little information from letters and a distant cousin.

Ella May was born 20 October 1861—203 days after the start of the Civil War. Her parents had a large estate. Her father (my great-grand-father) was a state senator in Missouri. The family had a large grove of maple trees from which sugar was extracted, and they were slave own-ers. Ella May and her thirteen brothers and sisters were wet nursed and nannied by a black woman. I wish I knew her name. If Ella May's atti-tudes had anything to do with what she learned in her care, the nanny must have been a spiritual giant.

Ella May married but had no children. One day a man came to the door with a four-year-old boy, asking Ella May to raise him because his mother had run off with another man. Homer Daugherty became Ella May and Jeptha's son.

A second child later appeared at Ella May's back door, a ten-year-old black child named Albert Washington. "Miss Ella," he asked, "could I come and live at your house? There are so many at our house I don't get enough to eat." Albert's family lived about a mile across the fields and hills. "Why yes, Albert, if it is all right with your folks," Aunt Ella answered. She rode horseback to the Washington cabin to ask about Albert. In dire straits, his parents agreed and Albert moved in with Ella and Jeptha. He was the first of several little black boys Ella raised, which might be surprising to us, considering her typical Southern background. I wish I knew the names of those other boys. She cared for the sick no matter who they were. One time, a black family lived in a house at the back of Ella's property, and a tree fell on the man of the house and broke his leg. Aunt Ella stayed with the family, nursing the man for six weeks in their home, which was probably not more than a cabin.

I am so proud to be related to Ella, a woman who rose above the inherited prejudice of her generation and culture.

I realized that because Granddad was the second youngest child in a family of fourteen, my mother would be among the youngest of the cousins. My mother was eighty-seven, and I knew of only two or three of her cousins who were still living—and they were in their nineties. I felt an urgency, that the time to find my stories was slipping away. In a phone conversation with my friend Vickie, I shared my desire to travel to my ancestral homes that spring or summer. Vickie wanted to go with me and even tracked down some special rates so that we could fly into our target area.

I felt excited but overwhelmed with the necessary preparations. I wrote letters to the addresses I found in Mother's papers, knowing that they were twenty or thirty years old, but hoping that someone was still alive who could help me. I even wrote public libraries and post offices in the small Missouri towns of Farber, Santa Fe, and Laddonia, hoping to find a contact. Of course, at this point I didn't realize how small some of these towns were. A number of them had no libraries and only part-time post offices.

The week before we were to leave, I hadn't received a single response to my inquiries. I didn't know what I would do when I arrived, but I felt guided and so kept trying to find leads. One day in the Family History Library in Salt Lake City, my sister Colleen and I were searching for information on Pike County, Missouri. Colleen looked up information on our grandmother's family to see if we could find anything more on this line. All we knew was that her father was William H. Tanner and her mother Mary Ann Crigler. We had been unable to find their marriage record, but Colleen went to check out some new marriage CDs the library had acquired. One CD contained both Missouri and Kentucky information, and by divine "accident" Colleen found the marriage of Mary Ann and William in Boone County, Kentucky. We had been looking in the wrong state.

At the same time, I found a book one of Mother's cousins, Kathryn Hutchinson Campbell, had written and donated to the Family History Library. Kathryn had donated just two others, one to the Daughters of the American Revolution in Washington, D.C., and one other to a library in the East; Salt Lake was certainly the only place where I would have found this information.

The book was packed with facts I was looking for. Kathryn had spent much of her life compiling information and writing down little stories and tidbits about the Biggs family. I was thrilled, but now I wondered why I was going on this trip in a week. I had just found basically all of the information I sought. Through a priesthood blessing, however, the Holy Ghost confirmed that I should go ahead, so I did.

Originally I had been scheduled to fly straight to St. Louis, Missouri, and return through Ohio, stopping off at Vickie's home there, but the travel agent mixed up the flight and scheduled me to fly both in and out of Ohio. I phoned Vickie and told her to meet me in Ohio instead of in Missouri. I felt a little frustrated, but very soon I realized that mix-up was also part of "the plan." There were no coincidences on this trip; it was full of divine help and intervention.

Boone County, Kentucky, where Mary Ann and William H. Tanner were married, was about a ninety-minute drive from Vickie's house in Dayton. I decided to visit the courthouse and look at the original marriage certificate, hoping to find other names on the record. Then we would leave for Missouri.

Florence is the county seat of Boone County and thus home of the courthouse. This courthouse was amazing. No one thought it at all strange that we were asking to see records. We signed in and then were shown steps to a basement filled with hundreds of large books, about eighteen inches by thirty inches, and five to six inches thick, all neatly organized and indexed. Before long a diminutive white-haired lady came down and asked what we were doing. I wondered if she was upset that we were there, but no, she was just protecting her life work. Mrs. Ann Fitzgerald and her husband had spent the last fifty years indexing and compiling those records.

We located the marriage certificate but found no additional signatures on it. After copying the certificate, I went upstairs to ask Mrs. Fitzgerald a question about the Tanners. She rattled off histories about the two Tanner families from that area and offered a guess as to which one she thought I would be part of. I was a little taken aback by the depth of her knowledge. "Wouldn't you like to come over to my house after I finish work and see what else I have?" she asked.

Though I appreciated her friendliness, I hesitated. It was early. What were we going to do for the rest of the day in this tiny town? Weren't we supposed to be off for Missouri? As if reading my thoughts, she asked,

"What do you plan to do for the rest of the day?" Then without waiting for an answer, she continued, "You should go over to the public library. You will probably find information there that will be of help." The public library, I wondered. What could they possibly have that would help? I got directions to both the library and her home, however, and promised to call back at 5:15.

Timidly entering the library, I asked, "Do you have any books on genealogy?" A rather bored librarian pointed to a room behind her. This room, we discovered, had been set aside solely for genealogical research! It had two filing cabinets, books, family records, films, and a treasure of information lining the walls. In a filing cabinet, I found long manila folders with family names on them—my family names.

Needless to say, I felt a deep debt of gratitude to Mrs. Fitz, as her friends call her. Let me share from my journal some thoughts on this guardian angel of genealogy in Boone County: "We met Mrs. William (Ann) Fitzgerald at the court house, a sprightly 94-year-old angel, truly one who lives the life of a Christian touched by the spirit of Elijah. . . . She goes to work each day at noon for 4 hours, driving herself the 8 to 10 miles. She told me that she helps anyone that asks, feeling that it is her responsibility. Her face literally glowed as we talked. I told her how I know that she is doing God's work, and I know that He is pleased with her. As we parted we hugged, and she kissed me. I was so touched. Touched by this beautiful daughter of God, who is filled with the Spirit of Elijah."

I went to bed that night, awed by the spirit of the day and a little overwhelmed by the help I'd received. But nighttime proved to be equally wondrous. All through my dreams that night people crowded around me, reaching out, touching me, and stroking my face. I felt their love for me, their concern, and my responsibility to them. During our travels and work in Kentucky, this experience continued nightly, until one morning I awoke realizing no one had been with me the previous night. I knew then that I had finished what I had come to do in Kentucky.

From Boone County we moved on to Clark County. There we found Dr. Doyle, who had spent many years gathering information on dozens of families that had come into Kentucky in the early part of this century. He was well known in the local genealogical society, and hundreds of people had written him letters over the years. He always tried to help.

He donated all his work correspondence and research findings to the public library in Winchester. Dr. Doyle made sure that many of the gravestones were copied, genealogies inscribed in family Bibles copied by hand, and family stories preserved.

In the Winchester Library, I read old plat maps and early pioneer land divisions, trying to figure out the burial sites of my ancestors. The names of old roads were clear, but those roads had been renamed, and local maps did not include the old names. I asked the librarians if they could help. Each in turn said no. But a woman who had dropped into the library for a minute heard me ask and said she knew the location of the farms I was looking for. Once again, I knew that her presence that day was not just accidental.

When we got to Bourbon County, Kentucky, we stopped in the little town of Paris, hoping to find a Baptist church with some records that I wanted. A local woman I stopped said, "Well, there are a lot of Methodist churches in the area. Are you sure you don't want Methodist? There aren't really Baptists here. Oh, it may be worth checking at the Duncan Tavern." I looked a little blank. She smiled, "There is a Daughters of the American Revolution library in the basement."

I would never have imagined that this very small town would have a genealogical library—especially one in a tavern! It was wonderful. Vickie and I were the only ones to sign in with the volunteer librarians in quite a few days. Though it was close to closing time and I could tell that the woman was anxious to leave, she also wanted to help me find out about Davis Biggs. "What other churches did he preach in?" she asked. From cousins' letters I knew: "Indian Creek and Silas Creek."

"Well," she said, "I'll tell you how to get there. You're lucky I'm on today. Those churches are so old that not many people know where they are. But I've lived here all my life and know the way." I felt compelled to see the churches where Davis had preached. I hoped to find some early records still kept at the churches that would give me personal information about him. Again I felt the guidance of the Holy Ghost.

Later, while searching a lovely country lane called Quisenberry Road in hopes of finding the old Quisenberry farmhouse, we kept coming to dead ends. I wanted to look at a gravesite that Dr. Doyle had copied information from. It was somewhere in this area, and I presumed that it would be on old Quisenberry land. We drove up and down the road but saw only the lovely tall trees that lined the road. Finally we stopped to pray, and then we pulled into a nearby driveway, also flanked by tall trees.

I felt drawn to a house on a little hill beyond. We knocked, but no one answered. "I know this seems crazy," I told Vickie, "but I am going to take a picture of this house and these beautiful rolling green hills." A bit uncomfortable with my picture taking, Vickie stayed in the car.

Shortly a man arrived home and asked what I was doing. I expressed my interest in examining family gravesites. Though he was only a tenant of the home, not kin to the original owners, he knew about some old gravesites at the back of the property. If we were determined, we could walk to them, but we would have to cross the bull field.

I wanted to see the graves so badly that even a bull could not stop me. As we walked towards the field, he called out, "What name were you looking for?"

"My grandmother was a Quisenberry," I answered.

"Did you realize that this is the old Quisenberry homestead?"

After climbing over boulders and crawling under fences to avoid the bulls, a reluctant Vickie at my side, we found five or six large tombstones in disrepair, the inscriptions mostly illegible. Fortunately Dr. Doyle had copied the information from the stones sixty years earlier. What mattered to me above all was just being there and feeling their spirit in this beautiful place.

From their stories, I had created visual images of these ancestors. I felt I knew them. Peggy Quisenberry had nineteen children and "is said to have wept most grievously because she could not 'even out'" the number to twenty.[4] Roger Quisenberry was born five months after Kentucky was admitted to the Union. During the War of 1812, twenty-year-old Roger was taken prisoner by the British and carried to Fort George, Kentucky. There he was compelled by the Indians to "run the gauntlet."[5] In his life he was known for his bravery.

Scrolling back two generations, I found Peggy's grandparents, the Eubanks. Richard Eubank was more than eighty years old when he and his wife, Polly, rode horseback from their home in Bedford County, Virginia, to visit their son Achilles (Peggy's father), in Clark County, Kentucky. That was in 1806 or 1807, when roads were primitive at best. Their son convinced them to settle in Clark County and built them a small house near his own. In 1830 Achilles' wife, Mary, died. According to the *Clark County Weekly*, "Achilles Eubank was 72 years old at the time his wife died but evidently he was a man of great energy and vigor and he soon considered remarriage." He wanted to marry Nancy Wear, "a fifteen year old orphan whom the Eubanks had taken in to their home and reared as their own child. His [seven] children strongly opposed his marriage to one almost sixty years his junior and this fact infuriated Achilles to such an extent that he divided his property among his children and migrated to the wilderness of Cooper County, Missouri." He and Nancy had six children before he died at age eighty-six. She would have been twenty-nine then.[6]

Unconventional remarriage seems to be a recurring theme in my history. James Quisenberry was only seventeen when he married Jane Burris, and together they emigrated to Kentucky, where they had thirteen children. When Jane became ill, a neighbor, Chloe Shipp, came to care for her and the children. After a long illness, Jane died. Fifty-one days later, James married twenty-six-year-old Chloe.

This marriage created much scandal in the little Kentucky community. At the time, James was the pastor of Stoner's Church. Some members of the church were so upset that they established a new congregation with a new pastor. To further complicate matters, the father-in-law of James's newly married daughter led this disaffected group.

But James and Chloe weathered the storm. Together they shared nineteen years and had eleven more children, giving James a total of twenty-four. Eventually softening toward James, his neighbors called him the leading contender for the title "father of my county." In the flyleaf of his Bible, he recorded the names, birthdates, and marriage dates of each of the twenty-four children; sixteen books listed under the heading "My Books"; and the names and birth dates of his thirty-one slaves.

To be honest, I was aghast to find so many slave owners among my ancestors. Dozens of wills attest to that fact. But I am grateful that slaves' names were recorded, allowing me to do the temple work for these Americans also.

When my dreams finally calmed down at night, I knew it was time to move on. I was sad to leave Kentucky, a place I had learned to love. Missouri was totally different. Vickie and I went into a courthouse in Bowling Green that was a total contrast to Mrs. Fitz's loving establishment in Florence. We had to beg before workers would take us up to the third floor where the oldest records are kept. Covered with layers of dirt and grime, two- and three-hundred-year-old records lay strewn over the floor, many in metal containers rifled long ago. The records that I needed were no longer there. It was a sad mess. I can only hope that in time someone in this area will catch the vision and do the work.

Most of the gravesites in Missouri were in extremely poor condition. One was in a pig pen and no longer accessible. My great-grandparents were buried in the little town of Farber, which has a large, new cemetery outside town. There we found memorial stones to these ancestors, though they had been buried in town. Thanks to descriptions in a book I'd found before leaving Salt Lake, we located the actual burial site, but it is now part someone's yard and part grassy field. We had no success trying to find someone in Farber who might know something about the original grave sites. I had always wondered why my family ended up in Canada, and in this place the Spirit whispered to me that in Missouri we would not have found the gospel. By now I also realized why I'd found the Biggs book in Salt Lake City before I left—Cousin Kathryn had recorded Missouri information and sites that would no longer be recognizable, and I needed to know that so that I could spend the time in Kentucky.

Elder Boyd K. Packer taught: "No one takes hold of this work without being susceptible to the blessings of the Lord. If you have problems with your own immediately living family, do all you can for them. Begin working in behalf of the Lord's family and good things will start to happen. . . .

". . . Members of the Church cannot touch this work without becoming affected spiritually. The spirit of Elijah permeates it. Many of the little intrusions into our lives, the little difficulties and the petty problems that beset us, are put into proper perspective when we view the linking of the generations for the eternities. We become much more patient then. So if you want the influence of dignity and wisdom and inspiration and spirituality to envelop your life, involve yourself in temple and genealogical work."[7]

During my trip I found extensive information on twelve lines. And the stories—oh, the stories were incredible. I know these people, I love them, I am excited to call them my friends, my family. I can hardly wait to meet them.

It is possible for all of us to have experiences with our ancestors like those I have had with mine. Our ancestors are reaching out to us; they depend on us to tell their stories and have their temple work done. They need us, and we need them.

NOTES

1. John Howie of Lochgoin, comp., *The Scots Worthies*, revised and corrected by James Howie, A.M. (Glasgow, Edinburgh, and London: Blackie and Son, 1851), 568, 570. See also J. H. Thomson, *The Martyr Graves of Scotland*, ed. Matthew Hutchinson (Edinburgh and London: Oliphant, Anderson & Ferrier, [n.d.], 121.

2. Joseph Smith, *History of The Church of Jesus Christ of Latter-day Saints*, ed. B. H. Roberts, 2d ed. rev., 7 vols. (Salt Lake City: The Church of Jesus Christ of Latter-day Saints, 1932–51), 6:184.

3. Boyd K. Packer, *The Holy Temple* (Salt Lake City: Bookcraft, 1980), 210.

4. Anderson Chenault Quisenberry, *Genealogical Memoranda of the Quisenberry Family and Other Families* (Washington, D.C.: Hartman & Chadick, Printers, 1897), 57.

5. Running the gauntlet was a form of Indian punishment or judgment. A gauntlet was a double file of warriors armed with clubs or other not immediately lethal weapons with which to strike at the runner as he ran by.

6. Kathryn Owen, "Who Was Who in Early Clark County," *Clark County (Ky.) Weekly*, 25 January 1980, 1.

7. Packer, *Holy Temple*, 179, 224–25.

Because I'm a Mother and I Love

CAROL R. GRAY

In the Church in the British Isles, members wear many hats because our numbers are few. While I was still a child in Primary, I was called as a Primary teacher. At age fourteen, I was called into the stake Young Women presidency. And before I was old enough to attend Relief Society, at age sixteen and a half, I was a regular Relief Society teacher. Those experiences helped to seal in my heart a testimony of my Savior.

My wonderful parents taught me as a child that the greatest thing we will ever do with our lives is serve our Heavenly Father. This service—whether in our churches, our homes, or farther afield—entitles us to our Father's companionship. I have learned that service is the secret avenue back to him.

At age twenty-nine, with four young daughters (the youngest six months) and my husband serving as bishop, I became very ill. I began to lose weight rapidly, and when I looked at myself in the mirror, I realized that my teeth were protruding. The doctors informed us that I was dying from cancer and had approximately twelve weeks to live. Nothing they could do would save me.

Those weeks were very traumatic for us as a family but also transforming. When you face death squarely in the face, your priorities fall into place. I realized that there were many things in my life that were not necessary. With my children, I never felt cross anymore. When I looked at my husband, I felt full of tenderness and deep gratitude. I loved them all so much. There did not seem any point in allowing

Carol Rosemary Gray, Fellow of the Royal Society of Arts, is chair and founder of Starlight UK Charities in the United Kingdom and in the United States. She is an advisor to the United Nations and to the British Ministry of Defense. She and her husband, Stuart David Gray, are the parents of seven children and the grandparents of seven.

anything negative to disrupt our lives. I learned to fill every second of my life with what mattered most. Our home truly became a tiny bit of heaven.

Obviously, the doctors were wrong about my life's timetable: I'm still here to tell the tale. A wonderful doctor performed an experimental operation—after all, I was dying anyway so it didn't matter what bits and pieces he took out and which he tied in knots. The operating team removed much of my blood supply system—I no longer have a jugular vein—and also my thyroid and several other parts of me that produced hormones. I'm now a mass of metal and rubber tubing inside. Every time I journey through the airport, I set off alarms and I'm frisked.

That radical operation saved my life. I'm a medical miracle, and quite regularly they haul me into a conference room like a specimen in a glass jar to prove that this operation can work—if the patient is very, very fortunate. They do not know that my Heavenly Father had much for me to do in my life. We talk about finding the teaching moments with our children. This period was my perfect moment for being taught by my Heavenly Father. I drew very, very close to him and learned to recognize the promptings of the Spirit.

After five years and three more children, the medical community realized that I wasn't going to kick the bucket, so they asked if I would serve as a bereavement counselor at a local hospice. Terminally ill patients can go to hospices to die with dignity and peace and, hopefully, without pain. I helped families prepare for the death of a loved one. I had many wonderful experiences with these families and often learned more from them than they learned from me.

One older couple in particular taught me a great lesson. The older gentleman, who reminded me of our prophet at that time, Spencer W. Kimball, was preparing to lose his wife of many years. I spent many hours at their home with them, talking, listening to them while they sang, watching this gentleman hold his wife's hand and tell her that he loved her. I listened while he told me how beautiful she was when they were younger and what they used to do when courting. One day, I received the phone call that I'd been dreading. "Carol, Carol, please would you come to the hospital? She's dying, and I don't want to be alone. Please, please will you come and be with us?"

I threw on my clothes and deposited my children with my next-door neighbor. (I had a very, very tolerant next-door neighbor.) Then I pulled my car out of the garage and into our lovely long driveway. At that time, we lived in an old Victorian house surrounded by an incredible garden. Whoever had owned this home before we did had loved gardening and had planted old English quince, roses of all varieties, including rambling roses, and fragrant, trailing honeysuckle. It was a typical English cottage garden, and I knew and loved every plant in it. Flowers lined the driveway, and I felt impressed to stop and pick a rose to take to the hospital. *Don't be silly*, I thought. *The woman is dying. She's not going to want a rose.* So I put my foot down on the accelerator, but again the feeling came, a little stronger: stop the car, pick a single rose, and take it to the hospital. But the urgency of the situation overrode the still, small voice. Out on the street, I pressed firmly on the accelerator and charged up the road in my car. Halfway up the road from home, I was in absolutely no doubt that the Spirit was prompting me—in fact, chastising me: "You turn this car around. You go back, and you pick a single, yellow rose."

I knew my garden very well. I had every color rose imaginable, except yellow. But my lovely neighbor had yellow roses, and I knew she would understand if I nipped over the wall, pinched one, and told her later. I turned back and raced up my drive. I jumped out of my car, and there before me, on one of my own beautiful, long-stemmed, pink rose bushes, was the most exquisite yellow rose I have ever seen, fringed with the most beautiful shade of pink all around the edges. I looked at the rose in total disbelief. Then I dived into my kitchen to get scissors, fully expecting that when I got back the yellow rose would have disappeared—a figment of my imagination. But no, it was still there. I cut that rose, added maidenhair fern and gypsophillia, wrapped it in cellophane, and put a bow on it. It looked quite beautiful. Then finally I drove to the hospital.

When I arrived in the hospital ward, the curtains were drawn. I peeked through and saw the old woman, obviously very sick and ready to die. The old man, clutching a very frail hand, had fallen asleep, his head lolling on the bed. It was such a tender scene that I didn't want to disturb it, so I placed the rose very gently by her hand and tiptoed out of the room. I headed for the Sister's office to tell her that I had arrived, but before I got there, I heard shuffling feet down the hall behind me. I turned to see the old man, tears streaming down his face, "Carol, how did you know? How did you know that today was our seventieth wedding anniversary? And always on our anniversary I have given my wife a single, yellow rose—how did you know?" I didn't know. I had no idea, but somebody up there did. I testify that our Heavenly Father loves you, that he knows you by name, that he knows you intimately. He knows of all your pains and sorrows and all your joys. He loves you without doubt.

Five years ago, the war in Bosnia was raging. Living in England, details of the conflict bombarded us via television all the time. The pictures were quite horrific. I imagined myself, as a mother, in those places, and I ached for their devastation, loss, and hurt. At this time, we were looking for a service project for our Relief Society sisters. As the ward Relief Society president, I wanted my sisters involved in a project that would bless the lives of many. We decided on an appeal for aid to send to the people of Bosnia. Within three weeks of starting, it grew from a ward appeal, to a stake, to a city, and then to an area appeal. Thirty-eight tons of aid were collected. Imagine your stake's cultural hall covered from floor to ceiling with donations—that's about thirty-eight tons. It had to be packed and boxed and parceled.

When our Relief Society started this appeal, I went through the priesthood line for approval from the bishop and then the stake president and eventually the area presidency. The brethren warned me each time, "Be very careful, Sister Gray. Do you know what you are taking on?" "No problems, brother," I would reply. "I will be fine." I asked for permission to store goods in the meetinghouse. The bishop said yes, thinking it would just be a corner cupboard job, which is quite honestly what I thought it would be. To deliver our donations, I had arranged with an established London charity that went regularly into Bosnia and Croatia. I had no intentions of accompanying our shipment even partway or going near a war zone myself. I have seven children and a wonderful husband. I am not a kamikaze housewife. I planned to collect the donations and let the sisters lose themselves in the service of others, which they did admirably.

Two days before we were to transport all of our aid to the London charity, they rang me and said, "Carol, we are really sorry, but we have run out of money. We can't take your aid." Everything we had gathered was stored in our ward meetinghouse. My bishop was sitting on diapers and milk formula. The family history center was closed because it was full of donations. The previous Sunday, when I had dutifully arrived early to put out flowers and organize the Relief Society room, I discovered that a wonderful GPO man, which is our equivalent of your Federal

Express, had very kindly dumped ten tons of aid in front of the chapel doors in the early morning hours. That Sunday I was the flavor of the month with the children and youth, who are always glad to skip classes. My bishop was less happy with me, though we did manage to move all the donations just in time to have sacrament meeting. I assured the bishop the meetinghouse would be clear by the next Sunday.

But now I had no means of transport. I was in an almighty mess. Because I didn't want to lose face with the brethren in my stake, I decided I had to deliver the donations to Bosnia myself. Drastic measures had to be taken. I sold my beautiful sports car and bought a twenty-eight-foot truck, not exactly a convenient size to take to town shopping afterwards. Many wonderful families joined with me, and we took 110 vehicles in all to transport our aid into Bosnia, a five-thousand-mile round-trip journey through Europe and the Balkans.

To go into these war zones was a big decision for me. My recently married daughter came along because she knows that I'm hopeless at directions. Turn me around in my back garden and I'm lost. I drove along with my parting promise to my husband ringing in my ears: this will be a one-time thing, an adventure of a lifetime. I will do my bit, and I will never, ever do it again. We went through minefields, under shellfire and sniper fire, and my stomach dragged along the floor as we went. I would never in a million years have thought Carol Gray, a sister who had never even gone to the temple without her husband, could do this thing.

On that first trip, I saw a group of children at the side of the road, and as we were passing, I grabbed a handful of sweets, threw them out of the window, and shouted "good day" to them in their language. I was horrified to see them fighting each other for the candy. I realized then that here was a group of children who had not had any proper food for a long time and who had never seen sweets. During that first convoy, I looked at those people, the devastation, and the nightmare that they were going through, and I knew that I had to return. I was overcome with the desire to help people. I knew that my Heavenly Father had gotten me into something that I wasn't, after all, going to be able to turn away from easily.

Now, I have a husband in a million; he gives me lots of space to be who I am. But how was I going to explain to him when I got home that I needed to go again? When I arrived home from that first trip, I ran down the steps and threw myself into his arms. I didn't say a word, and he said, "I know. Don't tell me. You have to go back." That was thirty-one convoys ago. It's amazing how the Lord gets you to do things bit by bit.

In those early days, we took in hundreds of thousands of food parcels to all the families around the front line areas. I chose to go to front lines because the families there were in desperate need, and yet no charities were going to them. I was naive; they were front-line areas because they were surrounded by minefields and were constantly being shelled. No wonder no one would go there. Nevertheless, we went in, prepared by our fasting, prayers, and blessings, and we were safe. These areas aren't as dangerous any more. The shelling has stopped—but the need is still desperate.

When the war was at its very worst, our food and medical supplies kept those people alive. We equipped the hospitals on the frontline with antibiotics, burn packages, and open-wound dressings. We kept those hospitals going, and it was a privilege. Now I'm involved with the rebuilding and re-equipping of schools, old people's homes, and medical centers, and supplying other desperately needed services.

I know that Heavenly Father opened doors that I couldn't have opened and that he stood by our side many times when we were in dangerous situations. Once I hadn't rung my husband for five days. That was dreadful of me, but I couldn't get to a phone because I was in a ravaged front-line area. Finally I was allowed to use a field phone that belonged to a doctor—he was busy working on someone who had had a leg blown off. Crouching beside him in the field, I rang my husband, "Hello, love, it's me. I'm fine." Suddenly there was the whine and loud thud of an incoming shell, followed by a large cloud of dust and rubble and searing heat and flames. We were cut off. No doubt my poor husband wondered if I had been blown up. I managed to get to another phone twenty-five kilometers down the road to call him back with reassurances.

I remember one trip to an orphanage in central Bosnia. Even though it was the middle of spring, we took Father Christmas to the children and we had lots of lovely presents and Swiss chocolate that we'd picked up from the Saints in Germany. The children, who hadn't had gifts for years, were sailing over the moon with delight—except for one little boy standing in the corner, cowering. Now, I'm an instant mom, so I went over and tried to get him to interact with me, to taste some chocolate, to accept a gift, but he wouldn't. In desperation and sadness, I turned to one of the helpers. She explained, "He came in nine months ago, clutching the severed hand of his mother." His home had taken a direct hit, and his mother, hearing the roof crashing down overhead, had pushed him under the large, solid, central table. There he was found with his family, no longer alive, buried in the rubble all around him. From that moment, this little boy had not spoken a word. Well, you can imagine, I struggled with the waterworks a bit.

At that moment, alarm bells shrilled out, announcing another shelling raid. Our convoy members were rushed out of the room. As I was leaving, I saw this little boy's eyes startle and his mouth part slightly, so I shoved in a piece of chocolate so that he would know that it was nice and not something horrible. I then dropped the chocolate bar at his feet and headed for the door. Before I got there, I felt a tug on my skirt. The little boy looked up at me and just said, "Momma." Those were very beautiful words to me. I came home from that trip with great designs to adopt him, but I never saw him again. I received a fax six weeks later to tell me that he had been killed in a shelling raid. He's happy now; he's with his family. And maybe, if I'm worthy, I'll meet him again, for my love for him burns as brightly now as it did then.

There is nothing that prepares you for the deep, haunted eyes of the people over there. They've lost everything, and I mean everything. I feel very lucky to have reared my children in the safety and comfort of England. We have food on our table every day. Our home is lovely and warm. The children have grounds to play on. I've a car to do my shopping in. And even more important, I have the gospel at my fingertips.

Who is the Lord going to use to help those who can't help themselves? Can he use those who can't even lift themselves up? Who does he need? He needs you and me, people who can go out and do. Service is wonderful, no matter where we serve. Not everybody is as balmy as I am and goes into a war zone. I've got a nickname with the personnel at all the borders. I'm "that mad Englishwoman." Five years ago, if you had told me that I'd be doing what I'm doing, I would have thought *you* had gone quite mad. I'm not special. I'm just a very ordinary English sister that happened to get involved. I'm hanging on to this work by its coattails, just hanging in there.

My work has led to many honors and job offers. I'm an advisor to the United Nations, the Ministry of Defense, and the peacekeeping corps in

Bosnia. But I haven't received these positions because I'm clever, or gutsy, or have any special talents. I haven't. I was a terrible student when I was young. I was one of those teachers' lunchroom horror stories. I sat at the back of the classroom and chattered all through lessons. But I have one thing in my favor: I'm a good mom. I can put my arms around people and tell them in their own language, "I'm here because I care and because I love you."

The stories are always the same. The picture is always the same. Can I turn away from families who have lost everything, from women just out of the rape camps where horrendous things have happened? They don't know what to do with themselves. They fall onto your shoulder and cry and sob and tell you their own individual tragedy. I don't understand their language, other than one or two phrases (usually an interpreter is with me), but this is what happens: I am able to give them love, and that is what they need and want most of all. They can be starving, without food for three days, but the fact that someone has come there and told them that they are loved means everything. Because I'm a mother and I love, I have been able to go into places where no one else goes.

It takes very little to make a difference in this world. You don't have to be a medical doctor, the president of the United States, or the British prime minister. The Lord needs women today to become involved. Women work from the heart, and we know how to make things happen. We touch people when they need to be touched. We lift them up when they need to be lifted up. We *must* believe in ourselves. We must serve from our hearts. Believe you are a daughter of God; believe you can make a difference. You surely will. The Lord loves me, and I am grateful for that beautiful fact. He loves you, too! Let his love fill your lives with spiritual teaching moments, that his companionship will be forever yours.

"Unto the Least of These My Brethren"

STACEY BESS

About eleven years ago, I began a career that changed my life forever. At age twenty-three, I had just earned a degree in elementary education—mostly to humor my mother and my husband. I had absolutely no intention of teaching school. I had been a stay-at-home mom since I was seventeen years old, and I liked it that way. But my mother kept urging me, "Honey, you are so young, and young marriages often don't work out. Just get a degree you can fall back on if you need to." So I enrolled at the University of Utah. Two days after I graduated, in the middle of winter, my husband said, "Honey, just go to the Salt Lake City School District and turn in your resume. It's the middle of the school year. They're not going to hire you." My mom, who was visiting, nodded, "No, they won't hire you." My response was, "Mom, I really want to rock my children like you did yours." My mom had brought a rocking chair over from England and had rocked all seven of her children in that chair. Even as adults, we still go home, climb into that chair, and feel loved by her.

That was the legacy I wanted to pass on to my children. But mostly to get Mom and Greg off my case, I went to the Salt Lake City School District. In my mind I could hear Mom saying, "They won't hire you. Don't worry. It's the middle of the school year." I walked into the building and handed my resume to the secretary. She looked up at me,

Stacey Bess taught at the school for homeless children in Salt Lake City for eleven years. Author of the book Nobody Don't Love Nobody, *she speaks throughout the country on service, children, and making a difference in the community. She and her husband, Greg, have four children, who range in age from eighteen to two. She serves as advisor to the Mia Maids in her ward.*

checked the paperwork, smiled, and said, "Honey, you are young." I said, "Yeah."

She looked down at my paperwork again. "You graduated two days ago?" Again I answered, "Yeah." She chuckled. "Well, it is the middle of the school year, and we're just about ready for Christmas break. We don't have any job opportunities, but it looks like you did your student teaching in a neat place, you have pretty good grades, and we'll consider you in the summer." I shook her hand and thought with relief, "Yes! I'm going home." As I headed toward the glass double doors in the district offices, a reflection caught my eye. Right behind me a very large gentleman was walking out of his office. "Miss Bess," he called, "come here." I turned and saw the sign above his door: Personnel Director, Assistant Superintendent. I followed him into his office and sat down. He stared intently at my paperwork. "You're young," he noted.

"Yes."

"Did you really graduate two days ago?"

"Yes."

"Would you like to be a teacher?"

I lied. "Yes."

He sat for a long time and then told me about a job opening at a school with no name, but I really wasn't listening because I wanted to stay home with my children. Finally he said, "Miss Bess, it is the middle of the school year. We don't have an opening, but I will put your paperwork right on top. And in the summer, we will call you back."

Elated, I shook his hand and grabbed the door handle. Then this gentleman changed my life forever. He said, "Miss Bess, sit down."

I turned. "Sir, did I do something wrong?"

He said, "No, but I'm about to."

I sat down again, slowly. "What?" I asked.

"Miss Bess, I am not supposed to do this, but I am going to offer you a job."

I was terrified. I looked down and noticed that my hands were shaking, so I sat on them so he wouldn't see. "Oh, Stacey," I said to myself, "don't cry in your first real job interview."

I swallowed over and over. "Sir, where do you want me to go?"

"Miss Bess, I'd like you to teach at the school for the homeless."

I lost the battle with my tears. The only thing I could get out of my mouth was, "Dr. Anderson,[1] I'm trained to be an elementary school

152

teacher. I'm not trained to teach grown-ups." He laughed. "Miss Bess, two, three, sometimes four hundred homeless children pass through this one school in a year."

I said, "Really?"

And I lied again: I promised him I'd think about the job. I shook his hand, and then I walked down the long hall to the parking lot. There I climbed into my car, held onto the steering wheel, and sobbed. All the way home, I'm embarrassed to say, I closed my eyes at stop signs and red lights and said to my Heavenly Father, "How dare you! How dare you send me there. I have no proven skills. I've never taught anywhere. How dare you do this to me!" Then I remembered my husband and my mother were in on it. I pulled into the driveway and saw my very sweet husband watching for me from the living room window. I was mad. I swung open the screen door just as he opened the front door. He looked at my face, smeared with tears and mascara, and said, "Oh, honey, you got a job, didn't you?"

"Yes, I did," and I sat him down on the couch and told him what I knew and how I felt about the homeless. He agreed, "No, I can't send you there, Stacey. We both know what it's like as you get off the Sixth South viaduct." Prostitutes and drug dealers. Mothers pushing carts. It's awful. "No, honey, you don't have to go there," he said.

I climbed into bed that night reassured that no one would ask me to take that job. About 2:30 in the morning, I woke up, tossing and turning, and couldn't go back to sleep for almost an hour. At 4:00 A.M. I woke up again, my heart pounding. After about four days of these night terrors, I got the message. My subconscious was saying, "Pay attention!" So I got up and knelt by the living room couch. I let go of my rebellious anger. This time, instead of telling my Heavenly Father what I would or wouldn't do, I listened for a very long time. I remember saying, "Heavenly Father, why me? I'm just a kid. I don't have any skills."

After the longest time, the answer came back, "You have been prepared for a lifetime. It is not your skills I am after. It is who you are inside."

I told Greg the following morning that I was going to take the job. Then I called Dr. Anderson and accepted.

He said, "I knew you would. Be there on January 3. The school is under the Sixth South viaduct. It doesn't have an address. You'll know it when you see it."

On my first day, I drove down the wrong side of the road under the viaduct. When I got to the end, I couldn't see any evidence of a school. What I did see were twelve boxcars in a row and railroad tracks everywhere. I was lost. I started to turn back when I noticed a line of cars parked bumper to bumper under the bridge. Puzzled because there were no businesses around, I watched for a minute. Car engines turned on and then tiny fingers rubbed fog from the windows. I was stunned. Families were sleeping in those cars—in Salt Lake City, Utah. Suddenly a small boy jumped out of one of the boxcars. I started to roll the window down. As he ran in front of my parked car, our eyes met, and he looked at me with the most horrid, hate-filled eyes. I froze. As I was trying to absorb that experience, out of nowhere a man tapped on my passenger window. He had two teeth, and a big hunk of scrambled egg hung from the side of his long beard. I screamed. Realizing that he had terrified me, he ran around to my side where the window was partly down and said, "Ma'am, are you lost?"

"I think so."

His beautiful blue eyes—the most beautiful I've ever seen—came to life, and he said, "Ma'am, are you the new schoolteacher?"

I couldn't lie. "Yes," I said.

He pulled open my car door and said, "Come on. People here are dying to meet you. Let me help you."

I handed him my briefcase, my open purse with a few dollar bills kind of hanging out, and my wire basket. Like a perfect gentleman, he helped me out of my car and wrapped his arm around me. "Ma'am, could I teach you how to live on the streets?"

I said, "Sure."

He said, "First of all, ma'am, don't ever give all your belongings to a total stranger." He looked me up and down. "You are a might bit proper. I have no idea why you're here." Then he pointed to my car and said, "Never leave your windows rolled down or your car doors unlocked."

I said, "Okay."

This lovely gentleman's name was Joe. Pointing to a battered aluminum shed, he said, "Always go directly to your school. Do your teaching and go home." But then Joe walked me in the opposite direction from the shed. After about forty feet, I started to get nervous. "Joe, where are we going?"

"Shhh. Follow me," he answered.

I did what he said. That naïve twenty-three-year-old followed a homeless man. I will be honest. I was so frightened I could hardly walk. We got to the far side of the viaduct where fifteen adults huddled around a fire. Gretchen, Jim's wife, was the cook. She opened their circle, welcomed me in, and lovingly wrapped her arm around me. "Honey," she said, "you're shaking. Are you cold?"

I lied, "Yes." I was terrified, not cold.

She said, "Honey, what is your name?" I told her. Then she introduced me to each of the mothers and fathers in the circle. Each told a bit about their child. Mostly it was something naughty, but each one, in their own way, said to me, "Please, love my child." Not one of them asked if I was a good reading teacher or if I knew a lot about math.

As I readied myself to go greet my new classroom, Gretchen held me against her and said, "Honey, I've just got one question. Where did you use to teach before?"

All eyes were on me. I looked down at the fire because I was so embarrassed. "Nowhere, Gretchen. I've never taught anywhere before."

She said, "Honey, you ain't going nowhere but up. You've started at the bottom."

I was sure that the Lord had sent me there, but it took all of the courage I had that first day to walk into my classroom and see the filth and sadness and loss and the toddlers picking stuff off the floor and eating it. Thirty-five children crowded in a corner around one boy who was entertaining them. "Ladies and gentleman," I cleared my throat, "my name is Stacey, and I'm your new teacher. Take your seats." They didn't move. The boy in the corner kept talking, and they kept laughing and listening intently to him. After I had called them to order three times, that very powerful young man finally said, "She's ready. Take your seats."

I was dying to see who was in the center of that attentive circle. As everyone took their seats, I discovered a beautiful, eleven-year-old young man named Zachary, the same boy who had earlier given me that withering glare in front of my car. He sat in the back of the class. I introduced myself with a scrapbook I had assembled for that purpose. I turned the pages, showing them pictures of my family and things that I loved. Then I got to my all-time three favorites, the three C's. "The first C is chocolate cake." I smiled at them. "Not in order, of course. My second C is children." No one smiled. "The third C," I told them, "is Diet Coke and, yeah, that might have been first." Still no one smiled. Suddenly a mouse scurried out from under the cupboard, ran across the floor, and raced across my feet. I screamed, climbed up on a little stool, and leaned against the chalkboard. I think I even swore. I'm not terribly proud of that, but, after all, a mouse *did* run across my feet. No one moved except Zachary. In the back of the room, with a ruler, he tap-tap-tapped on his desk.

The next day was no different. Day after day I faced this painful world and every night I went home crying. I complained to my family, "No one should have to endure these people. No one should have to see the sadness and the loss and the emptiness."

"Just get through the month, honey," Greg comforted me. "Then you can quit."

Hardest of all, at the end of every day Zachary would catch me by the door and shove me against the wall. "Go home, Proper. You don't belong here."

I watched and cried and cried and watched, and one day I had had enough. I called Zachary into my classroom after school. "Zachary, I need to talk."

He sat in my chair, put his feet up on my desk, turned his baseball cap sideways, and said, "Whadda ya want?"

I said, "Zachary, I'm having a hard time here. Help me. Just answer one question. Why do you hate me so much?"

He said, "Miss Stacey, please don't take it personal. I'm sure you're a fine teacher, but I hate all women."

I said, "That isn't fair, Zachary. I came that way."

"Miss Stacey, look over at the wall and imagine something. You're three or four years old, and your momma lines up all her kids. If she points to you, you look enough like her, and she keeps you. If you don't, she doesn't. I didn't. I love my daddy, Stacey, but he goes to different cities every year. You know, sometimes I've been in different schools seven times in one year. I have loved a lot of people, but then I always have to leave. I've decided never to trust anyone again." He took my hand. "I bet you're a good teacher, but I will not trust you." Then he left.

When I went home that night, I told my family about Zach. Nichole said, "Mom, don't worry about teaching him any math or reading or spelling. Just teach him about love and trust. Show him that people follow through when they say they will." What Nichole didn't know was that I didn't want to teach about trust. I didn't want to follow through. I wanted to get through the month and quit. But her words haunted me all that night, and the following morning I told him, "Zachary, I will stay. I want you to know that I want to leave, but I will stay and be the one person in your life who will prove to you that there are people who do love, who do stay. I will stay for you and for all the other Zacharys who pass through my school this year."

He laughed. "Sure you will."

For three months Zachary and I built a very sweet relationship. In fact, I was starting to fall in love with these people who filled my days. Then I received frightening news from my doctor. I had cancer in my neck, and it had to be removed right away.

I said, "Oh, Dr. Swenson, not now when I'm just falling in love with these people. I'm just catching on."

He said, "You'll go back. I don't know how far the cancer has traveled, but tell them that you will be back."

I sat on the floor in my classroom one morning with twenty-five students sitting against me, feeling my neck and rubbing their hands on my cheeks. But not Zachary. He sat in the back drumming rhythmically with his ruler. When everybody left, I grabbed his arm and pulled him towards me. "Don't touch me," he said bitterly. "You lied. I was trusting you and loving you and now you're leaving." I could have talked with this kid forever and it would not have helped.

When Greg and I went into the hospital, Dr. Swenson had said to Greg, "Please do not bring your young children. We'll be moving her from the surgery center into the recovery area, then into another recovery area, and finally to the cancer floor."

I was coming to after the surgery and had a trachea tube down my throat. My mother had told the staff that I was a fighter, so my arms were restrained. My leaden eyelids were still closed, but I could feel a drip-drip on my chest. The anesthesia kept me from thinking clearly, but my brain was shouting, *I'm bleeding, and no one's doing anything.* Then I heard giggling and talking, and I got angry. *You're all having a party, and I'm bleeding!* I thought. I listened more carefully and could hear my husband at the head of my bed and my mother near my wrists. I also heard an unfamiliar voice, a child's voice, that haunted me terribly, but I couldn't make out the words. I began shaking, and my mother held my hands very tightly. "Stacey, open your eyes and look straight up."

With effort I blinked and saw my dear friend Zach, who had bribed an orderly with five bucks and had broken onto the recovery area floor. There he stood over me, big tears splashing down onto my bandages. "Zachary," the doctor cautioned, "if you don't quit crying over her, we'll have to change the bandage."

The nurse pulled the tube out of my throat (I do not remember any of this) and I said, "Zachary, what are you doing out of school?"

"Teacher," he answered, "you told me you loved me, and I believed you. I came here today to make sure they keep you with us."

Zachary's arms were filled with wrapped and tagged presents. "Zachary, where did you get the gifts?"

"I just got them. That's all you need to worry about."

I fear that we have hosted many stolen gifts in our home. Zachary, now nineteen, is a remarkable, fascinating human being. He and I still talk on the phone quite often. Of course, he always calls collect. We have not cured him of that. He lives on the island of Kauai, in Hawaii, where he owns his own business. He has lived with us on and off for a few weeks at a time. One night just before I flew to Tennessee to address the National Association of Professor Educators (professors who train teachers), we talked. Nothing excites me more than teaching professors what teachers need to know to teach children better.

"Zach," I said, "I will tell them what you would like me to tell them. Why have you stayed so connected to me? What was it about my school that caused you never to forget us?"

"I don't know."

"Was I good teacher?"

"I don't know."

"Well, was I a good math teacher?"

"Did you teach math?"

I finally gave up on that concept. At the end of the phone call, as I do with each of my students or family members that call home, I said, "Zachary, I love you."

For about thirty long seconds, he didn't say anything. Then he answered, "That's what I want you to tell the people. You loved me. And when I was faced with life's choices of whether to be a success or not, I kept hearing your voice, 'I love you.'"

That night I kept waking up. My husband patted me and said, "That was a good thing, honey. Go to sleep. That was a good thing."

Zachary is still a very successful young man by my standards. I don't know whether he will experience homelessness again, but he has never forgotten the principle that I hold so dearly, that Christ holds so dearly: "Love one another."

My second school friend debunked every concept I ever had about homeless children. Children who have experienced loss build walls around themselves. To reach them you must creatively and tenderly chip away at their defenses, sometimes for weeks, sometimes for months. Not Alex.

I first met Alex at the bottom of the stairs as I went through the alarmed doors to meet my class. I very cautiously put out my right hand to hold his and said, "Hello, Alex. My name is Stacey. I will be your new teacher."

He yanked my hand, pulled me towards him, and said, "Wow, you're beautiful!"

His sweet brother, Anthony, standing behind him, was bashful and very embarrassed. I said to him, "It's okay."

We climbed to the first landing on the stairs. Again Alex took my hand, swung me around, and said, "I gotta tell you something else. You've got the greatest brown eyes I've ever seen."

Anthony was ready to have a nervous breakdown at that point. "It's okay. He's all right," I reassured him.

At the top of the stairs, Alex grabbed me by the hand one more time. "I'll go to class after I tell you one more thing."

"All right, one more thing."

"I have been kicked out of every school I have ever been in."

"You haven't!"

Anthony nodded his head. Alex continued, "Miss Stacey, I have a problem."

I wanted to say, "Oh, really?" But I responded evenly, "You do?"

"Yes. I have a problem with these don't-be-a-kid rules. Things like 'Shut up' and 'Sit down' and 'Don't bug your neighbor.'"

"Yeah?"

"Do you have those in your school?"

"Well, if I'm talking, I would like you to listen."

"Listen to me for a minute," he said. "Do you like to talk?"

"Yes, that's why I'm a teacher."

"So do kids. And if you listened more, you would learn more. Miss Stacey, do you like to sit still?"

159

"No, Alex. When I'm talking before an audience, I walk back and forth like a wild animal. I can't sit still."

"Neither can we."

I am so grateful that my homeless students don't sit at chairs or in assigned seats. I can let them move around wherever they want as long as they are learning.

Then he asked the most important question. "Miss Stacey, is there anybody in your life that you just love to bug?"

"Yeah, I'm married to him." Something told me that Alex would appreciate my latest prank. "Alex, I'm going to tell you what my two older children and I did the other night. We got a big, two-gallon pitcher of water and put it in the fridge. The next morning, when we could hear Dad singing in the shower, we tip-toed into the bathroom and poured ice-cold water all over him."

"Could I just ask you one question? Was he naked? Did he chase you?"

"Well, Alex," I said, wondering where this might lead, "he did. Wouldn't you run, if you had ice-cold water poured all over you?"

"I like you," he said.

We went into class and sat down on the floor. We were very late, and my teaching partner was just beginning "Jam Session." Jam Session is the students' time to say whatever they want, and I mean *whatever*. Alex's eyes got bigger and bigger as he listened. When we finished, he pulled me up off the floor, "Don't call this Jam Session anymore. I want you to call this Kid Power."

"Why?"

He said, "Grownups think *power* for kids is a dirty word. But if we had power, and you taught us how to use it, we wouldn't be trying to take it all the time."

He was right. I had just sat through a psychiatrist's session on teaching kids to use their power. I said, "Okay, we'll call it Kid Power now."

He went on, "My brother Joe tells me that I don't need an alarm clock. He'll be the alarm clock. To wake me up in the morning, he slugs me on the side of the head. At home I have no power. I will come to your class with no power, but I will expect it when I'm there."

I realized I was dealing with a very strong little spirit who had much to teach but who was also very damaged. Every day while I taught at the fifth-grade table, he would go over to the snack cupboard, look at me, almost daring me to watch, and take some food, which he put inside his clothing—in the cuffs of his socks, in pants pockets, up shirt sleeves. After two weeks of watching, I said, "Alex, we've got a little problem."

"Yes, we do. You've let me steal from you."

I knew why he was stealing. In our classroom we call it "creative taking" because we know why the children do it. Our job is to teach them to get past their loss so they understand why they take things. I said, "Alex, why do you steal food?"

"Miss Stacey, I don't eat what I take," he answered. "When I put the food against my body, it takes the emptiness away."

I knew that. I made a deal with him: "I will teach you how to get rid of emptiness and loss if you will keep your hands out of my cupboard." The other part of the deal was he could have the grand prize at the end of two weeks if he dealt with loss properly. You see, homeless children go through loss maybe seven times a year; you and I, seven times in a lifetime.

Alex was marvelous. For two weeks, he would come up to me and say, "I am empty," and I would hug him. Or he would come into class and say, "Joe's outside. He hit me this morning. Please go out and talk with him," and I would go out into the hall and very quietly say, "Joe, I'll beat the snot out of you if you touch him again." His brother Joe would smile and say, "I'm sorry. I know you love him," and it would stop for a little while.

At the end of two weeks, Alex said, "All right, I'm ready for the grand prize. I've been talking to my buddies, and I know that I can have just about anything, right?"

"Well, within reason."

"Good. Do you know who Karl Malone is?"

"Yeah, I know who he is."

"Well, I'm moving in two weeks, and I want to meet him."

"Oh, Alex, I only know *who* he is—but I will try."

"If anybody can do it, you can."

That night I called my friend Judy, who works with a volunteer group that had some connections to the Jazz office, and through much prayer and a beautiful letter to Mr. Malone, Alex and I were standing in the school lobby within about forty-eight hours of sending the letter. Alex was on the left, I was on the right. We were holding hands. I was shaking so violently Alex leaned over to me and said, "Knock it off."

"I'm nervous. Look at him."

"Teacher, he is a regular guy."

As I approached Karl Malone, my nose was level with his belt buckle. I offered him my hand. "Mr. Malone, my name is Stacey Bess. Thank you so much for coming to our school. Please come upstairs and give my students the talk that I've heard you give about staying in school."

After a long silence, he taught me an incredible lesson. "I have followed your career, and you should know better," he said. "Please do not hold me to a 'stay in school speech.' Don't let me hide behind my uniform, behind a podium, or behind my stardom. Let me come today and be Uncle Karl. Let me give your students what they truly need. Me."

I followed him into my classroom, leaned against the bookcases, and could not stop crying. He teased me relentlessly. Then I watched twenty-five little bodies climb all over him as he sat down on the floor. They took off his shoes and socks, measured his feet, his toes, and from his wrists to his elbows. And he loved them. He didn't care about the lice. He didn't care about the hepatitis or the tuberculosis. Like Christ would have, he sat on the floor and loved them. Only two times I got a little nervous. Little Curtis was looking at Karl's hand and I thought, "He's panicked about something." He turned it over and back, looking at one side and then the other. "Mr. Malone, one side of your hand is darker than the other." I just about swallowed my tongue.

Mr. Malone looked from me to Curtis. "Honey, when I sunbathe I just forget to flip over."

At one point Alex and Curtis were each on a leg, running their fingers through his beautiful, textured hair. Alex and Curtis have very fine, silky hair. I walked over and said, "Guys, let's give Mr. Malone just a little bit of space, shall we?"

A very large finger pointed in my direction. "You, go stand over by the bookcases and don't move."

I did what he said, which was so unlike me. Then I watched as they got to his mustache, each on one side. As they moved toward his nose I thought, "If they put their fingers in his nose, I will have a heart attack right here."

When Mr. Malone went to leave, he wrapped his arms around them, held them tight, and said, "I love you."

Alex, at age thirteen, has come back to my school. He didn't care about his cute teacher. The very first question he asked was, "Do you think Karl Malone still thinks I'm way bad?"—which is current slang for "way good." "You bet he does," I said. "You bet he still loves you."

People often ask me, "Don't you get sick when you have to walk past all those homeless grownups?" I don't because I have had the luxury of knowing them, of loving them. Every homeless adult who crosses my path has a story. Their stories tell me that their homelessness is due to being deprived of love and to devastating childhood experience. It is not a money issue. Being abused and deprived of love is a primary cause of homelessness.

My dear friend Sarah is the meanest, foulest-mouthed human being I have ever met. We were told when we moved into a new shelter, "Just steer clear of Sarah." One day I heard a loud, bellowing voice at the front desk swearing in the foulest language I had ever heard. It was early, before school was to start, so I came out of my classroom to see what was going on. It was Sarah demanding a coat. It was cold. The woman at the desk said, "No, Sarah, you live at the women's shelter. We help only *families* at the family shelter." Fuming, I walked over to the front desk and grabbed Sarah by the arm. "I have a coat, and I can give it to you."

"Who are you?" she asked

"I am the teacher."

"Is the coat good looking?" she demanded.

"I think so."

She came into my room and slammed the door shut. I was alone with Sarah! I had been warned. But I picked up the white, furry coat and draped it over her shoulders from behind. When she turned, I exclaimed, "Wow, you're beautiful!"

Tears rolled down her cheeks. "Nobody ain't *never* said that to me before. *You* are my friend."

I'm not sure if that was a curse or a blessing, because for the next seven or eight months she was my friend, and oh, was she my friend! I'll never forget two experiences. Once I was running down the sidewalk, late for school. She was running toward me with a vase. Two of my homeless friends came running to save me because we never know what Sarah will do. She plopped the vase down on my very pregnant tummy and said, "These are for you. I stole them."

"You didn't."

"Yes, I was walking past the nurse's station at the University Hospital, and I lifted them off the station, and no one said a word."

I wanted to say, "Honey, no one would dare say a word to you."

I could hear my male friends standing behind me, scoffing, "They're dead. Tell her they're dead."

I elbowed Kenny behind me and shot him a look: *Open your mouth one more time and you die.* Then I turned and kissed and hugged her. "Sarah, thank you."

As I walked into the shelter, Kenny said, "Why didn't you tell her those flowers were dead?"

"Kenny," I said, "Sarah has learned the most important lesson you ever learn in life. *I owe you back.* Sarah never knew that before. I gave her something as simple as a coat, and now she knows that she owes people."

Another day I was again racing in late. Sarah was sitting on the sidewalk, crying. I said, "Sarah, I'm late! But what's the matter? Do you need a hug?"

She said, "I can't bend over and get the medicine on my legs, and I need to put it on."

"I'll do it," I instantly offered. That was rash of me because I was pregnant and very prone to losing my breakfast.

When I lifted up her pant leg, I saw several ghastly, open wounds. I always keep rubber gloves in my bag because of the needles I find everywhere. As I put them on, I closed my eyes and thought, *Heavenly Father, don't let me throw up all over her. Just let me do this.* Through my mind flashed, *This is what the Savior did. He could feel just as sick as I do right now, yet he went to the poor and the suffering, and he served and he loved.* I had two minutes to put on that ointment and get out of there. I finished, hurried around the corner, and threw up all over. Once inside, I did not say a word to my teaching partner until she noticed my swollen eyes. She asked, "What's wrong? Did Sarah beat up on you?"

"No, I just had a neat experience," I said and told her about putting the ointment on Sarah's legs. I didn't tell her that I had prayed. When she looked thoughtfully at me and said, "That's what the Savior did, Stacey," it was another confirmation. I am where God wants me to be.

And what about my own children? There is nothing more painful than being away from them. But I know that the Lord knows that I am doing what is right. He has looked after us. Before I gave birth to my sweet McKenzie, I decided that I was going to quit, but I wasn't going to tell anyone. For eight years I had waited for this baby, and I was determined to rock her. As I left the shelter for the final time before my scheduled delivery day, I was greeted by Sarah and her anger. She grabbed me fiercely. Pressing up against me, she said, "I hate you."

"Why?"

"You are walking away, and you are not even saying good-bye." She was right. I was. I was going off to rock my babies. She said, "Before you leave I want you never to forget what I am going to tell you. Look into my eyes."

I looked into her irate, blood-shot eyes. She continued, "I want you to see the little girl that lives inside of me. The little girl that no one ever took the time to love, that no one ever took the time to reach, and no one ever took the time to teach. You are going to walk away from every little girl and boy that has a chance of turning out just like me. Before you have your baby, go lay your head down on the sidewalk and see if you hear the little girl that cries." As I tearfully walked away that day, she said, "You better think long and hard."

The following morning, I threw on my clothes without showering and grabbed my car keys. My husband sat up in bed, "Where are you going?"

I said, "I don't know, but I'll be back."

I drove all the way to the shelter. "What are you doing here?" my friend Jane said when I walked in. "You have a baby coming at 10:30."

I answered, "I don't know why. I couldn't sleep all night. I just needed to stand here for a few minutes."

"Well, as long as you're here, come back to the medical clinic. You can solve a problem."

I walked back to find dear Sarah. "Go ahead, Jane," Sarah demanded. "Tell her our plan." Jane is the one who picks lice out of my hair and gives me shots in the rear once a month so that I don't get hepatitis. She was the last person I would expect to say, "Stacey, we would like for you to strap your newborn baby to your chest and teach school."

I laughed. That was a ridiculous idea. But I smiled at Sarah. "I'll think about it," I promised.

On the way to the hospital, I said to my very conservative, proper husband, "I just want to pass an idea by you."

He said, "Over my dead body."

When McKenzie was four weeks old, I was sitting up in bed about 3:30 in the morning, unable to sleep. I kept saying to Heavenly Father, "Whose babies do I owe? You keep sending me these great children, and

165

I feel like I need to be serving them; and yet I feel such a pull to the others."

I got up and grabbed a legal pad from my husband's nightstand. Maybe if I wrote down everything I had learned about these people, if I kept a family record, I would be able to let go. So, for eight hours I wrote like a fool. And for the next five or six days I kept adding to the stack of papers. When, after much prayer, I was sure I was finished, I walked to my husband, prepared to hand him the paperwork and say, "We have a family record of all the children who came to live with us while their parents were either in jail or rehab." Instead, I put the papers in his lap and out of my mouth poured, "Now you will understand why I must strap this baby to my chest and teach school."

My husband, who at the time was not very active in the Church, looked at me, with tears in his eyes, and said, "I knew the minute that crazy idea came out of your mouth that that was what you were to do. The writing process was to let you know that you weren't finished. But," he added, "I have one request. With all that I've known and all that I've seen, please don't let them hold my baby." I understood.

When I pulled up to the shelter my first day back, I strapped on my newborn with a prayer that my baby would be safe.

John, one of my very favorite people on the streets, is a beautiful black man who tells me every Valentine's Day, "I love you and please tell me that if I had done everything right, and you were single, you would marry me." I always tell him yes. He opened my car door, took a look at my sweet baby McKenzie, and said, "Wow, we did a great job, didn't we?"

Then he carried her into the shelter like a proud daddy and handed her to none other than my dear friend Sarah. Jane was standing behind Sarah mouthing, "Don't let her hold the baby." I had to, I absolutely had to. There was such a feeling inside of me that I owed this baby to these people. So, I took all the blankets off, held her sweet little body up to Sarah's neck, and I whispered, "Sarah, babies are unconditional love. They are a gift from God. Feel her. Smell her. Kiss her sweet skin."

McKenzie, being the great nurser that she was, began to suckle Sarah's skin. Sarah cried and cried as she kissed and loved and smelled. Then she began naming all of her own children who had been taken from her. She handed McKenzie back to me and said, "Your baby will do more for your students than you will ever do." I knew that was a compliment. And she was right. My sixth-grade boys, who are the coolest of the coolest, always told me, "I'll never touch your baby. I'll never have anything to do with your baby." But I caught them rocking her and singing to her. They would write lullabies at night, and as long as I wasn't watching, they would sing. Little Marie, whose job it was to walk her mommy and daddy safely back and forth to the liquor store every night, wrote this in her journal: "My teacher is funny. She really likes her baby. You can just tell by the way she kisses her all over and leaves lipstick marks all over her head. Watching her makes me happy." But at the bottom she added, "I wish somebody would have loved me like that when I was little."

In one short line, this lonely little girl summarized the longing, aching wish of every one of these homeless children—and every member of the human family—to be loved all over, to be loved completely, and to be loved unconditionally.

When we go home, I believe the Savior will ask, "Who did you love in my name?" And if we cannot name names, if we cannot look him in the eye, we will be sad.

NOTE

1. Except for Karl Malone, the names of people in this account have been changed to protect their privacy.

Temple Attendance: Renewing Our Strength

CYNTHIA L. HALLEN

If the temple is the Lord's spiritual university, then its textbook is surely the scriptures. Although we do not discuss certain sacred matters outside of the temple, we may learn the language of the temple through scripture study. I find the prophetic words of Isaiah especially relevant. Isaiah 40:31, for instance, tells how Christ can lift us up through temple service: "They that wait upon the Lord shall renew their strength; they shall mount up with wings as eagles; they shall run, and not be weary; and they shall walk, and not faint."

Each phrase of this verse invites contemplation. The phrase "wait upon" can be read two ways: to "wait on" and to "wait for." Both apply to the temple. It is the place where we serve, or "wait on," the Lord and his children. It is also the place where we "wait for" the Lord, as we patiently prepare to meet him and to see his face. And as we serve in his house with all our hearts, we may look forward to receiving all our heart's desires.

Those who wait upon the Lord in the temple shall "renew their strength." One way the Lord renews our strength is by giving us new clothes. The new clothes represent covenants that provide a new identity in Christ and the promise of a renewed body in the resurrection. A recent scholarly edition of the Bible indicates that the word *renew* means "to exchange": "The Hebrew for this verb is used of changes of

Cynthia L. Hallen, an associate professor of linguistics at Brigham Young University, served a full-time mission in Bolivia and a Church-service mission for the LDS Translation Department. She is Relief Society president in the American Fork Stake and an ordinance worker in the Mount Timpanogos Temple.

clothes . . . , which can symbolize strength and beauty."[1] Thus, in Isaiah 52:1, we receive this charge: "Awake, awake; put on thy strength, O Zion; put on thy beautiful garments, O Jerusalem." Through temple ordinances, the Lord changes the faded old clothes of mortality into the glorious new garments of immortality.

In Titus 3:5, we read that the Lord saves us "by the washing of regeneration, and renewing of the Holy Ghost." In such ordinances as baptism, the Lord purifies us, lifting us up from the deep waters of sorrow and death. In other ordinances, such as confirmation, the Lord renews us. He changes our clothes, through the Holy Ghost, transforming us from fallen creatures into new creatures who are worthy through the atonement of Jesus Christ to wear the robes of righteousness.

The renewal of our strength spoken of by Isaiah includes the regeneration of our bodies. Our limbs are strengthened so that we can spiritually fly, so that we shall "mount up with wings as eagles" (Isaiah 40:31); the Lord promises us that we will "ride upon the high places of the earth" (Isaiah 58:14) as did Jacob and Enoch of old. Often in scripture, the mountains or the high places of the earth represent the Lord's temples (see, for example, Isaiah 2:2–3; Micah 4:1–2). As the Lord lifts us up on the wings of his spirit in the temple, our vision expands, our wisdom increases, our perspective deepens and broadens.

The Lord makes our feet "beautiful upon the mountains," or in the temples, so that we can "run, and not be weary; and . . . walk, and not faint" (Isaiah 52:7; 40:31). We run, as did Mary and the women at the tomb, with the good news that Christ, who was lifted up on the cross, has risen from the dead to lift us up into eternal life. Isaiah 52:7 describes the beautiful feet of the person that "bringeth good tidings, that publisheth peace; . . . that saith unto Zion, Thy God reigneth!" Bible commentary explains that this scripture refers to "messengers who ran from the scene of a battle to bring news of the outcome to a waiting king and people."[2] Our good news is that Christ has won the victory over sin and death. The temple gives us strength to proclaim those glad tidings to all nations, kindreds, tongues, and people.

Our feet are strong because we "walk and walk and walk" like the pioneers, pressing forward to the promised land.[3] Our knees are beautiful because we kneel daily and give thanks and pray and testify that the Lord has redeemed his people. Through temple ordinances, we walk and run and fly to lift up those who are in need. And when we are in need—when we feel weary, faint, weak, vulnerable, or helpless—the Lord lifts us up, not only like eagles on the wings of his spirit but also like lambs into his arms: "He shall feed his flock like a shepherd: he shall gather the lambs with his arm, and carry them in his bosom, and shall gently lead those that are with young" (Isaiah 40:11).

Let me share one memorable experience about how the Lord gently leads those that are with young. I served the last part of my mission in Cota-Cota, Bolivia, a minor suburb of La Paz, where many Aymará Indian people live. When I left Bolivia in 1978, I said good-bye to a beautiful Aymará family with four bright-eyed children, all of them Church members scarcely a year. Two years later as a student at Brigham Young University, I received a sad letter from my native missionary companion about a terrible accident in Cota-Cota. The gas stove had exploded in that family's one-room adobe house while the three youngest were inside taking a nap. Oscar, Susy, and Edgar were burned in the fire: Oscar escaped serious injury, but Susy and Edgar were severely burned. Their mother, Yola, had saved their lives by pulling the children from the burning house, but their injuries were severe. When I heard the news, I was inconsolable. I cried and cried. And I cried even more when I thought of the mother and father of those children. How must they feel?

I sought comfort in the Provo Temple, fasting, and praying, and weeping the entire session. I found some peace in an inspired prayer, when a brother said, "Bless the suffering, that friends will be sent to them."

Those words comforted me, but I did not realize their full significance until two years later when I had a dream in which I saw that Bolivian family dressed all in white. They were in the temple with the missionaries who had baptized them. I also dreamed that I moved from Provo into a house in the Avenues area of Salt Lake City, one block from the old Primary Children's Hospital.

I graduated from BYU that summer and several weeks later, I was offered a job in Salt Lake. In September 1982, I moved into the house on the Avenues I had dreamed of. One evening after work, I felt prompted to take a walk. I set out to stop and chat with one of my visiting teaching sisters, but when she was not home, I decided to watch the sunset from City Creek Canyon. As I walked, I saw ahead of me two children with a man and a woman. When they stopped at the canyon, I drew near and noticed that the children were a boy and a girl with glossy, dark hair and merry, bright eyes. When the girl began to run down the steep mountainside, the woman called out, "Susy, come back."

At the name Susy, my heart stirred with recognition. I asked the man, "Who are these children? Where are they from?"

"They are from Bolivia," he said.

I called out their names, and they turned to me. They were my little ones from Bolivia. Through Church fast offerings, the Lord had brought them to Primary Children's Hospital. The Lord knew how much I loved them; he had heard my prayers and the comforting prayer of the brother in the Provo Temple. He had led me to find Susy and Edgar out for a walk with their nurse and their social worker on the last night that they were in the hospital for inpatient care. Eastern Airlines donated my passage to take them back to Bolivia.

Since then all four children and their faithful mother, Yola, have received their endowments in the temple. All the children have served as missionaries in Bolivia. The words of a hymn came to me as a testimony after this experience:

Come, ye disconsolate, where'er ye languish;
Come to the mercy seat, fervently kneel.
Here bring your wounded hearts; here tell your anguish.
Earth has no sorrow that heav'n cannot heal.[4]

So many of my experiences of heaven have been in the temple, and I know of a surety that earth has no sorrow that the temple cannot heal, both for the living and for the dead, as we seek our Savior there.

NOTES

1. *NIV Study Bible: New International Version*, ed. Kenneth Barker (Grand Rapids, Mich.: Zondervan, 1985), 1073.
2. *NIV Study Bible*, 1093.
3. *Children's Songbook* (Salt Lake City: The Church of Jesus Christ of Latter-day Saints, 1989), 214.
4. *Hymns of The Church of Jesus Christ of Latter-day Saints* (Salt Lake City: The Church of Jesus Christ of Latter-day Saints, 1985), no. 115.

Grief Is a Personal Path

Carol Frogley Ellertson

I have no special knowledge of death and grieving, except what I have learned as I have grieved over losses in my own life. We all grieve differently; there is no one correct way.

We grieve every time we experience a loss—of a job, a marriage, a home, friends or family members, health, independence, reputation, financial stability, even dreams. Perhaps a child or family member has strayed from the Church. Loss is a fact of life.

I have never lost a child or a spouse in death, but I have experienced deep, debilitating, depressive grief. I first experienced deep grief—waking up every morning with a heavy pain in my chest—when my dear sister Marie, two years younger than I, was in a car accident involving a semi truck. She sustained multiple injuries and severe head trauma, and she had no heartbeat when they found her. Emergency personnel were able to resuscitate her, but she immediately slipped into a coma. I grieved but seemed to get stuck somewhere in the process. I visited her every day. We didn't know if she would ever wake up. Over and over I cried to God to bless her, but I couldn't feel any whisperings of comfort or premonitions for her future. She had been on the verge of graduating from Brigham Young University and was almost engaged. Her boyfriend visited her for a while but eventually lost hope and quit coming to see her.

My anguish continued each day for two months. Then one day I began to cry uncontrollably. For hours I cried and pleaded with the Lord in prayer, telling him that I just couldn't go on anymore not knowing if she would ever come back to us. In Luke 22:44 we read, "And being in

Carol Frogley Ellertson received her bachelor's degree in music composition and is completing a master's degree in ancient Near Eastern studies. A homemaker, she and her husband, Daniel N. Ellertson, are the parents of six children. She serves as her stake's music chair.

an agony he prayed more earnestly." Maybe the Lord knew that I could go no further. That night I dreamed that my favorite plant in my living room was dying. Despite daily care, the plant was wilting and turning brown. In my dream, I was very discouraged and decided to give up caring for the plant. But before I did, I watered it one last time. I dreamed I awoke the next day to a sunny morning. I entered my living room, and to my amazement, the plant now reached to the ceiling, green and full. The Lord had given me hope for my sister. When I woke up, I hurried to the hospital to tell my mother about my dream, but she had her own news for me. My sister had said the word *ouch* that morning.

Many months of recovery followed. My mother worked and worked with Marie and brought her back from death with faith and sheer will power. Essentially Mother reared her twice, patiently teaching her to speak and move again, sometimes defying doctors whose directions she felt were not in tune with what my sister needed. After months in the hospital, all Marie wanted was to go home. The doctors were sure she wasn't ready. My mother finally took her home against their wishes, and her recovery accelerated from there. She is now married, has two children, and teaches first grade. God gave us a miracle.

Many years later, when this same wonderful mother of mine was herself diagnosed with a brain tumor, I did have premonitions about the outcome. When I tried to pray for her recovery, I experienced such a struggle that I could not form the thoughts in my head or the words in my mouth. I knew there would be no miracle this time. Our family began a nine-month grieving journey toward her death. I would drive from Provo to Salt Lake nearly every day to help care for her. Though my sisters and I wanted to care for her during her remaining days, we couldn't possibly give her all that she needed. We had young families that we needed to go home to.

I remember feeling a lot of resentment during that time. I think this was how my anger over her coming death expressed itself. I resented those who came to take care of her because they represented my failure to do so, even though we could not have managed without them. I was angry with my father because he left at times during the day when I thought he should be at home helping us. I didn't understand the burden he had caring for her all through her fitful, sleepless nights. I resented friends who came to see her, especially those whom she had not seen for many years, believing they came only out of curiosity. I wanted to shield her privacy and dignity. Now I know these friends wanted to express their love and say their last good-byes. I even resented some family members, on the one hand for being too maudlin and on the other, for not being sufficiently sorrowful. I didn't realize that all my resentment was a product of my own heartache.

Anyone who goes through such an experience needs to be sensitive to the whisperings of the Spirit. My mother did not keep a journal, and I had planned to get much of her life story on tape. She was lucid and aware for months after her diagnosis. One day I was sitting in the temple when a strong feeling came to tape her memories as soon as possible. I considered going to Salt Lake that very day to begin taping, but I waited until the next day. When I got there, I found her mental function failing rapidly, and within two days she was no longer able to talk. I did get about two hours on tape, but had I come sooner, I would now have many more of her memories.

My mother waited to die until her family was all gathered. It was my father's birthday, and she stayed for the celebration. She had been largely incoherent for weeks, but that last day she wrote a birthday card for my father. My sisters and I think it was really written by our grandma, who had died many years before. The handwriting was Grandma's, and we definitely felt spirits there waiting to take Mother. We believe she put them off until the birthday was over. As she slipped away around midnight, she opened her eyes and stared intently at something and then was gone.

The fog of the previous nine months now became a depression. I knew that the Lord was near, but I was depressed nevertheless. When I read secular books or listened to tapes on handling death, they seemed to talk about grieving without God. The only way I could think to grieve was with God, with a constant soul cry to him day and night. And I felt him with me, but he would not remove my pain. The only way to healing was straight through it, no detours. I was like an inconsolable two-year-old who had stumbled and cut a nasty gash on her knee. A parent who runs to comfort a hurt child knows that the injury will heal in time. But the two-year-old knows only the pain and screams in agony, wanting relief. Parents can't take the pain away; they can only comfort the child until exhaustion and sleep take over.

As mortals, we are relative two-year-olds in the eternal scheme. The Lord knows that our losses and hurts are temporary. But we can't see that far ahead; all we can focus on is our pain, our exhaustion. We lose interest in life and its business. C. S. Lewis noted after he lost his wife: "No one ever told me about the laziness of grief. . . . I loathe the slightest effort. Not only writing but even reading a letter is too much. Even shaving. What does it matter now whether my cheek is rough or smooth?"[1]

When I grieved for my mother, I grieved not only for her loss but also for aspects of our relationship that I felt sad about, that I wish had been resolved. I thought that these kinds of feelings were unique to me, but this last year I have watched three close friends grieve similarly when they lost their mothers. We long to be one with our children and our parents; that is what the Atonement is all about, being at one. After some impressions and some dreams in which Mother has come to me, this longing in our relationship now feels resolved. In these special dreams, when she hugged me, I felt it physically.

When my father emerged from his fog of grief and took an interest in dating, I got a feeling in the temple that my mother wanted him to marry a certain woman he had been seeing and that I should do all I could to encourage that relationship. I didn't think this woman was seriously interested in him, but I was wrong. Now they are happily married.

Grief is a personal path. A friend of mine could not shake her depression after the birth of a stillborn son. After a year, she was extremely debilitated. Finally she was prompted to start reading past entries of her journal. A picture of herself as a happy, healthy, functioning woman emerged from the pages and influenced her thought processes positively. She emerged from her depression.

Another young mother I know lost her husband suddenly when he reacted to medication for surgery. She had three children under age three. A woman of great faith and testimony, she feels her husband very near, influencing her and her children. Well-meaning friends have told her that she isn't grieving properly because she doesn't appear to have gone through all the so-called "stages of grief." They are worried about her mental health, and yet she is functioning very well.

I have grieved over the death of my ten-year-old son's best friend, who played at our house every day. This boy, Steven, was riding his bike after school, on his way to meet my son at the bike path, when he was killed by a sanitation truck. My son came upon his body and subsequently blamed himself. I was blind-sided by the intensity of my feelings; that heavy pain in the chest was there again. The only thing that made me feel better was writing music for this boy. I also wrote a song after my mother died that led to a feeling of purpose and accomplishment. Letting grief be a catalyst to create can be very therapeutic. Music also helped to assuage my pain—not music that tried to cheer me up, but music that expressed anguish. In particular, I was moved by *The Symphony of Sorrowful Songs* by Henryk Górecki. Our Western culture doesn't allow me to weep and wail for days and throw myself prostrate on the casket like many Eastern cultures. This music is cathartic; it meets that need for me.

For others, art might help traverse the path to healing. A pioneer journal that detailed a terrible epidemic of sickness among the Saints moved artist Judy Law to portray through her work "the universality of pain as part of mortality." She also hoped to "somehow share [her] conviction that we live beyond earthlife; that we are not alone and forgotten in our struggles and suffering here, that help, comfort, and caring come to us from the real but unseen world that surrounds us."[2] She called her painting *And Sanctify to Thee Thy Deepest Distress* because as she began working, words and phrases of the hymn "How Firm a Foundation" kept running through her head:

> When through the deep waters I call thee to go,
> The rivers of sorrow shall not thee o'erflow,
> For I will be with thee, thy troubles to bless,
> And sanctify to thee thy deepest distress.[3]

The struggles we go through as we let go of our loved ones in death are universal. Without death we would not fully understand how much we love those who leave us. But how we endure the pain, the depression, the confusion, the guilt, and our deep, deep sorrow is as different and unique as each of us who passes through it.

NOTES

1. C. S. Lewis, *A Grief Observed* (1961; reprint, San Francisco: HarperCollins Paperback, 1994), 21.
2. Notes in possession of the author.
3. *Hymns of The Church of Jesus Christ of Latter-day Saints* (Salt Lake City: The Church of Jesus Christ of Latter-day Saints, 1985), no. 85.

Final Gifts:
Letting Go of Loved Ones

CAROL J. H. WEENIG

My intense interest in a healthy approach to death and dying began when my youngest daughter and I entered the University of Utah together as freshmen. My decision to attend college thrilled my mother. I would be the first on both sides of my family to get a college education. Six weeks before classes started, however, Mom had a stroke. During the three weeks that she lived, my family and I were on an emotional roller-coaster as we were told right up to the night she died both that she could be rehabilitated and that there was no hope for her recovery. In addition, we were given no options for her care. My mother did not die with the hope and dignity to which she was entitled.

Cardiologist Stephen Sinatra asked, "Must we view death in such an alien, let's-not-talk-about-it, don't-want-to-face-it kind of way? Can we not instead transform the final chapter of our life—the conclusion of our time here on Earth—from a frightening experience into a new spiritual awakening? . . . For when we each face up to our mortality, the process of dying can be a truly spiritual and healing experience, for both the dying person and the loved ones."[1]

After Mom died, my frustration and grief led me to seek a healthy approach to the process of dying. I wanted to learn how to do what Rabbi Zalman Schachter-Shalomi suggested, to "send our loved ones onward with our blessings rather than to become distracted by our own grief over their imminent departure."[2] Learning how to do this has

Carol J. Hansen Weenig is a certified health education specialist. She and her husband, David J. Weenig, a registered pharmacist, are the parents of four daughters. She serves as Relief Society president in her ward.

strengthened my faith and testimony in the sanctity of life, both mortal and eternal. It has taken away some of my concern about our mortal exit and replaced that concern with a desire to approach death with hope and dignity. There are some positive and practical ways to support those going through the dying process.

One of my first projects as a newly graduated health educator was to help compile, edit, and format a new hospice inservice and teaching manual. The hospice program is a very special way of caring for the dying, as well as for their families. A concept of care rather than a specific location, hospice considers everyone involved: the person who is facing death, the whole family, the doctor, nurse, and any other professionals or caretakers involved in the care of that dying person.

Hospice care enables the dying to stay at home, if they choose, and, wherever they are, to be surrounded and supported by their loved ones, who are also provided with support and guidance. The dying decide how and where they want to spend the rest of their lives. Hospice concentrates on achieving control over pain without impairing the patient's alertness. Because their physical and emotional comfort is addressed so thoroughly, the dying can concentrate on living life as fully as possible until life ends.

As I listened to hospice nurses share their experiences during this project, I realized that they considered it a privilege to participate in someone's death. Their obvious love and respect were profoundly spiritual and uplifting. Many of them practice and teach family members the methods advocated by Anya Foos-Graber in *Deathing: An Intelligent Alternative for the Final Moments of Life*. She believes that just as the Lamaze method teaches pregnant women and their husbands, who act as coaches, how to participate more actively in the process of birth, so a similar method of coaching allows both loved ones and the dying person to be purposefully involved in the process of dying.

One story in particular has stayed with me. As a young father approached death, his wife clung to him and sobbed out her grief and despair at the prospect of rearing their family without him. The hospice nurse quietly helped this young mother to her feet and led her out of the room. Gently she counseled this young woman, who in her panic had forgotten all she had learned and been prepared for in the previous six months. In essence, the nurse reminded her of what Foos-Graber advises: When the support person or "coach" (in this case the wife) becomes aware that death is near, say very quietly, "My dear, I want you to know that I love you very much, and I will miss you. Relax, breath[e] away all feelings of anxiety and know that this loving process will guide you to the other side. Reject nothing and just let everything happen naturally. Remember your spiritual teach[ings]. We have taken care of all your physical concerns so your passage may be effortless, focused and peaceful. Go in peace, dear one, and know that my love will follow you."[3] In addition, the nurse told the young wife that her husband had come to an acceptance and was ready to go, but he was holding back because of her fear. He couldn't leave her as she was.

Calmed and supported, the wife went back to the room, stood at the head of the bed, and holding her husband's face with both hands, tenderly told him through her tears that she loved him, that she and the children would miss him, but they would be all right. Then she gave him permission to go. He died very peacefully within minutes.

From hospice nurses I learned the greatest fears the dying have are concern for those they are leaving behind, fear of being abandoned or lonely, fear of suffering and pain, fear of dependency, fear of regression, fear of loss of self-control, fear of the unknown, and again, concern for the ones they leave behind. If we understand the dying process, we can help alleviate all those fears.

When dealing with a dying person, do not avoid the subject of personal death. Be human. It's all right to cry. Do not discourage the emotions of grief, either in the dying person, in the person's loved ones, or in yourself. Tears, anger, guilt, despair, and a whole array of feelings are natural reactions to the family disorganization that is taking place.[4] Recognize that shock, numbness, denial, self-reproach, anxiety and panic, sadness, loneliness, and depression are also normal feelings and behaviors associated with grief.[5]

Be willing to spend time listening to those who are grieving. Let the dying mourn. They need someone to listen quietly to their feelings and their fears. Follow up what they say in a very gentle way. Ask questions. Ask them to repeat statements if you don't understand. Don't be afraid to say, "I'm not sure I follow you. Can you explain that a little more?" Also respond to them in ways that tell them you accept what they are saying, feeling, or even seeing, and that you are not judging but only listening.[6] Sometimes to keep focused I have to remind myself, "I'm just listening! I'm just listening!"

Allow differences of opinion. Allow doubt. Allow questioning. Respect individual differences and personalities. Strange as it may seem, sometimes just silently sitting beside a person also facilitates communication. It can free the person to start talking. Recognize, however, the times when the person really doesn't want to talk. Don't push, but let the person know you are interested and will be there to listen whenever he or she wants to talk.[7]

In addition, use touch to convey your caring. Touch your shoulder with your fingers. Now take your palm and cup your shoulder. Can you feel the difference? Fingers are invasive; palms are comforting. When using touch, however, be sensitive to when it might be an invasion of privacy. Allow the dying person to remain in control.

Treat the dying person as a whole person. Physician William Ostler said, "It is as important to know the person who has the disease as to know the disease the person has."[8] That includes helping them to reach out to others and give as much as they can, as long as they can—within their limitations. Up until a week before she died of cancer, one woman continued to knit baby hats, booties, and small blankets to donate to the local homeless shelter. Doing for others helped her a great deal.

Share your religious convictions about faith, prayer, immortality, and death; answer questions as honestly as you can, but let the dying person take the lead and do not actively prescribe or try to convert as death approaches. Now is not the time. Also avoid fairy tales and supposedly comforting half-truths. This advice is especially important when you are talking with children who are watching a loved one die. Do not say that Grandpa is "going away" for a while. If that's so, when will he be back? Be sure you use the words *God* and *Heavenly Father* carefully. If children, in particular, hear you say, "God is going to take Grandpa," or "Heavenly Father needs Grandpa on the other side," their natural reaction is to stay away from God lest they be taken also.[9]

It is generally not a good idea to try to shield children from the painful experience of death. It is much healthier to prepare children by very gently explaining what is happening and then allowing them to say their own good-byes and express their love to a dying grandparent or other special people in their lives. That can be a therapeutic experience for both the dying and the children involved.[10] Deanna Edwards, in her book *Grieving: The Pain and the Promise*, says, "There are two groups in our society we overprotect: the very old and the very young. Amazingly, however, these are the two groups of people who meet death and loss naturally, without pretense, and can teach us how to grieve if we give them the opportunity."[11]

My little grandchildren were somewhat prepared when my mother died, but I was impressed by the way the funeral director explained to them what had happened. He drew a glove out of his pocket and put it on. The glove, he explained, was like their great-grandmother's body, and the hand inside the glove was like her spirit. Because her body had grown very sick and very old, it had separated from her spirit. Her body would be put in a special place in the ground, but her spirit would now live on in another place. Some day, because of a special gift that the Savior, Jesus Christ, gave us, her body and spirit would be reunited never to be separated again, and her body would be made well and healthy. If they lived worthily, they would see their great-grandmother again some day. His explanation also comforted the adults listening nearby.

You can help children by explaining that it is all right to feel sad or to cry—that you feel that way, too—and that it sometimes helps you to talk about it. Reassure your children that when *they* want to talk, you will be glad to listen. And then remember your own advice. Just listen. Children don't need sermons at this time as much as they just need to be listened to and accepted.

A very big part of supporting the dying is learning the dying person's wishes. Take care of any questions they may have over legal concerns or any other matters—relationships, material concerns, or any other areas of "unfinished business." Help them to resolve those issues.

And finally, learn the physical signs and symptoms of approaching death and what you can do to support your loved ones through it:

1. Dying persons spend an increasing amount of time sleeping. You can help by quietly sitting beside them and sometimes talking to them while they seem to be asleep. Speak normally but calmly.

2. You will notice a gradual decrease in food intake. Cravings come and go. Nothing tastes good. Meats are the first to go in their diet, followed by vegetables and other hard-to-digest foods. Finally the dying don't want even soft foods and liquids. Forcing them to eat or drink only causes them more discomfort. Instead, offer them ice chips or small sips of cool water. Wiping their face and lips with a moist washcloth sometimes helps. Remember to use a soft and *moist* cloth. A dry one is too abrasive.

3. Urine output will decrease. They may lose control of their bladder or their bowels as their muscles begin to relax. Remember, this is an area of great concern to them. Help them maintain their dignity. They can sense your negative feelings. Treat them how you would want to be treated in a similar situation.

4. They might become restless and pull at their bed linen. They might "see" things that you can't see. Medical professionals say this is a result of decreased oxygen to the brain and they are seeing people or things that don't exist. Perhaps, but I am convinced, both from personal experience and from experiences recounted by hospice nurses, that someone special *is* there to escort them home. You can help when they are restless by playing soothing music, gently massaging their foreheads, or even reading to them.

5. Natural metabolic changes can cause confusion; they may not recognize where they are or who is with them. You can help them if you identify yourself by name before speaking to them. Remind them of the day and time. It might even help to keep a light on in the room. Whenever you need to communicate something important for their comfort, such as it's being time for pain medication, speak softly but clearly and truthfully.

6. As oral secretions become more profuse and collect in the back of the throat, you may hear what has been called "the death rattle." Hospice nurses tell me that suctioning a dying person's throat may not only increase those secretions but also causes unnecessary discomfort. Instead, gently turn the person's head to the side and let gravity help to drain the secretions. Gently wipe the mouth with a moist cloth. Sometimes elevating the head of the bed or using a cool-mist humidifier to increase the humidity in the room will help. The sound of congestion does not indicate severe or new pain; it is a normal part of the shutting-down process.

7. A dying person's body will become increasingly cool to the touch. The skin may become darker in color, especially on the underside of the body. This means that blood circulation is decreasing in the extremities and being reserved for the vital organs. Cover the dying person with a blanket, but never use an electric blanket, which might burn them.

8. You will notice a change in a dying person's breathing pattern. It will become irregular with ten to thirty seconds of no breathing. This is Cheyne-Stokes Syndrome; it indicates a decrease in circulation. You can

help by elevating the head of the bed. Sit beside the person, hold their hand, and talk gently to them.

9. Reassure them of your love, let them know that you will be all right, that you will be able to go on with life, and give them permission to go. Don't be afraid of shedding tears, which are a natural and normal way of saying good-bye. Tears are honest expressions of your love and also can help you to let go.[12]

I was not with my own mother when she died. The mortuary where her body was taken, however, was owned by dear friends. The wife told me of the peace and healing she had experienced sitting beside her grandmother after she died and quietly sharing her thoughts and feelings. She asked if I would like to have some private time alone with my mother. I did. I knelt beside her casket for a long time. With healing tears streaming down my cheeks, I talked to her. It helped me let go and begin my journey to peace.

I have learned to recognize and accept dying as a natural part of life. I now see it as a birthing process where, as loved ones leave mortality, they are greeted with great joy on the other side, much as we rejoice at the birth of a new little spirit here on earth. We do not have to be only solemn bystanders, however. We, the living, can serve as support persons, to help ease the transition to the next life. As Psalm 30:5 says, "Weeping may endure for a night, but joy cometh in the morning."

NOTES

1. Stephen Sinatra, "Love Paves the Path to Death: A Spiritual Blueprint for the Final Journey," *HeartSense* (May 1997): 6.
2. Zalman Schachter-Shalomi quoted in Sinatra, "Love Paves the Path to Death," 7.
3. Anya Foos-Graber, quoted in Sinatra, "Love Paves the Path to Death," 7.
4. Earl A. Grollman, "Children and Death," in *Concerning Death: A Practical Guide for the Living*, ed. Earl A. Grollman (Boston: Beacon Press, 1974), 77.
5. J. William Worden, *Grief Counseling and Grief Therapy*, 2d ed. (New York: Springer Publishing, 1991), 22–24.
6. Maggie Callanan Pflaum and Patricia Kelley, "Understanding the Final Messages of the Dying," *Nursing* 16, no. 6 (1986): 29.
7. Pflaum and Kelly, "Understanding the Final Messages," 29.
8. William Ostler, quoted in Balfour Mount, "Whole Person Care: Beyond Psychosocial and Physical Needs," *The American Journal of Hospice and Palliative Care* 10, no. 1 (January-February 1993): 30.
9. Grollman, "Children and Death," 70.

10. T. Berry Brazelton, "He Won't Take His Medicine, She's Afraid of the Doctor," *Family Circle*, March 1998, 44.
11. Deanna Edwards, *Grieving: The Pain and the Promise* (American Fork, Utah: Covenant Communications, 1997), 119.
12. *At the Final Stage*, ed. Carol J. Weenig (Salt Lake City: Community Hospice, 1996), 1–8.

This Is a Test. It Is Only a Test.

SHERI L. DEW

My mother made me take piano lessons. And because I am her eldest and she had not yet been worn down by the thankless task of prodding five children to practice every day, my whining about hating to practice fell on deaf ears. The fact that I eventually studied piano for fifteen years is largely a tribute to Mother's resilience. I wish I had a dollar for every time she prophesied that I would thank her one day for all of the musical torture. As always, she was right. I have thanked her, again and again, for that introduction to the keyboard, because somewhere between those first bars of "Here we go, up a row, to a birthday party" and "Rhapsody in Blue," I fell in love with music, especially classical music, which in its more magnificent passages made my heart feel like it was going to leap out of my chest—in other words, it made my young spirit soar.

Here, again, Mother deserves all the credit. I couldn't have been more than ten or eleven when she gave me a stack of classical albums, introducing me to some of the great composers whose works were characterized by dramatic musical passages and what I call the Big Finish.

I would lie in front of the stereo for hours, listening to the third movement of Rachmaninoff's second piano concerto or his "Prelude in C# Minor," all the while imagining myself at a shiny black concert grand in Carnegie Hall. I pictured my debut there, standing ovation and all. I imagined that I would be humble but brilliant—brilliant enough to move an entire audience, including Mother, to tears. Somewhere in all

Sheri L. Dew is the second counselor in the Relief Society General Presidency. She grew up in Ulysses, Kansas, and graduated from Brigham Young University with a degree in history. A popular speaker and writer, she is vice-president of publishing at Deseret Book Company.

of my daydreaming, I caught a vision of how it would feel to play so beautifully that others' hearts would soar.

At that point, Mother no longer had to encourage me to practice. Once I had a vision of the possibilities, the motivation to master the piano came from inside. Am I saying that practicing suddenly was enjoyable? Absolutely not! It was often sheer drudgery. But I found a technique that helped me endure those tedious hours of practice, day in and day out. When I set out to tackle a new piece, I would master and memorize the Big Finish first, all the while visualizing myself in concert where the audience jumped to its feet at the last chord. Imagining how grand the Big Finish would be kept me going through months of rehearsal on technical passages that didn't provide nearly the same sense of drama but that had to be mastered nonetheless. In short, my progress on the piano and my motivation to practice increased dramatically when I caught a vision of my potential.

We are temporarily afflicted with the amnesia of mortality. But just as my spirit was stirred by the majesty of those dramatic musical passages and the possibility of performing them flawlessly, through the power of the Spirit we can often "catch a spark," as President Joseph F. Smith taught us, "from the awakened memories of the immortal soul, which lights up our whole being as with the glory of our former home."[1] It is the Spirit that will also shed light upon our ultimate potential—the grandest finish of all.

If, on the other hand, we are not able to catch a vision of the Big Finish, meaning a clear image of who we are and what we are becoming—how can we be willing to practice? Life, like classical music, is full of the difficult passages that are conquered as much through endurance and determination as through any particular skill.

Remember the announcements that used to interrupt your regularly scheduled television programming? "This is a test of the emergency broadcasting system. It is only a test. If this were a real emergency, you would be notified through this station." You've probably seen the poster that reads, "Life is a test. It is only a test. Had this been a real life, you would have been instructed where to go and what to do." It reminds me of a greeting card a friend gave me that shows a frazzled woman who says, "Mother told me there would be days like this . . . But she failed to mention they could go on for months at a time."

There are times when days feel like months and when life feels like the test that it is, days when the vision and hope of a Big Finish are dimmed by immediate demands, days when one might wish for a mortal exam that was a little more manageable.

For indeed, this life *is* a test. It is only a test—meaning, that's *all* it is. Nothing more, but nothing less. It is a test of many things—of our convictions and priorities, our faith and our faithfulness, our patience and our resilience, and in the end, our ultimate desires. In the long run, as Alma taught, whatever we truly desire, we will have. "I know that [God] granteth unto men according to their desire . . . ; yea, I know that he allotteth unto men . . . according to their wills, whether they be unto salvation or unto destruction" (Alma 29:4).

Thankfully, our experience here is an open-book test. We know why we're here, and we have from prophets ancient and modern an extensive set of instructions that never become passé or grow outdated.

Yes, life *is* a test of many things. But at the risk of sounding simplistic, may I suggest that the mortal experience is largely about vision—our vision of ourselves and our ultimate Big Finish. And vision is determined by faith. The firmer our faith in Jesus Christ, the clearer our vision of ourselves and what we can ultimately achieve and become.

The adversary, of course, is intent on obstructing our vision and undermining our faith. He will do anything and everything to confuse us about who we are and where we're going because he has already forfeited his privilege of going there.

A vision of our potential is central to survival, both spiritually and physically. I've always been curious about Lehi and his family. Just imagine the family home evening when he informed his wife and children that the Lord had directed them to pack a few belongings and foray into the wilderness, leaving behind their life of comfort. I doubt any of them were enthusiastic about the news. Can't you just imagine the dialogue?

"You want us to do what? To pack a few things and leave home?"

"Yes, that is what the Lord has asked us to do."

"Where are we going?"

"I'm not entirely sure. I know only that we must leave Jerusalem. And by the way, we'll need to travel light. So leave most of your things here."

"When will we come back home?"

"That isn't entirely clear. Perhaps never."

We know how Laman and Lemuel responded initially and in perpetuity. Why didn't Nephi, their younger (and presumably less mature)

187

brother, react the same way? He probably wasn't thrilled with his father's news, either.

The difference is a classic demonstration of the power of vision. While Laman and Lemuel rebelled, Nephi asked the Lord if he might see what his father had seen. He had the faith to seek his own vision: "I, Nephi, . . . did cry unto the Lord; and behold he did visit me, and did soften my heart that I did believe all the words which had been spoken by my father; wherefore, I did not rebel against him like unto my brothers" (1 Nephi 2:16). That vision, or sense of purpose, sustained Nephi through a life of trial and tribulation. It helped him pass the test, so to speak.

Joseph Smith was persecuted from the time he announced that he had seen the Father and the Son until he died a martyr. How did he do it? Let us never forget that his prophetic mission began with a vision. "I have actually seen a vision; and who am I that I can withstand God, or why does the world think to make me deny what I have actually seen? For I had seen a vision; I knew it, and I knew that God knew it, and I could not deny it, neither dared I do it; at least I knew that by so doing I would offend God, and come under condemnation" (Joseph Smith–History 1:25).

"Where there is no vision, the people perish," Solomon proclaimed (Proverbs 29:18).

And perhaps nothing is more vital today than having a vision, manifest by the Spirit, of who we are and what we can become, of our intrinsic value to the Lord, and of the unparalleled role we must play in these latter days. We are literally the offspring of God, his begotten sons and daughters, with the potential of exaltation (Acts 17:29; D&C 76:24). "The Spirit itself beareth witness with our spirit, that we are the children of God: and if children, then heirs; heirs of God, and joint-heirs with Christ" (Romans 8:16–17).

But how do *we* get a clear vision of who we are? How do we gain an eternal perspective compelling enough to move us to action and to govern our choices and priorities? From whence cometh the vision?

I'm sensitive to the issue of vision at the moment, because I'm going through that midlife eye crisis where I can't seem to hold things far enough away for me to read them. Because of my changing eyesight, I find myself turning on lights and lamps everywhere.

Light is a key to vision! And Jesus Christ is the ultimate Light, the "light which shineth in darkness" (D&C 6:21), the light which chases "darkness from among [us]" (D&C 50:25). Faith in Jesus Christ is the key to vision, to seeing ourselves as the Lord sees us. So to improve our vision, we must increase our faith in and connection to the Savior.

It is no accident that faith—not only *believing in* Jesus Christ but *believing* him—is the first principle of the gospel. President Gordon B. Hinckley has said that "of all our needs, I think the greatest is an increase in faith."[2]

"Blessed art thou, Nephi," the son of Lehi was told, "because thou believest in the Son of the most high God" (1 Nephi 11:6). In Alma's brilliant discourse we are told, "If ye will awake and arouse your faculties, even to an experiment upon my words, and exercise a particle of faith, yea, even if ye can no more than desire to believe, let this desire work in you, even until ye believe in a manner that ye can give place for a portion of my words" (Alma 32:27).

Can't you just hear the Savior saying, "If you only *want* to believe that I will do for you what I have said I will do, will you experiment? Try me. Put me to the test."

As Lehi and his family learned, their Liahona worked according to their faith in God (Alma 37:40). When they became slothful in their devotions and ceased to exercise faith, the marvelous works ceased. That is in keeping with divine law, for, as Elder James E. Talmage taught, "Faith is of itself a principle of power; and by its presence or absence, . . . even the Lord was and is influenced, and in great measure controlled, in the bestowal or withholding of blessings."[3] Therefore, let us not "be slothful because of the easiness of the way. . . . The way is prepared, and if we will look we may live forever" (Alma 37:46).

Looking. Seeing. Seeking our own vision.

We sometimes tend to define unbelievers as apostates or agnostics. But perhaps that definition is too narrow. What about those of us who have received a witness of the divinity of the Savior and yet deep in our hearts don't believe he will come through for us? We believe he'll do it for others—for President Hinckley, the Quorum of the Twelve, the stake Relief Society president—but not for us.

Have you ever carefully selected a gift for someone only to present the gift and have it fall flat? Perhaps a simple "Thanks" feels nonchalant and even ungrateful. Similarly, it must be disappointing to the Lord, who offered the ultimate sacrifice, when we by our unbelief essentially refuse his gift and therefore his offer of help.

Not long ago a friend who is a respected gospel scholar told me about a fireside he had given on the power of the Atonement. Two sisters came up to him afterwards and said, "What you have taught is great, but frankly it sounds too good to be true."

The Lord's gift to us *is* too good to be true—which makes a tepid reaction to that gift all the more regrettable. More than once Nephi chastened his older brothers for their unbelief: "How is it that ye have forgotten that the Lord is able to do all things according to his will, for the children of men, if it so be that they exercise faith in him?" (1 Nephi 7:12).

How indeed? It is a question we might ask ourselves. The Lord *can* do all things. But it is our faith in him, even our willingness to believe, that activates the power of the Atonement in our lives. "We are made alive in Christ because of our faith" (2 Nephi 25:25). I love Nephi's words when he tells his brothers, speaking of the Lord, "And he loveth those who will have him to be their God" (1 Nephi 17:40). Or in other words, those who accept him and his gift.

One would think it would be easy to embrace and have faith in the gift of the Atonement. But I fear that some Latter-day Saint women know just enough about the gospel to feel guilty that they are not measuring up to some undefinable standard but not enough about the Atonement to feel the peace and strength it affords us. Elder Bruce R. McConkie said that too often the best-kept secret in the Church is the gospel of Jesus Christ. Perhaps some of us don't know how to draw the power of the Atonement into our lives; others aren't willing to seek its blessings. And some don't ask because they don't feel worthy. It's quite the irony that the gospel of the great Jehovah, which contains the power to save every human being and to strengthen every soul, is sometimes interpreted in such a way that feelings of inadequacy result.

Do you remember the exchange in the animated classic *The Lion King* between the deceased King Mufasa and his lion cub, Simba, who turns to riotous living after his father's death? Simba sees his father in a vision, and when he attempts to justify his aimless lifestyle, his father teaches him a divine truth: "You have forgotten who you are because you have forgotten me." Truman Madsen has said that the cruelest thing you can do to a human being is to make him forget that he or she is the son or daughter of a king. There is a direct relationship between our personal experience with the Lord and how we see ourselves. The closer we grow to him, the more clear and complete becomes our vision of who we are and what we can become.

I have tender feelings about the connection between our faith in the Lord and the way we see ourselves, because I have spent much of my life struggling to feel that I measured up. Growing up, I was painfully shy. The phrase "social reject" comes to mind. To make matters worse, I hit five-foot-ten in the sixth grade. Five-foot-ten is not a popular height for a sixth-grade girl. I was a Mormon in a very non-Mormon community. The fact that I had a great jump shot didn't translate well socially. The guys were my best friends—but not my dates. And I was a farm girl. Though our little town had all of four thousand residents, there was a clear social distinction between the town kids and the country kids. I laugh about this now. But it wasn't very funny then. There was nothing cool about being a tall, sturdy (as Grandma used to call me), Mormon farm girl. I couldn't do what my friends did or go where they went. I was different, and for a teenager, different is deadly.

The summer after my sophomore year in high school I had an experience that convinced me I was destined to a life of mediocrity. Our small MIA went to Education Week at Brigham Young University, and one of the classes I attended was on the dreaded topic of self-esteem. One day, mid-lecture, the presenter suddenly pointed at me and asked me to stand and introduce myself. I could manage nothing more than to mumble my name and slump back down in my chair. It was pathetic.

I had obviously not demonstrated what the speaker was hoping for, so she pointed to another young woman in the audience—a tall, thin girl with beautiful, long hair. Poise oozed out of her cells as she stood and introduced herself, concluding with a gracious word of thanks to the speaker for her marvelous presentation. All the while I was thinking, "Oh, sit down. She didn't ask for a eulogy." But the comparison between the two of us wasn't lost on me. The lecturer only made things worse when she said, "It seems that the young girl from Kansas doesn't feel as good about herself as the girl from Salt Lake City does."

I can still picture myself in the back seat of our car as we drove home to Kansas. Between little bursts of tears, I contemplated the future, and things didn't look promising. I didn't measure up, and I feared I never would. Now I don't want to overstate things. I had great experiences growing up, and I had disappointing experiences—just like you. But I suffered with a deep feeling of inadequacy.

My insecurities followed me to college at the Y, and as a result I suffered socially, scholastically, and spiritually. When, during graduate school, a friendship ended in a disappointing way, I hopped in my little Toyota and drove home for a few days of consolation. For a week I moped around the house feeling sorry for myself. Then one afternoon I walked down to my brother's room and noticed his journal on his nightstand. Brad was thirteen, and I thought it might be fun to see what pearls of wisdom he had written. The entries were predictable—about sports and girls and motorcycles. But then I came to the entry he had made the day I arrived home unexpectedly from BYU: "Sheri came home from BYU today. I'm so glad she's home. But she doesn't seem very happy. I wish there was something I could do to help her, because I really love her."

As you can imagine, the tears began to flow. But the sweet emotions unleashed by my brother's words triggered an even more powerful sensation, for almost instantly I had a profound feeling of divine love and acceptance wash over me and, simultaneously, a very clear impression that I ought to quit focusing on everything I didn't have, because I had enough, and start doing something with what I did have.

For me, it was a profound moment. I didn't pop up and suddenly feel confident about life, but I couldn't deny that the Spirit had spoken and that the Lord loved me and felt I had something to contribute. It was the beginning of seeing myself with new eyes.

Now let's fast-forward a decade to my early thirties when I faced a personal disappointment that broke my heart. From a point of view distorted by emotional pain, I couldn't believe that anything or anyone could take away the loneliness or that I would ever feel whole or happy again. In an effort to find peace, comfort, and strength, I turned to the Lord in a way I had not before. The scriptures became a lifeline, filled as they were with promises I had never noticed in quite the same way—that he would heal my broken heart and take away my pain, that he would succor, or run to, me and deliver me from disappointment.

Fasting and prayer took on new intensity, and the temple became a place of refuge and revelation. What I learned was not only that the Lord could help me but that he would. Me. A regular, farm-grown member of the Church with no fancy titles or spectacular callings. It was during that agonizing period that I began to discover how magnificent, penetrating, and personal the power of the Atonement is.

I pleaded with the Lord to change my circumstances, because I knew I could never be happy until he did. Instead, he changed my heart. I asked him to take away my burden, but he strengthened me so that I could bear my burdens with ease (see Mosiah 24:15). I had always been a believer, but I'm not sure I had understood what, or who, it was I believed in.

President George Q. Cannon described what I experienced: "When we went forth into the waters of baptism and covenanted with our Father in Heaven to serve Him and keep His commandments, He bound Himself also by covenant to us that He would never desert us, never leave us to ourselves, never forget us, that in the midst of trials and hardships, when everything was arrayed against us, He would be near unto us and would sustain us. That was His covenant."[4]

And it all begins with the willingness to believe. "For if there be no faith among the children of men God can do no miracle among them" (Ether 12:12).

Do you believe that the Savior will really do for *you* what he has said he will do? That he can ease the sting of loneliness and enable you to deal with that haunting sense of inadequacy? That he will help you forgive? That he can fill you with optimism and hope? That he will help you resist your greatest temptation and tame your most annoying weakness? That he will respond to your deepest longing? That he is the only source of comfort, strength, direction, and peace that will not change, will not betray you, and will never let you down?

An unwillingness to believe that the Savior stands ready to deliver us from our difficulties is tantamount to refusing the gift. It is tragic when we refuse to turn to him who paid the ultimate price and let him lift us up. *Life is a test.* But divine assistance is available to help us successfully complete this most critical examination.

Since that difficult period ten years ago, I have had many opportunities to experience the workings of the Lord in my life. He hasn't always given me what I've asked, and the answers haven't always come easily. But he has never left me alone, and he has never let me down.

Each experience with the Savior leads to greater faith, and as our faith increases, our vision of and confidence about who we are grows clearer. The more we visualize and sense through the impressions of the

Spirit our ultimate potential, the more determined we become to achieve it. It's the difference between your mother hounding you to practice the piano and your reaching the point where you want to do it yourself. You simply will not be denied the ultimate reward.

Why is it vital that we as LDS women have a clear vision of who we are and what we are about and have a bedrock faith in the Lord Jesus Christ?

Sister Patricia Holland said something that I find profound: "If I were Satan and wanted to destroy a society, I think I too would stage a full-blown blitz on women."[5]

Is that not exactly what he has done? Hasn't he tried to discourage and distract us in every conceivable way? Doesn't he try to block our understanding of how spiritually sensitive our natures are, how anxious and willing the Lord is to speak to us, and how vital we are to the plan and purposes of the Lord? Satan wants us neutralized, because he knows that the influence of a righteous woman can span generations.

His stated purposes are clear: he desires to make us miserable like unto himself (see 2 Nephi 2:27). He wants us to fail the test, to give up any hope of the Big Finish. Peter delivered a no-nonsense warning: "Be sober, be vigilant; because your adversary the devil, as a roaring lion, walketh about, seeking whom he may devour" (1 Peter 5:8). Indeed, through eons of practice the adversary has perfected the arts of deception, deceit, despair, and discouragement.

Many of his tactics are bold and brazen and played out daily on everything from the internet to the nightly news. But despite the fact that the adversary's handiwork is outrageously displayed at every turn—pornography, abuse, addiction, dishonesty, violence, and immorality of every kind—many of his strategies are brilliant for their subtlety. "And others will he pacify, and lull them away into carnal security, that they will say: All is well in Zion; yea, Zion prospereth, all is well—and thus the devil cheateth their souls, and leadeth them away carefully down to hell" (2 Nephi 28:21). C. S. Lewis said something similar: "The safest road to Hell is the gradual one—the gentle slope, soft underfoot, without sudden turnings, without milestones, without signposts."[6]

See if any of the following techniques sound familiar:

1. As we have been discussing, Satan tries to blur our vision of why we're here and get us preoccupied with this life. He would have us

distracted by and involved in anything and everything except what we came for.

2. He wants us to feel insignificant—that no matter how hard we try, we'll never make much of a difference. Oh, sure, our work is necessary but not very important. *That is a big fat lie.* It is a diversion designed to keep us so focused on any perceived injustices that we completely overlook the opportunities and privileges that are ours, that we underestimate the vital nature of our contribution, and that we never come to understand the power we have to change lives.

Elder Henry D. Moyle said: "I have a conviction deep down in my heart that we are exactly what we should be, each one of us. . . . I have convinced myself that we all have those peculiar attributes, characteristics, and abilities which are essential for us to possess in order that we may fulfil the full purpose of our creation here upon the earth. . . .

" . . . that allotment which has come to us from God is a sacred allotment. It is something of which we should be proud, each one of us in our own right, and not wish that we had somebody else's allotment. Our greatest success comes from being ourselves."[7]

The world can make us feel that we're just another number—to the IRS, to the bank, to the guy who reads the gas meter. Every time I go to New York City on business, and though I love the pulse of that city, I feel swallowed up—by hundreds of skyscrapers that block the light from reaching the ground and by a sea of black limousines carrying important people doing important things. The sheer number of people can make you feel like a tiny blob in a mass of humanity. And yet the Great Jehovah, the creator of worlds without numbers, has extended the unparalleled invitation for us to come unto him one by one (see 3 Nephi 11:15). He who knows even when the sparrow falls also knows our names, our needs, and our desires.

The gospel, with its sanctifying and redeeming power, is available to all. "Thus we may see that the Lord is merciful unto all [I love that word] who will, in the sincerity of their hearts, call upon his holy name. Yea, thus we see that the gate of heaven is open unto all, even to those who will believe on the name of Jesus Christ" (Helaman 3:27–28). There are no qualifiers relative to age, appearance, intellect or talent, marital status, ethnicity, social standing, or church calling. When I think of the times in my life that I have felt excluded—because I didn't have the right marital status, or the right look, or the right social connection—it comforts me to know that the Keeper of the ultimate gate, the Host whose guest list I most want to be included on, has placed no limitations on my accessibility to him. He has invited *all* of us to come unto him, to learn to hear his voice, to attach and commit ourselves to him, and to ultimately enter his presence. During the Mount Timpanogos Temple dedication, President Gordon B. Hinckley said that in the temple there is no aristocracy, "only the aristocracy of righteousness."[8] All of us are eligible to come unto Him to the extent to which we seek to take upon us the name of Christ and reflect his image in our countenances. For he has promised, "Every soul who forsaketh his sins and cometh unto me, and calleth on my name, and obeyeth my voice, and keepeth my commandments, shall see my face and know that I am" (D&C 93:1).

3. Satan tries to wear us down by creating the image that there is nothing glamorous in enduring to the end. It's the very reason I learned the Big Finish first, to keep the ultimate reward in front of me so that I would keep practicing those difficult technical passages that required as much endurance as skill. I have always hated talks on enduring to the end because the very phrase makes life seem like drudgery rather than an adventure. And yet the most haunting regret imaginable would be to pass through the veil and, with the full sweep of eternity opened before our eyes, realize that we had sold our birthright for a mess of pottage, that we had been deceived by the distractions of Satan, and that the Big Finish would never be.

4. The adversary encourages us to judge and evaluate each other—a practice that is demeaning both to the person who judges and to the one who is judged. Recently a young woman whose marriage has crumbled told me how much she loves the gospel but how weary she is of feeling that she'll never be accepted because her life hasn't unfolded as she expected it to. If there is anyplace in the world where every one of us should feel accepted, needed, valued, and loved, it is as sisters in The Church of Jesus Christ of Latter-day Saints. We ought to give up telling each other how to live our lives. It is wonderful to talk about principles, which apply equally to each of us, but it is rarely helpful to suggest how those principles should be applied.

For example, our prophet has spoken clearly about the importance of building strong families. That's the principle. How that is accomplished, however, will vary from family to family. We could do more good by encouraging each other to develop our spiritual sensitivities so that we can receive inspiration about our own lives. The need for spiritual acuity is universal, for the Lord is in the best position to give advice.

5. Lucifer whispers that life's not fair and that if the gospel were true, we would never have problems or disappointments. Bad things shouldn't happen to good members of the Church, should they? The adversary would have us believe that with baptism comes a Magic Kingdom Club Card and that if our lives aren't like perpetual trips to Disney World, we're getting short-changed.

The gospel isn't a guarantee against tribulation. That would be like a test with no questions. Rather, the gospel is a guide for maneuvering through the challenges of life with a sense of purpose and direction. "I feel happy," President Brigham Young said. "'Mormonism' has made me all I am, and the grace, the power, and the wisdom of God will make me all that I ever will be, either in time or in eternity."[9]

6. The adversary attempts to numb us into accepting a sliding scale of morality. Sometimes rationalization overtakes even the best among us. "R-rated movies don't bother me," we sometimes hear. "I go for the story, or the music, and skip over the profanity and the sexually explicit scenes." Yet advertisers pay millions of dollars for a few seconds of airtime on the bet that during brief but repeated exposures to their products we'll be persuaded to try them. If sixty-second ads can influence us to spend money we don't have to buy things we don't need to impress people we don't even like, then how will minutes, hours, months, and years of watching infidelity, violence, and promiscuity affect us? The litmus test for entertainment of any kind is simple: Can you watch or participate in it and still have the Spirit with you?

7. The adversary promotes feelings of guilt—about anything. Pick a topic. You can feel guilty for having a large family—how can any one woman possibly care for eight or nine children? Or for having no children at all—you're not doing your duty. For working outside the home— don't you know what the prophet has said about mothers who seek employment? Or for choosing to stay home—what's the matter, no ambition?

Guilt does not originate with the Savior, who invites us to step to a higher way of living and a more ennobling way of thinking, to do a little better and perhaps a little more. Promptings that come from him are hopeful and motivating rather than defeating or discouraging.

8. Lucifer works hard to undermine our innate tendency to nurture

and care for others. His object is to get us so busy and caught up in the "thick of thin things" that we don't have time for each other. Voice messaging is efficient, but it doesn't replace a listening ear and a caring heart. If the adversary can cause us to focus more on our differences than on our similarities, if he can confuse us about who our sisters are and what their eternal potential is, if he can keep us so busy running from one commitment to another that we no longer have time for each other, he has made great strides towards neutralizing the strength and influence that we have.

We need each other. We need each other's testimonies and strength, each other's confidence and support, understanding, and compassion. It is as Martin Luther said: "The kingdom of God is like a besieged city surrounded on all sides by death. Each man [and woman] has [a] place on the wall to defend and no one can stand where another stands, but nothing prevents us from calling encouragement to one another."[10]

9. The adversary would have us hung up on perfection and stymied by the commandment to become perfect. He wants this glorious potential to loom as a giant stumbling block rather than the promise of what is ultimately possible—in other words, to make the Big Finish seem little more than a dream. Every prophet in this dispensation has explained that we should expect not to achieve perfection in this lifetime. The goal instead is to become pure, so that we are increasingly receptive to the promptings of the Holy Ghost.

The Savior doesn't want us to be paralyzed by our errors but to learn and grow from them. He sees us as works in progress. The faith of the brother of Jared was so strong that he was allowed to behold the Lord (see Ether 3:13). Yet prior to that remarkable event, there was a time when the Lord chastened him for three hours (see Ether 2:14). If the scriptural account had ended there, minus the "rest of the story," our impression of this righteous man would be different. The rest of *our* stories remains to be told. It is purity, rather than perfection, that we are seeking at this stage of our eternal quest.

10. Lucifer would have us so busy—with family, friends, careers, and every soccer league in town—that there's no time to live the gospel. No time to fast and pray, to immerse ourselves in the scriptures, to worship in the temple—all the things we need to do to "study" for our mortal test. In other words, he wants us to be a little more concerned with the

world than with the gospel, a little more interested in life today than in life forever.

11. He delights in portraying religion as something restrictive and austere rather than liberating and life-giving. He depicts the Father and the Son as aloof rulers rather than our deified Father and Elder Brother who love us, who have a vested interest in our future, and whose motive is to help see us through this life so that we are worthy to return to them. He paints eternal life as something out of reach, even other-worldly, something for prophets and a few other select people, a condition you and I could never hope to achieve. And he does everything he can to block the memory of our former home.

He loves it when we seek for security in bank accounts, social status, or professional credentials when ultimate security and peace of mind come only from a connection with the Lord Jesus Christ. He claims victory when we rely on others for spiritual strength—on husbands, leaders, friends, family members. He doesn't want us to find out how intimate our connection with our Father and Elder Brother can be and how palpable and sustaining their love is.

In short, he tries to keep us at arm's length from Jesus Christ. Oh fine, if we profess him to be the Savior—talk is cheap. And if the adversary can keep us so distracted that we never really seek, embrace, and commit ourselves to the Lord, then we will also never discover the healing, strengthening, comforting power available because of the Atonement. We will never know that because of the Savior we have access to everything we need to pass this test.

The antidote to the distractions of the adversary is Jesus Christ. Light *is* stronger than darkness. Jesus Christ illuminates our vision of who we are and why we are here and gives us courage to move forward in the journey toward our heavenly home. The potential reward *is* too good to be true, a Big Finish that makes Rachmaninoff pale by comparison.

Just as Satan's motives have been clearly identified, so are the Savior's, whose express work and glory is to "bring to pass the immortality and eternal life of man" (Moses 1:39). "He doeth not anything save it be for the benefit of the world; for he loveth the world, even that he layeth down his own life that he may draw all men unto him" (2 Nephi 26:24). The contrast between the Savior and Satan is stunning. It is the quintessential difference between light and dark, arrogance and

199

humility, self-interest and charity, power used to destroy and power used to bless. It is the battle between good and evil personified.

Eleven years ago President Ezra Taft Benson issued this charge: "There has never been more expected of the faithful in such a short period of time than there is of us. Never before on the face of this earth have the forces of evil and the forces of good been as well organized. . . . The final outcome is certain—the forces of righteousness will win. But what remains to be seen is *where* each of us . . . will stand in the battle— and *how tall* we will stand. . . . Great battles can make great heroes and heroines."[11] You have been called to live and work and raise families in the twilight of the dispensation of the fulness of times, and you are nothing less than the best the Lord has ever had. You are heroines in every sense of that word, which is why the Lord needs us to arise and be everything we can be. President Howard W. Hunter put it this way: "There is a great need to rally the women of the Church to stand with and for the Brethren in stemming the tide of evil that surrounds us and in moving forward the work of our Savior. . . . Only together can we accomplish the work he has given us to do and be prepared for the day when we shall see him."[12]

I believe him. The impact of righteous, determined, pure-hearted women today is immeasurable. It doesn't matter where you live, whether or not you have children, how much money you have, or how talented you think you are—or aren't. This is a day when the Lord and his kingdom need women who are firmly grounded in their testimony of Jesus Christ, women of vision who have their sights trained on the purpose of life. Women who can hear the voice of the Lord, expose the distractions of the adversary for what they are, and press forward with a sense of purpose and a desire to contribute. Women who are articulate as well as compassionate. Women who understand who they are. And where they are going. And are determined to not let anything keep them from getting there.

Good women all over the world are desperate for leadership, for role models, for the assurance borne out in lives well lived that families are important, that virtue is not outdated, and that it is possible to feel peace and purpose in a society spinning out of control.

We have reason to be the most reassured, the most determined, the most confident of all women. In saying this, I don't minimize our personal disappointments. But we know what we're here for. And we know that we are beloved of the Lord.

We are members of the most important and potentially influential women's organization in the world, the only such organization founded by a prophet of God and led by women who do so under the direction of, and therefore with access to, the power of the priesthood of God. Remember President Spencer W. Kimball's statement nearly twenty years ago about the vital role righteous women would play during the "winding-up scenes" of this dispensation. Well, these are the winding-up scenes.

I have a friend who is an executive with a Fortune 500 company. One day we sparred verbally over a definition of the word *power*. His response interested me: "Power is influence. If you have influence, you wield power."

If my friend is right—and I am inclined to agree with him—then collectively and individually we have tremendous power. The influence of the sisters of this Church is overwhelming. We need not be shy or apologetic about who we are and what we believe. Nowhere else in the world are there 4.1 million women who, because of their beliefs and vision of the eternal possibilities, seek after and defend all that is virtuous, lovely, of good report, or praiseworthy—women who are devoted to building, lifting, helping, and loving. Talk about influence!

Who is better suited to defend the sanctity of home and family? Who better prepared to celebrate virtue and integrity? Who better to demonstrate by example that women can be strong and savvy and articulate without being shrill, angry, or manipulative?

Are we not like Captain Moroni's armies who, though vastly outnumbered, were "inspired by a better cause, for they were not fighting for monarchy nor power but they were fighting for their homes and their liberties, . . . yea, for their rites of worship and their church" (Alma 43:45).

You and I compose a pivotal battalion in the army of the Lord! Remember what happened when Captain Moroni hoisted the title of liberty? "Behold, whosoever will maintain this title upon the land, let them come forth in the strength of the Lord" (Alma 46:20).

May we arise as sisters in this, the greatest cause on earth. May we go forward together in the strength of the Lord. More than ever he needs our faith and faithfulness, our vitality and our ingenuity, our unwavering commitment and conviction. We are witnesses of the Lord Jesus Christ, the living capstone of all that has come before us and a vital link to all that lies ahead.

This life is a test. It is also a glorious privilege. May we work toward the kind of Big Finish the apostle Paul described as he anticipated his journey back home: "I have fought a good fight, I have finished my course, I have kept the faith: henceforth there is laid up for me a crown of righteousness, which the Lord . . . shall give me at that day" (2 Timothy 4:7–8).

May we build and keep the faith. May we go forward together with a clear vision of who we are, what we are about, and how vital our contribution is to the Lord's kingdom. This is The Church of Jesus Christ of Latter-day Saints. We can make the difference the Lord needs us to make. I know we can. More importantly, he knows we can. For in the strength of the Lord, we can do all things.

NOTES

1. Joseph F. Smith, *Gospel Doctrine* (Salt Lake City: Deseret Book, 1939), 13–14.
2. Gordon B. Hinckley, *Ensign*, November 1987, 54.
3. James E. Talmage, *Jesus the Christ* (Salt Lake City: The Church of Jesus Christ of Latter-day Saints, 1949), 318.
4. George Q. Cannon, *Gospel Truth*, sel. Jerreld L. Newquist, 2 vols. (Salt Lake City: Deseret Book, 1974), 2:170.
5. Patricia Terry Holland, "'Many Things . . . One Thing,'" *A Heritage of Faith: Talks Selected from the BYU Women's Conferences* (Salt Lake City: Deseret Book, 1988), 17.
6. C. S. Lewis, *The Screwtape Letters* (Philadelphia: Fortress Press, 1980), 56.
7. Henry D. Moyle, *Improvement Era*, December 1952, 934.
8. Gordon B. Hinckley, Mount Timpanogos Utah Temple dedication, American Fork, Utah, 13–16 October 1996, in minutes recorded by Lowell Hardy.
9. Brigham Young, *Journal of Discourses*, 26 vols. (London: Latter-day Saints' Book Depot, 1854–86), 8:162.
10. Cited in Jeffrey R. Holland and Patricia T. Holland, "Considering Covenants: Women, Men, Perspective, Promises," *To Rejoice as Women: Talks from the 1994 Women's Conference* (Salt Lake City: Deseret Book, 1995), 105.
11. Ezra Taft Benson, "In His Steps," address to Church Educational System personnel, Anaheim, California, 8 February 1987.
12. Howard W. Hunter, *Ensign*, November 1992, 96.

"Get Thee behind Me": Thwarting Latter-day Deceits

TESSA MEYER SANTIAGO

The apostle Peter urged the early Christian Saints to "be sober, be vigilant; because your adversary the devil, as a roaring lion, walketh about, seeking whom he may devour" (1 Peter 5:8). Most of us recognize Satan's open warfare with good for what it is. In 2 Corinthians 11:13–14, however, Paul exhorts the Christians of Corinth to beware also of false prophets, "deceitful workers" who transform "themselves into the apostles of Christ. And no marvel; for Satan himself is transformed into an angel of light." Thus Satan, "the father of all lies" (Moses 4:4), can present himself as an angel, a counterfeit messenger of the Lord[1] supposedly on a divine errand in which he seeks the immortality and eternal life of men and women, but he is really on an errand to make all of us "miserable like unto himself" (2 Nephi 2:27). And how does he mislead us? By persuading us that we are following God's ways when, in reality, we are following the enticings of Satan. If the adversary can induce us to misinterpret our Father's errand for us, then we will never become what we are meant to be. To that end, subtle twists of the truth are even more effective than monstrous lies. I would like to examine a few of the deceits—the "wind[s] of doctrine . . . and cunning craftiness" (Ephesians 4:14)—by which Satan seeks to blind women's minds and distract their hearts, causing us to lose sight of our divine potential.

Tessa Meyer Santiago is a creative writer and a student at the J. Reuben Clark School of Law at Brigham Young University. She and her husband, Kevin Frank Santiago, are the parents of three children. She served a mission to Boston, Massachusetts, and teaches the Gospel Doctrine class in Sunday School.

DECEIT 1: DIVINE DEMANDS ARE RESTRICTIVE

According to the Gospel of Luke, God sent the angel Gabriel "to a virgin espoused to a man whose name was Joseph . . . and the virgin's name was Mary" (Luke 1:27). In a few short moments, young Mary learned that she had "found favour with God" and would "bring forth a son, and shalt call his name Jesus . . . [who] shall reign over the house of Jacob for ever" (Luke 1:30–31, 33). Surely this was shocking news. She was a virgin and promised to Joseph. At that time, tradition demanded that an unmarried woman found pregnant be made a public example. Mary could have objected or responded in a myriad of other ways. Instead, she replies, "Behold the handmaid of the Lord; be it unto me according to thy word" (Luke 1:38). What faith, what commitment to the will of God can be heard in her simple consent.

Cynics may say she had no choice: If God wanted this of her, who was she to refuse? Brigham Young clarifies this idea with truth: "It is a mistaken idea that God has decreed all things whatsoever that come to pass, for the volition of the creature is as free as air."[2] Mary might have refused. Just as Christ might have. "When he came in the flesh he was left free to choose or refuse to obey his Father. Had he refused to obey his Father, he would have become a son of perdition. We also are free to choose or refuse the principles of eternal life," Brigham Young explains.

President Young also refutes the common notion that choosing to obey the will of God is choosing *not* to exercise our independent agency. "God rules and reigns, and has made all his children as free as himself, to choose the right or the wrong. . . . Does it follow that a man is deprived of his rights, because he lists in his heart to do the will of God? [For instance,] Must a man swear to prove he has an agency? . . . I can manifest to the heavens and to the inhabitants of the earth that I am free-born, and have my liberty before God, angels and men, when I kneel down to pray, certainly as much as if I were to go out and swear. . . . [So] in rendering that strict obedience, are we made slaves? No, it is the only way on the face of the earth for you and me to become free. . . . All that the Lord requires of us is strict obedience to the laws of life."[3]

As Eliza R. Snow in hymn number 195 reminds us, "By strict obedience Jesus won the prize with glory rife: 'Thy will, O God, not mine be done,' adorned his mortal life."[4] Mary was great not only because she was chosen as the mother of Christ but because she positioned herself through her choices so that God could use her in his work. If we are to become women of Christ, we must learn to embrace the will of God. In return, Christ promises: "I [will] gather you as a hen gathereth her chickens under her wings" (3 Nephi 10:6).

DECEIT 2: THE WAY IS EASY

Alma teaches his son Corianton that it is "easy to give heed to the word of Christ, which will point to you a straight course to eternal bliss" (Alma 37:44). The word *easy* here may mislead some readers. Nephi teaches that the Lord works in plainness: he "worketh not in darkness" (2 Nephi 26:23) but "doeth that which is good among the children of men; and he doeth nothing save it be plain" (2 Nephi 26:33). Our Father's definition of *easy*, then, is clearly communicated concepts and expectations, simple directions that are easy to follow, and an outcome that blesses his children. Our Father's definition of *easy* includes, however, a significant exercise of faith, diligence, and endurance—the heartbreaking spiritual work required to enter the kingdom.

Satan, the author of confusion, would have us believe that an "easy way" is one of quick, instant gratification. But pleasure is not the purpose and goal of our existence. Joy is (see 2 Nephi 2:25). Satan wants us to confuse the two: shortchanging ourselves by trading in joy for pleasure. Standing in the grocery store checkout line, I read the following magazine covers: one easy exercise to a washboard stomach; sparkling windows in just minutes; thirty days to a slimmer you. And I buy into the myth of instant, pleasurable change, completely ignoring the fact that it's taken years of absolute neglect for my body and windows to get into their current states. I forget that the only instantaneous change I know of comes in that luminous instant when we are washed clean of sins through the Savior's redeeming blood. Yet, even then we must choose to remain clean. Satan would dissuade us from believing that work or endurance is part of the gospel of change. He wants us to expect that change is instantaneous. And then to be disappointed when it is not. If in our disappointment at finding work part of the equation, we abandon our efforts to become better, his work is done.

If the adversary cannot get us to abandon hope, he will entice us to cheat. By appealing to our laziness, greed, or pride, he would have us arrive at a worthwhile goal in the wrong manner. I have learned that it is not so much the destination but the way in which I journey that God scrutinizes. As a child, I often played a party game called blindman's bluff. Blindfolded, walking slowly with my hands stretched out before me, I tried to catch the other children in the room. Somehow, I managed to maneuver an eyelid, or wrinkle a cheek, so that I could peek. Of course, if asked "Can you see?!" I would lie. Lying somewhat lessened the thrill of catching my friends so quickly. Plus, every time I cheated, I heard a voice that sounded remarkably like my mother's whispering: "But you cheated, my darling. You could see."

When Satan sought to tempt Christ in the desert, he challenged him to turn stones into bread. Elder Jeffrey R. Holland explains the significance of this temptation: "Here Jesus experiences the real and very understandable hunger for food by which he must sustain his mortal life. . . . Why not eat? . . . Why not simply turn the stones to bread and eat? The temptation is *not* in the eating. . . . The temptation . . . is to do it *this way*, to get his bread—his physical satisfaction, relief for his human appetite—the easy way, by abuse of power and without a willingness to wait for the right time and the right way. It is the temptation to be the convenient Messiah. Why do things the hard way? Why walk to the shop—or bakery? Why travel all the way home? Why deny yourself satisfaction when with ever such a slight compromise you might enjoy this much-needed nourishment? But Christ will not ask selfishly for unearned bread. He will postpone gratification, indefinitely if necessary, rather than appease appetite . . . with what is not his."[5]

It is not that eating is wrong, or that it is wrong to want a house with a second bathroom or to seek a Harvard education for an academically gifted child. These are not unrighteous desires. What is wrong are the ways we sometimes attempt to gain the good things of the world: We would have them now, because everybody else apparently has them, and we are sometimes willing to forgo ethics and to compromise morality to obtain them.[6]

DECEIT 3: THE WAY MUST BE GRAND

The children of Israel were three months out of Egypt, grumbling and moaning, when "the Lord sent fiery serpents among the people, and they bit the people; and much people of Israel died. . . . And Moses made a serpent of brass, and put it on a pole" (Numbers 21:6, 9), providing a way for those who had been bitten to be healed. Still many of the children of Israel refused to look. Nephi comments: "The labor which they had to perform was to look; and because of the simpleness of the way, or the easiness of it, there were many who perished" (1 Nephi 17:41).

This year my husband Kevin and I decided to run a ten-kilometer race together. In preparation we have begun an exercise program devised by an authority from *Runner's World*. Unlike other exercise programs begun and abandoned, we have actually stuck to this one for three weeks, and the future looks promising. Here is why: the program allows us to exercise only thirty minutes a day for only four days a week. At first, Kevin, who once played basketball for Brigham Young University, found himself playing challenge games in his mind: "Well, it says to walk four minutes and then run one, but I can probably run two. In fact, I could probably pull off three. . . . Or maybe I'll just run until I throw up." He caught himself, realizing that such grandiose schemes would sabotage his efforts.

Later on, Kevin and I discussed how we damage ourselves by imagining that we are somehow better than the norm, that we can or need to run faster, swim longer, jump higher than required. Jacob said of the Jews that "they despised the words of plainness. . . . Wherefore, because of their blindness, which blindness came by looking beyond the mark, they must needs fall" (Jacob 4:14). How many of us cannot have family home evening unless there is a lesson, a hymn, a snack, and a colorful, neatly laminated job chart on the fridge? How many of us, launching a new scripture reading program, say to ourselves, "Okay, I'll read thirty minutes a day, and then I'll write in my journal, and then I'll study the Sunday School readings and the Relief Society manual"? After the second day, finding ourselves hopelessly swamped in our grandiose scheme, we abandon ship for some desert island with no scripture study at all. What about the meals we cook, the lessons we teach, the children we raise and the clothes we buy for them: how have we fallen because of our pride and stubborn insistence on doing things our way? In many cases, I find I have looked way beyond the mark, making the way not easy but fraught with difficulty and complexity where there should be plainness. The Lord counsels us: "Do not run faster or labor more than you have strength and means . . . but be diligent unto the end" (D&C 10:4).

Deceit 4: If I am an At-home Mom, My Home Must Be Perfect

Women who choose not to work outside their home sometimes labor under the misguided notion that the home itself reflects their mothering skills. They thus are bothered by the intrusion of children into the daily schedule of laundry, vacuuming, gardening, sorting, picking up, and putting away. Yes, a certain peace comes from living in an orderly, clean home. But I realize I have gone too far when I ban my son, Christian, from playing with his toys because his room is clean and I want it to stay that way.

My friend and visiting teacher, Gwen, has two beautiful daughters. This spring she also had a row of bright, cheerful tulips lining the front of her house. Maya, her four-year-old, one day brought her every single tulip bloom, leaving only headless stems to grace the front yard. Gwen said that just as she felt her body start to quiver with an imminent explosion, she thought, "What? Am I raising children or tulips?" President Ezra Taft Benson called the women of the Church home not to clean toilet bowls and wash dishes in immaculate houses but to teach children the gospel of Christ. If we think of ourselves only—or even primarily—as housekeepers, we neglect the next generation of souls.

Staying home also doesn't mean delaying the development of our God-given talents and abilities. Some husbands and wives believe—to the detriment of their own souls, the happiness of their families, and the health of their communities—that women who stay home have nothing else to offer the world. They mistakenly believe such women have no talents or that any talents they have must be used solely for the betterment of their families. They labor under the mistaken notion that "I have chosen to stay home to rear my children; therefore, I must delay the development of my skills and talents until I no longer have children at home." But a woman's circle of influence does not stop at the curb bordering her home. We must not underestimate the power and responsibility of our womanhood. We are equally under covenant both to rear and to teach our children and to recognize and develop our own considerable talents for the service of God.

DECEIT 5: WOMEN'S BODIES ARE TO BE ADMIRED FOR THEIR YOUTH AND BEAUTY

Perhaps one of the most discouraging struggles women endure is that never-ending battle with our own bodies. A woman's attitude toward her own body is fraught with misconceptions fueled by a world that celebrates an almost prepubescent female body as the ideal norm. Unfortunately for most of us, time moves on. We are no longer seventeen, a number of children have made their way through our birth canals, and gravity is exerting its inexorable pull. Whenever we look in the mirror, we are reminded of what we are not. Satan would have it just that way. He would have us think that because our bodies do not look a certain, supposedly desirable, way, they are not worth having at all. Thus, we enter into a war with our bodies, hating the very tabernacle our Father has given us, despising the flesh. If Satan can get us to fixate on our bodies, either in vanity or self-loathing, then he has caused us to misunderstand completely the role our bodies play in our salvation.

I was pregnant all one summer. I spent my time bobbing in the deep end of Deseret Towers' pool watching the women go by. I wondered why the women who had contributed the most to our society seemed to feel the least confident. Why did they cover their bodies as if in shame, disrobing only to plunge quickly down, their shoulders barely emerging above the waterline as they stood watching their children swim? Why did the freshman Deseret Towers' residents, young women who knew nothing of what breasts and hips and wombs are meant to do, rule, queens of the roost? In a better world, in a kinder, more saintly world, a mother's body would be kindly regarded, with respect and honor for what she has given, for what she has done. I am learning that a woman who mothers well gives all she has: body parts, internal organs, limbs. Some parts are temporarily donated; others, irreparably altered; most effects are permanent. And, if she lets this mothering sink into the marrow of her bones, if she allows the job of nurturing to wrestle with her spirit, a woman's soul is wrought in the image of God.

For me, having a woman's body has meant special tutoring in life and death. I have been pregnant four times. Each pregnancy ended in a surgical procedure. Three times out of four, my stomach and uterus have been cut open to retrieve, in all their bloody splendor, Julia, Christian, and Seth. Each time, I have entered the mother's valley of death, bringing my body under the knife, to lie still as someone cut into my flesh to release life from my womb. What should be a joyous moment is full of fear for me. At the birth of Seth, our youngest, I lay on the operating table trying so very hard to be brave. But I was petrified, and my body knew it: my pulse raced, I hyperventilated and vomited in an allergic reaction to the epidural. My eyes filled with tears. On one level, I desperately wanted to run from that certainty of pain and possibility of death. Yet I had no other choice if I wanted the life within me to live.

As I lay on the table, my mind filled with the image of Annie Dillard's tomcat, who would jump through her bedroom window at night covered with the blood of his kill. When she awoke she would find herself "covered with paw prints in blood." "I looked as though I'd been painted with roses," she recalled. Annie would ask herself, "What blood was this, and what roses? It could have been the rose of union, the blood of murder, or the rose of beauty bare and the blood of some unspeakable sacrifice or birth."[7] She never knew exactly how to read "the midnight canvas." And I never know when I am on that delivery table exactly what is happening to me. Am I the site of some unspeakable horror or some unspeakable joy? Paradoxically, I am both: An open womb, a uterus pulled out onto my abdomen; an immense pressure, an indignant cry, and a wrinkled old man's face that looks at me from beneath the hospital beanie like a Sharpei puppy. Only after I place my swollen, reluctant body on the table can I hear those first sounds of life. And no, the recovery is never swift in return for my heroism. My stomach has been bisected, the severed nerves need to learn to stop screaming. My bowels remain sluggish from the epidural; my head pounds from the allergic reaction I have known was coming since my first pregnancy.

As I battle through the pains, my body begins to make milk for the child who needs to be fed. When I am barely coherent, unable to sit up, the nurses bring my newborn to me. "He's hungry," they say. "Put him to the breast." So I struggle upright, ignoring the burning incision, to cradle the little body that was so recently inside me. I turn his mouth to me and do for my son what he cannot do for himself. And I understand a little more now how the Savior would "take upon him death, that he may loose the bands of death which bind his people" (Alma 7:12). The demands and duties of life, of the soul, take precedence over the travails of the body.

The third of my four pregnancies ended in death. On a long November Monday morning, I labored for ten hours, knowing that the end would produce only the misshapen fetus that my body in its wisdom knew to expel. While my body tried to perform the labor which it knew was necessary, my spirit keened. Medicine calls it a spontaneous abortion. But I have no name for the desolate feeling that clouded my spirit as my body labored. I knew only my baby would not be born the same week my Emperor tulips were scheduled to appear. I knew I could reshelve the baby name books and stop doodling "Nicholas Kevin Santiago" on sacrament meeting programs. I knew my sister-in-law and I would not give my parents their twelfth and thirteenth grandchildren a mere three weeks apart after all. But most of all, I knew I wanted with all my heart to have another child, and I grieved for what was not to be.

But I did not grieve alone. In that valley of desolation brought on by physical travail, I believe the Savior sent angels to be with me, to succor me in my infirmity: My sister who rubbed my back, changed the bath water, and who, while I was at the hospital, cleaned my house, did my laundry, and fed my children; nurses who looked at me with compassion, calling me "dear, sweet Tess," their words a consolation, "how sorry I am you are here"; women, who knew and had also labored in vain, whose eyes looked at me with a special sweetness; a doctor who, sensitive to my pain, chose to shield me from a surgical procedure in the sterility of his office and instead administered a blissful ignorance through anesthesia as he cleaned my womb of what had been the promise of a child. Most comforting of all, the Lord gave me a husband who held my hand and stood by, waiting and watching, feeling helpless to stop my pain, wishing he could endure for me. I found him sobbing in his office three days later; he too had lost a child. In all my pain, no one had noticed his. Yet, I believe we both felt the arms of the Savior around us healing our hearts in the aftermath of that dreadful week. We felt our neighbors' tears, their hearts aching, sorrowing for our pain; we heard the faint whisperings of another child in time; we learned lessons in patience from Him who would gather us in his arms as a mother hen would gather her chicks.

Could I have broken my heart to the will of the Lord another way? Would I have come so heavy laden and willingly to the Savior's yoke? I don't know. I do know that the death of a small, misshapen body brought light to my soul that perhaps could not have entered any other way. I cannot help but think, as I remember those births, that this human body, also can make us most divine—that the peculiar pains of a woman's flesh teach her exquisitely, intimately. What they teach she cannot know beforehand or even know that she needs to know. But when the pain subsides or is grown accustomed to, she realizes that some time during the darkest of nights or mundanest of mornings, knowledge has descended like the dews from heaven and enlarged her soul.

Unfortunately, the experience has also enlarged her hips and thighs. If she's anything like me, she bears the physical scars of that battlefield: the burst blood vessel on my left cheek appeared during labor with Julia. It still spreads spidery-red fingers across my face. The root canal brought on by my pregnancy with Christian left me with a porcelain crown. A seven-inch, maroon scar bisects my lower abdomen. Just below it is another, faded to flesh. Stretch marks ornament my breasts and hips like silver ribbons. My hips are two sizes wider, my feet a size bigger than when I was married—my very bones have expanded in response to my mothering. Some of the effects are temporary, just for the moments of pregnancy: the bleeding gums, the weakened bladder, the hair that falls out in clumps, the intermittent back pain, and aching hips. These pass in their time, but the memory remains.

In that memory lies the glory of this earthly body: though we may be resurrected in a perfect frame, the lessons taught me by my mother-body will rise with me. The sacrifice, the pain, the fear and faith of my mothering will sink into my soul and remain with me in the eternities. My spirit and this woman's body inseparably connected constitute my fullness of joy. Time writes its messages on all of us. Our very bodies have become our book of life, "an account of our obedience or disobedience written in our bodies."[8] To what have we been obedient? To the purpose for which we were made: to provide a body and a safe haven for the spirits entrusted to our care. If we mother well, we wear out our lives bringing to pass the lives of others. Of the physical fruits—our wider hips, our sagging breasts, our flatter feet, and rounder buttocks—we need not be so ashamed.

DECEIT 6: YOUTH IS THE OPTIMAL PHYSICAL AND SPIRITUAL STATE

In the book *Tuesdays with Morrie,* the author observes as he drives to visit his dying university professor that nobody on a billboard is over the age of thirty-five.[9] A subtle adversary has devised a world fixated on youth. Magazine covers present the faces of women, airbrushed to erase any trace of aging or wisdom. Hair is lightened, eyelids tucked, cheeks acid peeled. I pale in comparison. I am left, if I allow myself to be so influenced, feeling worthless, insignificant, unattractive in a sagging, stretch-marked body. Even though Nephi tells us, quite beautifully, that "death hath passed upon all men [and women], to fulfil the merciful plan of the great Creator" (2 Nephi 9:6), many of us cling stubbornly to vestiges of youth. Satan would have it no other way, for with age normally comes wisdom and the ability to live your life according to God's plan. Experience, sweet or sad, is a grueling schoolmaster.

About twelve miles south of Provo, Rose Bleazard Castagno rests in her daughter's bedroom. Grandma Rose is dying: diabetes, a diseased spleen, a hole in her eighty-four-year-old heart. Her life has been a stalwart example of faith: homesteading with Stanley, her husband, and an ice-house near Stansbury Island in the Great Salt Lake, four children and two miscarriages, widowed at age forty, a mission to England in her fifties as a single sister. She can ride a horse like a rodeo queen; she got me hooked on parsnips in my pot roasts. She has much to tell this world of endurance, faith, sacrifice, and the love of the Savior. Can I not learn more from her than from the celebrity on Jay Leno's show last night, a twenty-two-year-old movie actor with large, white teeth holding court while America watched?

Our culture would have us learn nothing from our experience. The "truths" it espouses are those of an adolescent world: true love is the pitter-patter of hearts as that tenth grader walks by your locker; if I no longer feel *that* every time I look at Kevin, then I must not love him. True beauty is young, unblemished, rosy cheeked and golden haired; if I do not fit that criteria, I must not be beautiful. True worth is being able to eat with the cool kids in the cafeteria; if I take a sack lunch, I am a geek. Style is the latest clothes with brand names ablazing; if I trade off wearing the same two dresses to church, I must not be stylish. Flair comes from breaking the rules; if I am absolutely obedient, I am dull. The list continues. Adolescent theories about worth, popularity, beauty, wealth, and rules masquerade as truth in our adult worlds. We need to recognize them for what they are and root them out.

Deceit 7: Better to make no choice than the wrong choice

When Satan was cast out of the heavens, he "sought to destroy the agency of man" (Moses 4:3). This was and will ever be his primary purpose. At every turn he seeks to undermine, confuse, and paralyze our ability to choose. He often does this by introducing fear into the choice process.

When Kevin and I started the arduous task of car shopping, we approached this venture, new to both of us, with all the diligence of deciding what college to attend or what to name our child. Actually our decision-making styles are considerably different: Kevin likes to deliberate painfully, considering every angle, determined to get it right. I just dive in with my eyes closed and hope I will be blessed for my courage, if not my intelligence.

Whatever our styles, our Heavenly Father's plan ably equips all of us to make choices; we are given opposition, agency, the gift of the Holy Ghost, time, and the Atonement to repent of any unwise decisions and their consequences. We have been taught that we are to make wise choices after prayer, deliberation, using our common sense; however, because most of us desire so strongly to make the right choice that the process is wrought with fear. Deciding what is right or wrong becomes very difficult for us. Deciding between two rights complicates matters even more.

Satan's strategy is to remove the Atonement from the decision-making process. He would have us believe that we have one and only one chance in which to get things right. Otherwise, we will be in his power. That unjustified but very powerful fear freezes many righteous women right in their tracks: should I marry this man, should I remarry, should I return to school, should I serve a mission, should I run for political office, should I leave this marriage, should I be raising my children this way, should I join this church? All crucial and significant questions to ask, all with large, sometimes eternal consequences. Because we desire to make the right choice, we make no choice until we know unequivocally that God has directed us. Unfortunately, most times God will not appear as a pillar of light to show us the way. He will speak to us through the gentle voice of his Spirit, perhaps best detected by a faithful, fearless heart. He has also promised that he will light the way through the darkness but only after we have taken the first steps. We must learn to act by faith to solve our earthly problems. Excessive fear of choice impedes our progress and nullifies the precious gift of agency.

To believe that a loving Father would give his children only one chance to choose wisely is the equivalent of asking my four-year-old son Christian to line up all the alphabet letters on our fridge in the correct order after showing him only once. Christian, in his eagerness to learn just like his older sister Julia, will do his earnest best, but I know he will make mistakes: after all, he still sings the song "lemon em o pee" and skips over fourteen, fifteen, and sixteen even though he has counted to twenty a hundred times in the last six months. He doesn't know or care that he is doing it wrong: he is delighted to be in the process of learning.

Adopting Christian's attitude is perhaps the greatest favor we may do ourselves regarding our agency. We must look at opportunities to choose as times for us to learn to use our agency wisely. If we continue to look at these choices as another chance to get it wrong, we will never progress beyond the fear of punishment into the gladness the gospel can bring. Many of us have progressed far enough in our spiritual lives, or at least in age, that the more obvious choices between right and wrong have already been made. We still, however, must learn to choose those things God would have us choose. In the decision-making process, the rejection of wrong and acceptance of right—meaning discovering the Lord's will for us—invests us with great personal spiritual momentum and confidence. We are then more fit to be used in our Father's kingdom. But we must learn first not to be afraid of our powerful responsibility to choose.

For some of us, the major decision to be made is whether to work or to remain home with our children. However we answer that question, once the decision has been made as prayerfully as possible, then that choice is over. What remains is the working out of that choice: how to mother or how to work and mother so that we can develop the qualities requisite for a woman of Christ. If every time we make a mistake on a project, or we spend hours sorting the toys into Ziploc freezer bags only to have the entire neighborhood descend en masse to unsort them, or we walk by our framed university diploma and wonder if we have chosen the wrong path—if every time something goes wrong, we run back to the site of our choice, wanting to dig it up and chew on it, like a dog to a buried bone, then we will find ourselves in constant motion but going nowhere. Perhaps we aren't going backwards, but we are at a standstill spiritually.

At times, we are so afraid to choose—because of the consequences—that we abdicate responsibility altogether for our agency. We would prefer not to choose. There are times that I wish Kevin would choose for me. Over the last few years, I have faced decisions about having another child, about whether to enter law school, about whether to return to teaching, about whether I should stop teaching. At each of these junctures, I have asked Kevin what he thinks I should do. Our conversation goes something like this:

"So, babe, do you think I should go to law school?"

"Oh, you would eat it up. You wouldn't even have to crack a book."

"No, I know I'll enjoy it, but do you think I should go?"

"Well, that's up to you to decide."

"But what will happen to the kids, and how will we do it as a family?" I ask.

"It's up to you. We'll manage if that's what you think we should do."

And there the conversation ends again: "It's up to you to decide." I hate that sentence. I wish sometimes Kevin would just tell me what to do: have another baby now, stop teaching now, write your book now—bring me my slippers now. But he doesn't. He leaves me to wallow in the marsh of my own choosing, turning options, listening to opinions, speaking to God in the car.

Why does he do this? Because when it's March, and the semester is three-quarters over, and I am two quarters behind, and students' papers litter the dining room table, I remember how I came to be there. Or when it's August, and one hundred degrees, and my hips are crumbling from the weight of the baby in my womb, in all my grumbling, I am brought back to the place of my decision. Revisiting that moment, I can say only, "Tessa, you chose this way. Now fulfill your responsibilities." Because my path has been of my own choosing, I must take full responsibility for the consequences. As I take the yoke of responsibility upon me, I am made able to bear the burdens of my choices. I come to understand that a loving Father will not desert his children in their time of need; that he will buoy us up as we work through this complicated maze of choice, agency, and personal responsibility.

I find it significant that our Father in Heaven rejected a plan by Satan that would have ensured the return of all his children. I envision a world under Satan's plan filled with Lamans and Lemuels: disgruntled because they had been told by somebody else what to do, even though that thing was good. When the hard times come, that world would fall to murmuring, rising up against the Lord's anointed because "they knew not the dealings of that God who had created them" (1 Nephi 2:12).

Some women, in a mistaken understanding of how the priesthood line of authority works, allow their husbands, or their bishops, or fathers to make their decisions for them. That is not a wise use of agency. Yes, we covenant to hearken unto the counsel of our husbands as they hearken unto the counsel of God. But we are entitled through our noble birthright as daughters of God to personal revelation and inspiration concerning our circles of influence. And we are duty-bound to work to obtain that inspiration, even at the peril of making a few unwise choices. At the judgment seat of God, our husbands will be called to give an account of their lives, not ours. Only we can stand before the bar of God to make an account of the earthly stewardships granted to us: our bodies, our children, our husbands, our intelligence, our talents, our time, our faith, testimonies and miracles, our communities, the sick and poor among us. These are our responsibilities, our chosen areas of stewardship. Some mistakenly believe that for a marriage to work, the woman must always acquiesce to her husband. Some remain silent, never challenging their husbands' ideas, believing they are being peace-makers.

If Satan can persuade a well-meaning woman to allow those around her to make her choices for her, then he effectively robs her of any spir-itual progress. She remains essentially a child, not knowing good from evil, not able to distinguish between the two and thus not able to teach her children how to choose or to equip them with the very vital skills of deliberation and decision. And so, the sins of a well-meaning but mis-led mother are visited on the children.

The scriptures contain many examples of women who understood the principle of choosing and then working through whatever consequences followed. For one, Eve "saw that the tree was good for food, and that it became pleasant to the eyes, and a tree to be desired to make her wise, she took the fruit thereof, and did eat" (Moses 4:12). As a consequence, she and Adam were cast out of the garden of Eden, with commandments to "worship the Lord their God, . . . offer the firstlings of their flocks, for an offering unto the Lord" (Moses 5:5), and "be fruitful, and multiply, and replenish the earth" (Moses 2:28). Upon heading into the lone and dreary world, Eve could have cursed a God who would desert his chil-dren. Instead, she "did labor with [her husband]" (Moses 5:1), "bare unto him sons and daughters" (Moses 5:2), and "was glad, saying: Were it not for our transgression we never should have had seed, and never should have known good and evil, and the joy of our redemption, and the eter-nal life which God giveth unto all the obedient" (Moses 5:11).

Agency is the supreme gift. Even our poorest choices can lead us to God in humility and gratitude for the Atonement. When Satan's origi-nal plan to take away all choice was frustrated, his second plan was to have us enjoy the power of choice but rob us of the humility wrought from suffering consequences. If we are to progress as women of Christ, we must exercise choice and learn from consequences.

So what is the solution? How do we overcome the temptations to misunderstand our role, to abdicate our responsibilities to choose, to take the shortcuts, to fear and doubt our own capacities? The task seems almost overwhelming. The solution, however, is quite simple: We need to believe, as strongly as we know Joseph saw God the Father and Jesus Christ in the Sacred Grove, that we are women of strength and power.

We need to recognize that fear and doubt come from the adversary, "for God hath not given us the spirit of fear; but of power, and of love, and of a sound mind" (2 Timothy 1:7). We need to rejoice in the privilege of our womanhood. Ultimately, we need to see ourselves as tools fit to build the kingdom of God. Julia Mavimbela, a black South African woman, wrote the following creed: "I give thanks to God that He has made me a woman. I give thanks to my creator that He has made me black; that he has fashioned me as I am, with hands, heart, head to serve my people. It can, it should be a glorious thing to be a woman."[10] Christ invites us in Doctrine and Covenants 6: "Fear not, little flock; do good; let earth and hell combine against you, for if ye are built upon my rock, they cannot prevail. . . . Look unto me in every thought; doubt not, fear not. Behold the wounds which pierced my side, and also the prints of the nails in my hands and feet; be faithful, keep my commandments, and ye shall inherit the kingdom of heaven" (vv. 34, 36–37). It is my prayer that we will be able to move ahead boldly like Eve, to make wise, thoughtful choices like Mary, to root out disbelief, fear, and doubt, and believe that we are fit for this kingdom.

NOTES

1. See LDS Bible Dictionary, s.v. "devil."
2. Brigham Young, *Discourses of Brigham Young*, sel. John A. Widtsoe (Salt Lake City: Deseret Book, 1941), 55.
3. Young, *Discourses of Brigham Young*, 55, 65, 225.
4. *Hymns of The Church of Jesus Christ of Latter-day Saints* (Salt Lake City: The Church of Jesus Christ of Latter-day Saints, 1985), no. 195; some capitals omitted for continuity of thought.
5. Jeffrey R. Holland, *Ensign*, February 1984, 69.
6. See Gordon B. Hinckley, *Ensign*, March 1990, 2.
7. Annie Dillard, "Heaven and Earth in Jest," from *Pilgrim at Tinker Creek* in *Readings for Intensive Writers*, comp. Susan T. Laing (Needham Heights, Mass.: Simon and Schuster Custom Publishing, 1997), 161.
8. Bruce R. McConkie, *Doctrinal New Testament Commentary*, 3 vols. (Salt Lake City: Deseret Book, 1965–73), 3:578.
9. Mitch Albom, *Tuesdays with Morrie* (New York: Doubleday, 1968), 117.
10. Carol Cornwall Madsen, introduction to Julia Mavimbela, "I Speak from My Heart," in *Women of Wisdom and Knowledge*, ed. Marie Cornwall and Susan Howe (Salt Lake City: Deseret Book, 1990), 63.

Lots of Stuff

MARY ELLEN EDMUNDS

I was thirty-six years old, comfortable with my life and career, when I was called to serve a mission in Indonesia. I didn't want to go on another mission, but once I found out that God wanted me to, I went. And I'm glad I did. I wouldn't trade my experience in Indonesia for anything. I spent about a month in Jakarta and then was sent to central Java. It was not an easy assignment. The high humidity reintroduced me to asthma and allergies. Mosquitoes for miles around heard I was in town and came over for the party. Cockroaches and rats were a part of everyday life. I struggled with using a hole in the ground instead of a toilet. "Bucket baths" in available water were scary, and electricity came and went without warning. I *murmured*. And worse than that. One night, shortly after I got there, I lay on my bed hurting and gasping for breath. After talking to Heavenly Father for quite a while, I screamed out, "What do you want from me?"

The next morning I took our very dirty three-speed fan to our old well to clean it. As I bent to take the fan apart, our neighbor approached, asking for water, as she did every day. I said, "Of course, come in. Take all you need; take all you want." She lived with her five children in the little place right behind us—a little shelter without windows, about ten feet by ten feet. Her husband didn't visit very often. *Suddenly it hit me hard.* Me, with my three-speed fan, complaining that the electricity wasn't always strong enough to run it. And this sweet soul, filling bucket after bucket of water to take to her little shelter. Me,

Mary Ellen Edmunds has served as a director of training at the Missionary Training Center in Provo, Utah, and as a member of the Relief Society General Board. A graduate of the College of Nursing at Brigham Young University, she has been a faculty member in that same school and has served full-time proselyting and welfare missions in Asia and Africa.

219

with a bed, clean water (once we boiled and filtered it), candles, a bicycle, a change of clothes for every day of the week. Me, with my knowledge that I was there only temporarily, that I would soon go back to my home, to electricity and discretionary time, to clean water and a kitchen, to fine twined linens and malls—and "lots of stuff."

What I learned from my neighbor at the well about materialism and consumerism, simplicity and consecration, has never left me. I am afraid of materialism. I fall into it so easily, and I want to climb away from it.[1]

THE PROSPER PROMISE

A thread runs all the way through the Book of Mormon; it is what I call the Prosper Promise: "And inasmuch as ye shall keep my commandments, ye shall prosper"—and they usually add "in the land" (1 Nephi 2:20). The Savior taught that God wants to bless us both spiritually and temporally. "I am come that they might have life, and that they might have it more abundantly" (John 10:10). *They* is *everybody*, not just you and me.

In Luke 12, the Savior shares with his disciples the parable of the rich man to warn them against covetousness. He says, "For a man's life consisteth not in the abundance of the things which he possesseth" (Luke 12:15). The rich man hoarded and coveted his possessions and lost his soul. Jesus then teaches, "Wherefore, seek not the things of this world but seek ye first to build up the kingdom of God, and to establish his righteousness; *and all these things shall be added unto you*" (JST Matthew 6:38; emphasis added). What things will be added? *Everything*. In Doctrine and Covenants 59, particularly, the Lord teaches that if we will be obediently cheerful, and cheerfully obedient, and thankful, the fulness of the earth will be ours (v. 18; see also D&C 104:14–15).

King Benjamin, in part of his address to his people, taught: "And moreover, I would desire that ye should consider on the blessed and happy state of those that keep the commandments of God. For behold, they are blessed in all things, both temporal and spiritual" (Mosiah 2:41).

President Joseph F. Smith repeats the principle in modern times: "It has always been a cardinal teaching with the Latter-day Saints, that a religion which has not the power to save people temporally and make them prosperous and happy here, cannot be depended upon to save them spiritually, to exalt them in the life to come."[2]

Is there anything wrong, then, with having an abundance of stuff—

"the good life"? Certainly not, if we believe what we read in the scriptures. In fact, often in the scriptures, people are described as being very rich. Helaman 6:9 is one example: "And it came to pass that they became exceedingly rich, both the Lamanites and the Nephites; and they did have an exceeding plenty of gold, and of silver, and of all manner of precious metals" (see also Alma 1:27–31).

How long does a Prosper Promise last? Readers of the Book of Mormon often get frustrated at the relentless cycles of prosperity and wickedness. One of the saddest examples is in 4 Nephi. The Savior's visit was followed by two hundred years of a Zion society. Everyone believed. There were no rich and poor; they had all things in common. Miracles were plentiful, and there was continual peace and no contention. "They had become exceedingly rich, because of their prosperity in Christ" (4 Nephi 1:23). First they sought Christ, and other riches followed. But then comes the downfall: "And now, . . . there began to be among them those who were lifted up in pride, such as the wearing of costly apparel, and all manner of fine pearls, and of the fine things of the world. And from that time forth they did have their goods and their substance no more common among them. And they began to be divided into classes" (4 Nephi 1:24–26). What a tragic end to two hundred years of a Zion society—peace, happiness, prosperity, urban renewal, unity, harmony.

THE UGLY FACE OF MATERIALISM

Pride, selfishness, greed, envy, contention, covetousness, excess, separation, and iniquity are everywhere. It's easy to look around us and point at others' excesses. We can always find somebody who has lots more stuff than we do—more toys, more money, more hair. But what about us? What about me? This is a very personal message. Why do I have so much more than I need of almost everything? Why do I so often forget that all I possess belongs to God? Why is it so hard for me to simplify? Why is the lure of shopping and possessing and consuming so powerful? Who *are* the Joneses? Who made *them* boss?

Elder Dallin H. Oaks's definition of materialism is helpful: "When attitudes or priorities are fixed on the acquisition, use, or possession of property, we call that condition materialism. . . . From the emphasis given to this subject in the scriptures, it appears that materialism has been one of the greatest challenges of the children of God in all ages of time. Greed, the ugly face of materialism in action, has been one of

Satan's most effective weapons in corrupting men and turning their hearts from God.

"In the first of the Ten Commandments, . . . God commands: 'Thou shalt have no other gods before me' (Exodus 20:3). . . . [This] commandment is a comprehensive prohibition against the pursuit of any goal or priority ahead of God. The first commandment prohibits materialism."[3]

President Spencer W. Kimball made the same point when he warned that our possessions could become false gods. "Whatever thing a man sets his heart and his trust in most is his god," President Kimball explained. We "see many parallels between the ancient worship of graven images and behavioral patterns in our very own experience. The Lord has blessed us as a people with a prosperity unequaled in times past. . . . Do we have more of these good things than our faith can stand?"[4]

Within two years of his arrival in the valley, President Brigham Young said to the Saints: "The worst fear that I have about this people is that they will get rich in this country, forget God and His people, wax fat [now he's getting personal], and kick themselves out of the Church and go to hell. This people will stand mobbing, robbing, poverty, and all manner of persecution, and be true. But my greater fear for them is that they cannot stand wealth; and yet they have to be tried with riches, for they will become the richest people on this earth."[5]

President Gordon B. Hinckley has quoted the phrase from 1 Timothy 6:10, "For the love of money is the root of all evil." He comments, "That's true. You get your mind on the things of the world and you lose the Spirit of the Lord in your work. It isn't money that He's talking about, it's the love of money, it's the covetousness, it's the greed, it's the desire to have more than you need which becomes the root of all evil. I hope you'll remember that all the days of your life."[6]

Some of us act as if we would have a tough time responding to the ultimatum: "Your money or your life!" How can we get so mixed up about what brings happiness?

Once upon a time, a dying man bargained with God to see if he could take one suitcase of anything with him to heaven. And he got permission. When he got to the pearly gates, Saint Peter said, "What's in the suitcase?" The man answered, "I got special permission to bring this." But Saint Peter insisted, "I just want to look in it." He opened it up and found it full of gold bars. Saint Peter was amazed. He said, "Why would you want to bring pavement?"

President James E. Faust teaches that "the relationship of money to happiness is at best questionable. Even the *Wall Street Journal* acknowledged, 'Money is an article which may be used as a universal passport to everywhere except heaven, and as a universal provider of everything except happiness.' Henrik Ibsen wrote, 'Money may buy the husk of many things, but not the kernel. It brings you food, but not the appetite; medicine, but not health; acquaintances, but not friends; . . . days of [pleasure], but not peace or happiness.'"[7]

"Set your affection on things above, not on things of the earth" (Colossians 3:2). "For where your treasure is, there will your heart be also" (Matthew 6:21). "In other words," Elder Oaks says, "the treasure of our hearts—our priorities—should not be the destructible and temporary things of the world."[8]

THE CONSUMER WAY OF LIFE

How does advertising affect you? Do you find that it often makes you feel dissatisfied? Do you find yourself wanting more stuff? A wonderful PBS program coined the word *affluenza* to mean an unhappy condition of overload, debt, anxiety, and waste resulting from the dogged pursuit of more.[9]

At first merely informational, advertising now seems to have as its goal creating feelings of dissatisfaction and insatiability. The word *consume,* after all, means to ingest, use up, waste, squander, or to destroy totally. And we're consumers. President Hinckley explains: "The adversary is clever and subtle. He speaks in a seductive voice of fascinating and attractive things."[10]

And what about credit cards, which allow us to live beyond our means? We have this new phrase: "Do you take plastic?" Sometimes I look in the mirror and say, "Am *I* plastic?" What is this doing to me?

An article entitled "Why the Devil Takes VISA" notes: "There is nothing wrong about consuming to live. We all have to do it. There's a wonderful Jewish tradition of 'consecrated consumption.' [But] many of us seem more and more focused on living to consume. [We seem bent on] consumption for pleasure, for the accumulation of resources exceeding [our] needs. Consumers are *made,* not *born.* A key component of today's [consumerism] is the proliferation of choice. [Have you noticed that?] Grocery stores that two decades ago stocked 9,000 items now stock 30,000."[11] No wonder it takes so long to shop.

How many of our choices are actually significant? What if we are inundated with so many choices—what to read, what to wear, what to watch, what to eat, where to surf on the Internet—that we are left without enough time for relationships, the scriptures, prayer, pondering, attending the temple? One way to interfere with our agency would be to inundate our minds with the spiritually irrelevant—tip us over with consuming choices.

Consumer living fosters values totally opposite from those our faith tries to teach us. Can we simultaneously seek and to some degree realize both instant gratification and patience? What about instant gratification and self-control? Can we be unsatisfied and contented at the same time? What about the need to learn to deny ourselves? What about pride?

C. S. Lewis described the pride of comparison when he said: "Pride is *essentially* competitive. . . . Pride gets no pleasure out of having something, only out of having more of it than the next [person]. . . . It is the comparison that makes you proud: the pleasure of being above the rest."[12] That is the point at which our attitude about our possessions changes, and we want more and better stuff than anybody else.

I read in the newspaper a few years ago about a man who bought a yacht for $29 million and spent $8 million refitting it, not because he wanted the boat, but because he wanted the best boat in the universe. He outfitted it with three elevators, a waterfall, and a small cinema that seats eighteen. He hired a crew of thirty-one and stocked enough food on board to feed fifty people for three months (if those people were from Java, he'd have had enough to feed fifty people for a year). He included a swimming pool, a hospital, and solid gold sinks and fixtures. When someone asked, "Why would anyone want a solid gold sink?" he replied, "It's sort of a little bit of an ego trip." And then he said, "I won't be spending much time on it—I'm very busy."

You can never get enough of what you don't need, *ever*. What you don't need never satisfies. We spend money we don't have to buy things we don't need to impress people we don't like—who don't come over.

CONSECRATED CONSUMPTION

Is it wrong and evil, then, to have nice things—or any things? Will we be kept out of the celestial kingdom if we have more than one home or car or TV or pair of shoes, or if we eat too much? I hope not! Can we get there only if we have *nothing*?

Elder Oaks notes: "The possession of wealth or the acquisition of significant income is not a mark of heavenly favor, and their absence is not evidence of heavenly disfavor."[13] Maybe you have more because God knows your heart, and he knows you will share—generously.

The prophet Jacob taught that acquiring riches was not evil if it was done for the right reasons and in the right sequence: "Before ye seek for riches, seek ye for the kingdom of God. And after ye have obtained a hope in Christ ye shall obtain riches, if ye seek them; and ye will seek them for the intent to do good—to clothe the naked, and to feed the hungry, and to liberate the captive, and administer relief to the sick and the afflicted" (Jacob 2:18–19).

"I do not consider there is anything too good for the children of God, if we don't worship it," Elder Andrew Kimball said. "It is the flaunting of rich clothing in such a way as to annoy those who are less fortunate in life that creates inequality [which is a synonym for iniquity] and hurts the feelings of the people. I do hope, my brethren and sisters, that we will endeavor to restrain ourselves in the follies and fashions of the world."[14]

"We may build a beautiful, spacious home that is far larger than we need," warns Elder Joseph B. Wirthlin. "We may spend far too much to decorate, furnish, and landscape it. And even if we are blessed enough to afford such luxury, we may be misdirecting resources that could be better used to build the kingdom of God or to feed and clothe our needy brothers and sisters."[15]

The gap is wide between those who have too much and those who don't have enough. Are we pulling away from those who need us? Are we forgetting how much we need them? "There is an interdependence," President Marion G. Romney taught, "between those who have and those who have not. The process of giving exalts the poor and humbles the rich. In the process, both are sanctified."[16] Mother Teresa understood this principle. She said, "[The poor] have taught us a different way of loving God by making us do our utmost to help them."[17]

I have been moved by examples I have seen. My dear neighbors in Indonesia saved a spoonful of uncooked rice every morning to share with those who were more needy than they. And they had only one meal a day. Cecilia, my neighbor and mentor in Africa, translated all the materials for our child health project, not for money but for love of God and neighbor. A Church member shares his jet plane so President Hinckley can go all over the world and visit the Saints in far-flung places. In these and so many other instances, I find myself asking, "Am *I* that generous? Would *I* do that?" It's so easy to say, "Well, if I had that much . . ." But if I'm going to be generous, I *will* be generous, no matter how much or how little I have. Some of those who have been the most generous to me have had little or nothing material to share.

Doctrine and Covenants 104:18 offers a chilling description of what hell might be: "Therefore, if any man shall take of the abundance which I have made, and impart not his portion, according to the law of my gospel, unto the poor and the needy, he shall, with the wicked, lift up his eyes in hell, being in torment."

Now is the time to share. Nothing belongs to us; it belongs to God.

THE JOYFUL USE OF GOD'S RICHES

President Ezra Taft Benson defines beautifully the relationship we should have with wealth: "Stewardship, not conspicuous consumption, is the proper relationship of man to material wealth."[18] Stewardship is taking care of all that Heavenly Father has shared so generously and abundantly with us and being faithful stewards. Someday he may kindly ask, "What did you do with all I gave you?" Will we answer, "Kept it, heh, heh. Never did wear everything even once, but I sure had a lot"? I hope not.

Consecrated consumption is the opposite of conspicuous consumption. We should joyfully enjoy, use, and share all that God has generously given us. Consecration might be described as keeping what we need and sharing the rest with others in a Godlike and Christlike way.

Elder J. Richard Clarke said, "It has always been the disposition of the true disciples of Christ, as they reached higher degrees of spirituality, to look after the needy."[19] Physical needs are not the only kind. Hunger and thirst also have a lot to do with the feelings in our soul.

"We can live simply so that others may simply live," reads a bumper sticker I saw. That's an important truth. We should try not to waste food and water, though it's hard for me to be careful when there's so much. If Utah has a winter with plentiful snow, it's harder to remember to be careful with water. Then I remember all the people I have known who've never had all the water they wanted to drink, let alone safe or cold water. We can learn to give away things we're not using anymore—

maybe even some of the things we *are* using. The effect of our tithes and offerings can be far-reaching. Can we spend less time and money on things which we don't really need? Probably. What one step can you take in the next week or month to begin changing your current spending or consumption habits? Wanting less is probably a greater blessing than having more; it's a condition of the heart.

Exploring this topic has been a soul-searching experience for me. This particular soul search has been going on for years. In every place God has sent me, people have struggled with temporal needs. And yet they seem so content so much of the time, so happy and generous. I ask God, "What do you want me to do with my abundance? What do you want me to do with all my stuff?" And his answer to me has always been three things. First, "Enjoy." Isn't that just like a loving Heavenly Father? "Enjoy all that I have shared." Second, "Appreciate it. Be thankful." What is it we haven't thanked him for in quite a while? Water? Electricity? Third is "Share." Share generously and often, in a Godlike and Christlike way. Gratitude is a great cure for greed. It really is.

Materialism isn't what we have: it's our attitude towards it. "Look[ing] at others with their lands and gold,"[20] focusing on things others have that we don't, can do bad things to us. We become crabby, selfish, and self-centered. We feel discontent. We could spend a whole lifetime without ever feeling contentment and satisfaction. I'd hate for us to miss those feelings.

My parents have taught me so much about all of this. Just three days after Christmas, my daddy went Home. Capital "H." I *miss* him. Someone said to me, "How old was your dad?" And I said, "He was ninety-five." And the person said, "Oh, well then." I wanted to give him my CTR biff: a knuckle sandwich garnished with several CTR rings. I now have two fathers in heaven. I pray only to one, but I talk to the other a lot. Everything that mattered to him, he took with him. So many times I've heard my parents say in their sweet and simple lives, "We have all we need. Our wants are simple. Bread and milk for supper." Daddy asked to be buried in a plain pine box with one rose on top, and we honored that request. He said he would haunt us if we didn't. He felt that funerals have become competitive, pushing people into debt for years to pay for fancy things. "I'm not going to be there very long," he said. "I just want a plain pine box." He also didn't want people to spend a lot of money on flowers. He didn't want them to spend money on him.

And so the last line of his obituary read: "Please, in lieu of flowers, take your family to dinner." That's my daddy.

The book of Acts contains a description of Zion. "And the multitude of them that believed were of one heart and of one soul: neither said any of them that ought of the things which he possessed was his own; but they had all things common. . . . Neither was there any among them that lacked: for as many as were possessors of lands or houses sold them, and brought the prices of the things that were sold, and laid them down at the apostles' feet: and distribution was made unto every man according as he had need" (Acts 4:32, 34–35).

We've got to do something to our hearts so that we will be comfortable in that kind of a society because that's what the celestial kingdom is—Zion. May God help us to simplify, to enjoy what we already have, to want to share our abundance with those around us. Enjoy! Appreciate! Share!

NOTES

1. I'd like to recommend several books to you on this subject: Faith D'Aluisio and Peter Menzel, *Women in the Material World* (San Francisco: Sierra Club Books, 1996); Peter Menzel, *Material World: A Global Family Portrait* (San Francisco: Sierra Club Books, 1994); Harold S. Kushner, *When All You've Ever Wanted Isn't Enough* (New York: Summit Books, 1986); and Hugh Nibley, "What Is Zion? A Distant View," chap. 2, *Approaching Zion*, vol. 9 of *The Collected Works of Hugh Nibley*, ed. Don E. Norton (Salt Lake City: Deseret Book, and Provo, Utah: Foundation for Ancient Research and Mormon Studies, 1989), 25–62.

2. Joseph F. Smith, "The Truth about Mormonism," *Out West* 23 (1905): 242, as quoted in Leonard J. Arrington, *Great Basin Kingdom* (Cambridge: Harvard University Press, 1958), 425, n. 16.

3. Dallin H. Oaks, *Pure in Heart* (Salt Lake City: Bookcraft, 1988), 73–74.

4. Spencer W. Kimball, *Ensign*, June 1976, 4.

5. Reported in James S. Brown, *Life of a Pioneer* (Salt Lake City: George Q. Cannon & Sons Co., 1900), 122–23; quoted in Bryant S. Hinckley, *The Faith of Our Pioneer Fathers* (Salt Lake City: Deseret Book, 1956), 13.

6. Gordon B. Hinckley, Korea Seoul missionary meeting, 22 May 1996; notes in possession of author.

7. James E. Faust, *To Reach Even unto You* (Salt Lake City: Deseret Book, 1980), 8.

8. Oaks, *Pure in Heart*, 74.

9. "Affluenza," PBS special, 15 September 1997, KCTS/Seattle and Oregon Public Broadcasting; notes in possession of the author.

10. Gordon B. Hinckley, *Ensign*, November 1994, 48.

11. "Why the Devil Takes VISA," *Christianity Today*, 7 October 1996.

12. C. S. Lewis, *Mere Christianity* (New York: Macmillan, 1960), 109–10.

13. Oaks, *Pure in Heart*, 75.

14. Andrew Kimball, Conference Report, October 1911, 82.
15. Joseph B. Wirthlin, *Ensign,* November 1990, 65.
16. Marion G. Romney, *Ensign,* November 1982, 93.
17. Georges Gorree and Jean Barbier, *The Love of Christ: Spiritual Counsels—Mother Teresa of Calcutta* (New York: Harper & Row, 1982), 23.
18. Ezra Taft Benson, *Ensign,* June 1987, 5.
19. J. Richard Clarke, *Ensign,* May 1978, 82.
20. *Hymns of The Church of Jesus Christ of Latter-day Saints* (Salt Lake City: The Church of Jesus Christ of Latter-day Saints, 1985), no. 241.

Until Debt Do Us Part

BERNARD PODUSKA

Finances, feelings, and relationships are interwoven. It might startle you to learn that finances are among the top four reasons leading to divorce in first marriages and the biggest problem in remarriages.[1] One study indicated that 89 percent of all divorces can be linked to quarrels and accusations over money.[2] And, unfortunately, divorce rates are rising. In California, for example, the estimate now is that 75 percent of all marriages will fail. The divorce rate in Utah is also very high—not as high as in California, but higher than the national average. So my interest in finances and debt is intimately connected to my concern for family stability. Why would finances, a temporal concern, affect the spiritual life of a marriage? President Brigham Young sheds light on this question: "We cannot talk about the spiritual things without connecting them with temporal things. Neither can we talk about temporal things without connecting spiritual things with them. Whether we are raising cattle, planting, gathering, building, or inhabiting, we are in the Lord and all we do is within the pale of his Kingdom upon the earth. Consequently it is all spiritual and all temporal, no matter what we are laboring to accomplish."[3]

When I first began teaching in the Family Science Department at Brigham Young University, we had a major called family financial planning and counseling. It was my task as a marriage and family therapist to teach financial counseling skills. In the course of running a small community clinic, we used computers to whip out all sorts of budgets for people with financial problems. But we found that within a month most

Bernard Poduska is an associate professor in the School of Family Life at Brigham Young University specializing in family finances and relationships. He serves as a high councilor in the BYU Eleventh Stake. He and his wife, Barbara Stagg Poduska, have reared five children.

of these budgets were failing. When we investigated why, we learned that the budgets did not work because we had put them together without considering the feelings and the relationships of the participants. We were merely number crunching. We discovered that a major problem in family finance is that people try to solve financial concerns with just numbers. Feelings and relationships, however, cannot be ignored. For example, envision a list of debts. You owe some to VISA, some to MasterCard, several thousand dollars on a car, several thousand on furniture, $150 to your husband's mother, and a couple hundred in dental bills. Now those are the numbers, but the feelings associated with those numbers are very different. The $150 owed to your husband's mother, although the least important debt to pay off from a financial standpoint because it isn't accruing any interest, still carries the strongest sense of obligation. In deciding upon a financial plan of action, you need to address *family* finances—feelings and relationships. These same factors should be considered when making purchases. A normal question you ask when purchasing is "Can we afford it? What does it cost?" A more important question in *family* finances is "Sure, this item is the most sensible selection, but how do you feel about it?" Unless both you and your spouse feel good about it, the cost is too high.

Remember that a marriage relationship is priceless. The first principle in family finances is that nothing is worth damaging the relationship over. Our stewardship to one another is a sacred covenant. Just for a moment, think of being in the celestial room of the temple. Imagine the Savior being physically as well as spiritually present with you. Imagine that He puts His arm around your shoulder and leads you to your husband. Then placing His hand on your husband's shoulder, He says to him, "This is my beloved sister," and calls you by name. "I want you to love her as I have." He then turns to you and says, "And this is my beloved brother," and He calls your spouse by name. "I want you to love him as I have." And then perhaps He joins your hands together, saying, "I want you to love one another as I have loved you." In that moment, you are married. He didn't ask you to buy each other clothes and dishes and cars and houses. He didn't ask you to make millions of dollars for each other. He merely asked you to love one another as He loves you. When marital relationships have this spiritual dimension, finances take on a new meaning.

When we have financial problems, we often wonder, "How did we get into this mess?" No one intends to get into a mess. We all plan to be frugal and well organized. Unfortunately, however, in the United States we often learn how to earn money but not how to manage it. Consequently, financial problems are usually behavior problems rather than money shortage problems. Our habits lead us to chronic indebtedness. No matter how hard we try, we always seem to be in financial hot water.

In the Old Testament, we find the counsel: "Thus sayeth the Lord of hosts; Consider your ways. Ye have sown much and bring in little. Ye eat, but ye have not enough; ye drink, but ye are not filled with drink; ye clothe you, but there is none warm; and he that earneth wages earneth wages to put it into a bag with holes. Thus sayeth the Lord of Hosts; Consider your ways" (Haggai 1:5–7). Thus the second principle in finances is, If you continue doing what you have been doing, you will continue getting what you have been getting. You have to change your behavior to get out of chronic financial problems. To paraphrase Mark Twain's statement on literacy—A wealthy man who does not manage his money has no advantage over a poor man.

One of the first behavior problems is impulse buying. We live in a world of advertising that tells us what we need and that we need it right now. So we go out and buy it without counting the cost. Or, if we do stop to consider our financial resources, we look at our income in terms of gross amounts. People say, "I make $2,000 a month," or "I make $50,000 a year." Thinking in terms of gross amounts creates the illusion that we have lots of money. We forget that Uncle Sam wants some of it, and the state wants some of it. Current research in Utah indicates that in earnings, about three hours out of an eight-hour work day are spent just paying taxes—property taxes, sales taxes, income taxes, you-name-it taxes. We talk about our proposed expenditures, however, without taking taxes into account. "Hey, I make $2,000 a month. I should be able to afford a lousy $325 monthly payment on this new car." I advise couples to translate all payments into the monthly income that they would have to earn to make that payment. For example, to clear $325, you probably need to earn around $500. If you are making $24,000 a year, $500 is one week's worth of work per month, or one-quarter of your income. So for the five years that it will take to pay for that car, you become an indentured servant. In colonial America, you'll remember, indentured servants were those poor souls who could not afford passage on a ship to begin a new life in the colonies, so they traded their services for the price of passage. In essence, they said, "I'll tell you what. If you'll pay the way for me now so I can travel to the American colonies, then I'll be your servant there for the next five years." That's exactly what we do when we sign a contract for a car.

Another related behavior problem is that we qualify for loans that we don't qualify for. Let me explain. When you apply for a loan at a bank, the loan officer will ask you to list your current monthly payments. So you and your spouse will dutifully list your payments—credit card payments, department store payments, car payments—and you come up with $500 a month going out for debts. The bank officer says, "You're really close, but you're a good Latter-day Saint family, so, by golly, we're going to give you the loan." You and your spouse smile at each other as you leave the bank, give each other a nudge, and say, "It's a good thing we didn't tell them about the boat payments." The boat payments are $200 a month, and the name of the boat is the USS *Tithing*. Because tithing is a charitable contribution, it need not be listed as a contractual debt. If it were a contract on a boat, you would not have qualified for that loan. So you just qualified for a loan that you don't qualify for. If you start adding other religious obligations that don't have to be listed, such as missions, food storage, and fast offerings, like many other Latter-day Saint families you will find yourself financially overextended, even though the bank said you qualified for a loan. You are now strapped with loan payments you can't meet.

Most people use credit cards to make up the difference. Credit cards also allow us to live a lie. In the old days, workers got paid in cash. When the cash ran out, the buying stopped. But with the advent of credit cards in the 1960s, we began to purchase things without having first earned the money to pay for them. As a result, we increased our standard of living, and we liked that increase. It was nice. In reality, when you go into debt, you are in effect saying to the bank, "I would really like to live at this other, much higher standard of living, but quite honestly, my income would never support it, and so unless you as a bank pour tens of thousands of dollars into my budget, I'm not going to be able to live like that. And I really want to live like that."

As time went on, debts grew. Somehow men had been given the impression that they were essentially irrelevant at home anyway; if they wanted to feel significant in this world, they had to leave home, go forth, and make lots of money, as if being a good provider meant that the first question God plans to ask fathers beyond the veil is "Hey, how much money did you make down there?" Most Americans soon found that they could no longer sustain their standard of living and the debt load on just one income. So the United States became a country of two-income families. Our quality of life dwindled as our standard of living increased. Credit cards (instant loans) allow us to live a lie.

The non-lie is to limit purchases to your level of income. A quick rule of thumb to help you live honestly and authentically is, If you can't pay it off in a year, you can't afford it. The best option is to save and pay cash. Let's illustrate with buying a new car. Family A takes out a loan to pay for the car. They will make $200 payments monthly for two years, and they get to drive home in that slick, new car. (Note that this option violates our rule of thumb: if you can't pay it off in one year, don't buy.) Family B begins depositing $200 a month into their savings account. At the end of a year, they have $2,500 because they've earned some interest. They then go to the car dealer, put down half the cost of the car with their savings, and take out a contract for one year. Family C puts $200 a month into their savings account every month for two years, and then they go to the dealer and pay cash for the car. Family A finances the whole thing, Family B finances only one year, and Family C saves for two years instead of financing. Notice, however, that all three families have the same budget—absolutely identical $200 car payments each month. The only difference is that A is paying interest and C is earning it.

People do the same thing with Christmas. They will rack up $1,200 on a VISA card at Christmas time and then spend the whole year, $100 a month, paying it off, plus paying interest. They get it all paid off by next Christmas and then rack up another debt. What's the difference between $100 a month to VISA and $100 a month into savings? It's the I-need-it-and-I-need-it-now behavior. The solution is to get out of the loop in which you are always in debt and always going in debt. Move into the savings loop. All you have to do is endure one lean year while you are saving up; then you are on the other side of that loop. It's either debt forever or savings forever.

The behavior most in need of change is overusing credit cards. In just the past few years, credit card use has risen dramatically. In 1970 Americans had $131 billion worth of consumer debt (debt that excludes mortgage debt). Twenty-eight years later, we now have 1.2 trillion dollars worth of consumer debt. That much money is hard to imagine. If you watched the propeller of an airplane spinning at two thousand rpms, you'd have to stand there for one year before it went around a billion times. So if you want to see a trillion, you'd have to stand there for a thousand years. It's an incomprehensible amount.

In addition to consumer debt, people are increasingly declaring bankruptcy. Last year, 1.3 million families in the United States went into personal bankruptcy. And we live in the most prosperous times in the nation's history. Why so much bankruptcy? Primarily because no matter how much we earn, we seem to spend more. A spending inflation is rampant, and the amounts are becoming astronomical.

Heed these danger signs of credit abuse: First, do your installment payments total 20 percent or more of your disposable income? Disposable income is the money left over after paying taxes and tithing. For most of us, anything beyond a car payment puts us into financial trouble.

Second, do you think of your line of credit as money you can use? People used to set aside three months of income as an emergency fund. Now we think of our credit line on our credit cards as our emergency fund. "Well, if something happens, we've got $4,000 left on the card." We act as if that's our money rather than our debt. We believe they really are *credit* cards rather than *debt* cards. That allows us to operate with a phantom income. We have this additional phantom way of purchasing things without having earned the money to do so.

Third, do you consistently pay no more than the minimum due each month? The interest paid to banks for credit card use is enormous. Banks have never had a gold mine like credit cards. Adding annual bank card fees, the interest you pay, and the percentage the retail stores are required to pay with each credit card purchase, a bank could be pulling in up to 28 percent on a credit card loan. Think of interest as a cut in your pay. In addition, you did not get anything tangible for that money; you merely are paying for the opportunity of using someone else's money.

Besides avoiding credit card debt, it's important to determine the true cost of an item before making a purchase. We all brag when someone asks how much our car cost, "Oh, I got it for $12,000, and it was a steal." We act as if that was the actual cost of the car. Yes, the list price was $12,000, but that didn't include 6 percent sales tax. That adds another $720. Property taxes also need to be added. Insurance costs have now tripled from the old junk heap that we used to drive. Maintenance costs have also gone up. Tires will cost more. The newer car may also get lower gas mileage. The list goes on and on. The true cost, when you add the interest for the next five years alone, is probably closer to $22,000 than $12,000. The same thing happens when you buy a computer. "Got the computer for only $1,500!" But did you count the cost of a desk to put it on, a printer, paper, a modem, and all the items you had to have to get it running just right? The true cost is the total package. You should determine the total cost, not just the sale price.

Along these same lines, be sure to estimate the cost per use of an item. If you buy a $15,000 boat and use it twice that year, that's $7,500 per use. If you use it two more times that year, then you've dropped the price to only $3,750 each time you take it out. Now, it might cost you $100 an hour to rent a boat at Lake Powell, but at the end of an eight-hour day, the bill is only $800, not $15,000 plus maintenance and property taxes, sales taxes, gasoline, insurance, and so forth. Consider carefully the cost per use. Would it be better to rent? to share? to borrow? to buy something used?

Once you've analyzed how you got into a financial mess, the next question is, How do we get out of it? Consolidation loans? Remember that your financial difficulties resulted from behavior problems, not money problems. A consolidation loan can give you a breather and take the pressure off. Basically, the loan allows you to consolidate all the VISA card and MasterCard bills into one low-interest loan, which isn't so low but is lower than the credit cards. The problem is, you still have the credit cards. If your behavior hasn't changed, the credit card debt gradually creeps back up until the cards are maxed out again. Now, however, you also have the consolidation loan—and double the debt. Consolidation loans are effective only if behavior has changed.

Rather than a consolidated loan, consider accelerated payment plans and the fold-down method to get out of debt. The accelerated payment plan consists of putting extra money with your payments on a loan or debt to pay it off sooner than the allotted repayment period. When you make a normal monthly payment, a large portion goes to pay interest, while only a small portion goes to pay off the principal. The accelerated payment plan works because when you add money to your payment, all the extra money goes to your principal. As you reduce the principal in this manner, you will not have to pay interest on the principal that you have paid off. For example, let's say you had a $100,000 mortgage with a 10 percent interest rate for thirty years—a conventional mortgage loan. The total interest—just the interest, not the $100,000 that you borrowed—is an extra $216,000, making the total payback about $316,000. (This is a good illustration of the true cost of something: the house cost you $100,000, but borrowing the money to buy the house costs you an additional $216,000.) Your monthly payments would be $877. If you were to add just an extra $25 a month into your payments, making them a little over $900, you'd end up paying off the loan in twenty-five years and ten months instead of thirty years. The bonus is that you'd pay $179,000 total instead of $216,000.

People say, "Where would I get that extra $25 every month?" All of us have extra expenditures in our budget we can cut out if we want to. My favorite illustration is what I call the $22,000 snack. It's summertime, and one of your children wants half a Popsicle in the morning (10 cents), and then with lunch you serve Koolaid and a homemade cookie (8 cents and 7 cents), and then for an afternoon snack the other half of the Popsicle (another 10 cents), plus later a bowl of ice cream for a treat after dinner (15 cents). That day's snacks total 50 cents. Most mothers would say, "One Popsicle, a cookie, a glass of Koolaid, a bowl of ice cream—that's not much!" But in a family of six, it adds up to $3 a day. Three dollars times thirty-one days equals nearly $100 a month in snacks. And that's just for Popsicles, cookies, and Koolaid, not Big Gulps, Slurpies, and potato chips. It all adds up to $1,200 a year, or for eighteen years of raising the children almost $22,000 to be budgeted for snacks. This far-fetched example isn't meant to suggest that you should cut out all snacks. They can be an important part of family life. It simply illustrates where money can come from to add to principal payments. We can cut back on some of those little luxuries that we've come to see as necessities: extra services on the phone, cable TV hookups, fast food meals and pre-packaged mixes, gasoline for driving places when we could just as easily walk.

Now let's talk about the fold-down method, which I consider a first principle of salvation as far as helpful truths in this world. Suppose you owe approximately $10,000 to a list of creditors. Your monthly payments are, say, $50 to VISA, $250 to MasterCard, $225 to Penneys, $850 in furniture loans, and so on. You only owed VISA $50, and with the January payment, VISA is paid off. What typically happens in a family is that someone will say, "Hey, we've paid off the lawnmower. Now we can get the snowblower." If we buy the snowblower, we don't get rid of our debt. All we do is transfer the debt from one creditor to another creditor. And payments just go on and on. The fold-down method, however, will help us change our behavior. We are used to that $50 a month going out, so instead of buying something else, we fold it down into the payments of another debt. We've been paying $100 a month to MasterCard; we make it $150. With that extra folded-down money, the MasterCard is paid off in February. Now we have $150 available and we fold that down into Penneys and annihilate that debt.

Even if you don't get everything paid down completely, usually after several months of folding down payments you are able to breathe again. You've gone from seven creditors down to three or four. Most debts cannot withstand this kind of attack. If you continue to make these payments—since your budget is used to it—then once your debts are eliminated you can start putting the payments into your savings accounts. The payments will then fold up rather than fold down. In no time you will have enough in savings so that you don't have to use your credit cards anymore. You don't have to take out loans anymore. You can be your own banker.

In paying off creditors, you can select items to be paid off first from both a feeling standpoint and a bottom-line practicality standpoint (what is the most pressing, what is costing the most interest). You may, as in our earlier example, owe $150 to your mother-in-law or a brother who is close to you. The debt may be interfering with your relationship, so you may want to pay it off first, even though there's no interest accruing on it. Paying off smaller debts first will free up some money, even though you're paying higher interest on some of the other loans. Crossing off debts gives you a psychological boost, a feeling that, hey, at least we're paying something off. As you pay off your debts, do not give in to the temptation to make additional purchases. Consider this a non-purchase period with every penny being devoted to getting out of debt once and for all. Use all your loose change, garage sale profits, tax returns, whatever extra money you can scrape together to fold into accelerated payments. If you do, you will save a huge amount in interest. Another nice benefit of the fold-down method is that reducing your debt load to a level where you can again breathe will do wonders for your marital relationship. In addition, working on a goal as a team is a great relationship strengthener.

After you have gotten out of debt, and you have changed your financially self-defeating behaviors, consider one last principle. To obtain financial freedom, you must determine what is sufficient, what is enough—enough car, enough house, enough income. Determining what is sufficient results in a closed-ended budget; never being satisfied results in an open-ended budget. With an open-ended budget, if you make $5,000, you'll spend $10,000; if you make $35,000, you'll spend $40,000; and on and on. You never arrive anywhere; you just keep making more money and spending more than you earn. That is why it is called open-ended. In contrast, with a closed-ended budget your income continues to go up but your spending levels off because you have decided, that's enough. That's enough furniture. That's enough house. We could qualify for and afford a much bigger house, but this is enough house. We could afford to buy a much more expensive car, but hey, this is enough car.

One sociology professor asks three questions: Do you expect to eat more than one kind of food each day? Do you have more than one pair of shoes? Do you have access to some kind of personal transportation? If you can answer yes to those three questions, in terms of standard of living you are in the top 10 percent of all the human beings that have ever lived on earth. And yet we want more and more and more. The house that your mother and father raised you in was most likely around twelve to fifteen hundred square feet. Now we look at houses that are three to four thousand square feet as a standard. Today the average Utah home costs $160,000, not because builders couldn't construct smaller, less expensive homes but because that is what buyers demand. When we look for a house, we don't say, "What is enough for us?" We say, "What is the biggest house we can qualify for?" When we are finally able to say "This is enough for us," we free up discretionary income that will keep increasing as our income increases. We will have money uncommitted and available for other uses.

Thoreau said it best: "Money is not required to buy one necessary of the soul."[4] When we think of all we are buying, all the toys we are accumulating, keep in mind that none of them is going to go with us. These are merely things of the temporal world, necessary for now but not needed in the eternal scheme of things.

I began in this essay talking about the relationship between money and marriage. Let me end on that same note. One of my favorite quotations comes from President Spencer W. Kimball: "Marriage . . . means sacrifice, sharing, and even a reduction of some personal liberties. It means long, hard economizing. It means children who bring with them financial burdens, service burdens, care and worry burdens; but it also means the deepest and sweetest emotions of all."[5]

NOTES

1. See Stan L. Albrecht, Howard M. Bahr, and Kristen L. Goodman, *Divorce and Remarriage: Problems, Adaptions, and Adjustments* (Westport, Conn.: Greenwood Press, 1983).
2. Marvin J. Ashton, *Ensign*, July 1975, 72–73.
3. Brigham Young, *Journal of Discourses*, 26 vols. (London: Latter-day Saints' Book Depot, 1854–86), 10:329.
4. Henry David Thoreau, *Walden and Other Writings of Henry David Thoreau*, ed. Brooks Atkinson (New York: Modern Library, 1937), 293.
5. Spencer W. Kimball, *Marriage* (Salt Lake City: Deseret Book, 1980), 8.

New Talents:
Fun, Fear, and Fulfillment

JANICE KAPP PERRY AND DOUGLAS C. PERRY

JANICE: An important part of life is discovering our talents. Through the years I have discovered the talents of my husband, Doug, and they have been totally different from my own. When we started dating, we went ice skating. Doug went right out on the pond and began doing figure eights; I could never get my ankles to stay up straight. Later in our marriage, he became a roller skater. He dressed in a tuxedo and performed in roller skating dance reviews. He bought me the best kind of skates and gave me lessons, hoping that I could perform with him. It just wasn't me. Either I lacked talent or desire or both. Fortunately for Doug, just before the review, a woman recently returned from her mission needed a partner, because I never would have made it.

Doug is also tenacious about learning languages. He plays several brass instruments. He's a racquetball champion. In later life, he has taken up canoeing, bicycling, and computers. Two years ago, at age sixty-one, he took up roller-blading. I see him going off on his roller-blades, and I just say a prayer. He's good, but he *is* sixty-three now.

I love Doug, but I often don't share his enthusiasm or talents. I have had to find my own strengths. As Doug and I travel through the Church,

Janice Kapp Perry and Douglas C. Perry are the parents of five children. Sister Perry received her musical training at Brigham Young University and has produced numerous albums and songbooks of gospel-related music. She has served as ward Relief Society president and sings with the Mormon Tabernacle Choir. Brother Perry, a music major when he met Janice at BYU, graduated with a bachelor's degree in Russian. He worked for many years as a computer programmer and analyst before taking over the family music business in 1980. A former bishop, he serves as ward activity chairman in their Provo ward.

we see women with beautifully decorated, well-organized, clean homes. And I think, *I wish that were my talent.* But I do only the bare minimum in that area so I'll have more time for the things that I truly love. Our Relief Society bulletin a few weeks ago reported, "Sister Edwards, who had back surgery, said she's well enough now to be up and cleaning out a few drawers." And I thought, *Wow, I've never felt that good.*

Recently a news reporter from the *Provo Herald* came to my home to interview me for an article about how mothers influence their children's creative abilities. She had already interviewed my brother, Gary Kapp, who is an artist. I said, "What did Gary say?" She answered, "Basically he described your mother as a cheerleader." "That covers it," I replied. Our mother gave us a belief that we had talent. Gary said she made him feel as if his first painting were a Rembrandt. He was in junior high then. I felt my first little song was the best song my mother had ever heard. She loved every song I wrote. If she knew I had just finished one, she'd say, "Play it over the phone. I can't wait until I get there to hear it." When I finished playing it, she would exclaim, "Oh, it's one of your best." Sometimes I knew it wasn't, but I always loved to call Mother for a bit of reinforcement. She put up half the money for my first album. She believed in us so completely that she second-mortgaged her home when we wanted to put on the play *It's a Miracle.* I can't believe we let her do it.

Perhaps we were most affected by the way she pursued her own talents. Mother was a widow for twenty-one years. Shortly before she died, she and I were in her bedroom one night, reviewing her life. Amazingly, she still felt happy and optimistic, looking forward to the next step. We reviewed the many spiritual ways that she had prepared herself. Then we talked in depth about how she had enjoyed her talents, how they had made her happy. When Dad died at fifty-seven, she had developed enough talents to fill her life happily for the next twenty-one years. In fact, on the day my dad died, she said, "I have my choice. I can be sad during these next twenty or thirty years, or I can decide to see how much I can accomplish." And accomplish she did. She had always loved music and the piano. She and Dad had played in a dance band for twenty years, and I played with her for a while after he died. She belonged to a senior citizens' fun band that traveled all over. She played for anyone who needed an accompanist. She also made quilts for every grandchild and crocheted and knitted for everyone.

After Dad died, she went on a full-time mission. When she came home, she learned how to be an excellent genealogist, researching and entering more than forty thousand names for temple work. She didn't have time to sit around and feel lonely.

Mother and I wrote a song together right at the end of her life. She said, "Down the path from each one of us, there's an old woman waiting. Her happiness depends on us, because she is us grown old." This song was the last thing we did together—and she made me promise I'd pay her royalties! She died a week later, so I have given her royalties to genealogical research. I call my version of our song, "The Woman You'll Be Someday."

> I see an old woman rocking there,
> The sun shining softly on her silver hair.
> I wonder the secrets she holds deep inside.
> Is she smiling or hiding a tear in her eye?
> She watches our day as her story unfolds,
> For you see, she is you grown old.
> And with every decision you make today
> You're creating the woman you'll be someday.
> Just for now the old woman depends on you.
> She waits and she watches as you make her dreams come true.

A lot of people who think they have no talents discover them along life's little twists and turns. Trying one thing leads to another. That's pretty much how it was for me. I loved playing ball until I was almost forty, and then I broke my ankle playing basketball with my nephews. While I was out of commission, I wrote the music for our ward roadshow, and my life turned in a whole new direction. When I told Doug I wished I'd started writing music sooner, he said, "No, those first years were your research phase. You were experiencing the things that you now write about." He was right. We'd reared our children. My father had died. One of our children had died. We'd reared foster children. All these experiences refined and taught me while my love for music was simmering. For years Doug and I had been focused on getting our children started singing, playing instruments, and even writing music—following their interests. That was the right time for us to do that. Then our last child went to school, and I was actually home alone. *I have five or six hours a day free to choose something I want to do,* I thought. It was a great feeling. That was the moment for *me*.

After the roadshow, I wasn't sure of my direction for a while, but one day the ward music director asked our son Steve to sing a solo in sacrament meeting. I decided to try to write a song for him. It was well received, so I tried again. When I had written a few pieces, I published them. That was a big step for me. When I first started writing, I sent all my songs to the Church music office. They responded, "Brighten your own little corner. Use your songs in your family, in your ward, in your stake. If they are good, we'll hear about them." That was wonderful advice. Our ward needed a temple song for Primary, and so I wrote "I Love to See the Temple." Another stake needed a missionary song for the kids at stake conference, so I wrote the army of Helaman song. I just kept doing little things that were needed right where I was and enjoyed being able to contribute. Somehow my songs found their way into a little larger arena than our Primary.

In time I had enough for an album of songs. After the album was recorded, I started receiving requests to speak. I was terrified. I would have played ball in front of anybody, but I didn't know how to stand up and talk about my music. Doug assured me that any woman in the Church can stand up and bear her testimony about what she personally has learned. But for at least two years, I let my fears hold me back. Eventually I risked it. And it was truly scary, start to finish. So I had to decide whether to keep doing it and overcome my fear or just quit trying. I kept trying. It took five years for me to overcome my fear of speaking. And I still wouldn't *sing* in public. Then a wise old Hawaiian woman chastised me when I declined to sing a solo at a Church meeting. Holding back was a sign of pride. Just stand up, do your best, and look to the Lord for your approval, not the world, she instructed me. So I took her advice, and I've been singing ever since and overcoming that fear.

For a time I was happy, contentedly doing everything that I loved. Then one day I read a brief article in a doctor's office called "Feeling the Fear but Doing It Anyway." Challenge yourself, the article suggested, to do something way beyond your abilities and see how far you get. Any little distance you cover will be a victory. I told Doug about the article, and he suggested that I try out for the Tabernacle Choir. I nearly fell off my chair. That *was* out of reach—something I'd never even considered.

But I asked around and learned that try-outs included three parts. First is a written test. I did that and passed. Then they require a home demo tape. So I did that and was told I passed. Next they would call me for a personal audition when there was an opening. After waiting two and a half years, I wrote in my journal, "I tried out for the Tabernacle Choir. I made it two-thirds of the way, and that was a victory." And I closed that chapter.

Several weeks later, I received a call inviting me to a personal audition. Talk about fear. "You'll always wonder if you don't try," Doug said. I was fifty-five. Choir members generally aren't accepted after age fifty-five because members have to quit at sixty and they like you to serve five years. Doug went with me to audition. The person before me had the most exquisite, well-trained voice. I said, "Douglas, let's go before she comes out because I cannot do this." The door opened, Doug took my hand and pulled me into the audition room. I had never known fear like that. As I sang my audition, I thought, *Whose voice is this anyway? It's not mine.* I knew I had not done my best.

Afterwards I cried, certain that I would never sing in the Tabernacle Choir. Two weeks later, to my amazement, I received a call to sing in the choir. Sister JoAnn Ottley works with new choir members who may need a little extra vocal help. She called me in right away. I said, "Sister Ottley, when I auditioned, I was too afraid even to do what I can do. For my peace of mind, tell me, how did I get in the choir?" She answered, "Well, we could tell you were afraid. We knew your musical background from your written test, and we had heard your tape. But sometimes we hear a voice that won't hurt the choir, and we feel we can bring you along with us . . ." She paused a moment and then smiled, "The bottom line is we pray over every person who auditions, and if the Lord says yes, you're called. So work hard and be at peace."

I've now had five beautiful years in the choir that I wouldn't have had if I had listened to my fear. I'm almost sixty. Soon I'll have to quit, but I'll have been on a wonderful European tour first. If my fear had held me back from the audition, I would have missed it all. So don't let your fears hold you back. Oliver Wendell Holmes said, "Many people die with their music still in them."[1]

To find your talents, think, *What brings me compliments? What comes more easily to me than to other people? What seems familiar to me?* I believe we might have brought some of what we did in our premortal lives here with us, inside of us, somehow a part of our individual, immortal spirits. Occasionally when I write music, I feel that I have heard it before. Look for the things at any age that interest you.

Good intentions are not enough; we must begin. Too often we're always getting ready to live. Before we know it, time runs out. Rabindranath Tagore wrote, "I have spent my days stringing and unstringing my instrument while the song I came to sing remains unsung."² So don't wait. Think of something you've never done before but secretly want to do and then take steps toward it. Any distance you cover will be a victory.

About a year before Sister Camilla Kimball died, she attended a dinner at the Church Office Building. She was bent over and had an oxygen tank with her. Her daughter was with her to help her. During the meal, however, she told me that she was having the best time taking oil painting lessons, painting the four seasons as they looked from the back door of her apartment. I said, "Is that a new talent or something you're adding to?" She answered, "Oh, it's brand new and it's very exciting." Anything she accomplished, she told me, would go with her when she left this life and give her a little head start.

A year ago, a Relief Society president from St. George visited to videotape me talking about developing talents. Her husband, a very shy man, came with her. I could tell right off that he was a good man. He sat back and listened as I talked. When they returned home, he told his wife that he had thought of something he wanted to try as a new talent—metal sculpture. She was pleased, feeling that he sat back too much; she had wanted him to be more involved in life. He started collecting what we might consider pieces of junk. Several months later, he brought us a sculpture that he called "The Tree of Life" with an explanation of what it meant to him. The next year he made sculptures for his children, neighbors, and friends. On a recent visit to St. George, he presented Doug and me with a new sculpture, "Cosmic Saw," and a framed explanation of its meaning. He seemed like a new person.

Ten days afterward, his wife called to tell us that Sid had been killed instantly in a car accident. I couldn't believe it. He had seemed so alive and so interested in his new talents. Later I phoned and said, "Tell me about him. Tell me what his life was like." I wanted her to have a chance to talk about him. Among other things, she said, "Developing his talents made him come alive, gave him a purpose for his everyday life, his spare time. The work brought joy to him and to many people who received his sculptures." She added that his sculptures would be treasures for his children.

A few months ago I saw an ad in the *Deseret News* about a Call-a-Jazz-Game contest. I read sports pages from three papers every day. Top to bottom. And I thought, *I could do that. I know how to write. I want to be a sports writer. Think of all the fun people I could meet.* So I stayed up late that night. I watched the Jazz–Houston game, took six pages of notes, wrote my article about the game, and got it in to the Jazz office the next morning. I thought it was a pretty decent article. The first-place winner would get to sit on press row and cover the Jazz–Clippers game. The winning article would appear in the *Deseret News* the next day. It would be fun to win. The second-place winner would get Jazz tickets for the whole family; third place, a Jazz cap; and fourth, a book on the Jazz's last season. I won fourth prize. And I thought, *Well, so much for that. I won't do that anymore.* Then I thought, *Wait a minute. I loved doing that. I'm going to call and find out the date for next year's contest.* Maybe in the next portion of my life I can be a sports writer. If you don't ever hear about me as a sports writer, you'll know it wasn't because I didn't try.

As we're working toward our large aspirations, we need to enjoy the small experiences along the way. Let me give you two examples. Of all my experiences with the Tabernacle Choir, singing in the finest concert halls in the United States and Europe, the experience that touched me most was in Salt Lake City. The Sunday before Christmas, the Make-a-Wish foundation brought a little girl to the Tabernacle to hear the Sunday broadcast. Afterward, she came up to the podium, and we sang a special arrangement of "Silent Night" for her. As she stood there with her mother's arm around her, I thought, *All the big events in the world don't compare for me to this one small focused moment.* I've heard my Primary songs sung at general conference, but I've also heard them at the American Fork Training School, sung by disabled children who could hardly learn or form words but had tears streaming down their faces while they sang.

Don't forget to have fun with your talents too. I have a whole collection of songs I hope the world will never hear. Once, Doug and I were to do a Christmas program at the Utah State prison, and I thought, *What can I do for them? Spending Christmas at prison, how would that be?* I wrote a song to the tune of "Jingle Bells" called "Prison Cells." It went

247

something like, "Prison cells, prison cells, ugly drab and gray. Still it's Christmas in my heart. You can't take that away," and so on. It was silly, but it was fun.

This couplet, quoted by Sister Norma Ashton, gives good advice: "I'll be content if I can just learn / Which bridges to cross and which to burn."[3] In your pursuit of your talents, keep that in mind. Take risks and have fun, but don't try to do too much. Burn a few bridges. Let me end with the comforting words of the Master that I put into a song, entitled "Do Not Run Faster":

I thought that I could do it all, complete each task, accept each call.
I never felt my work was done, until I had pleased everyone.
I told myself I must be strong, be there for all to lean upon,
But in the end I came to see, that's more than God requires of me.
He has said:

Chorus
Do not run faster than you have strength.
If you grow weary, what have you gained?
You will have wisdom and strength enough,
If first you remember to fill your own cup.

DOUGLAS: Living with my wife, Janice, and her talents has always been interesting. Before I met her, she was already a fine musician and a great athlete. I guess, if the truth were told, she probably should have become a professional athlete—she was just born thirty years too soon. I'm sure she could have quarterbacked her high school football team and taken them to the state championship—she's that good.

So in between her music and her other talents, sports occupy a lot of her life. During the 1998 NCAA finals, she was flipping channels watching the University of Utah Utes play in the championship series and the Utah Jazz play on another channel. I came into the room and needed to know something. "Honey," I said, and asked her the question. She didn't respond—she was still changing channels. "Honey?" Still no response. I said, "Jani, do you love me?" Still no answer. I shook her shoulder gently and finally got through. "Hmm?" she said. I asked again, "Do you love me more than basketball?" Without looking up she said, "College or pro?"

Developing talents can be painful—it can also be a pain for the people we live with. If we can learn to see the humor in our experiences, we'll be better off. Here's a case in point. Soon after we were married, Janice and I moved to Pacific Grove, California. I was in the army and studying Russian at the Army Language School at the Presidio of Monterey. We lived in a tiny, cracker-box home. Our bedroom was our living room and dressing room with a curtain across part of it to hide our clothes. We had a bathroom, a tiny kitchen, and a front and back door. Every day, new bride Janice worked to perfect her cooking skills, and each day she'd ask me, "Honey, what would you like for supper?" One day I suggested she bake some homemade bread. My mother had taught me how to make bread, so I wrote down the recipe for Janice and left for school. All day I thought about coming home to aromatic, delicious homemade bread.

When I entered the kitchen door that evening I smelled nothing. No wonderful aroma. I went down the hall to the living room/dressing room/bedroom and found Janice crying on the bed. She just pointed to the kitchen. I walked back to the kitchen and noticed what I hadn't seen the first time. There on the counter were two brand-new, glistening aluminum loaf pans, and way down in the bottom lay this *dead bread*. I picked up one of the loaf pans and discovered that the pan itself had been basted both inside and out. It slipped out of my hands and thunked onto the kitchen floor. "Did you forget to cool the scalded milk before you put the yeast in?" I called to Janice. I was sure I had told her.

Then I laughed—a big mistake. The bedsprings squeaked, and I heard footsteps coming. I'm smart, though, and I nipped out the kitchen door. She bounded down the hall, scooped up that wad of bread, and from the doorway threw it at me. I was somewhere between the azaleas and the rhododendrons, but with her arm and aim, that dough smacked me on the back of the head. When I regained consciousness, I was face down with my head near a rose bush. I could hear her in the kitchen fumbling with the other loaf tin. I knew my life was in danger, so I quickly rolled over and in self-defense grabbed the first dough wad, lying there covered with grass, leaves, and dirt. Her second lob missed me, and I threw the first wad back at her. Then we threw these big, gooey globs of bread back and forth. At first she was trying to kill me, and I was just trying to survive. But as we continued to hurl them at each other, the globs hit in midair and coalesced. After that, we'd throw it, and it would elongate in the air and wrap itself around us as it landed. We started to laugh, and before long we were laughing so hard we couldn't even stand up. So it was we learned that joy can come after pain. I had a headache for three days, but Janice eventually did learn to bake good bread.

Developing talents takes time. You can cook some things by holding them at a rolling boil on the stove till they are done. You can slap them on the table with a little butter and salt, and they're edible but not wonderful. Most things benefit by simmering, taking some time with the proper herbs and seasoning, allowing for the blending of flavors. In the same way, our talents develop over a period of time. As a boy I read an anecdote about the great Italian opera singer Enrico Caruso. When he first performed in America, a woman approached him after the concert and said, "Oh, Mr. Caruso, you sing so wonderfully well. I'd give my right arm to sing like that." He said, "My dear lady, one arm would not be enough. You see, I've given my entire life to be able to sing like that." It takes time.

We also need to keep focused. Let me tell you about focus. Ten years ago, Janice and I were in Cuzco, Peru, which is 12,000 feet above sea level. At 12,000 feet you get headaches and can't think straight—you do funny things. We were with our son (who had just completed his mission) in a motel room with three single beds and lamp tables between. We said our prayers and tried hard to get to sleep. During the night I heard a terrible cry, "Honey, please come quick. I think I'm having a stroke." I sat bolt upright with a gallon of adrenaline tearing through my system. I ran down the hall to the bathroom, looked in—and laughed. There was my sweetheart having a stroke, and all I could do was laugh. That's awful. I said, "I'll be right back." I raced back into the room, grabbed what I needed, went back to the bathroom door, and said encouragingly, "Sweetheart, if you'll take *my* glasses off and put *your* glasses on, I think the stroke will go away." It did! Perhaps that's a little bit of what the Lord had in mind when he said, "Let thine eye be single." Stay focused.

Staying focused on talents means being persistent. Have you ever wondered why someone has a particular talent and you don't? Toward the end of my mission, a companion who spent no time studying French said to me, "Elder Perry, you are so lucky to be able to speak so well." I looked at him, and all I could think was, *Well, the harder you work the luckier you get.* I had studied French two hours a day every day of my mission except two, when I was too sick to get out of bed. If you work consistently, good things will happen.

250

In Ether 12:27, as a part of a wonderful discourse on faith, Moroni shares with us a great and comforting lesson: "And if men come unto me I will show unto them their weakness. I give unto men weakness that they may be humble; and my grace is sufficient for all men that humble themselves before me; for if they humble themselves before me, and have faith in me, then will I make weak things become strong unto them." He gives us weaknesses so that we can overcome them and thus become like our heavenly parents. Heavenly Father never does something for us that we should be doing for each other. Why? He wants both the giver and the receiver to grow. He wants us to develop the capacity to give and to receive.

Thoughtful practice makes perfect. My first missionary companion, Robert Harris of Provo, used to say, "We are intelligent to the degree that we put truth into practice." I pondered that a lot during my mission and added this: "Practice produces habits." We do something consciously for a time, and then it enters what I call our "habitory." Besides patterns of behavior, habits can include patterns of thought and desire. I have observed that good habits seem to increase our intelligence. They enhance our ability to do things without conscious effort. If that is true, then bad habits must decrease our intelligence and are to be avoided at all cost.

Another point: In striving for a Christ-centered life, we need to be balanced. We need time for self-development and time to serve others. Best of all is to combine both—developing our talents while serving other people. We should pray for such opportunities to give unselfishly and without fanfare. Our oldest son, Steven Kapp Perry, had no apparent singing talent as a young boy. When he was in the second grade, he couldn't always carry a tune. But he never refused when someone asked him to sing. Through the years he worked hard to develop his voice and the Lord was gracious; now, as a full-time playwright and composer, he sings confidently and well.

Developing our talents is fulfilling. I once had an eighth-grade trombone student named Russ. He was shy, untidy, unkempt, never looked at me, and his trombone sounded like the moan of a dying cow. He was absolutely the worst I had ever heard, and he sat in the ninth chair of nine trombones. But he did practice and improve consistently. As his playing improved, he gained confidence. Gradually his appearance improved, his clothes became neater, he began to comb his hair, and the pimples on his face disappeared because he was washing it. He began to look people in the face and smile. The girls noticed that he was good looking. And his trombone began to sound like a trombone. By the end of the eighth grade, he was playing first chair trombone and running for student body president. What a difference the development of a talent can make.

Opportunities to develop talents can come at any age. During the last fifteen months, I have been studying Italian. I had one or two private lessons a week for the first three months and have been reading and studying on my own for the past year. I've acquired a number of native Italian friends and call them on the phone and talk to one or more almost every day. I heard a mission president's wife relate how President Spencer W. Kimball told us we could learn a language to be able to bear our testimony to others. Get a Book of Mormon in the target language and one in our native language, he said. After having a native or competent speaker help us to produce the sounds and read the spellings of the target language, we should begin each study session with prayer and read a verse in our language followed by the same verse, out loud, in the target language. He promised us that if we would read out loud consistently and try to understand each verse before moving on to the next one, by the time we finished the Book of Mormon we would be able to speak the language.[4] I bear testimony that this is true. I have read the Book of Mormon in English, French, German, Russian, Spanish, and I'm in Helaman, the second time through, in Italian.

Too often we compare our weakness to someone else's strength. We look at another person's Ph.D. talent and give up because ours is only at the kindergarten level. We must remember that every Ph.D. began in kindergarten. If you are the Ph.D., don't shine your light in other people's eyes. Years ago movies were shown in darkened theaters and ran continuously. Usherettes with hooded flashlights guided patrons through the dark to empty seats. The usherettes were instructed to point the light at their own heels and to walk slowly so the patrons could follow the light on the floor. Sometimes a new usherette would walk too fast and lose the patrons. Realizing what had happened, she would turn and, instead of pointing the flashlight on the floor to guide them, would point the light back in their eyes so she could see them, just compounding the problem. We must not point the Ph.D.-level light of our talent in the eyes of a kindergarten-level talent.

The scriptures are replete with counsel from the Lord about talents. If we want to develop talents, we need to be clean before God. We need to repent because, as it says in Doctrine and Covenants 50:28–29, "No man is possessor of all things except he be purified and cleansed from all sin. And if ye are purified and cleansed from all sin, ye shall ask whatsoever you will in the name of Jesus and it shall be done." God loves us and wants us all to become like he is. We need to work to do so. Moroni wrote, "Deny not the gifts of God, for they are many; and they come from the same God" (Moroni 10:8). Our talents are among these gifts. Pray, fast, and consider what talent the Lord would have you develop.

NOTES

1. Oliver Wendell Holmes, quoted by Spencer W. Kimball in *Miracle of Forgiveness* (Salt Lake City: Bookcraft, 1969), 16.
2. Rabindranath Tagore, quoted by Spencer W. Kimball in *Miracle of Forgiveness*, 16.
3. Norma B. Ashton, *Ensign*, September 1989, 24.
4. I have been unable to find the exact source of this quotation, but I bear testimony that it is true and that it works.

Anchors in the Sea of Family Life

KATHLEEN B. JENSEN

The traditions we create in our homes become anchors to ground us in a world of turmoil and stress. I'm convinced that an ordinary, perhaps ho-hum, home and an exciting, spiritually uplifting home aren't significantly different. The former just lacks the essential small things—the traditions that enliven, lift, and stabilize families.

A tradition that has become an anchor in our home is what goes on at our kitchen table. It's a wooden trestle table with benches on both sides and a chair at each end. It's been in use for more than twenty years, and it shows the effects of eight children. Eating dinner together as a family is a very important part of our family life.

Twenty-three years ago when we built our home, my mother strongly suggested that we not put a bar in our kitchen. I disagreed because I thought a bar would be convenient and cute. She pushed the matter by saying she didn't want my kitchen to become a short-order, fast-food kitchen. She made me promise that if we put in a bar, we would still sit down together as a family and have dinner. I thought she was being a little old-fashioned, but she made her point: "Have dinner with your family."

I don't know of any scripture that tells families to eat together, but after being reared in a home where that happened and being a parent in a home where I try to make it happen, I know that it's a good thing for families to do.

I like to cook, which helps, but we are busy people with busy children, and time is always the challenge. It does take some planning to make it

Kathleen Bushnell Jensen has taught first grade and served as PTA president. She and her husband, Marlin K. Jensen, a member of the First Quorum of Seventy, are the parents of eight children. She serves as her ward Relief Society president.

all happen, but it also doesn't have to be a gourmet feast every night. Sometimes on busy nights it's grilled cheese and soup. And we've even had Pizza Hut help us out on occasion. But the key is that we eat together. We turn off the TV and the music; and if the phone rings, the answering machine gets it. We sit in our places, and everyone has a certain spot. If someone isn't there, he or she is missed. We bless the food, and then we eat and talk and eat and talk—and talking is just as important as eating. I don't know how families stay close without a table. It's where everything from current events to personal traumas and even manners is brought to life. And then there are dishes to do—which we assign as a rotating blessing—and someone feeds the cat and dog, and someone sweeps the floor. At that point, everyone goes his or her merry way. It isn't a big deal, but we have connected as a family.

I think it's sad that people can live in the same house and yet live parallel lives. I know of a couple who while attending counseling sessions to save their marriage were advised to buy a wonderful dining room table and use it. That is the closest I can come to scientific evidence to support my point.

We did put in a bar, and sometimes we use it; but, eating together as a family is the rule, not the exception. Does it take a little more work? Yes. Does it take a little more time? Yes. Is it worth it? Many times over.

My sister Jane once did some volunteer work in a home for troubled youth. She found that the teenage boy she had been working with was having a birthday on the day of her next visit. She stopped at a local bakery, had his name put on a cake, and topped it with candles. She sang "Happy Birthday" to him, and the cake was shared with everyone there. What she considered a simple gesture of fun and goodwill touched this young man very deeply. He told her he had had only one other birthday cake in his whole life. I couldn't help wondering why his own parents hadn't brought it to him. Where were their traditions?

Think of traditions as the frosting on the cake. Traditions might well be one of the small things by which great things come to pass. A tradition can be as easy as pancakes on Saturday morning. If it's St. Patrick's Day, they ought to be green and shaped like a shamrock; other times they look like Mickey Mouse or somebody's initial. Many of our family traditions are based on holidays with extended family on both sides. We have a piñata at New Year, an Easter egg hunt with the cousins, a family reunion at Lake Powell every summer, Christmas stockings with our

255

names on them, shopping and lunch with Grandma Jensen on our birthdays, planting a garden in the spring, weeding in the summer, picking raspberries, eating caramel corn at Grandma Jensen's on Halloween, riding in our hometown parade on the 4th of July—either on a decorated bike or a family float. The parade route is unique; it goes around the park twice, in case you miss something the first time. Our list goes on and on, and I hope yours does, too.

I have often thought that car trips have brought our family together, whether we are going camping, or to St. George, or Jackson, or wherever. Getting there is part of the fun. I admit I may have a huge tolerance for pain, but car trips create forced togetherness, and in this busy world, togetherness is hard to come by.

In the car we play the alphabet game, eat treats, sing songs, and listen to music. Things we do repeatedly become traditions. Even our treats have become predictable. I don't think we have been on a road trip in the past twenty-five years without apples and a paring knife, red licorice, and squirty cheese with Triscuits. The creative possibilities with this last treat are endless. We make designs with the cheese, spell names and initials of family members and others, and make triple and even quadruple deckers. We carry on until the cheese squirts no more. Squirty cheese at home has little appeal. I must admit I find it rather gross, but in the car, it has a life of its own. We are barely pulling out of the driveway when Marlin says, "Break out the treats!"

Time spent in a car can be good family time. We live in the country, and so there is a little drive time connected to almost every lesson or appointment. Through the years, that one-on-one conversation counts as uninterrupted quality time that I treasure. Cell phones and in-car TVs have started to invade that space. We mustn't let them—if we have them, we can turn them off!

Reading has been a tradition in our family. Reading to someone allows us to share a common story line and also creates a closeness. We have found naptime for preschoolers and bedtime for older children are prime time. I'm convinced that along with gospel stories and scriptures, children should be exposed to the fabulous world of children's literature. No child should grow up without knowing the nursery rhymes, Curious George, Dr. Seuss, Richard Scarry, *Sylvester and the Magic Pebble*—the list goes on and on.

I have a husband who shares this love of books and has read to the children as well. He loves adventure books, and so do they. It helped so much at night when he was there to take either the older or the younger children. Then we each read. We are almost to the point of just older children. I'll be sad when no one wants a bedtime story.

I have fond memories of reading *The Secret Garden* to our children when they were in grade school. We were in the bedroom of one of the girls, and our sons, Matt and Ryan, had chosen not to come in because we were reading "a girl's book." We read several chapters each night and were getting to the good part when one of the boys yelled out, "Louder, please!" They were into it as much as we were—*The Secret Garden* was not gender specific.

My memories of being read to as a child are very warm and pleasant. I hope our children have similar feelings. I must admit I am very touched when I see our son and his wife reading to their young daughters. They are making their traditions.

I'd like to read a quotation that I have loved forever:

> You may have tangible wealth untold;
> Caskets of jewels and coffers of gold.
> Richer than I you can never be—
> I had a Mother who read to me.[1]

I have a friend who reads novels to the family on car trips. Once they went to Colorado over Easter, and she said they laughed all the way to Denver reading *The Education of Littletree*.

A tradition we have had a harder time establishing is reading the scriptures as a family. Our goal is to meet every night at 8:30, read scriptures, and have family prayer. Family prayer is the perfect way to end a day—and we all agree that we feel good when we read the scriptures. But in reality, we fall very short. Marlin always says that our family specializes in 1 Nephi. I can't begin to tell you how many times we have regrouped, started over, and tried again. It all sounds so easy on paper, but in reality, we are not home, or someone is sick or grumpy, or you name it. I think Satan tries very hard to sabotage our good efforts. We do keep on trying, however, and as President Gordon B. Hinckley said, "Do the very best you can."[2] I do think it is a great anchor to read the scriptures together.

When I asked Kate, our seventeen-year-old, what she thought anchored our family, she said, "I know you won't believe this, Mom, but

I think family prayer does." I was surprised because half the time when it's time to pray, Kate is on the phone. We wait and wait in the family room, and by the time she gets there, she's the only one in the mood to pray.

We are all so human; prayer and scripture reading sound easy, but they take a lot of effort, like every other good thing.

Family home evening is a tradition whose merits I value deeply. Family home evening has been a tradition in our home for more than two decades. We've had fun ones, terrible ones, indoor ones, outdoor ones, long ones, short ones, mad ones, organized ones, and disorganized ones. Our lessons have always been fairly short, with games and songs to extend it. On any given Monday evening we could wonder if any good was coming out of home evening, but the cumulative effect of years and years of ten-minute lessons is quite remarkable. We need to hang in there.

Sometimes the traditions we've started make me tired. Last February I felt myself wearying a little bit. In the past, we've always given a little Valentine present to each family member. They would find their name attached to the end of a string and then follow their string through the dining room, den, living room, bedrooms, etc., until they found their Valentine. With four of our children married and our last child almost nine, I thought perhaps this tradition could be put to rest. So last February 14th I announced that we would just hand them their Valentine with a great big kiss (no strings attached)! Allison, thirteen, and Sarah Jane, nine, were totally sad that I would wear out while they are still in their prime. They jumped into action and had the whole house completely strung within minutes. Shortly after we had finished our chase, our oldest son, Matt, popped in with our two darling grand-daughters. We had a little Valentine for them, and Matt said, "Mom, don't just give it to them. Where are the strings?" So the strings have been brought back by popular demand. Traditions do have power.

We are creating traditions whether we want to or not. A rule that has become a tradition has to do with movies. Some years ago our family decided not to see any R-rated movies. Knowing that each of our children has made a personal decision to keep that tradition is an anchor for all of our family.

Sometimes I wonder about the value of green pancakes, and egg hunts, and squirty cheese. We can grow up without such things, but if we believe that the family is preeminent, then we should be doing everything we can to anchor our family spiritually.

Creating anchors for our family doesn't take a lot of money. It doesn't really take a lot of creative genius. It does take time, and it does take a strong desire to make it all happen.

We can create wonderful anchors even if we live alone. I grew up in a single-parent home, and I know firsthand that a loving mother is capable of creating a spiritual, loving, and intact home. The biggest drawback as a single mom is the lack of time. Although the time problem is universal, it hits single and working moms the hardest.

In *The Road Less Traveled*, M. Scott Peck points out that love is work. Love is a verb, an action word.

If we love our family enough, we will be willing to pray with our family, read with our family, cook for our family, spend our time with our family, and do whatever it takes to anchor them. Effort and desire are the main ingredients in making things happen for our family.

I'm convinced that great families don't just grow up following the course of least resistance. They are works of art. Luckily we have some wonderful help in shaping them—the Holy Ghost. He is always our first line of defense. If we don't get a confirmation of what we're doing, then we must change our course. We are human, and we can change bad patterns. Don't let them become the traditions that we pass on.

Marlin recently ran into an old childhood friend. The conversation quickly turned to why they liked their growing-up years so well. His friend said he had thought about it a lot and had decided it was because "we had everything money couldn't buy."

Money gives us a quick thrill, and I have to admit I like it. But buying things, even a new house or a new car, doesn't fix a broken heart. Money can't fix people. If money could fix the scars of a neglected childhood— the birthday cakes not baked, the love not given, the stories not read— we would go into debt to make ourselves whole and well. If we have deficiencies from our past, which everyone does, let's not pass on the pain—let's break the cycle for the sake of the next generation. Let's love our families enough to give them everything money can't buy.

While our family was serving a mission in Rochester, New York, in 1994, my mother became ill and died. My sisters took care of the distribution of her estate and the sale of her home. Upon returning to Utah at the end of our mission, one of the first things I wanted to do was "go home" to my childhood home. Our daughters felt the same, so we headed to Clearfield. Everything seemed so familiar, even turning up 100 North as I had done a thousand times before. As we approached the house, we saw a strange car in the driveway, my favorite tree had been cut down, there were no begonias in the flower boxes, and the roses were gone. I thought to myself, "How dare they! Ownership shouldn't give one that kind of license!" We all had a sick feeling in our stomachs. Grandma's house wasn't Grandma's house. We slowed down but didn't even stop. It wasn't home.

Yet it took only a few minutes to realize that the warm feelings I have about home are still there, even though "home" had drastically changed. They have nothing to do with the structure and the yard but are all wrapped up in the people—Mom and Dad and my brother and sisters, great neighbors and our ward family—and the memories of all the wonderful traditions we had in our home. It is my prayer that we too may create the spiritual anchors of loving traditions for our families, anchors that will help to secure all of us in an increasingly storm-tossed world.

NOTES
1. Strickland Gillilan, "The Reading Mother," *The Best Loved Poems of the American People*, sel. Hazel Felleman (Garden City, N.Y.: Garden City Books, 1936), 376.
2. Gordon B. Hinckley, *Ensign*, November 1996, 69.

Refuge

SHAUNA U. FRANDSEN

As mothers in Zion, what can we do to shelter our children from the storm? How can we make our homes a refuge against the dark world outside? I know a sister whose thirteen-year-old son in junior high school, without obvious cause, suddenly became defiant, belligerent, and negative. He was caught in a darkening world. He started hanging out with a tough crowd at school, swearing, drinking, and using drugs. The parents found they had no relationship with this son who had changed so dramatically from his preteen years. They tried counseling, but that seemed to make matters worse. The mother quit her job so that each day she could pick up her son after school and take him directly home, protecting him from outside influences. Her son resented that.

One night while praying to her Heavenly Father asking what she should do, the mother felt impressed that she should love her son and tell him so. But she knew he would not listen to her, because they had no communication. When they did talk, it was in anger. Frustration and fear flooded the mother with anger whenever she looked at her son and saw what he had become. She simply did not have a relationship in which she could say to him those words, "I love you."

Each time she prayed, the feeling persisted: "Tell your son you love him." But she just couldn't find the right moment.

One night she went downstairs to get the laundry. Her son's bedroom was next to the laundry room, and the door was open. The mother went in, looked at her sleeping son, and said quietly, but out loud, "I love you

Shauna Ushio Frandsen, a member of the Relief Society General Board, received her master's degree in education from the University of Utah. She teaches kindergarten at Jordan Ridge Elementary. She and her husband, Ronald Mackay Frandsen, are the parents of three children.

even if you don't know it. Regardless of what happens, I will always love you." *There*, she thought, *I finally did it. I've said, "I love you."* She felt good. Even if her son was sleeping and could not hear her, she felt good just to say those words.

Everything changed for her because every night thereafter, when she was sure her son was asleep, she would tiptoe into his room and tell him she loved him, sometimes lightly stroking his hair, sometimes kneeling by the bed to gently hold him, taking care not to wake him.

Often, he stayed out late with his awful friends. She would wait until she heard him come home and then wait a bit more until he was asleep. She would then sneak into his room to tell her sleeping son that she loved him.

Those moments became the high point of her days.

The son turned fifteen, moved from junior high to high school, and in the transition, made some new and better friends. His attitudes slowly changed, his grades improved, and he even chose to enroll in seminary. Each high school year got better and better; his disposition became more positive. He graduated from high school and seminary and was called to serve a mission.

One day shortly after he returned from a successful mission, some neighbors visted their home for advice. They had a wayward daughter and did not know what to do. They remembered the difficult times this family had with their son during junior high and wanted to know how to handle the situation.

The mother told them, "You just have to weather it. Somehow, they outgrow it; it just passes." But as she continued in this vein, her returned missionary son interrupted, "Mom, that's not it! Don't you remember? Every night you would come into my room and say, 'I love you.' I *waited* for you every night. I waited until you came down to say 'I love you' before I went to sleep." His mother's love had been his refuge against a darkening world, a shelter from the storm, a light beckoning him home.

After the Honeymoon: Crazy Glue for Marriages

JAMES M. HARPER AND COLLEEN HARPER

A newspaper cartoon pictures a married couple introducing themselves to another couple, explaining, "Bob and I didn't want to drift apart like other couples, so we crazy-glued ourselves together." In a trying, frantic world, we may need even more than crazy glue to keep our marriages together. We'd like to share a few ideas that have helped us and other couples who have come to us for advice in our different professional practices.

First let's dispel a few myths about what makes a good marriage. Conventional wisdom tells us that certain personality flaws—a man's insensitivity, in particular—are the underlying cause of marital stress. Research findings, however, indicate that no personality traits in either men or women predict marital happiness or marital stability. Conventional wisdom also tells us that men and women differ in their needs for intimacy. In fact, research shows that the major difference between men and women lies not in their ability to be close and intimate but in the way they handle conflict. Conventional wisdom further predicts that the more alike you and your spouse are, the more happy and compatible you will be as marriage partners. Actually, it's not similarities or differences that count but how you handle differences when

James M. Harper and Colleen Harper are the parents of five children. Brother Harper is chair of the Department of Family Sciences at Brigham Young University. He received his Ph.D. in counseling psychology and has been a hospital consultant. Sister Harper received her master's degree in social work and counsels children and families. She serves as a Relief Society teacher. Brother and Sister Harper served together when he was called as president of the Korea Pusan Mission.

they do arise. So it's not whom you marry but how the two of you handle your differences that matters most in a marriage. Or to put it another way, although whom you marry is important, how you cope with conflict is far more crucial.[1]

Now let's look at two myths about marital conflict. First, conventional wisdom says that problems early in marriage tend to get better with time, so it's best to ignore them at the beginning. Actually, problems usually worsen over time, so it's best to deal with them as early as you can when they're easier to handle. And second, conventional wisdom tells us that if there is enough love and commitment between two people, nothing can get in the way of marital happiness. But research shows that although love gets a relationship off the ground and is always a necessary ingredient over time, it is not sufficient fuel to keep a marriage flying. Once again, the single best predictor of marital stability and happiness is not love but how well couples manage the differences that inevitably arise in a relationship.

DEALING WITH DIFFERENCES

JIM: In the 1970s, social scientists Satir, Stachowiak, and Taschman studied families to see why some were healthy and others weren't. Their findings reversed prevailing views on healthy family patterns. These researchers videotaped a number of families—some who were in family counseling and others who reported happy marriages and successful children—while they were planning a family vacation. The researchers then asked a panel of experts—psychiatrists, psychologists, and marriage and family therapists—to categorize the families as healthy or troubled. Convinced that conflict was an index of troubled relations, the experts did poorly. To their surprise, the research team discovered that healthy families do argue; they express feelings; they talk freely to each other. The troubled families, on the other hand, tiptoed around issues. They were afraid to let their emotions out and didn't know how to resolve their differences.[2]

In *How to Make a Good Marriage Great*, psychologist Victor Cline says, "Good marriages are not problem-free. In fact, I suspect that there are really no great differences in the number and severity of problems in the marriages of those who divorce and those who do not. The difference is in the individual's commitment, energy, and skill in creating joy and continuing love in their relationship—despite whatever disasters booby-trap them along the way."[3]

Most of us have tried badgering those we love to make them meet our wants and needs. We usually talk to our spouse about what he or she is not doing, rather than requesting a specific change. What results is a lot of justification and excuses. I, for instance, have become an expert at developing excellent excuses for why husbands have difficulty taking out garbage. Talking to people about what they are not doing rarely convinces them to change.

The best way to handle differences is to be direct about what you want or need. The language isn't so hard: "I want . . ." and then you fill in the blank. "I want you to take out the garbage next Thursday morning when it's garbage day." With that phrasing, you generally can expect three responses. First, you might still get justifications for noncompliance, such as, "I try to get to work by 7:30 A.M. on Thursdays, so it is really hard for me to get the garbage out"; second, the person might simply say no; and third, the person might actually agree to take out the garbage. Making excuses is the most common response. If that happens, summarize what you think you've heard, without refuting it, and then repeat your request. Eventually, if you continue to make your request without letting yourself get angry, the other person will commit. "Okay, I will take the garbage out!" If you get a "no" response, try to discover why it is difficult for the other person to do what you're asking. Learning to ask directly for a want or need has helped hundreds of couples that I've had the opportunity to work with professionally.

First principles. In addition to direct requests, understanding the following concepts will help you deal with differences.

1. Opinions and feelings are neither right nor wrong. Both partners' opinions and feelings are equal in value, and both are probably somewhat distorted. You, not your spouse, get to choose how you feel and think, even if someone tells you that you should feel or think another way. On the other hand, you also need to accept full responsibility for your feelings. Blaming your partner for your feelings ("You make me so angry!") is one of the most serious roadblocks to successful conflict resolution.

2. Pay attention to how you or your spouse uses feelings, particularly anger, to mask other feelings or to manipulate. Anger covers other feelings—like hurt or fear—that need to be addressed. Your angry spouse may be trying, intentionally or unintentionally, to hide his deeper emotions from you. So if your husband is angry, try to get past the anger and

visualize the hurt or fear inside him. Anger will also get people off your case. If I explode in anger when you ask me to take the garbage out, you're going to withdraw quickly, and I'm off the hook. Anger is also a way to stop unwanted behavior in others. If the kids are being chaotic in the next room, yell at them and they'll stop. The only problem is that you'll have to get more and more extreme over the years because they'll learn to tune you out. Be honest about your feelings, and be fair. Don't use anger to manipulate or intimidate others to get your way.

3. Needing to win conflicts in marriage will always make you a loser. Conflict can help marriage partners in many ways. It can expose core issues, motivate more effective solutions, and give the couple a chance to grow closer. The goal should never be to win but to increase intimacy and closeness. This may seem backwards, but if you and your partner will work through arguments, you will be rewarded with new insights into each other and increased closeness. Couples who challenge each others' thinking will find more creative, satisfying solutions to those common conflict areas of money, sex, in-laws, and child-rearing.

4. Aggression and verbal and emotional abuse are destructive. If needed, sign a nonaggression pact. The biologist Maturana's definition of violence may surprise you. He says that violence is holding an idea to be true in such a way that another's idea is wrong and must change.[4] By that definition, some of us may recognize that we are guilty of aggression.

5. The wounds men and women suffer in relationships are similar. You may say, "My husband is sort of like an alien from outer space. I don't understand him." The popular view is that men prefer not to be open about feelings while women tend to overreact; in reality, both hunger for intimacy and connection, for acceptance, support, and affection.

Yet men and women use very different methods to get what they need. Men have a harder time handling conflict, and women have a harder time tolerating emotional distance. In the face of conflict, men often feel uncomfortable with their emotions and withdraw; women when upset want to work through a problem, sharing their hurt and thoughts. They prefer to talk, trying to get it all out. Men may experience this persistence as harassment. They usually want to solve emotional problems quickly, not talk them to death. Typically, men will offer a solution, and they may try to talk you out of your feelings either by applying logic ("If you would just look at it logically, you wouldn't feel that way") or by suggesting a course of action ("If you'll just do such-and-such, you won't feel that way any more"). That's if they haven't withdrawn first. Remind yourselves that even though your methods may be very different, your relationship goals are the same: acceptance, support, and emotional closeness.

Fighting fair. Besides these general principles, we have identified several rules for effective conflict resolution in families.

1. Identify sensory data. Don't say to your partner, "You're angry at me. I know you are." Instead, say what you see or hear: "The tone of your voice is loud. You have an edge to your voice. You're looking at me with that furrowed brow." That is sensory data, what you see or hear. Then you can share how you interpret your partner's behavior. Those interpretations are *your* thoughts and *your* feelings.

2. Stick to one issue. Remember the purpose of conflict is to gain fuller understanding, satisfying solutions, and greater intimacy. Don't bring up the past or harp on sensitive subjects. Colleen no longer reminds me about my many failures to take out the garbage in the midst of other things we are trying to resolve.

3. Diffuse destructive anger; don't just withdraw. If you need some space and time, say to the other person, "I need some space to cool off, but I will come back at a certain time and we'll talk about this and work at resolving it."

4. Stonewalling is not fair. That means suddenly clamming up and refusing to talk. (Husbands are typically very good at this.)

5. Don't ever name call or swear.

6. Avoid long speeches. I often tell married couples in the heat of conflict, "You know, you just gave quite a long speech. What's the most important message for your partner to hear out of that?" The response is frequently something that the words never said, like, "I want him to know that I'm scared," or "I want him to know that I love him," or "I want him to know that I need to be loved." I'll reply, "I didn't hear those words. Why don't you put that in just one sentence? Tell him, 'I want to be loved,' or 'I need to be needed,' or something like that?" Because the message is short, concise, and bottom line, he will get it, maybe for the first time. He just couldn't wade through all the long speeches.

7. Don't involve a third person if your purpose is to get the person to join with you against your spouse, or if it allays your anxiety so you won't work it out with your partner, or if you are violating the boundaries of

your marriage by sharing too personal information without your spouse's permission.

8. Do not withdraw sex, love, or money as punishment.

LEARNING TO LISTEN

COLLEEN: Most of us spend a lot of time listening, but few of us know how to listen well. If I jump in with a "Yeah, but . . . ," then I'm not listening in a constructive or helpful way. Our son is a debater. Whenever he gets in debate mode with us, we have to remind him, "Oh, you're in the debate mode now, huh? You're trying to shoot down all of our arguments, and you're not really listening." Early in our marriage, Jim thought that when he disagreed with what I was saying, he needed to interrupt with his opinion. That usually led to a pretty good argument instead of a resolution. Jim also realized that as I was telling my story, he was logging in his head the points he was going to make. If you are listening as if you were a lawyer or a debater, you will be using the word *but* either out loud or in your head. Lawyer-listeners do not get the other person's full story. Learn to see and hear your partner's perspective. When somebody starts talking, face the person, make eye contact, try to "listen to" facial expression and body language as well as words, and do tracking behaviors (like nodding your head or saying "Uh huh") so the other person knows you are with him or her. Listening is not a passive role. It takes energy, focus, and intelligence, not to mention self-control.

Another element of listening is to acknowledge the other person's experience. That doesn't mean saying, "Oh yeah, I had the same thing happen to me," and off you go telling your bigger and better experience. Just acknowledge what the person is saying in some way, like "That sounds difficult," or "What a funny thing to happen," or "That was pretty upsetting." Remember also to acknowledge what the person feels: "You must have been terrified!" Our daughter was in a car accident. She came home crying, upset, and fuming at the person who had hit her. As I looked at her, however, I knew that the whole experience was scary for her. I said, "It was really scary, wasn't it." That was the real issue.

Invite more information. "Tell me more about it." One day our second son came home and announced, "Today I got in a fight at school." Before I had learned to invite more information, I would have asked immediately, "Have you been suspended?" But if I had done that, he would have stomped off angrily with a "Oh yeah. You always expect the very worst from me." Instead I tried inviting more information, "What happened?" "I was going through the halls," he began, "and I saw this big ninth grader picking on a little seventh grader. I just got so mad I went over, and I picked up the ninth grader, and slammed him against the locker, and I told him he'd better never do that again, or he'd answer to me." My son was six foot three. I suspect he was successful in stopping the ninth grade bully.

Another element in good listening is to summarize for accuracy. "So what I hear you telling me is that you saw this situation, you went there, and you pushed the guy against a locker and told him not to manhandle the other guy." This is a good time to ask questions. You could say, "Is there anything else?" to get more information or ask an open-ended question about that experience. At some point, of course, I'm going to ask my son if he got suspended, because I want to know.

Avoid asking "why" questions. "Why did you get a dent in the back of the car?" How can you answer that? "Oh, I just thought it would be fun to do today." It's much more helpful to ask, "How did it happen?" "What happened?" "Who was involved?" Most of the time we don't know why things happen, so we either have to make up an excuse or tell a lie, if we're a youngster. What? When? and How? questions are much better.

GROWING AND DEVELOPING

Marriage partners and the marriage relationship are always evolving. You cannot assume that your spouse is the same person today as when you married. Nor are you. In fact, marriages don't last unless partners are willing to grow and change as they undertake different developmental tasks through the years. We have grouped these tasks into four stages.

JIM: In a marriage's early years, couples must establish a couple identity, sort out roles, and establish their own family traditions and rituals. Of paramount importance to the survival of the marriage, they must develop conflict resolution skills. Learning to manage finances, another developmental task of early marriage, can be a good place to start on conflict resolution skills. Other opportunities to practice these skills will not be in short supply.

Let me illustrate with a story of a skirmish early in ourmarriage. I grew up as an only child. Because my mother's pregnancies occurred before medical science learned how to deal with the Rh factor, she had at least six miscarriages before she was finally, amazingly, able to carry me to full term. My mother and father ran a family business together and shared domestic chores equally, so I learned early to help around the house and to cook. Cakes made from scratch were my specialty. When I was about eleven, I taught myself to bake bread while my mother was away at a meeting. Mom was quite surprised to come home to find a warm, edible loaf on the counter. In later years, I came to marriage confident, maybe even somewhat arrogant, about my cooking.

Colleen was equally confident. She grew up in a large farm family. The boys did the outside chores, like feeding the animals and tending the farm, while the girls kept the house clean and cooked meals. In college Colleen majored in home economics education. So when we married, she already knew how to cook plus a great deal about foods and nutrition. Our first fight was over how to prepare a pizza. I, of course, had learned the "only true" way to make pizza. I knew that "apostate" groups made pizza other ways, but imagine my shock at discovering that Colleen was one of them. Our fight over that pizza was our first attempt to resolve a conflict. We were certainly novices. It's good to remember those experiences in your early years. They help you realize now, years later, that you are different—you have developed.

COLLEEN: A major task of the middle years is agreeing on how to raise and discipline children while still keeping marriage a first priority. Babies and small children and teenagers can be needy, and sometimes they must come first; however, if children *always* come first, your marriage will begin to suffer. Remember that at some point your children will no longer be living with you—at least you hope so. Our eighteen-year-old son once threatened angrily, "I'm going to move out. I don't like living here any more." And I said, "Go ahead. Move out." He quickly changed tactics: "No. I'm going to live here until I'm fifty-five!" He won. I was terrified.

One night at supper, Jim and I had a disagreement in front of the children. I don't remember what it was about, but I remember slamming down a plate so hard it broke. The children stopped chewing and looked frightened. "What's the matter?" I demanded. Nobody responded. "Are you afraid of something?" I pressed on. Finally one child ventured, "We're afraid you and Dad are going to get a divorce." My anger melted away, and I assured them we were not headed for a divorce. "We're just having a problem right now and we'll work it out. We're committed to working out our problems instead of divorcing." The middle years can be particularly stressful. Remember, however, that the very best gift we can give our children is to make our marriage relationship strong.

During these middle years of marriage, spouses also need to promote each other's personal growth, even though they're probably doing different things. Whether you are in the home or in the workplace, working together or separately, personal growth helps keep a relationship alive. Yet as we protect individuality, we also need to maintain intimacy.

Next come the Sandwich Years. Jim had a more stuffy title, but I'm *in* these years, and I feel squished and sandwiched in between two bready stages of my life as I try to manage children starting out on their own while also caring for the needs of aging parents who need help. This is the time when parents launch their children, one major developmental task of these years. And then, just when you think the house is going to get bigger and you make plans for the extra bedrooms, you end up tending grandchildren, letting married children move back to save for a down payment, or caring for an aging mom or dad. This is also a time to find new interests and identity. For years, your social life has revolved around the children's activities—basketball games, piano recitals, dance rehearsals, homework. In this stage, you're not as focused on them. It's time to renegotiate your relationship with your spouse and determine how you are going to enjoy life now it's just the two of you. Finding new interests you can share will be important.

JIM: The later years involve still different issues. People often assume that issues in marriage are similar across the life cycle, but a study I'm involved in indicates that couples deal with much different issues in their later years than they did earlier.[5] For instance, older couples report that they seldom argue. They've probably identified each other's "hot spots" and have learned to ignore them or have worked through them. Older couples also know they've weathered both ups and downs in marriage and now want to review their lives together, remembering the satisfying times.

OPENING SPACES FOR EACH OTHER

COLLEEN: Biologist Humberto Maturana defines love as opening space for the existence of another.[6] When we criticize someone, we start closing space. If the purpose is to motivate a change, criticism isn't effective, anyway. We can't change anybody but ourselves. Judith Sills, author of *Loving Men More and Needing Men Less*, believes there is no such thing as constructive criticism. One zinger will erase twenty acts of kindness. If you hear, "Because I love you, I'm going to tell you something," brace yourself. Unless it's something that can be fixed immediately with

271

a napkin or a safety pin, I'd rather not know. Most criticism is better left unsaid. Consider also *how* you request changes or point out a problem. Instead of saying, "We wouldn't have so many money problems if you'd just balance the checkbook" (a hurtful "constructive criticism"), you could say, "You know, I get anxious when the checkbook isn't balanced" (identifying how the behavior affects you) or "Maybe we could work on it together" (offering help). Pointing out a problem need not sound like blaming.

A critical attitude can be an unconscious bad habit. For a week, keep track of how many times you are positive with your spouse, children, or others. You might be surprised. Often we think we are being positive when we really aren't. Lately I've noticed my youngest daughter tensing up whenever I am around. I started paying attention and realized that I have been critical of her lately because I'm worried about her. She's turning thirteen and becoming a typical teenager. I just hate to see my youngest entering those difficult years, even though she's not really doing anything wrong. It isn't her behavior but my criticisms and wary attitude that are straining our relationship.

Let me repeat: The only person we can change is ourselves. But don't despair! Little personal changes can lead to gratifying changes in relationships. Picture a mobile. If one piece changes, the others have to adjust.

When Jim and I first got married, I stored up all of my anger and irritations, like stuffing a big garbage bag, and about every six weeks I dumped it all on Jim. "And do you remember that two weeks ago you didn't take out the garbage?" Jim would feel bad and apologize, but nothing would change. Then I would begin collecting irritations again. Finally I decided to change my attitude and behavior—at least about the garbage. I would deal with what was current. I learned not to store up grievances to bring out later. Last week I reminded Jim to take out the garbage, but when I came home he'd forgotten. We have two cans, and both were overflowing. In the past, we would have had a fight. It's no longer that big of a deal. Taking out the garbage has never been high on Jim's priority list, but I love him anyway.

CONNECTION RITUALS

JIM: It takes energy, commitment, and positive communication to create what we call connection rituals between a husband and wife. First of all, may we recommend what we call ten-second kisses, not pecks on the

cheek? No doubt ten-second kisses were common while you were courting or in your first year of marriage. Try them again now. You might be
thinking, *If I did that, my husband would immediately sweep me up and take
me to the bedroom*. But there is a difference between affection and sex,
and you need to work that out in your relationship. Affection becomes
increasingly important over the life span of a marriage while sex
becomes less important. Connection rituals of some kind focus on affection needs.

A connection ritual that Colleen and I developed revolved around
my work schedule. When we moved into our present home, it took a
while to get draperies up on the picture window in the living room. One
day, the neighbor across the street said to Colleen, "You know, my kids
always pay attention to your home about the time your husband leaves
for work and then again when he comes home." "Why is that?" Colleen
asked. "Well," she replied, "because they can always find you 'making
out' in the living room then."

Besides daily rituals, leave space in your planner for romantic days.
Create time for intimacy and sexuality. *The Complete Idiot's Guide to a
Healthy Relationship* (which is actually a fairly decent book) advises: Date
your husband and make it a grand seduction.[7] Get away for a weekend, if
you have to, to find time for each other. Or hang a sign on the door that
says to the kids that this is Mom and Dad's time. Not necessarily for sex
but just for time to connect. An important element in intimacy is taking
time to sit and talk with each other about the day, about the things you
read, the experiences you enjoy. Make connections with each other.

Now let's talk for a minute about timing and pacing. Years ago
a researcher named Ray Birdwhistle studied the nonverbal exchanges
that move a man and a woman in the American culture from their first
contact (usually holding hands) to sexual intercourse. He identified
twenty-six steps and concluded that the pacing and rhythm in moving
through the steps, like a dance between the two of you, is important.
Birdwhistle also discovered the importance of sequence. Have you
ever been fixing dinner and your husband began initiating step fifteen?
You probably said, "Stop that. Now's not the time. Are you trying to be
affectionate or is this about sex? What is this?" What he doesn't understand is that it is important to start at step one rather than jumping to
fifteen.

COLLEEN: When my mom was teaching me about sex, I asked her,

"Well, is it as good as candy?" For me, at that young age, candy was the best thing in life. She answered positively, "Oh, Colleen, it's better." My mom helped me have a good attitude about sexual intimacy. And you know what? Sometimes it wasn't as good as candy, but as we worked at it, it has gotten better and better. After twenty-seven years, it is still an important part of our relationship. As you get older, you will need to plan time for this relationship. I struggle with a chronic illness and am often fatigued. We have to plan for times when I am not exhausted. If you are not in the mood, cuddling and being loving can help. Remember, if you don't use it, you're going to lose it—especially as you grow older.

The most important three-letter word in marriage, however, is *fun*, not *sex*. Keep childlike playfulness alive in your relationship and be serious about not being serious. We must carve out free hours just to be together and protect that free time from conflict and problems. We've had the experience of clinging, crying children or pouting teenagers who don't want you to leave. Tell them that you will be nicer to be around and better parents if you can go out and have time together. It's true. Jim and I once went out just after we had had a fight with one of our children. I began to disagree with Jim's handling of the problem when he stopped me. "You know, this time is for us. I know we need to deal with and concentrate on his problem soon, but can we shelve it for now and just be together and enjoy each other?" We did.

While serving in Korea, we attended a mission presidents' seminar where our General Authority instructor asked, "What's the most important meeting that you have?" We raised our hands and suggested zone conference and other missionary meetings, but those weren't the answers he wanted. Then we started guessing, "Well, . . . family home evening? . . . Sunday worship meetings? . . . What?" Finally he instructed us: "The most important meeting in a week is date night with your spouse. When you leave the mission field, the only people you are going to take with you are your family members. The most important relationship you have is with your spouse. You need a date night every week." Jim and I looked at each other. We had been serving about a year—a very busy year caring for our small children and a large mission. We hadn't "dated" very much. We followed this counsel and were blessed.

Share both spiritual experiences and goals. Face your relationship towards the temple. The Proclamation on the Family gives wonderful advice about relationships. When was the last time you read it? Pray together and separately. Strengthen your testimonies.

Preserving hope

Jim: Each relationship has a hidden reservoir of hope. Even when couples fight over how to make pizza, or how to discipline the children, or about whose work is more important—even when it appears to outsiders that they have lost that reservoir of hope, each partner continues to hold inside a hope that the relationship will improve.

Plan to tap that hidden reservoir of hope. If you simply fly through life accepting whatever it brings, the influences of the world that compete with marriage time and marital quality will overwhelm you. If family life is tense and children fight and argue, that often reflects the pace of Mom's and Dad's lives. When our children were younger, their arguments over minor things—for instance, drawing a line in the middle of the seat of the car and daring the other, "If you put your little finger over this line, I'm going to slug you in the mouth"—was a signal that maybe we'd said yes to too many presentations, too many meetings, too many commitments. Slowing down, giving more attention to our relationship, decreased the tension and minor skirmishes. Nourishing and protecting your relationship will guard your reservoir of hope.

Set aside regular time for friendship, sexuality, and fun so your hidden reservoir of hope can grow. The husband in one couple I worked with was approximately fifty-five, a professional with a heavy schedule and a counselor in a bishopric. The wife was a few years younger and very involved in her activities. For many months they had spent relatively little time together. We called his receptionist from my office and made an appointment for her in his schedule. They weren't sure that they really wanted to spend time with each other, yet deep down they still harbored hopes for their marriage. As soon as they committed to protect a certain time during the week for each other, that hidden reservoir of hope in each of them began to grow, and they found ways to reconnect.

Let me end with a few words about my relationship with Colleen. We met when we were sophomores in high school. I rode a bus sixty miles every day to get from my little town in Montana to the high school across the border in Idaho. Colleen, the principal's daughter, was always there to greet me with a big smile as I got off the bus and entered the high school doors. One night I missed my bus home and was a bit traumatized about how I would get the sixty miles home. When I went into the office to call my parents, the principal offered to take me home. Gratefully, I rode in the back seat with Colleen. She was sitting as far to the other side of the car as possible. The closer we got to my home, the louder her father turned up the radio. When we were about two blocks from my home, Colleen quickly said to me, "Would you go with me to the preference dance?" Her father had known that she was going to invite me and was trying to give her the courage to ask. Colleen will tell you we've been pretty good friends ever since. That means a lot to me. I can testify to you that marriage can be that sanctuary where you find your best friend, the place where you learn what the doctrine of celestial marriage means.

NOTES

1. Howard Markman and Clifford I. Notarius, *We Can Work It Out: Making Sense of Marital Conflict* (New York: Putnam, 1993).
2. Virginia Satir, James Stachowiak, and Harvey A. Taschman, *Helping Families to Change* (New York: Jason Aaronson, 1975).
3. Victor Cline, *How to Make a Good Marriage Great* (Salt Lake City: Bookcraft, 1996), 5.
4. See Humberto R. Maturana and Francisco Varela, *The Tree of Knowledge: Biological Roots of Human Understanding* (Boston: Shambhala Press, 1992), 246–47.
5. In my work at the university I have been involved in studying a group of about 750 aging couples from across the United States. We have been following them for approximately three years.
6. Maturana and Varela, *Tree of Knowledge,* 245.
7. Judy Kuriansky, *The Complete Idiot's Guide to a Healthy Relationship* (New York: Alpha Books, 1998).

"When Daddy Comes Home": Making Space for Divorced Fathers

Jody N. Reid

In cases of divorce, children all too often end up paying the price for the poor choices of their parents. These children usually love both parents, need both parents, and feel overwhelming stress and uncertainty concerning their future relationships with them. Fifteen years ago my first marriage ended. Over and over I heard, "You and your former spouse will hate each other." "Your child has lost his father." I heard all bad news, no happy endings, no suggestions for compromise. I am writing this essay, not because I have all the answers, and not because all situations admit to a single formula for success, but because I believe opening spaces for fathers is the single most important thing a woman can do following a divorce to create a happier future for her children. Divorced parents can facilitate for their children strong and healthy relationships with their other parent. I've seen it happen.

How? It takes a lot of work, the same kind of work that a marriage takes. Relationship work—with the child and with the former spouse. It's not the cooking-dinner kind but the what-you-say-while-you're-eating kind of work. Most divorced women find it relatively easy to work with their children, but working with a former husband definitely will provide a challenge. I believe for the sake of our children we must accept that challenge. The benefits of good relationships with fathers are clear. Dads are undeniably important.

Our children are half mom and half dad. Who they are is tied up in

Jody N. Reid received her bachelor's degree in biological sciences from Stanford University and her master's in library and information science from Brigham Young University. She and her husband, David Reid, have a combined family of five children. She serves as a Primary teacher.

who their parents are, and how they feel about themselves is tied up with how they feel about their parents. Whether their parents share the same house or just the same continent, children never divorce a parent. They must be nurtured and allowed to dwell on all of the positive qualities that led each parent to decide to marry in the first place. All of us—and this includes former spouses—are mixtures of good and not so good, strong and weak. Think of why you married your former husband. That's good to do even within a working marriage. Hang on to the memory of *that* person and instill it in your children. Feel that strength and that beauty. Your children's future healthy self-image is tied to their ability to love that person. To develop self-love and appreciation, to enjoy happy and balanced lives, they must feel good about the sum of who they are. Who they are is linked to the parents they come from.

Mothers who love their children enough can figure out ways to work toward that kind of Christlike love that will allow them to forgive their former spouse, a person who has inevitably wounded them deeply and often almost indelibly. The closer they can come to achieving that kind of love, the closer they can come to realizing success in other relationships—with their families, friends, and perhaps a future spouse. Love, like truth, can make us free. Pray for help and keep praying. Your prayers will be answered. You might not like the answer, but it will be the Lord's will. I believe with all my heart in Nephi's promise, "The Lord giveth no commandments unto the children of men, save he shall prepare a way for them that they may accomplish the thing which he commandeth them" (1 Nephi 3:7).

After my divorce, I prayed. The answer I received was simple: You must always love your ex-husband. Short and sweet. We are supposed to love everybody, aren't we? Yes, but how could I love him again?

Divorce is one of life's unexpected tragedies. However much we may want to control the self-destructive actions of another person, we cannot. That would negate choice and make us followers of Satan's ways. Most of us have enough trouble controlling our own actions. People make choices after they decide to marry, and our futures are never assured. I was married in the temple to a returned missionary. Sounds good, felt right. Now, however, in the aftermath of its tragic end, I have learned to view my marriage as exactly that—a tragedy, more like death or illness—rather than dwelling upon it as ghastly mistakes, sins committed, badness on the part of either of us. This perspective makes it easier to take stock of the situation and move on. Our children live every single day in the wake of our decisions. We must prayerfully strive to put together the pieces of our family and to build for the children the conditions that will help them live happily and productively.

All these ideas sound great. But talking about this fifteen years after the divorce is a far cry from waking up to a new day, a fresh pain, and uncertainty about whether you will ever, for the rest of your life, make it through a day without tears. Feelings of pain, anger, and betrayal are intense. Knowing these things, don't be afraid to live again. Let Christ lift you.

Let's look at one family that has experienced a divorce. Mom is raising the children, working full time, and trying to live the gospel. Dad is living in an apartment and has fallen away from the Church, but he's enjoying himself. He really makes it fun for the kids to visit, and they have a good relationship with him. In fact, they cry when they come home. So what happens to Mom? She's poor, she's tired, and she's, quite frankly, becoming bitter. She wants to point out what a creep Dad really is, especially after she takes the youngest child to the park and he points out a beer can as grown-up pop like they have at Dad's. She wishes she could divorce her *children* from their father.

What's going on? Here Mom is doing the right thing, and it's backfiring right in her face. Does she want the children to have a better relationship with Dad? No! She never wants them to visit again. His bad influence is wreaking havoc on their lives—and hers. Again, it is a matter of perspective. It is so easy to get exhausted by the tough side of life that even living the gospel can be just one more job to get through in the day. It's time to reassess. Mom needs to ask herself, Why do I live the gospel? What does it give me? Are my children seeing the richness it adds to my life? Heavenly Father created us to have joy. If living the gospel does not make us truly happy, how can any of us, in an intact marriage or after divorce, expect our children to embrace its precepts? And after a divorce, how can we expect an inactive parent to want to return to fellowship? The challenge, in my mind at least, is clear. We must learn to live joyously. It doesn't take money, and it doesn't take magic. It takes perspective, flexibility, humor, laughter, sharing, love. We need to step back from the enormity of our difficulties and disappointments to savor the small moments. Healing and joy will return to our lives.

Children will see the difference between fun and happiness. Often we give our children way too little credit. If we trust them to be wise, we allow miracles to happen. Refusing to give up hope for change and encouraging a better, more honest relationship with his children may help an inactive spouse to find his way back. Aren't we all strong and weak, good and not so good? Aren't even former spouses sometimes lost sheep? We need to pray for them.

Does the dad who shows little interest in his children need some help? Once we get past our anger, wounds, and fears and turn our emotions toward a Christlike love for our former spouse, almost all the suggestions and principles that help involve fathers in family life apply after divorce. It's a matter of learning to let go of our past and inventing a future in the best interests of our children, our former spouse, and ultimately—a sort of free bonus—ourselves. Everyone benefits.

But what if you face the very worst possibility? What if your former husband is a bad, bad influence on your children? Should you oppose his relationship with them? Each situation is unique, but as you prayerfully decide, I offer two thoughts. First, are you being totally honest with yourself, or are your fear and anger overriding your faith? Second, give your kids credit. You've taught them well. They know what is right and what is wrong, and they are much stronger than you know.

It was our decision that dictated who our children's other parent would be. Remembering that makes it easier to assess our actions and change for the better. Situations and people can change. Never underestimate your children's capabilities as a force for good, and never underestimate the power of your love. But most of all, remember the Savior. The past is done, but the future is ours to live as closely as we can to what Christ would have us do. The gospel gives us strength to overcome the challenges in our lives. Our tools are prayers, scriptures, the inspiration of priesthood holders in our lives, the counsel of our leaders and prophet.

Our children need their fathers. Their fathers need them. Our Christlike love and actions, our generosity, and our faith can give each one the other. Everyone benefits. The Savior said, "Peace I leave with you, my peace I give unto you: not as the world giveth, give I unto you. Let not your heart be troubled, neither let it be afraid" (John 14:27). These words are for each of us, no matter what we might face. May Christ truly lift us up. It's our choice to let it happen.

Divorce and the Hero Principle

ELIZABETH A. DALTON

Nine years after a temple marriage to a returned missionary I met at Brigham Young University, the impossible happened. I became a single mom. I clearly remembered sitting in sacrament meeting as a teenager staring at the one or two single moms in our ward and their children. To me, these children seemed more wild and unruly than the other children in our ward. Because there had been no divorces in my immediate family, a single-parent family seemed strange. I still remember thinking, *That will never happen to me*. But it had. I even found myself sitting on a row at church with two very wild and unruly little girls—my Sara, age six, and my Susan, age two.

I was a single mom for four years. In 1994, I remarried. My husband, Steve, has three young children, I have two, and recently we had a baby boy of our own. We are facing the challenge of blending families in a "yours, mine, and ours" home.

Through my trials, I have gained greater wisdom and empathy for others in similar circumstances. I want to share with you stories from my life and my work as a divorce mediator in hopes that divorced or divorcing Church members will gain perspective, hope, and motivation to walk a higher road and find healing.

HEALING FROM DIVORCE

The pathway to healing from the event of divorce requires you to learn in greater depth the gospel principles taught and exemplified by our Savior. To ultimately find peace, you must walk a higher road, guided

Elizabeth A. Dalton is an attorney and family mediator in Highland, Utah. She and her husband, Steve Brunt, have a combined family of six children. She serves as first counselor in her ward's Young Women program.

at every step by the Holy Ghost. The Savior is describing that pathway to healing when he says "strait is the gate, and narrow is the way, which leadeth unto life, and few there be that find it" (Matthew 7:14). For me, healing came only after I chose to walk a higher road.

When faced with the immediate event of divorce, you stand at the crossroads where higher and lower roads diverge. Do you want to be a "divorced person" with all the attached embarrassment, shame, and stigma that is attached to that label? Or do you want to be a person who went through divorce but grew spiritually and moved past it? The choice is yours. Many choose to walk a lower road and remain victims of divorce. They choose to suffer pain longer than is helpful for themselves or their children.

For me, the healing process primarily involved self-forgiveness. As a naive nineteen-year-old, I married impulsively. I did not listen to my parents or understand the warnings of the Spirit. To forgive myself, I needed to let go of the pain, betrayal, and disappointment of the past. I needed to regain a sense of self-worth and my identity as a daughter of God. There was a point in counseling when I visualized giving my pain and sorrow to the Savior and allowing his atonement to work in my behalf. Although most of the pain from my divorce is gone, some of it will never go away. For me, that pain reminds me always to listen to the Spirit. What purpose will your pain serve for you?

For many women, the path to healing also includes forgiving others. The most challenging divorces for Latter-day Saints occur when one spouse has broken sacred covenants and betrayed the other, as in cases of adultery or homosexuality. The wounds of betrayal are deep and real.

As a divorce mediator, I sometimes ask couples to design a healing plan. This task clearly separates those who want to walk a higher path from those who want to hurt and seek vengeance through litigation. Those who take me up on the offer realize that to heal wounds and create peace, the unfaithful spouse needs to do repair work and the faithful spouse needs to let go of anger and pain through forgiveness.

Look creatively for ways to heal wounds caused by your former spouse. You do not need a mediator or the cooperation of your former spouse to design a healing process for yourself. Many healing plans involve postdivorce counseling. In one case, the faithful spouse concluded that a Caribbean cruise would help her heal her pain; the unfaithful spouse gladly wrote out a check. In another case, an unfaithful husband purchased a new bedroom set for his former wife to symbolically repair the damage. As another example, after eighteen months of litigation and not speaking to one another, the faithful spouse started her healing when her unfaithful spouse offered a sincere, heart-to-heart apology in mediation. The couple then settled their case in forty-five minutes. In another case, an unfaithful mother significantly repaired the wrong she committed in breaking up the family by designing a parenting plan that provided the dad generous time with their children.

Don't allow conflict to sidetrack you from the higher road. In a divorce context, it doesn't take much to start a fight—and fights can have devastating effects on children. A year ago, I had a case where the divorcing couple had spent months fighting over a huge collection of CDs. Meanwhile, their two teenage sons to escape the conflict turned to drugs and other unacceptable behavior. Fighting over possessions is destructive, but my saddest cases are those in which the parents fight over the children.

A technique my husband and I invented to quell the never-ending quarreling and contention among our children can be applied in divorce settings. If fighting and quarreling begin among our children, we simply say, "Who will be the hero and end the fighting?" At first, we gave out immediate "hero" rewards. Now, being the hero in the family has evolved into a reward in itself. I have seen this principle work miracles in troubled families. For several years, various judges have referred cases to me that at first I thought could not be resolved, cases involving polygamy, child kidnapping, and physical and sexual abuse. I have seen miracles occur; I have witnessed families heal from severe trauma.

What was the secret in these miracle cases? There was a hero. In most cases, there emerged a mom who wanted to end the contention and begin the healing process for her children. In the cases of child abuse, the mothers wanted their children to heal and not be labeled as victims. Instead of alienation and separation from the father, these mothers desired that their children learn to be strong and assertive in protecting themselves. The mothers saw a need for their children to heal the father–child relationship and trust the world again. With the added intervention of counseling, these moms began the process of ending the cycle of abuse by turning a sick father–daughter relationship into a healthy one.

If healing can occur in such extreme cases, I have great hope for healing in less extreme situations. If you are experiencing conflict, I challenge you to become the hero. The hero's journey is challenging and full of obstacles. Sometimes you have to start over completely in how you deal with your former spouse. To begin the hero's journey, you must choose to walk the higher road, the road the Savior walks.

At the time of my divorce, my former husband and I were both trial attorneys. With our daughters in the middle, we could have waged a mean and nasty court battle. Fortunately, I had learned about mediation and took additional training as a divorce mediator. The first divorce case I mediated was my own. My former husband and I decided to put aside our intense feelings of anger and disappointment and settle our divorce ourselves. Based on my training, we created a new, co-parenting relationship based on the following principles:

1. We leave the past in the past, taking from the past only the lessons it teaches.

2. We focus our conversations only on our children and their needs.

3. We treat each other with respect and do whatever we can to build trust with each other.

4. We trade favors and build good-will with each other (for example, we save seats for each other at school programs).

5. In conversations with our daughters, we focus only on the other parent's strengths. In other words, we say only positive things about the other parent.

6. We have a no-conflict rule. We problem-solve instead of fight.

7. We follow the Golden Rule—we treat each other as we would like to be treated.

8. We recognize that relationship problems are best solved one-on-one. Therefore, we do not involve others in our problem-solving efforts.

9. If one or both of us neglect one of our principles for a time, we don't quit. We start over and recommit to our co-parenting principles.

As a result of our commitment to these principles, our two daughters, now nearly fifteen and eleven, have recovered in large part from their divorce experience. They have good grades and are focused on being kids. To them, we had a "good divorce." I believe my daughters are "making it" because my former spouse and I consciously choose not to squabble and are 100 percent focused on being parents.

We aren't always perfect co-parents. We are still learning how to do it. Sometimes I'm the hero and help resolve conflict; sometimes my former husband is the hero and focuses me back on track. When you create a co-parenting relationship, you begin mending a broken home. You restructure the family, allowing the children to grow up in two homes. If your goal is healing and peace, two moms, two dads, new siblings, and new grandparents can mean a greater abundance of love and support for your children.

HEALING BLENDED FAMILIES

The present statistics on divorce are scary. Currently 65 percent of first marriages end in divorce. The majority of those divorcing will remarry, but at least 75 percent of second marriages will fail. Even when you have made a wise choice in a second partner, significant external factors stress a second marriage.

One frequent stressor is ghosts from the past. If you are a single mom, the best wedding present you can give your next spouse is to resolve as many issues from your first marriage as you can. Create and then focus on a healing and recovery plan. Resolve co-parenting issues that are causing contention.

Another challenge often arises when a real mom and step-mom begin rearing children together. A real mom is like a mama bear with her cubs—everyone knows not to mess with a mama bear's cubs. Yet a step-mom functions in the role of a mother when Dad has the children. That is a reality. The children I have interviewed in my practice tell me that, for the most part, they appreciate the support of two moms. If problems have developed, the healing process begins with respect. If the moms can focus on the children, define roles, and agree on the times when each will be in charge, they can have a successful working relationship.

Big challenges arise when parents are not honored and respected. In a blended family, it is essential to honor all the parents involved. Not only is this good advice, it is a commandment—honor thy parents. I once encountered a case where a step-mother, because of her own insecurities, forbade her new step-children ever to speak of their deceased mother. She threw away all the former mother's belongings and tried to erase her memory. The step-mother's actions had tragic consequences for the family; the children felt unwanted and left home as soon as they could.

It is important to respect the natural bond children have with their parents. In my daughter Susan's bedroom is hung not a small picture of her dad but a large portrait of him. My husband, Steve, Susan's step-father, helped her hang this portrait. If you obey the commandment to honor parents, loyalty conflicts will end.

I am often asked what a parent should do when a child refuses to have a relationship with the other parent, refuses even to see him or her. My counsel is that your primary duty is to teach your children to honor their parents. Honoring does not mean you have to agree with the parent's behavior or choices, but it means giving a fair opportunity for a relationship to happen and heal.

Difficult challenges arise when you try to blend children. Many children do not want a new step-brother or step-sister—let alone a new step-parent. If you are a step-parent, do not impose a relationship on a step-child. Allow the step-child to guide the development of the relationship. After remarriage, consciously create a new family by taking trips together, enjoying new family traditions, and participating in fun activities as a new family. Relationships are built on a shared history of experiences.

As a wife and mother in a second marriage, I compiled an open-ended list of what has made a successful blended family for us. So far, my list includes the following:

1. Be committed to the Lord and his gospel.

2. Anchor your marriage on the principle of commitment—not just for better or worse or for richer or poorer. Plan on experiencing challenges you never thought would happen.

3. Cherish your marriage as sacred. Creatively find ways to spend time alone to nurture your marriage.

4. Be united as a couple and as the parents in your household. Accept it as a given that your own children will strive to tear apart your new marriage at various times.

5. During the first year of your new marriage, focus on having fun and building new relationships. During the second year, you can focus on the more administrative duties of family life. If you do the fun part correctly, you will discover that encouraging step-children to do chores and behave appropriately will be a lot easier.

6. Do not hold back on your love. Don't expect instant acceptance. It is difficult at first to love children that are not yours and for them to love you. It requires a higher level of love on everyone's part.

7. Create family traditions unique to your blended family.

8. Go on several trips together just as a family.

9. Be fair and do not show favoritism.

10. Pray for guidance from the Spirit. Pray for the softening of hearts.

11. Look for ways to unify the family.

12. Be patient. Understand that it can take five to seven years to blend families.

13. Never, never give up.

Whether healing from divorce, rebuilding shattered lives, learning to share your children, or trying to blend two families, you choose the path you will take. Perhaps Robert Frost describes it best for me in "The Road Not Taken":

> Two roads diverged in a wood, and I—
> I took the one less traveled by,
> And that has made all the difference.[1]

Choosing to walk the higher road is not easy, which perhaps explains why it is often less traveled. The higher road requires you to take responsibility for where you are now and where you have been. You have to ask others for support and rely on them—you cannot heal alone. However, if you walk the higher road, you become stronger and wiser. Ultimately, you discover that you are not walking alone; the Savior walks beside you.

NOTE
1. *The Complete Poems of Robert Frost* (New York: Henry Holt, 1949), 131.

Lead, Guide, and Walk Beside: Women as Leaders

ARDETH GREENE KAPP

Several years ago, while participating in a women's conference, I was approached by an older sister who asked, "How did you make it through middle age?"

I responded, "I don't know; I haven't arrived there yet."

Observing the obvious, she replied with a knowing smile, "Oh, you've made it all right—you just don't remember."

Now, years later, in another conference, I might be asked how I'm handling older age. Yes, there are some things I don't remember, but over the accumulation of years of leadership in this Church, I have learned some things that I shall never forget—things planted deep in my heart. Many insights, experiences, and important lessons over the years have helped me in gaining a deeper understanding and an eternal perspective of women leaders and priesthood authority.

We share a remarkable time in Church history and in the history of the world. We are experiencing a broader concept of leadership. For some it may require a new way of thinking. We are living in a time when our voice, our influence, may be far more powerful than ever before—if we are prepared.

President Spencer W. Kimball, speaking to the women of the Church, addressed us with these stirring words: "To be a righteous woman is a

Ardeth Greene Kapp, former Young Women General President, received her bachelor's degree from the University of Utah and her master's degree in education from Brigham Young University. She has served on the BYU faculty in the College of Education and also on Church curriculum planning and youth correlation committees. She also served with her husband, Heber B. Kapp, when he was called as president of the British Columbia Vancouver Mission.

glorious thing in any age. To be a righteous woman during the winding-up scenes on this earth, before the second coming of our Savior, is an especially noble calling. [Note that he speaks of our *calling*.] The righteous woman's strength and influence today can be tenfold what it might be in more tranquil times."[1] Leadership involving councils, cooperation, and men and women working together will increase.

We do not live in tranquil times, but they are *our* times—wonderful times as we consider the Lord's plan and system relating to women leaders and priesthood authority.

Can you imagine the emotion that could mount in a discussion about women leaders and men in authority in the climate of our society today? In the world there will continue to be confusion about men's and women's roles in the home and in society. But in the Church, eternal principles are in place that clarify our responsibilities and provide order, opportunity, and direction. It is through priesthood authority that we are lifted up and "set apart" from the world. In view of the ever-increasing challenges and the need for leadership in an expanding church, President Gordon B. Hinckley admonishes us: "In this world, almost without exception, we must work together as teams. It is so obvious to all of us that those on the football field or on the basketball court must work together with loyalty one to another if they are to win. It is so in life. We work as teams, and there must be loyalty among us."[2]

As Elder Dallin H. Oaks explains, "The Lord's servants must do the Lord's work in the Lord's way or their efforts will come to naught."[3] The Lord's way calls for men and women to be directed by priesthood authority and to receive inspiration from the same source.

President Gordon B. Hinckley issues this call: "Stand strong, even to become a leader in speaking up in behalf of those causes which make our civilization shine and which give comfort and peace to our lives. You can be a leader. You must be a leader, as a member of this Church, in those causes for which the Church stands."[4]

Effective leadership is hard. It's sometimes frustrating. It can be lonely, and when we are starting out, there are many lessons to learn. Years ago I was called and set apart as a Laurel advisor. I was young. It was not my first calling in the Church, but it was the first time I remember having such a compelling desire to magnify my calling. My class of twelve girls decided to have a fashion show to raise money for our stake building project. We even got Rose Marie Reid, a nationally renowned fashion designer who was a member of the Church, to agree to come and narrate our little show.

As the word spread, the project became bigger than we had ever expected. It was the first time I realized that to talk is easy, but to organize, plan, lead, manage, and succeed in accomplishing what you want to have happen are far more demanding. With more questions than I had answers for and more people than we had room for and more responsibility than I had experience for, I felt for the first time the heavy weight, the load, that accompanies leadership. I was in over my head.

It was then that I went to my Father in Heaven in earnest prayer. I went out into a secluded spot in nature, where I felt the most fervent prayers have always been offered, and there poured out my heart. Not having cleared the project or even discussed the plan through the proper channels, I accepted full responsibility. "Father in Heaven," I pleaded, "if you will just see me through this crisis so the young women will not be disappointed and the guests will not be dissatisfied and the bishop will not be unhappy with me, I promise I will never get myself involved in anything of this magnitude again."

Our Father in Heaven heard the prayer of this fledgling leader. The fashion show was a great success; it was even written up in the *Church News*. But I learned from that hard lesson, years ago, that it is not intended that we carry the load of leadership alone—not in the Church, in the home, not anywhere. I learned that the greatest source of help for any leader comes when we turn to our Father in Heaven and seek his help. "Lead me, guide me, walk beside me" is a familiar phrase.[5]

When we learn and follow the true order of heaven set up for leadership in the Church, our Father will lead us, guide us, and walk beside us. And when we have done the best we know, even in our inexperience and sometimes poor judgment, I testify from years of experience that he will see us through. He watches over us and has us in his keeping.

In the Church there are many resources available when we understand priesthood authority and Church government. I believe the Brethren are looking to the women of the Church, asking us to study the doctrine of the priesthood and understand it. Elder James E. Talmage explained: "It is not given to woman to exercise the authority of the Priesthood independently; nevertheless, in the sacred endowments associated with the ordinances pertaining to the house of the Lord, [it is clear how dramatically] woman shares with man the blessings of the Priesthood."[6]

From the writings of Brigham Young we read, "The Priesthood of the Son of God, which we have in our midst, is a perfect order and system of government, and this alone can deliver the human family from all the evils which now afflict its members, and insure them happiness and felicity hereafter."[7]

He said another time: "There is no act of a Latter-day Saint—no duty required—no time given, exclusive and independent of the Priesthood. Everything is subject to it, whether preaching, business, or any other act pertaining to the proper conduct of this life."[8]

The heavens are not closed to women as long as our hearts are open to the Spirit. The prophet Joel recorded the promise of the Lord: "I will pour out my spirit upon all flesh; and your sons and your daughters shall prophesy, . . . your young men shall see visions: and also upon the servants and upon the handmaids in those days will I pour out my spirit" (Joel 2:28–29). I bear testimony of this promise. More is required of us as women than simply to wait in some back room until called upon.

If there is any question about the worth of a righteous woman's influence, her value, and her insights, consider the words of President Gordon B. Hinckley, speaking to the women of the Church: "I feel to invite women everywhere to rise to the great potential within you. I do not ask that you reach beyond your capacity. I hope you will not nag yourselves with thoughts of failure. I hope you will not try to set goals far beyond your capacity to achieve. I hope you will simply do what you can do in the best way you know. If you do so, you will witness miracles come to pass."[9]

President Hinckley further reminds us: "We are here to assist our Father in His work and His glory, 'to bring to pass the immortality and eternal life of man' (Moses 1:39). Your obligation is as serious in your sphere of responsibility as is my obligation in my sphere. No calling in this church is small or of little consequence."[10]

We are called to take a stand, to contribute, to be accountable. This is not a time to ride the tide or to retreat. "They who are not for me are against me, saith our God" (2 Nephi 10:16). This is not a tranquil time but rather a time to participate in a meaningful way in councils, in our communities, and in our individual spheres of influence. And how broad is this influence? It begins in the home and moves out well beyond the walls of our homes, beyond the margins of our fields and the borders of our towns and cities.

No one talks to everyone, but each one of us talks to someone, and we pass the word along. The lyrics of the hymn "Behold! A Royal Army" convey the need for our united effort working together, counseling together, multiplying effectiveness as we approach the challenging days that lie before us:

> And now the foe advancing,
> That valiant host assails,
> And yet they never falter;
> Their courage never fails.
> Their Leader calls, "Be faithful!"
> They pass the word along;
> They see his signal flashing
> And shout their joyful song:
> Victory, victory,
> Through him that redeemed us!
> Victory, victory,
> Through Jesus Christ, our Lord![11]

Yes, through modern technology we pass the word along from border to border, far and wide, and from one generation to the next. May our own words and our actions regarding women leaders and priesthood authority contribute to the victory and never weaken the line.

Today, as in times past, women shoulder responsibilities for the mission of the Church. Of our responsibility, President Kimball, addressing the sisters, said: "Much of the major growth that is coming to the Church in the last days will come because many of the good women of the world (in whom there is often such an inner sense of spirituality) will be drawn to the Church in large numbers. This will happen to the degree that the women of the Church reflect righteousness and articulateness in their lives and to the degree that they are seen as distinct and different—in happy ways—from the women of the world. . . .

"Thus it will be that the female exemplars of the Church will be a significant force in both the numerical and the spiritual growth of the Church in the last days."[12]

When we as women attune our ears to the words of prophets as from the voice of the Lord himself (see D&C 1:38), we are lifted, elevated, and magnified in our possibilities and opportunities. From our homes will come children who have been nurtured and prepared as leaders for generations to come. There is nowhere that our influence is more important to the Lord's work than in our homes, but it must not stop there. A righteous woman's influence extends beyond the home.

LEADERSHIP IN CHURCH CALLINGS

Consider this statement from President Gordon B. Hinckley as we attempt to place a value on the contribution that can be made by women: "What a resource are the women of The Church of Jesus Christ of Latter-day Saints. . . .

" . . . You bring a measure of wholeness to us. You have great strength. With dignity and tremendous ability, you carry forward the remarkable programs of the Relief Society, the Young Women, and the Primary. You teach Sunday School. We walk at your side as your companions and your brethren with respect and love, with honor and great admiration. It was the Lord who designated that men in His Church should hold the priesthood. It was He who has given you your capabilities to round out this great and marvelous organization, which is the Church and kingdom of God. I bear testimony before the entire world of your worth, of your grace and goodness, of your remarkable abilities and tremendous contributions."[13]

The Lord directs his work in heaven and on earth through the priesthood. Sometimes sisters may abdicate their responsibility to fully magnify their callings because they interpret loyalty to the priesthood to mean that they should simply take direction from those in authority. We use the term *priesthood* interchangeably as we speak of priesthood power, authority, and holders of the priesthood and may not accept responsibility for receiving inspiration and helping to advance the work by speaking up.

On the other hand, there are those in authority, bearers of the priesthood, who may not understand the place of women leaders called by priesthood authority and so do not benefit from the power and blessing of a united effort. This must not be. Understanding priesthood is a blessing to men and women.

I learned something of my responsibility in relation to the priesthood in one of my first meetings with the Presiding Bishopric more than twenty years ago as a counselor in the Young Women General Presidency. I was new in my calling and felt somewhat overwhelmed as we approached that first meeting. I had a certain responsibility that was to be an item on that day's agenda. I waited anxiously with pen in hand to receive any direction. I was prepared to follow without question. I spoke briefly to the matter when called upon and then waited for Bishop Brown's response. He listened, paused, leaned forward in his chair with his hands folded on the table in front of him, and then asked, "Ardeth, in view of what you have presented, what is your recommendation?" At that time in my experience I had never anticipated that the Presiding Bishop of the Church would ask for my recommendation. This was a daunting responsibility about which I was to learn more.

I was anxious and nervous and felt the weight of my calling. I thought of my nephew Kent. On his second day of kindergarten, Kent told his mom he had pains in his stomach and didn't want to go to school. Before treating the symptoms she determined to ascertain, if possible, the cause. "Kent," she asked, "what are you feeling?" He explained his concern very clearly. "Mom," he cried, "I'm afraid of the hard work and the big boys." I could relate to his feelings.

A young sister who had recently been called as ward Relief Society president spoke to me of her concerns. "I am much younger than most of the sisters in my ward," she said. "I am inexperienced. How do I do it?" She might have asked, as others have, "How do I honor and sustain priesthood leaders, and how do I contribute so I will be heard? How can I be courageous and bold but not overbearing?" These questions are not unfamiliar to women called to positions of leadership. Should she interpret supporting the priesthood to mean going along with a plan she has concerns about, without expressing her views? I think not. It means studying, preparing, seeking, asking. Inspiration is available to those called to lead, women as well as men, when we seek it earnestly, ask prayerfully, and work diligently. And having prepared in mind and heart, we speak up in the spirit of the work.

We read in the scriptures that if we are prepared we shall not fear. Brigham Young explained: "If you want the mind and will of God . . . , get it, it is just as much your privilege as of any other member of the Church and Kingdom of God. It is your privilege and duty to live so that you know when the word of the Lord is spoken to you and when the mind of the Lord is revealed to you. I say it is your duty to live so as to know and understand all these things."[14]

Consider the theme young women are repeating worldwide in many languages as they speak of making and keeping sacred covenants and preparing to receive the ordinances of the temple. Could that theme have sprung from some academic study of teenage growth and young girls' social needs? We know that things of that nature come through the promptings of the Holy Spirit after much preparation. When led by the Spirit in our callings, we learn things we didn't know on our own. Vision and revelation come by the power of the Holy Ghost, which is bestowed on *all* members of the Church through the laying on of hands. As the Lord declared, "On my servants and on my handmaidens I will pour out in those days of my Spirit; and they shall prophesy" (Acts 2:18).

The power of inspiration is one of the resources available to my young Relief Society friend. I wanted to help her know how to avail herself of that resource. "Tell me about your call," I asked. She said, "The bishop gave me a wonderful blessing. I feel the weight and responsibility for all the sisters in the ward, and I don't even know them." Her voice revealed her concern as well as her dedication.

Consider the unique and significant elements related to the common yet remarkable process followed in calling people, men and women, to leadership in this church. As we consider the setting-apart blessing, we are drawn to a deeper understanding of the meaning and the blessings associated with the authority of the priesthood. "The laying on of hands, for example, is a tangible representation of the link necessary to transmit a blessing, gift, or priesthood authority from one person to another."[15]

What is it that sets us apart as leaders in the Church from a leadership position in any other organization? It is just that. We are *set apart*. We are lifted up, given access to blessings, inspiration, and revelation to do the Lord's work in the Lord's way. Through Christ we are lifted up (see Moroni 9:25). The setting apart by priesthood authority provides a different arena in which to do our work. The principles are different from those of the world. The practices are different. And the outcome is different.

Another important blessing is the process of being sustained. President Hinckley tells us, "It may appear as a somewhat perfunctory exercise. But I remind you that it is an act of grave and serious importance, an act required under the revelation of the Lord."[16]

Our sustaining of others as indicated by a raised hand should temper our judgment, increase our patience, and seal our lips against any murmuring and our thoughts against any criticism of those we sustain. Our having been sustained by others should strengthen our faith and increase our confidence. In this spirit we work together, men and women.

MEN AND WOMEN WORKING TOGETHER

It is not a new discovery, and it comes as no surprise to anyone, that men and women think differently and see things differently and respond to life differently. We are supposed to. The insights, the unique perspectives, experience, and points of view of both men and women are needed to accomplish the work. We need to understand our differences as being complementary and unifying, not divisive and separating.

Bruce C. Hafen, speaking at the BYU Women's Conference in 1985, shared this insight: "Consider the implication of [the cliché] a woman leads with her heart, a man with his head. This essentially says that a woman can't think and a man can't feel. Just as it is good for a man to have tender feelings, it is good for a woman to have a thoughtful, probing, and well-educated intellect. Masculinity has no monopoly of the mind, and femininity has no monopoly of the heart."[17]

Still, we have differences. One area of difference became obvious to me in comparing men's and women's journal entries. When I was sixteen years old, my father was serving as bishop, and one night six young missionaries came to our home to stay overnight before leaving for their field of labor miles away. Following that memorable occasion, I took to my journal and wrote pages and pages with all the details of an Elder Kapp, who had been one of the six elders. Years later, at the first opportunity, I searched his journal to discover what he had written of that historic occasion. Finally I came upon the page and read these words: "Met the bishop's daughter and she is cute and fun but kind of young." Even allowing for the fact that he was an obedient missionary focused on his work, this seemed to be a rather brief report of the experience. Just the bottom line, so to speak.

We have in our family the separate journals of my grandfather and grandmother, describing how they left Utah in a wagon with their young family and headed north to Canada. Reading their individual accounts of the same day, one would wonder in many cases if in fact they were on the same journey. Their accounts were so different—yet they were equally significant.

Of course, there will be occasions when men and women won't see eye to eye, for whatever reason. There may be occasions when the opportunity to express one's recommendations is not made available.

But how we respond to priesthood leaders can have a tremendous influence, I believe, on the opportunities to participate, to be heard, to learn from others, and to contribute. In conversation with some priesthood leaders, I learned about natural reactions to certain leadership styles and how responses can be influenced.

The first leadership style is that of a woman who is overbearing and difficult to work with, maybe a person full of "zeal without knowledge," as Brother Hugh Nibley speaks of. The obvious reaction of other leaders would be to minimize or even avoid interaction with this leader.

The second leadership style is that of the woman who is passive and does not contribute. It is almost as though she were invisible. The reaction is to ignore her and expect nothing from her.

The third style is that of the leader who sees her role too narrowly, too stereotypically, as fragile and delicate as a porcelain doll. The reaction of other leaders is patronizing and overprotective; they might put her on a pedestal and thereby limit her growth.

The fourth style is that of the sister who is very team oriented, shares a joint stewardship, and behaves as a co-leader whose contributions are vital. She is well prepared and speaks up. The reaction from other leaders is to actively solicit her counsel and help. She works with others interdependently and synergistically.

It would be well, I believe, to take a reading occasionally on our leadership style and consider the degree to which we are all responsible for the working relationship we have with other leaders.

We need not think and feel the way others do to have our contributions be of value. We don't all need to see things the same way to maintain good relations.

I recall one meeting with priesthood leaders when I left the room feeling somewhat discouraged, misunderstood, and a bit annoyed. Walking past a plant in the hallway, in my discouragement and without thinking, I reached out in frustration and hit one of the leaves on the plant. Have you ever been that frustrated or discouraged? Let me tell you there is a lesson to learn in every situation. The very next day, when I passed that plant in the hallway—you may not believe this but—the whole plant was wilted and had turned brown. It appeared dead. Someone must have forgotten the need for water, but the timing was perfect for the lesson. I paused in amazement. The plant seemed to speak to me, "If you become discouraged, you will kill the Spirit within, and if you lose the Spirit, the life needed to sustain you as a leader will soon die."

Eliza R. Snow warned of this danger in her lyrics to the hymn "The Time Is Far Spent":

> Be fixed in your purpose, for Satan will try you;
> The weight of your calling he perfectly knows.
> Your path may be thorny, but Jesus is nigh you;
> His arm is sufficient, tho demons oppose.
> His arm is sufficient, tho demons oppose.[18]

After my experience with the plant, the sister who was with me on that occasion would from time to time smile and say, "Now remember, don't hit the plant." It has been a good reminder in times of frustration.

There may be, unfortunately, circumstances when the opportunity to be heard is not made available. Even being heard is not necessarily the same as being understood. An example given by Elder M. Russell Ballard offers insight into how we might work more effectively. Elder Ballard tells of a stake presidency who were going into a priesthood executive committee meeting to tell the brethren how a seminar for temple preparation could be held. They described the meeting: "They [the brethren] just sat there, listening to us, without any expressions of support or excitement." In their next presidency meeting, the stake presidency counseled together on how the situation could be improved. In the president's words: "It occurred to us that we had the habit of telling the high council how we were going to do things, as opposed to counseling with them and receiving their ideas and input. . . . At our next priesthood executive committee meeting we approached the temple preparation seminar in a different way. We asked for their suggestions and recommendations, and then we sat back and waited for them to respond. At first they were hesitant—this was a new way of doing things. But soon momentum began to build and the ideas began to flow. . . .

"After the meeting one of the brethren came up to me and said, 'This is one of the most productive meetings I have ever attended.'"[19]

Surely the same principles would apply to an auxiliary presidency presenting an idea to a bishopric or stake council, or even a parent working in a family council.

I am reminded of a time when as a Young Women General Presidency our preparation time had been lengthy—months long, including counseling with our priesthood leaders on what we knew were some of the weightier matters of our calling. It wasn't the style of the jewelry or the size of the manual or the color of the flags that consumed our thoughts or took our time. Those things are nice and yes, important, but must not be confused with the weightier matters.

The time arrived for the final presentation. But we worried (having invested so much) about being close-minded or biased in our opinions and not receptive to further counsel from our priesthood leaders. We knelt in prayer before the meeting and asked, "If this proposal is right, may the ears of our priesthood leaders be open; but if not, let them be closed, that we may not go amiss."

At the conclusion of the presentation, which was well received, as we prepared to leave, one of the priesthood leaders thanked us for our work and said, "Today, sisters, you have opened not only our eyes but also our ears." This statement by one who had not been aware of our earlier prayer was a witness to us that we had been directed by the Spirit in weightier matters.

President Hinckley speaks of what we know to be the weightier matters. He says, "The purpose of all our work is to help the sons and daughters of God find their way along the road that leads to immortality and eternal life." And he continues, "But when all is said and done, our greatest responsibility as leaders in this Church is to increase the knowledge of our people concerning their place as sons and daughters of God, their divine inheritance and their divine, eternal destiny."[20]

Without strong leaders, how can the "weightier matters" be conveyed to congregations new in the faith? And how are those leadership qualities to be developed worldwide?

The Lord's hand is evident in all that is taking place at this historic time. I have been around long enough to remember when all matters pertaining to the women's organizations were funneled through the ward and stake auxiliary leaders to the auxiliary leaders at Church headquarters. From Salt Lake we received bulletins and specific direction on what to do and when. People came to the great MIA June conference from far and wide. (It doesn't seem so far and wide now, considering how the Church is expanding and extending throughout the nations of the world today.) There we received all we needed to know to run the programs, including the scripts and sometimes even the props.

When those things ended, it was a difficult time of transition for some. The communication line was changed. To accommodate the growth of the Church, the responsibility for making decisions had to be carried by the local leaders, within established principles and guidelines. We learned that there was only one organizational channel, and that was the priesthood channel. Auxiliary leaders on the ward and stake level would now counsel with their local priesthood leaders. Leaders, men and women, would be prepared to receive direction for their stewardships locally and seek inspiration individually.

THE COUNCIL SYSTEM

Today there is an increased emphasis on the importance of the council system: ward councils, stake councils, and all other means of counseling together. The idea of councils is not new to our thinking. It harks clear back to the Great Council in Heaven, which we attended as spirit children of our Heavenly Father. And this year, for the first time, auxiliary leaders and priesthood leaders are meeting together as a council in the Saturday night leadership session of stake conference. This is an historic time, a wonderful time.

In an effectively working council, men and women share the vision and are united on what they want to have happen. Having a sense of ownership encourages the commitment to become part of the solution, not part of the problem. Members draw from each other's experience and inspiration, and in the process everyone grows.

In Elder M. Russell Ballard's recent book, *Counseling with Our Councils*, which I recommend to every adult member of the Church, we learn more of this heaven-inspired system of leadership. He explains: "Each council member has a responsibility to be spiritually in tune when taking part in council meetings so that he or she can make a positive contribution to the issues being discussed. . . . As we do this, our councils will be conducted in a spirit of love and compassion and will follow the example of the Lord, who 'counseleth in wisdom, and in justice, and in great mercy' (Jacob 4:10)."[21]

Did you notice how he says "*each* council member"? (emphasis added). That clearly includes the women who are present by assignment in the fulfillment of their callings. Elder Ballard writes: "Too many women leaders are underutilized and unappreciated, at times because priesthood leaders don't have a clear understanding or an enlightened view of the significant contribution the sisters can make. They too bear the mantle of presidency, and they have been set apart and blessed to assist the priesthood in bringing women and their families to Christ."[22]

The most effective councils are those in which every person's input is valued. A father shared with me the outcome of a family council in which his family determined together to develop a family mission statement and a motto. Each member participated in the council, making recommendations and contributing to the discussion. It became the unanimous decision of the council that the recommendation of the eight-year-old, even though there were teenagers with more experience, was ideal for their family. The motto was "Do what is right no matter what." Would that simple motto from a Primary child be considered inspirational? I think so.

Sister Janette Hales Beckham, former Young Women General President, often admonished the women of the Church to become "righteous, problem-solving women of faith." Ponder that statement: "righteous, problem-solving women of faith." Over the years I have found three steps to be helpful in organizing one's thoughts in preparation to participate in councils.

First, make observations. After thoughtfully considering and studying an issue prior to the meeting, be prepared to express as succinctly as possible the matter as it appears to you. Make certain it is an important matter that needs the benefit of counsel—many things do not. Your preparation will invite competence in your presentation.

Second, express concerns. Within your area of stewardship, you have not only an opportunity but a responsibility to address those things that may be limiting factors in accomplishing the work. We have a responsibility to express concerns, and when we do so in the spirit of our calling, they become the concerns of others. As we counsel together, needs and resources can be appropriately matched.

Third, make recommendations. Since that first meeting years ago with Bishop Brown, I have tried never to go to a meeting without having thought through what would be my recommendation in view of my present knowledge. Then, of course, I have been ready and willing to modify, adapt, or adjust my thinking. It is every leader's right and responsibility to seek and receive inspiration to make recommendations. When you do this, you become identified as a leader who takes responsibility— who is a problem solver, not a problem carrier.

Of course, our recommendations may not always be approved. There may be times when, after prayerful consideration, a name is submitted but not approved and further prayerful consideration is required. This should not put in question one's inspiration or the inspiration of the presiding authority. It more likely confirms the worthiness of the one whose name was submitted; however, other circumstances known to the presiding authority sometimes result in a different direction. It may be a matter of timing. I've learned that even when a recommendation or a proposal is right, the timing may not be, and at a later date we see the wisdom in the direction given.

I would caution against ever succumbing to the influence of the adversary by allowing a feeling of discouragement, resentment, criticism, or offense to creep in. It helps no one if we harbor resentment or hurt because our ideas are not readily accepted. Negative feelings, if allowed to smolder, can be destructive to the Spirit. Remember the message of the wilted plant: We can lose the life and light that comes from the Spirit if we are not mindful. Refusing to be offended by things that may not go our way will protect against the destructive influence of the adversary.

Responsible leadership requires thinking. In the mission field I would occasionally ask the missionaries, "Ere you left your room this morning, did you think to pray? And when you prayed, did you stop to think?" [23] Thinking, pondering, and praying are all part of the preparation for our council meetings, and a woman's voice when spoken in the spirit of her calling places her in a position to be valued, to contribute, and to make a difference.

When time is provided for counseling together on things dealing with the weighty matters of home and family and building the kingdom, we are more likely to be led by the Spirit. When an unnecessary amount of time is spent on plans, programs, parties, and posters, we may be caught up in doing things right but not in getting the right things done. The weightier matters must not be left to the mercy of those things that seem to demand immediate attention.

I believe the adversary would like, if possible, to keep us busily engaged in a multitude of "good" things if that would distract us from the *essential* things, the things that make all the difference. Some things matter more than others. Instead of thinking, "What shall we plan? What shall we eat? What shall we do?" we should first ask the question, "What do we want to have happen?" What we want is to lead our Father's children along the path toward immortality and eternal life. With every

302

decision, we might ask, Will this program, this activity, this plan, move us toward or away from the goal? With all my heart I bear testimony of this principle as it applies to every effort we make in becoming effective leaders. Our administrative responsibilities must not rob us of our ministering opportunities. As we strive to pattern our leadership after Jesus Christ, the *perfect leader*, let us visualize in our minds and try to identify with his tender, inspiring example as he went about empowering others; healing and succoring others; inspiring and motivating others; dining and socializing with others; praying with others; serving others.

The purpose of a council becomes effective when the talking and planning are followed by the going and doing. I learned of a group of young women some time ago who were discussing a service project. But they weren't talking of painting houses or mowing lawns, as worthwhile as those activities may be. One young woman, new to her calling, sensing the weight of her responsibility as a leader among her peers, spoke up about learning to do things the Lord's way. She pointed out to the girls: "We have Maria, who belongs to our class, and she hasn't been out for two months. Furthermore, her family doesn't even know where she is. For two months she has been a missing person." This young leader, who might have been looked upon as only a child, said, "Why don't we pray for her?" Another one of the girls said, "Why don't we pray for her and fast for her?" Then a third one participating in the council added, "Why don't we all write to her?" The Young Women leader, who later confessed that sometimes we grown-ups lose some of our childlike faith, explained to the girls, "We don't know where she is. We don't know where to send the letters." But she went on to support the young women by saying, "We will go as far as we can." So they fasted and they prayed, and they wrote letters and sent them to the girl's home.

It should be no surprise to learn that a call came shortly thereafter from a family member, reporting, "Maria has called home. We know where she is. She is coming home."

Do you think it made any difference to that girl that there were letters from her peers waiting for her, carrying the message that she was wanted and loved? The leader reported that Maria showed up at school the following Tuesday for the first time in two months. Is it possible that the fervent, earnest prayers of an anxious family in behalf of a precious child might have been answered through the inspiration given to a young leader in council with her peers? Surely this is the Lord's way.

303

When we become involved in counseling together on the weightier matters of the kingdom, we are led by the Spirit, regardless of our age or our gender.

Consider these compelling words of President Boyd K. Packer, speaking to the women of the Church in a general conference: "We need women who will applaud decency and quality in everything from the fashion of clothing to crucial social issues.

"We need women who are organized and women who can organize. We need women with executive ability who can plan and direct and administer; women who can teach, women who can speak out.

"There is a great need for women who can receive inspiration to guide them personally in their teaching and in their leadership responsibilities.

"We need women with the gift of discernment who can view the trends in the world and detect those that, however popular, are shallow or dangerous.

"We need women who can discern those positions that may not be popular at all, but are right."[24]

I think of Eliza R. Snow, of whom President Joseph F. Smith said, "She walked not in the borrowed light of others but faced the morning unafraid and invincible."[25] There are many Eliza R. Snows among us today, and there can be many more. The Lord's way is not to limit opportunity but to expand it just as fast as we are ready. Our contribution as sisters is essential to building the kingdom.

If there is ever a time when women leaders question their value, their worth, and the importance of their contribution, let the words of President Hinckley resonate loud and clear: "I invite every one of you, wherever you may be as members of this church, to stand on your feet and with a song in your heart move forward, living the gospel, loving the Lord, and building the kingdom. Together we shall stay the course and keep the faith, the Almighty being our strength."[26]

This call from a prophet of God is for each of us, not for someone else. It is for now, not later. The call is for you, and for me, for our voice, our influence, our goodness. Do you hear the call in your heart and in your mind?

Let us go forth with optimism and patience as we stand together, serve together, and prepare to counsel in unity with men and women as never before. Directed by the priesthood of God, knowing it is the Lord's way, we can face the opposition boldly, nobly, and without fear. Let us not be weighed down but lifted up (see Moroni 9:25). In our leadership responsibilities, beginning in our homes, I testify that Christ will lift us up beyond our natural abilities to accomplish our work—which is, in reality, his work.

NOTES

1. Spencer W. Kimball, *My Beloved Sisters* (Salt Lake City: Deseret Book, 1979), 17.
2. Gordon B. Hinckley, address at Brigham Young University devotional, Provo, Utah, 17 September 1996.
3. Dallin H. Oaks, *The Lord's Way* (Salt Lake City: Deseret Book, 1991), 5.
4. Gordon B. Hinckley, in *Church News*, 21 September 1996, 3.
5. *Hymns of The Church of Jesus Christ of Latter-day Saints* (Salt Lake City: The Church of Jesus Christ of Laltter-day Saints, 1985), no. 301.
6. James E. Talmage, "The Eternity of Sex," *Young Women's Journal*, October 1914, 602.
7. *Discourses of Brigham Young*, sel. John A. Widtsoe (Salt Lake City: Deseret Book, 1954), 130.
8. Young, *Discourses of Brigham Young*,133.
9. Gordon B. Hinckley, *Teachings of Gordon B. Hinckley* (Salt Lake City: Deseret Book, 1997), 696.
10. Gordon B. Hinckley, *Ensign*, May 1995, 71.
11. *Hymns*, no. 251.
12. Kimball, *My Beloved Sisters*, 44–45.
13. Gordon B. Hinckley, *Ensign*, November 1996, 70.
14. Young, *Discourses of Brigham Young*,163.
15. Richard O. Cowan, "Instructions on Baptism for the Dead," in Robert L. Millet and Kent P. Jackson, eds., *The Doctrine and Covenants*, vol. 1 of Studies in Scripture Series (Salt Lake City: Deseret Book, 1989), 493.
16. Hinckley, *Teachings of Gordon B. Hinckley*, 69.
17. "Women, Feminism, and the Blessings of the Priesthood," address delivered at the Brigham Young University Women's Conference, Provo, Utah, March 1985.
18. *Hymns*, no. 266.
19. M. Russell Ballard, *Counseling with Our Councils* (Salt Lake City: Deseret Book, 1997), 85.
20. *Teachings of Gordon B. Hinckley*, 117.
21. Ballard, *Counseling with Our Councils*, 66.
22. Ballard, *Counseling with Our Councils*, 92–93.
23. See *Hymns*, no. 140.
24. Boyd K. Packer, *Ensign*, November 1978, 8.
25. Joseph F. Smith, as quoted in Ardeth Greene Kapp, "Drifting, Dreaming, Directing," in *Blueprint for Living: Perspectives for Latter-day Saint Women*, ed. Maren M. Mouritsen (Provo, Utah: Brigham Young University Press, 1980), 88.
26. Gordon B. Hinckley, *Ensign*, November 1995, 72.

Developing Christlike Leadership Skills

CHERYL BROWN

Developing is an interesting word—a present participle, if we want to be precise about grammar. What's important about this particular participle is that the agent, the person or thing causing the development, is ambiguous. In my own life so much of what I have been called to do has been, and is still, beyond my current knowledge and abilities that I have to recognize this fact: Developing is not just a matter of my making goals and then working hard. The Lord has declared, "For behold, this is *my* work and *my* glory—to bring to pass the immortality and eternal life of man" (Moses 1:39; emphasis added). As baptized members of The Church of Jesus Christ of Latter-day Saints, called to be leaders of families, Church, and society, we can take comfort that the Lord is an agent in our development. We are not on our own. It is *his* work and *his* glory to be with us, to help us.

Developing can be painful. It means change, and change often implies recognizing something about ourselves that needs to change, perhaps because we as leaders may have unintentionally hurt someone. Hurting others makes us feel bad. So developing often requires repentance and frequently sorrow.

In this regard, let me share an experience from my mission that profoundly affected me. A wonderful little family was very interested in the gospel. The family included a mother and father, a toddler, and a close relative of the mother. I had been working in a very wealthy area of the

Cheryl Brown is an associate academic vice president of Brigham Young University. She has worked in many international capacities and has served several times as a ward Relief Society president.

country. Among the rich, few had been eager enough for the gospel to be brought to baptism. I was therefore excited when this little family in my new area showed genuine interest in the gospel and began to come to church in preparation for baptism. I very much wanted them to be baptized. The last missionary discussion, "Be Ye Therefore Perfect," dealt, among other things, with keeping the Ten Commandments and paying tithing. Tithing was often a problem for new contacts, but, because this family had a statue prominently displayed in a lovely front yard grotto, I was much more concerned about teaching the commandment to have no graven images. On our first evening visit to their home, candles had been burning in the little grotto as a sign of devotion. I worried that the commitment to have no graven images might be a hurdle for the family, especially the wife.

Finally the time came to teach the last discussion. I do not remember which of us taught the concept about having no graven image, but I do know that I did not make any special efforts nor forcefully step in to emphasize the meaning of the teaching. We simply committed the family to keep all the commandments and be baptized. The family members were interviewed, found worthy, and baptized. It was a wonderful, happy day for a wonderful family. I was thrilled.

The week after the family's baptism, we scheduled a visit to help them get started holding family home evenings. As we stepped off the bus and started up the street toward their home, my heart sank. There in the front yard, glowing brightly in the darkness, were candles illuminating the statue in the lovely little grotto. I knew that I had made a mistake. We should have taught the Ten Commandments more forcefully. I had been prompted to stress the principle about graven images. I could see now how my desire to ease their way to baptism had made it more difficult for this family to understand and live the truth. Understanding the correct principle and committing to obey it *before* baptism would have been much easier, both for them and for us.

We taught the family better that night, but I was transferred too soon afterwards to be sure that the teaching had been accepted. As I left the area, I felt heartsick. I vowed never to be cowardly in that manner again, and I continued regretting the difficulty I had caused this dear family.

One day in my new area, I recounted this story to a recently arrived missionary. As I told him of my sorrow for having made the path harder for this sweet family, he said, "You shouldn't feel so bad."

Shocked by his lack of concern, I inquired, "Why not?"

"Well," he asked, "at the time you gave that last discussion, you didn't feel bad about what you had done, did you?"

"No," I answered, thinking back. "I didn't feel bad until after the family was baptized and I saw those candles burning in their yard. Then I realized how much stronger the family would have been if I had been stronger, and I felt terrible."

"Well," he said, "you shouldn't feel so bad now—because it's obvious you've grown! You didn't feel bad when you were making the mistake, and now you do. So you're one step up from where you were. You should feel good about that."

I have used this one-step-up lesson hundreds of times since then to keep myself going and growing when I felt like despairing about the faults in me that keep popping up. When I start feeling bad about the consequences of a mistake, I've learned to start feeling good about feeling bad. The sorrow that brings repentance is a good thing, and it's always one step up from where we were when we made the mistake. Repentance is a necessary part of developing Christlike leadership skills.

This principle works in the lives of all good leaders. In both the early-day Church and the latter-day Church restored in our times, Christ has selected great leaders to carry on his work, and those great leaders have modeled for us how to develop by repenting.

I love, for example, the story of Peter in the New Testament—Peter, the rock, the fisherman, the impetuous. It was Peter who declared through the power of revelation at Caesarea Philippi, "Thou art the Christ, the Son of the living God" (Matthew 16:16). And it was Peter who, at the Last Supper, swore loyalty, saying, "Lord, I am ready to go with thee, both into prison, and to death" (Luke 22:33). But later, after Jesus was taken, Peter thrice denied knowing his Lord. "But a certain maid beheld [Peter] as he sat by the fire, and earnestly looked upon him, and said, This man was also with [Jesus].

"And he denied him, saying, Woman, I know him not.

"And after a little while another saw him, and said, Thou art also of them. And Peter said, Man, I am not.

"And about the space of one hour after another confidently affirmed, saying, Of a truth this fellow also was with him: for he is a Galilaean.

"And Peter said, Man, I know not what thou sayest. And immediately, while he yet spake, the cock crew.

"And the Lord turned [this moment must have been absolutely shattering], and looked upon Peter. And Peter remembered the word of the Lord, how he had said unto him, Before the cock crow, thou shalt deny me thrice.

"And Peter went out, and wept bitterly" (Luke 22:56–62).

But Peter developed. From then on, he testified unfailingly. He healed the sick. He had the revelation and the necessary confidence to send the gospel to the Gentiles over the opposition of many Jewish converts. As the Lord's representative, he was thrown into prison just as he had sworn he was willing to do, and he died for his testimony of the Savior. In fact, tradition has it that he was crucified head downward because he felt himself unworthy to be crucified in the same position Christ had been. Peter, the denier, developed into Peter, the rock, the sure leader and follower in the footsteps of Christ.

Joseph Smith, the greatest leader of this dispensation, also had to develop through repentance. For example, Joseph tells in his personal history of one early occasion of repentance: "In consequence of these things, I often felt condemned for my weakness and imperfections; when, on the evening of the above-mentioned twenty-first of September, after I had retired to my bed for the night, I betook myself to prayer and supplication to Almighty God for forgiveness of all my sins and follies" (Joseph Smith–History 1:29).

This repentance, as you recall, immediately preceded the appearance of the angel Moroni and the revelation of the Book of Mormon. Joseph was developing into a leader the Lord could trust with something bigger.

Another instructive example was when, following a disagreement with Emma, Joseph was unable to translate until he returned to the house and set things right with her.[1] The Lord's leaders repent. The Lord's leaders develop. If we are to become Christlike leaders, we must change; we must repent; we must develop.

I once worked at a camera shop and photographic studio. I enjoyed watching the photos developing. To get images to appear, light was passed through the negative onto paper, specially treated to be sensitive to light. Then the paper, which looked no different from how it had looked before the light was shone on it, would be placed in a developing tray filled with carefully measured (and, I might add, noxious) chemicals. In the developing tray, images would begin to appear, faintly at first and finally, depending on the amount of time left in the tray, clearly. As members of the Church, we are specially treated paper that has been exposed to the light. We are each now in the "developing tray" where specially selected and measured experiences envelop us. If we trust the "Master Developer" and stay in the tray, even though some of the chemicals are noxious and many experiences seem harsh, the image, *his* image, will begin to appear. We will have "received his image in [our] countenances" (Alma 5:14). We will become like him.

As leaders, what does it mean to become like him? We must develop his leadership skills. Two pairs of such skills are, first, justice and mercy, and second, authority and advocacy.

In his *Lectures on Faith*, the Prophet Joseph Smith talks about the attributes of God as being knowledge, faith or power, justice, and judgment.[2] I think I understand in part why knowledge, faith, and judgment would be attributes of God, but I have always preferred thoughts of God's mercy to the idea of his justice (I figure I might need mercy more). Until I read the *Lectures on Faith* I did not realize what a blessing justice is. If God and Christ were not just, we could not trust them, because we would not know what to expect from them. We would be bewildered by possible capriciousness. But the God of Israel is not a capricious God. Even our Lord's grace, his divine mercy, is not meted out on a whim. We must petition him with a broken heart and contrite spirit. The Lord is and must be just. And because he is just, we can have confidence in him.

I remember hearing in a sacrament meeting of a young man whose summer employer had grossly misrepresented his job, which he had termed ditch digging. Instead, the work was mucking out a sewage drainage system. The pay was poor, the work grueling, and his boss hypocritical, dishonest, and crude. But the young man could not afford to quit, and it was too late to find another job. One night when he came home, the injustice of it all overwhelmed him, and he began to complain, bitterly outraged that this man could get away with his deceit. In the midst of his angry complaints, his father stopped him. "Don't destroy your own goodness over this," his father said. "This man will get his fair reward, and you will get yours. When all is said and done, you will have the fair reward for your work—if not here with this man, then when you come before the Righteous Judge. Nothing truly good you do will go unrewarded. And nothing bad that man has done will escape just consequences." The young man never fretted again about that season's work. He knew he would be recompensed fairly, that the Lord would make sure all things were set right.

So how do we develop the principle of being just as leaders? We have neither the strength nor the calling to punish and reward as the Lord does. But we do have it in our power to treat all people with the same full measure of respect, concern, and love. As a teacher of language teachers, I work with people from many countries and cultures, and I have learned to tell when people expect less of those from different places, races, or ethnic groups. Those from whom less is expected know it, too. Not to believe equally in the goodness and ability of all groups and classes of people is the very heart of chauvinism. To become like Christ, we must be just in our thoughts of, and respect for, others.

Our Lord and Savior is also merciful. On this subject, Joseph Smith states: "But when the idea of the existence of this attribute [mercy] is once established in the mind it gives life and energy to the spirits of the saints, believing that the mercy of God will be poured out upon them in the midst of their afflictions, and that he will compassionate them in their sufferings, and that the mercy of God will lay hold of them and secure them in the arms of his love, so that they will receive a full reward for all their sufferings."[3]

How does this description of mercy apply to us as leaders trying to be Christlike? If I substitute the term *leader* for the word *God* and insert *labors* and *efforts* in place of *afflictions* and *sufferings*, we can more clearly see what the consequences of mercy in leadership might be: "But when the idea of the existence of this attribute [mercy] is once established in the mind it gives life and energy to the spirits of the saints, believing that the mercy of *the leader* will be poured out upon them in the midst of their *labors*, and that *she* will compassionate them in their *efforts*, and that the mercy of *the leader* will lay hold of them and secure them in the arms of *her* love, so that they will receive a full reward for all their *efforts*." I particularly love that phrase, "so they will receive a full reward for all their efforts." Leaders need to have compassion, or mercy, on others' efforts. As a leader you have no doubt noticed an inevitable tension between trying to develop the potential of those you work with and trying to achieve a perfect program. A prayerful leader seeks a degree of balance between those things. If our programs do not have some modicum of excellence, people will not want to participate in them or be involved with them. On the other hand, if opportunities to grow are withheld from those with potential but not perfection, we have lost the goal for which most programs exist. For that reason, developing the skill or attribute of mercy, particularly with efforts, is essential to a Christlike leader.

The second pair of Christ's leadership skills I'll discuss are authority and advocacy. This pair points out a very important characteristic of leaders: they interface those above them with those below them. In a hierarchy, authority comes from "above" to a leader, who then deals with those supposedly "below" him or her. The need for advocacy comes to a leader from those below and is practiced in dealing with those above. Let us observe how Christ handled his being "above" others. Abinadi stated, "I would that ye should understand that God himself shall come down among the children of men" (Mosiah 15:1). Christ took his authority and came down to "be with" us, to experience all that we experience, to suffer all that we suffer, to truly understand us as we are and where we are.

As leaders, we must do the same. We need to be "with" rather than "above." With regard to doing this, I long ago learned two rules of leadership. First, never ask anyone to do something you would not be willing to do yourself. In other words, never ask someone to scrub floors or take someone a meal if you would be unwilling or consider it unnecessary to do it yourself. Remember that Christ was willing to "come down among the children of men." He did not ask us to do something he was not willing to do himself.

The second rule modifies the first: Never do for others something they could do for themselves. Christ also practiced this principle. For example, the Lord commands the brother of Jared to build barges. The Brother of Jared does so but asks for help with two final details— providing light and air. The Lord immediately tells him what to do about the air, but he turns the other matter back to the brother of Jared, asking, "What will ye that I should do that ye may have light in your vessels?" (Ether 2:23). The brother of Jared must think, must work, for a solution. He must develop faith. He finds and prepares sixteen stones and takes them to the Lord. The Lord touches the stones. Jared sees his finger and is then invited into the Lord's full presence. Note that the Lord does not do for the brother of Jared what this leader could and should do himself, because it was not, after all, just the lighting of the barges that the Lord was ultimately after. It was the developing of the light within the brother of Jared. So we must allow thinking, work, and development of faith and light in those we lead.

What about advocacy? What does it mean to be an advocate leader? How do we follow Christ's leadership in this matter?

Christ is our advocate. In Doctrine and Covenants 38:4 he states, "I am Christ, and in mine own name, by the virtue of the blood which I have spilt, have I pleaded before the Father for [you]." By virtue of the blood he spilt, Christ became our advocate. I was surprised to find that Christ claimed this role for himself five different times in the Doctrine and Covenants, generally stating very directly, "I am your advocate with the Father" (D&C 110:4; see also 29:5; 32:3; 45:3; 62:1).

What kind of sacrifice will we make to be advocates for those "under" us? Do we plead before the Father in behalf of each person for whom we have stewardship? How can we lead them if we don't pray for them? And in what other ways can we be their advocates? Can we sit in councils and not say anything about their needs, hopes, or desires? When we call in visiting teaching reports or have quarterly visiting teaching interviews, do we speak of their needs and what we have observed? Do we think of ourselves as their advocates? Do we even go to the interviews? How can we advocate our sisters' needs if we do not communicate with those over us? Elder M. Russell Ballard has talked much about "counseling with our councils," urging all to both listen and speak during council discussions.[4] To be Christlike leaders, we must learn to be advocates for those we serve.

I am grateful to have Christ as our leader. Because he is just, we can trust him; because he is merciful, we don't have to fear; because he is willing to bring down his authority and be with us, we know he understands; because he is our advocate, we can take that precious "one step up" from the mistakes we make. May we come to be like him, developing, receiving his image in our countenances, that "when he shall appear, we shall be like him" (1 John 3:2).

NOTES

1. B. H. Roberts, *New Witnesses for God*, 3 vols. (1909; reprint, Salt Lake City: Deseret Book, 1950), 2:136–37.

2. Joseph Smith, *Lectures on Faith*, comp. N. B. Lundwall (Salt Lake City: Bookcraft, 1959), 127–28.

3. Smith, *Lectures on Faith*, 130.

4. See M. Russell Ballard, *Ensign*, November 1993, 76–78; *Ensign*, May 1994, 24–26.

House of Glory, House of Light, House of Love

TRUMAN G. MADSEN AND ANN N. MADSEN

TRUMAN: Like you, we are keenly aware that the subject of the temple is both intimate and sacred. In 1893, at the time of the dedication of the Salt Lake temple, Elder Franklin D. Richards said: "The temples are full of telegrams from the heavenly world for you. . . . The blessings of heaven are treasured up there, and these temples are the great repositories of eternal life, glory, honor and immortality, waiting for the children of God to come up and bring their offerings of broken hearts and contrite spirits, and draw upon those treasures."[1]

ANN: When Elder Richards wrote that in 1893, there were three operating temples in the world. Today there are about fifty operating temples and as many more under construction or announced. This seems to be just the beginning. Our access to temples will dramatically increase with these many new temples. In this amazing multiplication, temple dedications will no longer be rare. They may still be once in a lifetime, but now that glorious experience will happen to Latter-day Saints all over the world.

How can we prepare ourselves for the wonderful experience of temple worship? Let me answer that question by describing how my love for the temple began and how Truman helped me prepare for my first visit to

Truman G. Madsen and Ann N. Madsen are the parents of three children and a Navajo foster son and the grandparents of sixteen. Brother Madsen, an author and lecturer, is a professor emeritus of philosophy at Brigham Young University. He serves as president of the BYU Fifth Stake. Sister Madsen, an Isaiah scholar and poetess, has taught ancient scripture at Brigham Young University for more than twenty years. She serves as a visiting teacher and teaches the sixteen-year-olds in Sunday School.

the house of the Lord. He gave me a copy of the Doctrine and Covenants to study two hundred underlined verses that referred to the temple. There were hours of tutoring in front of the University of Utah institute building between classes. And there was a fireside series on temples at the old Eighteenth Ward in Salt Lake City, where two of the lectures were given by a young Truman G. Madsen.

Did I have a hunger for the treasures of the temple? Oh yes! And was it satisfied? With a feast!

TRUMAN: In the final lecture of that fireside series, entitled "Personally Vital Temple Purposes," I was astonished to hear myself say in public, "In the temple I was inspired to go to Ann Nicholls and ask her to marry me." That was news to everyone—including Ann. It was even news to me. I gasped. She gasped. We have since said to our children that we had a temple courtship as well as a temple marriage.

ANN: On a beautiful June day in 1953 Truman led me to an altar in the Salt Lake Temple so that we could kneel across from each other and look into each other's eyes and into the clear blue eyes of President David O. McKay as he officiated at the ceremony that would bind us to one another from that day to this moment and then forever, according to our faithfulness.

TRUMAN: Our long experience in temple worship together began on that day forty-five years ago. We'd like to share with you some of what we have learned in that time.

As a framework, we'll consider the following questions:

How does the temple help us see ourselves as we really are?

How does the temple help us better understand the role of women in the plan of salvation?

How do we find Christ in the temple and how do we approach him there?

What level of purity is necessary before we enter the temple and how will the temple further purify us?

How do we access the light and truth that is in the temple?

What can we learn in the temple about praying?

How does our love for our families and those we serve expand through temple worship?

How do we take the temple home with us and how can the teachings of the temple transform our homes?

HOW DOES THE TEMPLE HELP US SEE OURSELVES AS WE REALLY ARE?

ANN: In the temple we are taught the beauty of holiness, the grandeur of virtuous lives. We sometimes live far beneath our spiritual potential,[2] and when we fall short, Satan reminds us of our inadequacies and seeks to pull us down to even lower levels. Yet "daily a voice [in each of us] demands that we ascend, that we rise to the peak of the mountain."[3] Isaiah invites us powerfully, "Come ye, and let us go up to the mountain of the Lord, to the house of the God of Jacob; and he will teach us of his ways, and we will walk in his paths. . . . Come ye, and let us walk in the light of the Lord" (Isaiah 2:3–5).

TRUMAN: Jesus the Christ spoke of himself as a temple. Likewise he chooses that highest of names for us: "Know ye not that ye are the temple of God, and that the Spirit of God dwelleth in you?" (1 Corinthians 3:16). "The elements are the tabernacle of God; yea, man is the tabernacle of God, even temples" (D&C 93:35). That is the vision he offers us of the radiant beings we can become.

Everything that we can say of Christ he promises us in potential. In his dedicated temples the power of his life and atonement and spirit enters our lives, and his endowment of power gradually transforms us into his likeness. Two powerful words, "as if," are part of our temple experience. It is "as if" Christ himself personally ministers and administers every promise and every covenant to us.

ANN: We *can* learn to be like Christ. He has "called us to glory and virtue," as Peter explained, and has "given unto us exceeding great and precious promises: that by these [we] might be partakers of the divine nature" (2 Peter 1:3–4). His temple ordinances act as a compass, to point the way. It is not a crooked path. It is straight and narrow, and it requires our hearts, total commitment, and faith.

Elder Henry B. Eyring says it so well: "It is uncomplicated. We simply submit to the authority of the Savior and promise to be obedient to whatever He commands."[4]

When Thomas asked Jesus, "How can we know the way [or the path]?" He replied simply, "I am the way" (John 14:5–6).

TRUMAN: The temple helps us see ourselves as we really are, divine children of our Heavenly Father with the potential to become like him. It teaches us that this is how God sees us.

Two little girls were sitting together in Sunday School. One whispered to the other, "My grandfather is the prophet." After thinking that over the other replied, "My grandfather is God."

In the eyes of our heavenly parents we are noble children, children of destiny. Just as we see great promise and good in our children and perfection in our grandchildren, he says to you: "You're wonderful just as you are! You're beautiful now! You can become a queen!"

ANN: One afternoon in the New England Mission home, Truman invited me to join him at the close of a missionary zone leaders' meeting. He found me upstairs in our room, exhausted.

As Truman left, I sank to my knees and said simply, "If you have something you want me to say, Lord, just tell me and I'll say it. But I'm running on empty." I had learned such prayers are answered. I started to go down, and I remember right where I was on the stairs when I had an unmistakable impression, "Tell them they are my sons." And in a flash I knew as never before what it meant that I was his daughter. The power of that experience still resonates in me.

TRUMAN: As spirits, we are born of heavenly parentage. In the quickening processes of the temple we become Christ's—in mind, spirit, and body. Thus, when Joseph Smith first sent the Twelve to England he instructed them to teach: "Being born again comes by the Spirit of God through ordinances."[5]

The highest ordinances of rebirth are given to us in the temple. Jesus submitted to all these ordinances, received the powers of godliness, and after the Mount of Transfiguration said, "All power is given unto me both in heaven and in earth" (Matthew 28:18). He said to his disciples at the climax of his life, "Be of good cheer; I have overcome the world" (John 16:33).

If we submit in that same pattern, we, through him, can overcome the world. How is it done? Modern revelation tells us. "For whoso is faithful unto the obtaining these two priesthoods of which I have spoken, and the magnifying their calling, are sanctified by the Spirit unto the renewing of their bodies" (D&C 84:33).

Joseph Smith taught that through this process we become a new creation by the Holy Ghost and that the fulness of the Holy Ghost is given in the temple (see D&C 109:15). We are purged of sin and sinfulness and we are prepared for his presence. We are enlightened by his Spirit. And we are transformed by it. He even taught that this process has, as he put it, "visible effects."[6]

317

I have seen beautiful, white-haired sisters in the temple and have thought to myself, *Who can believe that there is anything but exalting truth in our temples when they see a face like yours?* Their faces are the mirror of consecrated lives. My grandfather once remarked that a photo gallery of such women would convert the world to Christ.

HOW DOES THE TEMPLE HELP US BETTER UNDERSTAND THE ROLE OF WOMEN IN THE PLAN OF SALVATION?

TRUMAN: Hugh Nibley has studied world ritual for more than fifty years. One of his illuminating articles on the temple appears in the *Encyclopedia of Mormonism*. He speaks of the temple as "Eve's show." This insight not only is emblazoned in the temple ordinances from first to last but is presupposed by them.

Our understanding of Eve is a radical inversion of many other religious traditions. The Pearl of Great Price describes God breathing into Adam the breath of life, or *ruach* in Hebrew. Joseph Smith taught, however, that when *ruach* is applied to Eve, it should be translated as *lives*.[7]

Patricia Holland adds an important insight about the nature of Eve's motherhood: "Could we consider this one possibility about our eternal female identity? . . . Eve was given the identity of the mother of all living years, decades, perhaps centuries before she ever bore a child. It would appear that her motherhood preceded her maternity, just as surely as the perfection of the Garden preceded the struggles of mortality. I believe *mother* is one of those very carefully chosen words, one of those rich words, with meaning after meaning. We must not, at all costs, let that word divide us. I believe with all my heart that it is first and foremost a statement about our nature, not a head count of our children."[8]

So Eve is a magnificent mother, but she is more. She is the life of those around her, her husband most of all. She feeds him, clothes him, loves him. But men are alive in at least three ways other than physically: intellectually, spiritually, and creatively. Woman innately has power to enliven, quicken, nourish, and magnify all these lives. In the temple we learn from Eve many essential roles of womanhood.

Some will argue, Was not Eve the terrible cause of the fall of the human race? Is she not justly maligned? Is not woman intrinsically evil?

On the contrary. The temple teaches there is something intrinsically good, even divine, in woman. She is the heroine who led the way into this obstacle course of mortality. Eve and then Adam would partake of the fruit, with drastic, yet ultimately glorifying, consequences. In the book of Moses, Eve sees unerringly and comforts Adam: "Were it not for our transgression we never should have had seed, and never should have known good and evil, and the joy of our redemption" (Moses 5:11). Eve in truth is inspired. What could be more Christlike than her sacrificial decision to seek the redemption of our Father's family rather than avoid the bitter cup? A woman was the first to taste death and the first to witness resurrected life. That is no coincidence. It is a lasting testimony of God's trust in woman.

Hence the temple doctrine is unequivocal. Eve receives and gives. She is an equal partner. She did not leave the garden for trivial, selfish gratification but to open the way for the birth and rebirth of the whole human family.

A woman's blessings in the temple are transcendent.

The ultimate relationship for a man and a woman can be found in temple marriage. Many traditions tend toward a negative view of marriage as an embarrassment, a necessary evil. But in a temple perspective, God commands the grandeur, the celebration, and the perpetuation of marriage and family. Women and men are equal partners: a king only with a queen, a priest only with a priestess, a patriarch only with a matriarch. This is the eternal truth: God glories in the sanctity and beauty of woman.

If only you could have this wave of divine recognition and approval and trust fill you to the brim! It is one of the treasures of the temple. The more you look for it there, the more you will find it.

HOW DO WE FIND CHRIST IN THE TEMPLE?

ANN: Anciently the children of Israel, led by Moses, built a sanctuary. We often refer to it as a "tabernacle," but in Hebrew it is called *ohel moade*, or the "tent of meeting"; it was the place where Moses met the Lord and spoke with him "face to face." Our temples are also places where we can come into his presence.

In the Doctrine and Covenants we read, "My glory shall rest upon it; . . . my presence shall be there, for I will come into it, and all the pure in heart that shall come into it shall see God" (D&C 97:15–16).

TRUMAN: Elder John A. Widtsoe taught that it is a glorious promise that those who enter the temple shall see the face of God. But, he wrote, what that means to most of us for now is that "the pure in heart who go into the temples, may, there, by the Spirit of God, always have a wonderfully rich communion with God."[9]

How do we prepare ourselves to one day enter God's presence? One essential way is attending the temple. Modern revelation teaches: "Therefore, sanctify yourselves that your minds become single to God, and the days will come that you shall see him; for he will unveil his face unto you, and it shall be in his own time, and in his own way, and according to his own will" (D&C 88:68).

ANN: We are to come to the temple in reverence, open-souled, able to cultivate silence. President James E. Faust taught us at the General Young Women's Meeting in 1998: "Hold your soul very still and listen to the whisperings of the Holy Spirit. Follow the noble, intuitive feelings planted deep within your souls by Deity in the previous world. In this way you will be responding to the Holy Spirit of God and will be sanctified by truth."[10]

We are asked to be quiet and speak only in whispers in the temple. It is easy to sense why. It is so that we can learn to be comfortable communing. It is to help us find Christ in the temple.

Some years ago I wrote these lines:

> Would God have us know silence?
> In this time of brazen bells
> Does He invite us
> To a place apart
> To bend in some secluded spot
> To listen?
> Is snow descending
> Soundlessly
> His lesson?
> When He calls to us
> In the still, small voice
> Elijah heard,
> Will we not have to wait,
> With Elijah,
> For surcease
> From the wind, fire and quake
> Of our daily din
> That our Lord's
> Own mild, yet piercing voice
> Might shimmer
> In our souls?

> God
> Whispers into enraptured silence,
> "Be still
> And know that I am God."

TRUMAN: We must all learn when to speak and when to keep silent. Once when I gave Ann a blessing, these words came to me: "You will know when to speak and when to keep silent." We are counseled, "Remember that that which cometh from above is sacred, and must be spoken with care, and by constraint of the Spirit . . . ; wherefore, without this there remaineth condemnation" (D&C 63:64).

We must show the Lord how far he can trust us. He surrounds our temple covenants with sobering requirements that we keep in our hearts what is sacred.

WHAT LEVEL OF PURITY IS NECESSARY BEFORE WE ENTER THE TEMPLE?

ANN: When you think of purity, you might think of a newborn baby. Can we as adults somehow learn to approach the purity of a child? We must strive for purity of heart, purity of mind, purity of language, and purity of behavior. How can we attain conscious innocence?

The Lord has said, "Prepare yourselves, and sanctify yourselves; yea, purify your hearts, and cleanse your hands and your feet before me, that I may make you clean; that I may testify unto your Father, and your God, and my God, that you are clean from the blood of this wicked generation" (D&C 88:74–75).

We need to know what clean feels like in order to get our bearings in this sometimes muddy world. We dress in white in the temple to represent purity. We offer broken hearts and contrite spirits, as pure as we can be, and that is acceptable to a loving Father.

Isaiah says it so well: "Wash you, make you clean; put away the evil of your doings from before mine eyes; cease to do evil; . . . relieve the oppressed, . . . plead for the widow. Come now, and let us reason together, saith the Lord [Jehovah]: though your sins be as scarlet, they shall be as white as snow" (Isaiah 1:16–18). That is pure.

TRUMAN: Our weekly opportunity to cleanse ourselves is at the sacrament table. How does the sacrament help us in the purifying process? It reminds us regularly of our commitment to be cleansed by Jesus' blood, shed for us in the Atonement. We all know that blood stains, but the blood of Christ purges us and purifies us.

After the birth of our daughter Mindy's third child, her doctor said to me, "Your daughter is hemorrhaging. We can't stop the bleeding. A hysterectomy could save her, but she might not survive that surgery."

"What are you telling me?" I asked. "I'm telling you to pray," he answered. We prayed and administered to her. Mindy, frightened, anxious, and weak was trying to calm herself. She began whispering the sacrament prayers. As she lay there bleeding, she reached the phrase, "that they may do it in remembrance of the blood of thy Son, which was shed for them" (D&C 20:79). Revelations come in hospitals. Mindy was given a new understanding of the life-giving power of Christ's atoning sacrifice. She was healed, and she returned to the sacrament and the temple with added insight and gratitude.

ANN: By partaking of the symbols of Christ's body and blood, when attended by the Spirit, we are washed clean, rinsed from the grime and filth of the world in completion of the changing process we call repentance. We give away all our sins that we may know the Lord. The tiny cup of water offered us in the sacrament is enough to gradually cleanse the "inner vessel"—that part of us that only the Lord sees.

TRUMAN: As Joseph Smith and Oliver Cowdery bowed their heads in the Kirtland Temple they heard the sweetest words of acceptance we can pray to hear: "Behold, your sins are forgiven you; you are clean before me; therefore, lift up your heads and rejoice" (D&C 110:5).

Throughout our lives we can continue the refreshing and regenerating process of becoming pure. We're promised that the time can come when we will have "lost every desire for sin" and will even "look upon sin with abhorrence."[11]

ANN: "What are these which are arrayed in white robes?" we are asked in the book of Revelation (7:13). We think of those made pure through temple worship.

President Boyd K. Packer has written: "Our labors in the temple cover us with a shield and a protection both individually and as a people."[12]

President Carlos E. Asay of the Salt Lake Temple wrote in a recent *Ensign* article: "I like to think of the garment as the Lord's way of letting us take part of the temple with us when we leave. It is true that we carry from the Lord's house inspired teachings and sacred covenants written in our minds and hearts. However, the one tangible remembrance we carry with us back into the world is the garment. And though we cannot always be in the temple, a part of it can always be with us to bless our lives."[13]

From the pristine white clothing worn inside the temple we take this precious part to be with us night and day. It is a daily reminder of what we have seen, heard, and felt. It shields us from the fallout of evil in the world. It helps maintain the radiance we have glimpsed in the house of the Lord.

HOW DO WE ACCESS AND UNDERSTAND THE LIGHT AND TRUTH THAT IS IN THE TEMPLE?

TRUMAN: The temple is called by the Lord "a house of learning" in which we will be "*perfected* in [our] understanding" (D&C 88:119; 97:14; emphasis added).

Elder John A. Widtsoe was given a patriarchal blessing when he was a little boy in Norway. "Thou shalt have great faith in the ordinances of the Lord's house," he was told.[14] Later in life he became an able soil chemist. He had tried in vain to find a formula that would pull together many years of research. He suggested to his wife, Leah, that they go to the temple and "forget the failure." In the temple the formula came to him as pure intelligence. Out of such experiences, he said, "I would rather take my practical problems to the House of the Lord than anywhere else."[15]

He testified: "The endowment is . . . so packed full of revelations to those who exercise their strength to seek and to see, that no human words can explain or make clear the possibilities that reside in the temple service. The endowment which was given by revelation can best be understood by revelation; and to those who seek more vigorously, with pure hearts, will the revelation be greatest."[16]

It is common knowledge that keeping the Word of Wisdom is a prerequisite for entering the temple. Our emphasis on the health benefits, the "run and not be weary" promise at the end of the revelation, sometimes obscures a related promise: "And shall find wisdom and great treasures of knowledge, even hidden treasures" (D&C 89:19).

Joseph Fielding Smith, as president of the Salt Lake Temple, often spoke of his favorite scripture: "That which is of God is light; and he that receiveth light, and continueth in God, receiveth more light; and that light groweth brighter and brighter until the perfect day" (D&C 50:24).

One night Elder Harold B. Lee sat with the president of the Manti Temple looking up toward the floodlighted spires. A dark storm raged around them. The temple president said, "You know, Brother Lee, that temple is never more beautiful than during a storm."[17]

Jesus said that he is "the light [that] shineth in darkness and the darkness comprehendeth it not" (John 1:5; D&C 45:7). In the Greek, this reads "the darkness did not overtake the light." In other words, no engulfing darkness can totally obliterate the divine light that is deep in us. And in his temple our light cleaves unto his light, our truth embraces his truth, and our virtue loves his virtue (see D&C 88:40).

Anticipating the first temple in our dispensation the Lord said: "If thou shalt ask, thou shalt receive revelation upon revelation, knowledge upon knowledge, that thou mayest know the mysteries and peaceable things—that which bringeth joy, that which bringeth life eternal" (D&C 42:61).

The mysteries of godliness are locked in the ordinances of godliness.

ANN: Robert L. Millet helps us understand one way we access and understand the truths that are presented to us in the temple. He writes: "We do not see things as *they* really are; we see things as *we* really are."[18]

Taking our covenants seriously transforms *us*. I heard anthropologist Professor Merlin Myers explain this once. Simply put, he said: "Scientists use mathematical symbols, a symbol system to let themselves into reality [truth]."[19] But the most powerful symbols transcend mathematics.

1. Ordinances are a symbol system (baptism, sacrament, temple ordinances, etc.).

2. Ordinances contain patterns of action or modes of behavior.

3. We act and are conditioned, and only then do we see into reality or truth.

4. Then a transformation occurs in us so we can see as God sees.

That means finally the "temple goes through us" after many times of our "going through the temple."

Our five-year-old grandson was taught in a recent Primary Sharing Time that each of us has two bodies and that they are alike. Later, as he left the house to go to church, he said excitedly, "Mom, I'm going to feed my spiritual body!" That sums it up.

The temple is the Lord's university. For entrance you do not need to have a 3.8 grade-point average. To qualify, the Lord asks only that you bring a broken heart and a contrite spirit to his altar. You must be willing to consecrate yourself, with the integrity to keep sacred things in your heart and with a tremendous desire to serve the Lord Jesus Christ.

"Therefore," says the Doctrine and Covenants, "in the ordinances thereof, the power of godliness is manifest. And without the ordinances thereof, and the authority of the priesthood, the power of godliness is not manifest unto men in the flesh; for without this no man can see the face of God, even the Father, and live" (D&C 84:20–22).

Sister Wendy L. Watson taught us a related truth at a recent BYU devotional. "When you interact with someone repeatedly over time, it changes you. That's why what you watch on TV or read or see in magazines is so critical. So watch what you watch. Be careful with whom or what you are interacting. These recurrent interactions change your cells. They change your soul. They change your countenance."

She continues with a question: "So, who would you most want to be like? Whose image would you like engraven on your countenance? . . . The Savior entreats us to come unto him. . . . He wants us to have increasingly repeated interactions with him, and to really get to know him. And because he never changes, the changes that would occur through our interaction with the Savior would all be in us. . . . As we really come unto him, we can become like him."

She goes on to say that the Savior is the ultimate and only true and living agent for change. He is the source of all change for good. "His desire is for you to change, to have a change of heart, a change of nature . . . in fact, he did all that he did so that you could change."[20]

Thus we are taught "that through the power and manifestation of the Spirit, while in the flesh, [we] may be able to bear his presence in the world of glory" (D&C 76:118).

Isaiah asks us who can dwell with God in everlasting burnings and answers the question powerfully: "He that walketh righteously, and speaketh uprightly; . . . that shaketh his hands from holding of bribes, that stoppeth his ears from hearing of blood, and shutteth his eyes from seeing evil; he shall dwell on high" (Isaiah 33:15–16).

I love Truman's account of his first encounter with this brightness in the temple. I cannot tell it as well as he, but I can feel it.

TRUMAN: I was sitting alone in the celestial room of the Salt Lake Temple after receiving my own endowment. I had only begun to grasp the meaning of the experience, but gradually, I felt a burning of light and peace—more penetratingly than ever in my life. I felt as if I hardly wanted to breathe or move, and I sat there like a statue lest I somehow break or diminish the flow of brightness.

ANN: I had a similar feeling at the dedication of the Washington Temple in November 1974 when President Spencer W. Kimball prophesied there would be thousands of temples. I wanted to linger in the room at the close of the dedicatory services, a room so full of light. It was almost impossible to go away from the glory I felt.

WHAT CAN WE LEARN IN THE TEMPLE ABOUT PRAYING?

TRUMAN: The Lord calls his temple a "house of prayer" and teaches us to come there for "the offering up of your most holy desires unto me" (D&C 88:119; 95:16).

We can take our deepest concerns to the temple and spread them before the Lord and expect to come away lightened in both senses of the word: no longer carrying burdens of care and with an understanding of the course we should take. Have you felt such reassurance and solace?

Elder Franklin D. Richards said: "If occasion should require, if sorrow, affliction or distress overtake, we may go to the House of the Lord and find a panacea that can be found nowhere else for the ills of mortal life."[21] Seek this solace.

One day a sister in our ward commented on how beautiful our seventeen-year-old Emily was and how happy she was to see her each day at the temple open house. I didn't know what she meant. We had been there as a family on the first day of the temple open house, but I had no idea that every day from then until the dedication Emily had walked from high school up to the temple, just to be there. When I asked her, "What did you do there? Why did you go each day?" She answered simply, "I went through the regular tour and then I would sit in the celestial room as long as they would let me—just to feel the presence of the Lord, to pray, to commune."

Have you ever felt like that? Have you been drawn to the temple like our Emily? Each day she would start for home but end up in the temple. It was like a magnet to her. It was wonderfully habit-forming.

ANN: Feeling this closeness to the temple is not automatic, but it can be sought after, if we seek with all our hearts. "And ye shall seek me, and find me, when ye shall search for me with all your heart. And I will be found of you" (Jeremiah 29:13–14).

Little by little the Lord reveals himself to us and in turn, we present ourselves to him, revealing as much as we dare until we are able to lay it all before him.

Let me tell you about a wonderful word in Hebrew which embodies our finally being able to open ourselves to the Lord. It is *hinunee*. It is the common answer of prophets when the Lord calls them to be his messengers. Abraham said it. Samuel said it. Isaiah said it. It means, "Behold, here am I," with the implicit intent "I am at your service, what will you have me do?" It is another way of saying, "Thy will be done." Christ said it first when he offered himself in the heavenly council to do for us what we could not do for ourselves.

To open ourselves to the Lord entails risks and costs, because once we offer, we will be sent and we become responsible. But once we go, we are on his errand and he promises to bless us. He wants us to succeed— to return to him. He weeps or rejoices over us just as we do over our children (see Moses 7:28–40).

So in the days ahead, when there is no other way to approach the Lord to tell him what you are willing to give, just whisper, *hinunee*. It is another way of saying, "Behold the handmaid of the Lord; be it unto me according to thy word" (Luke 1:38).

TRUMAN: Joseph Smith once said, speaking of our not asking enough or being thankful enough in our prayers: "We have not desired as much from the hand of the Lord through faith and obedience, as we ought to have done, yet we have enjoyed great blessings, and we are not so sensible of this as we should be."[22]

Sometimes in the temple we feel like we are praying in the Garden of Eden and life is all beauty and goodness. And sometimes, it is as if we are praying in the Garden of Gethsemane, and it is too hard to bear. Either way, the temple is a retreat and a place of Christ's intensive care, where his rays come together in focus and peace. When we taste consolation in the temple, we will recognize it later as we kneel at home and seek to commune with him there.

ANN: There is a window where I routinely pray. I have been watching spring come as I kneel there each day. The trees begin with a pale green fuzz and there are red and yellow tulips peaking up, sometimes through snow. One day I watched two deer nibbling on our flowers. One morning recently, as I prayed in this sacred place, all at once I realized that I was feeling precisely as I do in the temple. It was such an electric moment. It was almost as if I *was* in the temple. I had begun praying just before dawn. As I continued in prayer the sun suddenly came over the mountain. First its brightness dazzled me, even with my eyes closed and then I felt its warmth. It took my breath away. It was such a ready symbol of God's presence.

I have been pondering lately about what *glory* means. "And the glory of the Lord shone round about . . ." (D&C 76:19) or "I was clothed upon with glory."[23] Maybe we miss tiny bits of glory when we fail to notice sunrises and sunsets. I think I had a tiny glimpse of glory in that moment at my window. And the silence of the morning at first light was a necessary preparation. My mind was like a clean slate.

What about praying for each other? Joseph Smith taught the sisters in Nauvoo "it grieves me that there is no fuller fellowship—if one member suffers all feel it. By union of feeling we obtain power with God."[24] Jesus said, "Be agreed as touching all things whatsoever ye ask of me" (D&C 27:18).

Recently I wrote to a friend who is seriously ill: "This morning we were in the Mount Timpanogos Temple, and stood in that unique sacred circumstance to pray for you. How blessed we are to live in a time when we walk out of the world into such holy precincts and feel the glorious difference. And then reenter the world with the determination to keep the holiness with us."

My friend Shirley says she often prays for something while she is in the temple and receives her answer later, outside. So the temple becomes the channel through which our prayers ascend, and later we can access the answers somewhere else. I love that concept.

HOW DOES OUR LOVE FOR OUR FAMILIES AND THOSE WE SERVE EXPAND THROUGH TEMPLE WORSHIP?

TRUMAN: President Howard W. Hunter said that "the purpose of the temple is to reunite the family of God." He also said, "In the ordinances of the temple the foundations of the eternal family are sealed in place."[25]

A dear friend of ours, Mary Finlayson, was asked to write on the Spirit of Elijah. She wrote: "I have spent the last four years in an effort to knit together my grandfather's unravelling family, and I have loved every minute of it. . . . I will never forget the feelings of family I had when they arrived at the Lion House [for our first family reunion]—feelings of love without conditions, complete belonging, and an overwhelming desire to serve each one in any way possible. . . . I don't know how it works but I suddenly saw why we are led by our prophets to do these things. I now believe that those feelings that surge up in us as we gather our earthly families, [now living or gone ahead] are a type. At some point, if we continue to grow toward it, we will feel those same automatic feelings of sacrificial love toward everyone we encounter. In short, I think we're just practicing on our blood relations for the real thing. At some point, we will gaze at any face and recognize instantly our kinship, sprung from the same Father."[26]

ANN: What do you think about as you sit waiting for a temple session to begin? Once, as I sat bathed in the silence, I looked again at the name of the person for whom I had come. I felt a sudden kinship, though two hundred years separated us in time. I whispered in my heart to her through the thin veil, "Welcome to this beautiful temple, Sarah. I hope that you will love it as I do." Since that singular day when I sensed her reality, I try to reach out to the person for whom I am officiating. I tell her how I pray that she will accept the covenants and love them. I tell her how grateful I am that I can do this for her because it is such a blessed opportunity for me to ponder anew the wondrous truths that I have treasured for many years. There are many quiet moments throughout the endowment ceremony when no words are being spoken. In these times she will see the endowment with spirit eyes enlightened by her time in the spirit world. And I will search again, using all the capacity a body provides. I will inquire, "Lord, what do you have for me here today?" We will both have a unique opportunity through this sacred pattern to better understand godliness.

Even the arithmetic of our temple service teaches us. Only once do we receive our own endowment. From that moment, each time we enter the temple—hopefully hundreds of times—we enter to serve others. This is the pattern of Jesus, who reaches out to all of us as our Savior. In our small reaching, beyond ourselves to our families and those we serve, we can learn to become saviors on Mount Zion.

I heard a wonderful story of Ghandi which illustrates this transcendent giving principle, a more complete consecration. Ghandi was traveling on a slow-moving train in India when one of his sandals slipped off and tumbled down the embankment. One of his followers started to jump down to retrieve it as the train lumbered along, but Ghandi restrained him. He quickly unfastened the other sandal, tossing it beside the first so that whoever found it would have a pair. I want to learn to feel like that.

TRUMAN: The world assumes that our relatives are dead, gone, and indifferent to us. It is just the other way around. They are alive—perhaps more alive than we. They are close at hand and concerned about us.

Joseph Smith taught: "Enveloped in flaming fire they are not far from us. They know and understand our thoughts, feelings, and motions and are often pained therewith."[27]

Yes, and surely they rejoice with us as well. I can testify that as the air is thinner on high mountains so the veil is thin in the temples of the Lord.

Our loved ones in the spirit world know what this life is like. They are not, the Prophet teaches, "idle spectators." They yearn over us. My good counselor, James Harper, tells the story of a woman who was baptized as proxy for her mother, a mother who had been handicapped and terribly difficult to live with. Her daughter felt both healing and forgiveness in that process.

ANN: Our family shared a tender experience as we went to the temple to perform baptisms, endowments, and sealings for the family of my grandfather's uncle John Pearson. Before we took our grandchildren up to the temple to be baptized for the Pearson family, I read to them from my grandfather's missionary journal, which he kept while serving his mission in England. In his journal, he wrote of each member of that family and how he loved them and longed to bring them into the Church. We assigned each grandchild a name from these entries; they saw the people for whom they would be baptized through my grandfather's eyes.

The sunny morning when we went to the temple in behalf of my grandfather's family was almost exactly one hundred years since my grandfather had written these things in his journal. I told our grandchildren that Grandfather Nicholls was a fine missionary who died shortly after his return home. Surely he had plenty of time in the spirit world to complete the teaching begun in 1894. As we went into the font area some missionaries were just finishing but lingered to watch our family. Later they approached me and said, "We could feel the presence of the Pearson family as you did those baptisms. Thank you."

TRUMAN: As I stood waist deep in the font, inviting my granddaughters and then grandsons to join me there, one by one, it all seemed like closing a circuit—like coming home. Perhaps I sensed a little of what Wilford Woodruff describes in the St. George Temple; it was as if the baptismal room itself was charged. Swept up in the feeling, I wept, and made a mistake in the wording, but was grateful to be kindly corrected. Later with my hands on still-moist heads I felt the blessing of conferring the gift of the Holy Ghost. It was not perfunctory. It was reality.

ANN: As we were leaving the temple I pointed out the bas-relief of the Samaritan woman at the well with Jesus. It is on the far wall in the waiting room of the Provo Temple so our grandchildren had to peek inside to see it. I asked them, not having any idea what they would answer, "Why do you think they have that story in the temple?" I had nothing particular in mind. Instantly, one of those guileless, intrepid souls spoke right up. "Because Jesus is telling her who he is and that's what happens in the temple. He tells us who he really is."

TRUMAN: God unites us by love. Satan's whole work is to separate and isolate us by discord, anger, hate, and the clamor for rights. All of us know what isolation feels like. We need to know what the unity of love feels like. I believe that it is impossible to feel the Spirit of the Lord and not feel love. And perhaps vice versa. When we know what love feels like we cannot help loving others. Love is contagious.

ANN: We all have moments when we feel like no one loves us. "Nobody loves me, nobody understands, nobody cares." But in the temple it is different. God's gentle, unfailing love fills his house. We can access it there: we can open ourselves to God's love as his children. Christ cares for us precisely because he participated in what we are going through. He yearns to gather us under his wings and nourish us, to "encircle [us] in the arms of [his] love" (D&C 6:20; 3 Nephi 10:4).

Temple workers themselves contribute to this feeling of love and caring. I remember entering the Frankfurt, Germany Temple. The man at the recommend desk, whose gray hair and lined face showed he had survived World War II, extended his hand to shake mine as he said, "Velcome to the house of the Lord." I wept as I sensed the reality of entering God's own house.

TRUMAN: Do you think those who are in the temple every day feel that love in a special way? Do they feel it constantly? We heard a fine temple president, Elder Carlos E. Asay, and his wife explain their view. President Asay spoke of the endowment as an "exchange of love." God loves us enough to give us commandments and make covenants with us that will inspire and can ultimately exalt us. Keeping covenants keeps us from sinning. We should be willing to honor the trust extended in eternal covenants by keeping them. Is this not "an exchange of love?" he asked.

ANN: What a touching moment it was for me when a dear friend confided about a year after her husband's death: "He adored me." Then weeping, she continued, "Now nobody feels that way about me any more." I could feel some of her devastation. All I knew to say was, "The Lord loves you deeply. Pray to feel *that* love in his house."

President Asay also taught us, "The temple is the bridge between heaven and earth—the seen and the unseen—and the bridge is love." We feel such love for the Lord Jesus Christ, who pleads our cause before our Father. I know he truly loves me. He truly loves you. The Spirit helps communicate that love.

TRUMAN: Such love is a taste of immortality. As Elder Parley P. Pratt wrote, the Spirit "develops beauty of person, form and features."[28] A sensitive temple worker once shared with me a glimpse of this ultimate blessing. He had officiated in the presence of many aged and infirm and arthritic couples as they performed sealings. He felt admiration but also sympathy for their slow-moving, patient labor. Then he suddenly saw them as they would be in the resurrection. He could hardly find words: "They were exquisite . . . splendid . . . youthful . . . lovely."

TRUMAN: Elder Henry B. Eyring tells of a mother who was driving down a freeway hardly able to see through her tears. She had just visited her son, a convicted murderer, in prison. "Why, why?" she cried out. "Why am I the mother of such a son?" And a voice from on high replied, "Because you are the only one on this planet who will go on loving him."[29]

There are ways, too deep and poignant to describe, that the Lord's temple service can reach the hardest of cases, bring faith to the faithless, and hope to the hopeless. Christ teaches in holy places that he never gives up. Neither should we.

ANN: Covenants bind us by love. Elder Henry B. Eyring once said that he had been taught that covenants were like a business contract, in which one person agrees to do something and the other agrees to do something else in return. But after serious reflection, he felt something new, something more powerful about our covenants with God. Covenant keeping is not a cold business deal but a warm relationship, bound by love.

Elder Eyring explained, "The Lord, with whom I am blessed to have made covenants, loves me and you with a steadfastness about which I continually marvel and which I want with all my heart to emulate." He goes on to say, "We are blessed by the Abrahamic covenant, and we are bound by it. But we are not bound by compulsion. We are bound by his love for us and by the love He evokes in us."[30]

All other virtues spring from this Christlike love. We forgive, we have mercy, we have empathy, we are willing to lift and bless and help when we are filled with that love. How can we give in to anger or impatience when our hearts are brimming with love? No wonder the scripture cries out, "Pray . . . with all the energy of heart, that ye may be filled with this love" (Moroni 7:48). We can pray daily for that sweet selflessness. Charity never stops, never fails. It even reaches back to us from beyond the veil.

HOW CAN WE TAKE THE TEMPLE HOME WITH US? CAN OUR HOMES BE HOLY?

TRUMAN: We've had the privilege of attending three temple dedications, two with our family. The latest was the Mount Timpanogos Temple dedication, which we attended with a whole row of our children and their children. As the services progressed, we looked across that row and saw their upturned faces as they sang, "The Spirit of God Like a Fire Is Burning." At the conclusion we overheard Max, then age ten, whisper to his mother, "Thanks for bringing me here!" We were knit closely that day. We were one. We remembered that President Lorenzo Snow instructed little children to give the Hosannah Shout at the top of their lungs because that would be the way they would greet Jesus Christ at his second coming.[31]

ANN: Our homes can, like the temple, be holy sanctuaries in this far-from-holy world. Bruce Hafen, when he was provost at BYU, described the world today as a polluted river. We are like fish swimming in the pollution, often carried by a current of which we are only vaguely aware, until someone swims against the current. Then we see the contrast.[32]

The Lord has commanded us: "Behold, it is my will, that all they who call on my name, and worship me according to mine everlasting gospel, should gather together, and stand in holy places" (D&C 101:22).

How is a Zion built? By producing and gathering the "pure in heart." Eliza R. Snow learned from the Prophet that the curse on the earth would not be lifted all at once, but that each time we dedicate a temple we lift the curse a little. Our homes can be the minitemples, the points of light that will recreate a little bit of heaven on earth leading to the Millennium. All of us are "home-makers." We make a home wherever we eat and sleep. There are several things we can do to help make our homes holy.

TRUMAN: We can help make our homes holy by dedicating them. Ann and I have painted, fixed up, shined, and then dedicated each of our homes. We were really dedicating ourselves to the purposes of the Lord in our family. We even dedicated our temporary apartment in Jerusalem. All the things we say, the prayers we offer, the blessings that are given, the feelings we experience—both good and bad—accumulate in our homes and are felt by those who come there. We add something to the sum each day. That's a sobering thought.

ANN: We can help make our homes holy by setting priorities. Family is first. Someone must be primarily responsible for dividing the tasks that keep a home going—no matter how many machines we have to cut down our work. We can't all abdicate everything. Orderliness, cleanliness, music, social life, decor—the abundant life is far different from merely existing in a space together. Someone or ones *must* have that as a priority or it will never happen.

Is home a place of beauty? Is home just a place to eat and sleep? Is there no lovely corner to curl up in to read a book? If spring is lagging outdoors, can we bring it inside with a pot of daisies or daffodils on the table for dinner—not for company, just because it's spring? If family is first then shouldn't there be flowers for family? You will notice the temple grounds are alive with beauty. So can our homes be.

TRUMAN: We can help make our homes holy by creating order and fixed points to count on.

In the temple we learn a planned sequence. Do we have such fixed points in our home regimen? When do we sit together and share? Everyone in the family can count on family home evening as a fixed point in their week for planning family events and simply to celebrate being together.

ANN: What about dinner time? Let's dine together! What a novel idea! Before you say, "Our family just can't," think about it. There is such an emphasis on good nutrition these days. We fill our freezers with well-balanced meals in individual, dated packets and then run in all directions, leaving each person to heat a nutritious meal in the

334

microwave and eat it on the run all alone. Isn't nursing our babies a type that should teach us something? We have to do that together. From infancy to adulthood, we communicate through food. Dinner is a time to share. It's a time for bonding. It's an informal temple preparation class.

TRUMAN: We had a fixed point at our house that worked for us—5:30 P.M. was inviolate. Everyone worked around it. That was our family's daily appointment to eat dinner together; that was when we had family prayer; that was when we read the scriptures and were spiritually fed. But I think what we all remember best was that we talked. We did not let the urgent rob us of this important time together.

We can help make our homes holy by living what we've learned in the temple. When we keep our temple covenants, they help us to cheerfully, patiently reverence one another at home. We become sanctifying influences to each other and all who come there. We quietly learn to live celestially, like Christ, creating a little bit of heaven on earth. Patience and prayer are part of the process.

ANN: When the Provo Temple was to be dedicated, we made plans to prepare our family for what we anticipated as a once-in-a-lifetime experience. We had a series of family home evenings focusing on the temple: one honoring our ancestors; one celebrating our wedding day, complete with photo album, ring, the story of our courtship, and so on; one explaining what we could of the activities that would go on in the temple. The culmination was a family visit to the temple open house—the first time our children would actually be able to enter the Lord's House with us. In preparation we each bathed carefully, washed our hair, put on all clean Sunday clothes, and drove to the temple. We explained to our children that this kind of cleanliness was part of the symbolism of purity which is essential for entering the presence of the Lord in his house.

TRUMAN: We learned an unexpected lesson from this experience. We arrived to an empty parking lot. There we were, all scrubbed, clean, excited, and expectant. But the door was locked; it was a Monday. What a let down. But the lights were all on so I went to look inside, pressing my nose against the glass. There was the temple president, showing his own family through the temple. Seeing us, and having compassion, he invited us to join them. We knew for a moment how it felt to be denied entrance to the temple. And just as suddenly, we experienced more joy than we had prayed and planned for.

ANN: Our homes can become holy places and still be lived in. They can be clean, orderly, and reverent—within the parameters of keeping happy, growing children in them.

As a grandmother I remember the first time the whole family came for Thanksgiving dinner to our newly remodeled house. The paint was fresh, and there was not a mark on any wall. I had foolishly hoped to preserve its pristine appearance for a week or two. As they all left, I gasped at little muddy footprints that ran the length of the new silver gray carpet and handprints on the walls and windows and mirrors. My newly clean home! But then I caught myself. I've learned to cherish fingerprints.

TRUMAN: Orson Pratt gives us a wonderful vision of glorified homes in the future: "In the latter days there will be a people so pure in Mount Zion, with a house established upon the tops of the mountains, that God will manifest himself, not only in their temple . . . but when they retire to their [homes], behold each [home] will be lighted up by the glory of God, a pillar of flaming fire by night."[33]

CONCLUSION

TRUMAN: We have spoken of the ideal, the vision. It may seem remote, distant, even utterly beyond us. But we can have a foretaste in this world. As Joseph Smith admonished: "Let these truths sink down in our hearts, that we may, even here, begin to enjoy that which shall be in full hereafter."[34]

Ponder these confirming words in a letter to a remarkable woman, Eliza R. Snow, from apostle Wilford Woodruff. The letter was written fifteen years after she became a widow, and thirty years before her death. Note the sense of fulfilled promises and the allusions to the temple.

"Thy soul has been inspired by the spirit of God and eternal light and truth. Thy lamp hath been lit at God's holy altar where the oil was pure and the spirit free so thou couldst weigh eternal truth . . .

"Thy words and testimony will live and speak in flames of holy fire. Ere long thou wilt be clothed with immortality and clothed with light. Thy garments are clear of the blood of fallen man. Thy soul is as pure as the crystal stream that flows from its snowy bed. Thou hast been true and faithful and are sealed unto eternal life and secured unto thyself a crown of glory. No power shall take it. It awaits thy coming. Soon this blessing will be thine. Ah, what joy!"[35]

ANN: No wonder Eliza could say to the women of her day and to us:

"We are women of God, women fulfilling high and responsible positions, performing sacred duties."[36]

We finish with the invitation with which we began: Come, let us go up to the temple where the Lord will teach us of his ways, and we will walk in his paths until we have learned them (see Isaiah 2:3).

Jesus moved from grace to grace to become more and more. And when a sick sinner asked, "Lord, if thou wilt, thou canst make me whole," He replied, "I will. Be thou whole" (see John 5:6). We, too, can be made whole. The temple is absolutely necessary for that to happen in our lives. It is the finishing of our faith. It is the crowning of our lives on earth. It is the only place on earth where our families can be knit together, bound by a love which Jesus has demonstrated once and for all in the Atonement.

In that holy house we can see ourselves as we really are; we can find Jesus Christ and understand who he really is; we can understand a new level of purity and learn to pray with power. As we search the teachings we receive, we will know how to overcome the devil and, ultimately, how to part the veil.[37] The temple is the bridge of love between this world and the next.

May we invite you with the words of Isaiah: "O house of Jacob, come ye, and let us walk in the light of the Lord"—the sunshine of his love (Isaiah 2:5).

I have tried to describe my feelings about the temple in the following lines:

> In the temple
> The quiet closes round me
> like fog.
> God's house reverberates
> with silence,
> filled with echoes
> from the faithful
> who have followed the light
> to here, like a star.
> White, we come clothed in white
> to this place,
> of radiant light.
> Dear Host
> of this Heavenly House,

if I come,
clothed in the pure white
of a new lamb,
with my heart as new,
may I, too,
be lighted?

NOTES

1. Franklin D. Richards, *Collected Discourses*, ed. Brian H. Stuy, 5 vols. (Burbank, Calif.: BHS Publishing, 1987–92), vol. 3, 12 February 1893.
2. See Brigham Young, *Journal of Discourses*, 26 vols. (London: Latter-day Saints' Book Depot, 1854–86), 9:33.
3. A. J. Heschel, *Israel: An Echo of Eternity* (New York: Farrar, Straus & Giroux), 225.
4. Henry B. Eyring, *Ensign*, May 1998, 68; see also Mosiah 3:19.
5. Joseph Smith, *Teachings of the Prophet Joseph Smith*, sel. Joseph Fielding Smith (Salt Lake City: Deseret Book, 1938), 162.
6. Joseph Smith, *The Words of Joseph Smith*, ed. Andrew F. Ehat and Lyndon W. Cook (Orem, Utah: Grandin Book, 1991), 4.
7. Smith, *Words of Joseph Smith*, 203.
8. Jeffrey R. Holland and Patricia T. Holland, *On Earth As It Is in Heaven* (Salt Lake City: Deseret Book, 1989), 94.
9. John A. Widtsoe, "Temple Worship," *Utah Genealogical and Historical Magazine* 12 (April 1921): 56.
10. James E. Faust, *Ensign*, May 1998, 89.
11. Smith, *Teachings of the Prophet Joseph Smith*, 51; Alma 13:12; 27:28.
12. Boyd K. Packer, as quoted in Carlos E. Asay, *Ensign*, August 1997, 22.
13. Asay, *Ensign*, August 1987, 22.
14. Quoted in Leon R. Hartshorn, *Exceptional Stories from the Lives of Our Apostles* (Salt Lake City: Deseret Book, 1972), 277.
15. John A. Widtsoe, *In a Sunlit Land: The Autobiography of John A. Widtsoe* (Salt Lake City: Milton R. Hunter and G. Homer Durham, 1952), 177.
16. Widtsoe, "Temple Worship," 63.
17. Personal conversation with Truman G. Madsen.
18. Robert L. Millet, *Alive in Christ: The Miracle of Spiritual Rebirth* (Salt Lake City: Deseret Book, 1997), 28.
19. Merlin Myers, devotional address, Brigham Young University, Provo, Utah; notes in possession of author.
20. Wendy L. Watson, "Change: It's Always a Possibility," devotional address, Brigham Young University, Provo, Utah, 7 April 1998; notes in possession of author.
21. Richards, *Collected Discourses*, vol. 3, 12 February 1893.
22. Smith, *Teachings of the Prophet Joseph Smith*, 90.
23. Joseph Smith, *History of The Church of Jesus Christ of Latter-day Saints*, ed. B. H. Roberts, 2d ed. rev., 7 vols. (Salt Lake City: The Church of Jesus Christ of Latter-day Saints, 1932–51), 1:133.

24. Smith, *Words of Joseph Smith*, 123.

25. Howard W. Hunter, *Ensign*, February 1995, 2.

26. Mary Finlayson to Ann N. Madsen, 17 April 1995.

27. Smith, *Teachings of the Prophet Joseph Smith*, 324.

28. Parley P. Pratt, *Key to the Science of Theology* (Salt Lake City: Deseret Book, 1948), 101.

29. Personal conversation; used by permission.

30. Personal conversation; used by permission.

31. Lorenzo Snow, in Journal of B. H. Roberts (uncataloged), April 1893, 193.

32. Bruce C. Hafen, devotional address, Brigham Young University, Provo, Utah; notes in possession of author.

33. Orson Pratt, *Journal of Discourses*, 16:36.

34. Smith, *Teachings of the Prophet Joseph Smith*, 296.

35. Wilford Woodruff, *Wilford Woodruff's Journal, 1833–1898*, ed. Scott G. Kenney, 9 vols. (Midvale, Utah: Signature Books, 1983–85), vol. 5, July 1857.

36. Minutes of Relief Society Organization, Salt Lake City, Archives of The Church of Jesus Christ of Latter-day Saints, 1842; notes in possession of author.

37. Sheri L. Dew, address in Logan, Utah, March 1998; notes by Mindy Davis.

Hearing the Voice of the Lord

HEIDI S. SWINTON

Twenty-two years ago, a tall, grave-faced doctor walked into my hospital room, sat down in the plastic bucket chair next to my bed, and took my hand. He looked at me for a few moments. We'd met just the day before when I came into the hospital at 2 A.M. pregnant with twins and in labor at seven months. My doctor had retired, and this high-risk specialist had taken over my case.

There I was, a young mother with one son who had just died and another son who was fighting for his life on a respirator. Two months premature, he couldn't breathe, and he had a hole in his heart and a litany of other problems. After miscarrying five babies, I had seen these twins as a blessing to make up for all the heartache and broken dreams. Now I was facing even deeper loss and disappointment.

I will never forget what the doctor said. "Heidi, I want you to know this. You have one son all the way home. That may be no comfort to you right now, but, believe me, in the years ahead, you will come to understand and know what it means. I have a teenage son, and I wonder if I will get him all the way home. Yours is already there." Over the days and weeks that followed, many friends called and came to see me and sent flowers and beautiful cards. But it was those words, "all the way home," that made the difference.

The doctor was speaking, but it was the Lord I was hearing. In Doctrine and Covenants 1:38 we are told, "Whether by mine own voice or by the voice of my servants, it is the same." The truth of eternal life

Heidi S. Swinton, a graduate of the University of Utah, has coauthored, compiled, and contributed to many books on Church subjects. She serves as a member of the Melchizedek Priesthood/Relief Society Curriculum writing committee. She and her husband, Jeffrey, are the parents of four sons.

borne to me that day was a spiritual witness from God. In the depths of my grief, the voice of the Lord sounded in my ears. "All the way home" spoke volumes to me then; it continues to speak to me today.

I count much of my life from the experience of the death of my eldest son. It was then that I really began to understand personal revelation. The questions "Why?" and "How could this happen?" begged for answers, yet my soul searched for more than just resolution. Suddenly mortality took on a different dimension, became part of the plan but not all of it. Eternal glory and its promises now included a face and a name: Christian Horne Swinton. To be with him, I needed to get all the way home myself.

That focus didn't require a U-turn in my late twenties or even a sharp turn. He called for me to increase my willingness and my ability to have ears to hear, to listen. At one time, all of us knew the Lord's voice. We cheered in the premortal existence when Christ presented the Father's plan. We heard it there; we are living it here. I have no doubt that we are tied to the heavens by revelation. We sometimes call that spiritual tie "being in tune."

When the Savior spoke to the Nephites, his voice "did pierce them that did hear to the center . . . yea, it did pierce them to the very soul, and did cause their hearts to burn" (3 Nephi 11:3). I have felt that pure revelation. We have been guided, encouraged, shielded, and taught by the voice of the Lord. When we choose to have ears to hear, we step forward on the path that leads all the way home.

Revelation is a fundamental principle of the Church. Some revelations may open the heavens in a way that can't be ignored; others come as thoughts or ideas. Some promptings come when least expected, often when we're busy doing other things. Impressions may come in the car, in the kitchen, or on our knees. We may "hear" in a crowded room or in the middle of a cluttered day. Time and place are really only mortal terms. Revelation reaches through the veil, reminding us of who we are and where we want to go.

I'd like to share six truths I have learned about listening to the Lord. First, I don't need to see Jesus Christ to know he is there or to know of his love for me. I need only listen, for he has said, "My sheep hear my voice, and I know them, and they follow me" (John 10:27). We need to hear the voice of the Lord so that he can direct us all the way home. "Come unto Christ" is a phrase we all know well. Nephi, as he spoke of the way to eternal life, said, "After ye have gotten into this strait and narrow path, I would ask if all is done? Behold, I say unto you, Nay; for ye have not come thus far save it were by the word of Christ with unshaken faith in him, relying wholly upon the merits of him who is mighty to save" (2 Nephi 31:19). Following the word of Christ is another way of saying, I hear.

I see this truth in the experience of Peter in the New Testament. Jesus has been teaching the five thousand and feeding the multitude with a few fishes and loaves. He then sends his disciples ahead, out on the Sea of Galilee in their fishing vessel, while he goes up "into a mountain apart to pray." In Matthew we read: "And in the fourth watch of the night Jesus went unto them, walking on the sea. And when the disciples saw him walking on the sea, they were troubled, saying, It is a spirit; and they cried out for fear. But straightway Jesus spake unto them, saying, Be of good cheer; it is I; be not afraid. And Peter answered him and said, Lord, if it be thou, bid me come unto thee on the water. And he said, Come" (Matthew 14:25–29).

I picture Peter scrambling over the side of the boat before walking on the water. Jesus has called to him: "Come." Water churns at Peter's feet, choppy waves surround him, the wind is blowing. His attention is drawn from the Savior to the dark, frothy water below. Distracted and losing focus, Peter begins to sink. Jesus reaches out and lifts him up.

The world calls it a miracle that Peter walked on water and stops there. But the scene says so much more about hearing the voice of the Lord. "Come," says our Savior. We've heard that call. "Come . . . that where I am, there ye may be also" (John 14:3).

Peter stepped out onto the water. Later, he became the valiant and dynamic leader of the Church and witness of the risen Lord. But he had to walk on unfamiliar territory to get there.

So do we.

When the Savior calls us to come, we sometimes need to turn, or change direction, and then press forward. "Follow me, and I will make you fishers of men," Jesus said to Peter and Andrew, James and John as he called them to leave their nets (Matthew 4:19). To Enoch he was even more pointed: "Prophesy unto this people, and say unto them—Repent . . . for their hearts have waxed hard, and their ears are dull of hearing, and their eyes cannot see afar off" (Moses 6:27). What was the result? A whole community heard that voice, "Come closer." "And the

Lord called his people Zion. . . . and lo, Zion . . . was taken up into heaven" (Moses 7:18, 21).

And that is the second truth. Hearing the call to come has everything to do with how close we are to the Lord—close in distance and close in heart. If we can't hear his voice or feel his presence, we need to move closer.

Often the voice is so significant that the time, place, and setting are indelibly marked in our minds. I will always remember hearing the chair scrape across the floor in the hospital as my doctor sat down to try and help me put my life back together. At other times, His voice is a gentle prompting or a sweet spirit that whispers of peace. At these moments, we err in thinking we imagined our feelings, or that we simply feel better. The source of our strength is clear: "I the Lord am with you, and will stand by you" (D&C 68:6).

What does that mean in our everyday experience? President Brigham Young said: "If we would know the voice of the Good Shepherd, we must live so that the Spirit of the Lord can find its way to our hearts."[1] How we do that is clearly outlined: repent, live the commandments, live up to our covenants. Or, again as Brigham Young said: "Live so that [your] spirits are as pure and clean as a piece of blank paper that lies on the desk before the inditer, ready to receive any mark the writer may make upon it."[2]

President Joseph F. Smith, sixth president of the Church, said of his own experience receiving revelation: "I fervently believe that God has manifested to me in my present capacity, many glorious things, many principles and oftentimes much more wisdom than is inherent in myself; and I believe He will continue to do so as long as I am receptive, as long as I am in a position to hear when He speaks, to listen when He calls, and to receive when He gives to me that which He desires."[3] These important steps put revelation within the reach of each one of us: Be receptive; be in the right position to hear; listen; and receive when he speaks.

What stands in our way of receiving? In the Doctrine and Covenants 66:10, we are counseled: "Seek not to be cumbered." *Cumbered* is a good word to contrast with *Come. Cumbered* sounds weighted down with purses full of problems, programs, wants, needs, responsibilities, challenges. Every day we have long lists of things to do. Do this or that, come to this and drop off that, stop here, pick up there . . . you know the list. Fractured lives that live by the needs of the day have no peace. How can we hear the Good Shepherd's voice in our hearts when the Spirit has to take a number just to get on our day's list? *Come* means, "Lay aside the things of this world," as the Lord said to Emma Smith, "and seek for the things of a better" (D&C 25:10).

It's all about turning our lives over to God. If we yield our agency to Christ, he will, as President Ezra Taft Benson said, deepen our joy, expand our vision, quicken our minds, lift our spirits, comfort our souls, and pour out peace.[4] What a promise. "Pour out peace." Is there anyone who has enough peace in her life? Peace is the opposite of *cumbered*. He will lift our spirits if we will but listen. For centuries people have tried to find peace by sequestering themselves from the world, perhaps in a remote hamlet or other sanctuary. But peace is not a place; it is a state of mind. It is knowing that the Lord's promises are true and then living worthy to receive them. Such commitment is usually found over the side of the boat, out on the water.

The story of Naaman, captain of the host of the king of Syria, is a good example (2 Kings 5:1–14). When Naaman came to the prophet Elisha to be cured of leprosy, this mighty warrior was not invited in. Instead, "Elisha sent a messenger unto him, saying, Go and wash in Jordan seven times, and thy flesh shall come again to thee, and thou shalt be clean" (v. 10). A man of considerable wealth and power, Naaman, outside "with his horses and with his chariot," was angry that Elisha did not pay deference to him: "Behold, I thought, He will surely come out to me, and stand, and call on the name of the Lord his God." Besides, Naaman further objects, "Are not Abana and Pharpar, rivers of Damascus, better than all the waters of Israel? may I not wash in them, and be clean? So he turned and went away in a rage" (vv. 9, 11–12). Naaman's humble servant, knowing the Lord was speaking through his prophet, counseled him, saying, "If the prophet had bid thee do some great thing, wouldest thou not have done it? how much rather then, when he saith to thee, Wash, and be clean? Then went he down, and dipped himself seven times in Jordan, according to the saying of the man of God . . . and he was clean" (vv. 13–14).

Pride stands in the way of hearing the voice of the Lord. We so easily get caught up in what we think we need and what we think we want. We have a tendency to give a wish list to the Lord and expect our soft-spoken demands to be met. We want the water to be smoother, we want the wind more calm, and we want to be called to serve in a big name river. Listening suggests otherwise. Humility and meekness are manifest in "Thy will be done."

For the most part, it is a still, small voice that we hear. Elijah's experience in 1 Kings is our model: "And he said, Go forth, and stand upon the mount before the Lord. And, behold, the Lord passed by, and a great and strong wind rent the mountains, and brake in pieces the rocks before the Lord; but the Lord was not in the wind: and after the wind an earthquake; but the Lord was not in the earthquake: And after the earthquake a fire; but the Lord was not in the fire: and after the fire a still small voice" (1 Kings 19:11–12). The secret is to have ears to hear.

The still, small voice can be heard above the noise of the crowd or in the quiet of our silent prayers. It can catch our attention when we're thinking about something else or sound so loud that we will change direction and go another way. It is a miracle, really, one that reminds us who we are because of who is talking and who we will become if we will listen. The world may march on Washington crying loudly for attention, but the still, small voice speaking to the hearts of the Saints will have a far greater impact.

We usually associate Brigham Young with the call to come to Zion. His own call to the Restored Church came by the prompting of the Spirit. Samuel Smith, brother of the Prophet Joseph Smith, first introduced Brigham to the gospel, but the Lion of the Lord, as he would be known, wrestled two years for his own witness of the truth. How long do we keep on listening?

Brigham Young's answer and witness finally came through the simple testimony of a humble missionary, Eleazer Miller, a man whom Brigham described as being "without eloquence . . . who could only say, 'I know, by the power of the Holy Ghost, that the Book of Mormon is true, that Joseph Smith is a Prophet of the Lord.'" Said Brigham Young of that defining moment, "The Holy Ghost proceeding from that individual illuminated my understanding, and light, glory, and immortality were before me."[5]

President Gordon B. Hinckley, when being set apart as a stake president, was counseled by Elder Harold B. Lee to listen for the still, small voice. President Hinckley recalls, "I remember only one thing he said: 'Listen for the whisperings of the Spirit in the middle of the night, and respond to those whisperings.' I don't know why revelation comes sometimes in the night, but it does. It comes in the day as well, of course. But listen to the whisperings of the Spirit, the gift of revelation, to which you are entitled."[6]

And that leads us to the third truth: Hearing the voice, we must hearken.

Twenty-seven years ago, a fresh graduate from college, I was preparing to leave for a prestigious journalism program in the East. It seemed to be the next logical step in my life. I had been the editor of my college newspaper and an intern with the *Wall Street Journal*. Frankly, I was a news junkie, and I was on the cutting edge of opportunities opening for women in all professions, the media in particular.

So there I was, sitting in the living room of my home, reading a newsmagazine. I will always remember that day, 4 September 1971. In my journal I wrote: "Today I read an article about Gloria Steinem [a political columnist]. She was on the cover of *Newsweek*. . . . I read the whole article, becoming more and more convinced I want to be just like her. Respected, influential, famous. And rich. To top it all off, she's beautiful."

My entry then takes a turn. "While I was sitting on the couch thinking about Gloria Steinem, her picture staring up at me from the cover, a voice spoke to me, a voice through my thoughts that said, 'That's how the Devil gets to people like you; he leads them away from the work of the Lord.'"

That unexpected thought so startled me that I got up from my mother's cozy blue couch and left the room. Later, settled in a long, hot bath, I was back to reading *Newsweek* and planning a career worthy of a cover story. Again I heard in my mind the quiet voice, the same words, the same caution, "That's how the Devil gets to people like you; he leads them away from the work of the Lord."

What I had heard was a personal revelation from the Lord. *Heard* is the appropriate verb: I heard but did not hearken. The next day I got in the car and drove East. Alma's counsel to the people applied to me, "A shepherd hath called after you and is still calling after you, but ye will not hearken unto his voice!" (Alma 5:37). Three days later I knew I had done the wrong thing, but it took months to get the courage to hearken.

Peter jumped over the side of the boat and walked on water. I got in the car and drove the interstate to Washington, D.C., to attend graduate school in journalism. "My sheep hear my voice . . . and follow me" some-times begins by first going the other way.

The fourth truth: What we often hear is how to help others.

We've had thoughts or impressions come to us—call, go visit, say this, write a note, bear testimony of Jesus Christ. There's no question where such promptings come from; there's no question how we feel when we respond. We are all busy; the question is, Busy doing what?

A Christmas Carol by Charles Dickens shows clearly the folly of think-ing only of ourselves. As you remember, Jacob Morley comes back as a ghost on Christmas Eve to warn his partner Scrooge of his misguided ways. The ghost laments, "I cannot rest, I cannot stay, I cannot linger anywhere . . . ; and weary journeys lie before me!"

"'But you were always a good man of business, Jacob,' faltered Scrooge. . . .

"'Business!' cried the ghost, wringing his hands. . . . 'Mankind was my business. The common welfare was my business; charity, mercy, forbear-ance, and benevolence, were, all, my business. The dealings of my trade were but a drop of water in the comprehensive ocean of my business.'"⁷

Last spring I rushed into Relief Society just before the meeting was to begin. I sat down next to Eileen, new to the ward and the wife of our home teacher. She smiled at me and asked, "How are you today?" It was a stressful time at the Swinton home. Two or three deadlines behind, I was heavily cumbered. I wondered momentarily how honest I could be with Eileen. I smiled and said, "You know, I am at the point where I simply am going to start buying socks because I don't have the time to wash them, and I will never have time to match them."

She looked at me startled. She had on the tip of her tongue the usual, "Oh, that's nice." But I hadn't answered, "Fine," so she just stammered "Oh," and then the opening hymn began and we got caught up in the meeting.

The next morning my husband got a phone call at his office. It was Eileen. "I don't know what's going on at your house right now," she said, "but I am going to bring dinner to you every night this week. Will six o'clock be all right?"

Now I know Eileen is as busy as everybody else, but amazingly, that night and every night for a week, dinner showed up at the Swintons. I told the boys not to eat it all at once. We needed leftovers. And I needed the message Eileen brought me—that the Lord was mindful of me. If we are listening only for promptings about our own lives, we may miss a message sent to someone else by way of us. That kind of listening—Eileen's kind—means attending to the second great commandment, "Love thy neighbor as thyself."

Christ knows us. But he may not calm our troubled waters. He didn't calm the seas for Peter. But he did reach out to him. Think about it. When we respond to the voice of the Lord, do we only listen for those things we want to hear? Those things that fit our needs as we see them, that solve only our problems as we understand them? Do we ask, "Make things easier"? And when he doesn't, do we say, "He isn't there!"? Or worse, "He doesn't care"?

It's fair to say life is hard. Not long ago, the members of the Church celebrated the strength and fortitude of the pioneers who came west to build Zion. They gathered in Kirtland, hearing "Come." They gathered in Missouri and were forced to leave. They settled in Nauvoo and were driven again.

The Lord used those hardships to prepare a people, build them into a force, and teach them to hear his voice inviting, "Come." Their destination was not Salt Lake; it was celestial glory. The experience of Laleta Dickson, a member of the tragic Willie Handcart Company trapped in the early snows of winter, moves me deeply. "When morning came, Father's body, along with the others who had died during the night, was buried in a deep hole. Brush was thrown in and then dirt. A fire was built over the grave to kill the scent to keep the wolves from digging up the remains. I can see my mother's face as she sat looking at the partly conscious group. Her eyes looked so dead that I was afraid. She didn't sit long, however. . . . When it was time to move out, Mother had her family ready to go. She put her invalid son in the cart with her baby and we joined the train. Our mother was a strong woman, and she would see us through anything."[8]

I have stood on the harsh Wyoming hillside at Rock Creek where her father is buried and felt the chill of the wind as it whips across that rugged landscape. How did they press forward? The Lord speaks of these courageous women in latter-day revelations when he says, "For mine elect hear my voice and harden not their hearts" (D&C 29:7).

How do we do that? By turning to Christ, for he has promised us, "I will go before your face. I will be on your right hand and on your left, and my Spirit shall be in your hearts, and mine angels round about you, to bear you up" (D&C 84:88).

Another truth, the fifth: We are never alone. Not here, not now, not tomorrow. We've heard the promise, "Draw near unto me and I will draw near unto you" (D&C 88:63). There can be no greater sensitivity to our every need nor any greater succor.

In the center of Salt Lake are nine stakes in what is called the Inner City, part of the Pioneer Welfare Region. It's an urban area filled with challenges. This past year, part-time missionaries from fifty-six surrounding stakes have been called as Inner City missionaries to provide help with home and visiting teaching and to teach welfare principles of self-reliance. Into this band of now more than two hundred missionaries was called a bank executive and his wife to help a bishop of a ward near the freeway in an industrial part of town.

Jump over the side of the boat. They heard the call.

The young bishop, with only ten active Melchezidek priesthood holders in his ward, gave the couple eight families to visit. The couple, a dignified man used to wearing a cashmere coat and his equally elegant wife, went to the first home. This family had a father in jail, sons in a detention center, and a mother struggling to find work and care for her small children. The missionary couple were at a loss how to help. In the next family, the story was similar. And so on through a handful on their list. They went back to the bishop, and the husband said, "We can't help these people. I'm a banker. I'm good at financial and estate planning. I can help with tax issues. These people don't need me. Don't you have someone I could really help?"

The bishop looked at them. I can imagine his silent plea, "Don't walk away from us. We can't make it without you." He said, "I prayed about your assignments and those were the names that came. Give it two more weeks. See if there isn't something you can do." Then, almost as an afterthought, he said, pointing to the list of names, "Have you been to see this sister?" The man shook his head. "She's in the hospital. Her leg was amputated. Would you go see her for me?"

The missionary couple went to the hospital and into the woman's room. She was asleep, so they sat down by her bed to wait. She eventually stirred and woke to see two strangers. "The bishop sent us," the banker said, trying to reassure her. She began to weep. After a moment, through tears she explained, "I went to sleep with a prayer in my heart.

I am so alone. I feel so desperate. I told the Lord I couldn't go on—didn't want to. I said to him, 'If the bishop would just send someone . . .'" That couple left the hospital with new ears.

Hearing the voice of the Lord is a witness to us that he lives. This is the sixth and most important truth of all. To come to know Jesus Christ we must serve him with whole-souled devotion.

Mary, when visited by the angel, said, "Behold the handmaid of the Lord; Be it unto me according to thy word." She went to Elizabeth who, filled with the Holy Ghost, "spake out with a loud voice, and said, Blessed art thou among women, and blessed is the fruit of thy womb" (Luke 1:38, 42).

What of Mary Magdalene at the tomb where she said, "They have taken away my Lord, and I know not where they have laid him." And then later in the garden, "Jesus saith unto her, Woman, why weepest thou? whom seekest thou? She, supposing him to be the gardener, saith unto him, Sir, if thou have borne him hence, tell me where thou hast laid him, and I will take him away.

"Jesus saith unto her, Mary." I love that part. I can hear kindness and care in his voice. "She turned herself, and saith unto him, Rabboni; which is to say, Master" (John 20: 13, 15–16).

Joseph Smith was introduced to the Savior in the Sacred Grove. "This is My Beloved Son. Hear Him!" (Joseph Smith–History 1:17). Listen to him, said our Father in Heaven. Follow him. The magnitude of that moment is staggering. Our Father in Heaven visited this earth to introduce Jesus Christ to the world, to those who would listen. Think what that means. We focus keenly on Joseph Smith receiving that vision. But for what purpose? So that we, too, would listen and would know our Lord and Savior's voice.

His voice is often in scriptures. I use my scriptures, in part, as a journal of revelations to me. I write in the margin the date that a specific verse touched me or answered a longing to know. I will note a name or an experience so I can remember the context. Isaiah 43:2–3 has a host of dates by it: "When thou passest through the waters, I will be with thee; and through the rivers, they shall not overflow thee: when thou walkest through the fire, thou shalt not be burned; neither shall the flame kindle upon thee. For I am the Lord thy God, the Holy One of Israel, thy Saviour."

And this one: "Woe to them that go down to Egypt for help; and stay on horses and trust in chariots, because they are many; and in horsemen, because they are very strong; but they look not unto the Holy One of Israel, neither seek the Lord!" (Isaiah 31:1). There's no question what the Lord is saying: This is my beloved Son. Hear Him, not the choruses of the world. Listen to Jesus Christ. He will help us find peace and comfort. He will be our strength and our compass. Listening is an expression of our faith.

As I stood by the side of my son's grave in the cemetery, his tiny blue casket surrounded by flowers, I was aware of gathered family and friends, their sorrow so apparent. That day my husband and I were being asked to turn, to hearken, and most of all to believe. During the delivery, Christian had suffered from a brain hemorrhage, and tests had shown that the damage was severe. "He will never be able to run and walk like his twin brother may," the doctors had informed my husband at the hospital across town from mine where he held vigil over our newly born sons, "but we may be able to keep him alive." Jeff asked if there was somewhere he could go to be alone. They showed him to a small office. He was "out on the water." He knelt and poured out his feelings to his Father in Heaven. He spoke of our righteous hopes for a family and then he said, "But if Christian's work is done, we are ready to accept that." He walked out of the office and over to the isolette where Christian lay. The signal on the heart monitor flattened out. Christian had heard the voice as did Peter, "Come." Come all the way home.

Several days later in the cemetery, we heard the voice of the Lord in our hearts—a still, small voice spoke of peace and a promise found in John, "Peace I leave with you, my peace I give unto you: not as the world giveth, give I unto you. Let not your heart be troubled, neither let it be afraid" (John 14:27).

I bear testimony of this sixth and ultimate truth: Jesus Christ "the good shepherd giveth his life for the sheep" (John 10:11). He set forth his gospel; he took upon himself our sins. By him, through him, because of him and his atoning sacrifice, we may receive eternal life and exaltation. I believe with all my heart that my Redeemer lives. He is the Son of God, the Redeemer of the world, the Savior of all his Father's children. I have heard his voice and recognize his call to each one of us: Come. Come all the way home.

351

NOTES

1. Brigham Young, *Discourses of Brigham Young,* sel. John A. Widtsoe (Salt Lake City: Deseret Book, 1941), 431.
2. Young, *Discourses,* 41.
3. Joseph F. Smith, as quoted in Joseph Fielding Smith, *Origins of the Reorganized Church* (pamphlet), (Salt Lake City: Deseret News Press, 1909).
4. See *I Know That My Redeemer Lives* (Salt Lake City: Deseret Book, 1990), 203.
5. *Teachings of the Presidents of the Church: Brigham Young* (Salt Lake City: The Church of Jesus Christ of Latter-day Saints, 1997), 315.
6. *Teachings of Gordon B. Hinckley* (Salt Lake City: Deseret Book, 1997), 556.
7. Charles Dickens, *A Christmas Carol* (New York: Stewart, Tabori & Chang, 1990), 33–34.
8. Laleta Dickson's History of William James of the Willie Handcart Company, Archives of The Church of Jesus Christ of Latter-day Saints, 1856, n.p.; spelling and grammar standardized.

Gospel Doctrines:
Anchors to Our Souls

MARLIN K. JENSEN

Perhaps the schooling I have received at the hands of a strong and wonderful mother, an accomplished and caring wife, and six charming but opinionated daughters is my greatest qualification for participating in a women's conference. At the very least, I feel well briefed regarding women's issues! I must admit that their lives and love (and that of our two sons) are my greatest inspiration and, next to my relationship with God, my strongest motivation to do right.

My subject is something I feel strongly about and see great value in, but not something I necessarily exemplify. Many times in recent years I have been encouraged by President Spencer W. Kimball's wise observation that "we would not have much motivation to righteousness if all speakers and writers postponed discussing and warning until they themselves were perfected."[1]

DOCTRINE SHAPES BEHAVIOR

Although my formal training was not in the behavioral sciences, the gospel has caused me to spend a good deal of my time in this life trying to understand my own behavior and that of those around me. From the scriptures I have learned that gospel teachings, sometimes called doctrines, are powerful shapers of human behavior. President Boyd K. Packer stated the principle beautifully in a conference address: "True doctrine, understood, changes attitudes and behavior."[2]

Marlin K. Jensen has been a member of the First Quorum of the Seventy since April 1989. A former lawyer and farmer, Elder Jensen and his wife, Kathleen Bushnell Jensen, are the parents of eight children.

A good example of this truth is found early in the Old Testament in the story of Joseph, one of Jacob's twelve sons. You will no doubt remember how Joseph was sold into Egypt by his jealous brothers. He ended up being blessed by the Lord and becoming the prosperous overseer of the household and business affairs of Potiphar, an officer of Pharaoh.

In the midst of this good fortune, Joseph was confronted with a moral temptation in the person of Potiphar's wife. Finding herself alone with Joseph, Potiphar's wife cast her eyes upon him and said, "Lie with me."

Joseph's response to her provides a model for all who encounter moral temptation. The record simply says, "He refused."

Joseph then explained his refusal. "Behold," he said, "[Potiphar knoweth] not what is with me in the house, and he hath committed all that he hath to my hand; there is none greater in this house than I; neither hath he kept back any thing from me but thee, because thou art his wife: how then can I do this great wickedness, and sin against God?" (Genesis 39:8–9).

Joseph's rhetorical question not only speaks volumes about his sterling character but also helps explain why he had one. Can there be any doubt that Joseph had been taught the doctrine that God is our Father, that we are his children, and that he has created a plan for our lives? In this telling moment, as Joseph wisely exercised his agency, he obviously wasn't worried about the possibility of disease, unwanted pregnancy, or even incurring the wrath of disappointed parents. His thoughts and motives were much higher, much more noble—what would his Heavenly Father think? How could he possibly offend Him? The influence of doctrine on our behavior can likewise be great and eternally beneficial.

Perhaps that is why early in this dispensation the Lord said to the Saints, "And I give unto you a commandment that you shall teach one another the doctrine of the kingdom" (D&C 88:77). Since we can't teach what we haven't learned, an important implication of this commandment is that we all must acquire a basic knowledge of gospel doctrine.

LEARNING THE DOCTRINE

For many years Elder Bruce R. McConkie's book *Mormon Doctrine* has been a much-used reference work in our home. It is a comprehensive and valuable compendium of gospel teachings. More than thirty years ago, when Sister Jensen and I were in our first year of marriage, we attended an institute class taught by Elder McConkie at the University of Utah. I still have my class notes containing Elder McConkie's comments explaining how the book *Mormon Doctrine* came to be. He told of his love for the teachings of the scriptures and how, as a young college student, he would walk to and from the campus giving himself talks on various gospel topics. In time, he began to organize and write them down, and eventually he compiled the book, which has guided countless Saints in their study of gospel truths.

I have often thought that as helpful and remarkable as Elder McConkie's book is, there is one compilation of doctrine that for me is more important than his. That is my own personal book of Mormon doctrine—the one I have written in my own head and heart and in the margins of my scriptures, the one I can draw on in my moments of need and when I want to teach the doctrines of the kingdom to others. Elder McConkie's knowledge of saving truths will help save him; mine will help save me. I must pay the price to acquire such knowledge just as he did. So must you.

This principle was forcefully illustrated for me early in my experience as a Seventy when I served on a committee at Church headquarters with Elder Marion D. Hanks. The committee met weekly, and our meetings usually began with prayer and an invitation by Elder Hanks for committee members to share gospel insights we had acquired during the preceding week. Being new and unsure of myself, I was very quiet for the first few months. Then one week through my personal scripture study I gained an insight I felt was worthy of sharing. When Elder Hanks called for our participation that week, I ventured to share what I felt was a fairly impressive morsel of truth. To my surprise and chagrin, positive feedback from the other committee members was totally lacking. As I looked pleadingly at Elder Hanks, I asked, "Is what I have shared perhaps something you had already thought about?"

"Well, yes," said Elder Hanks, with a grin spreading over his face, "probably for the first time in about 1948!" Then, seeing my crestfallen countenance, he came with great charity to my rescue. "But that doesn't matter," he said. "*You* needed to think about it too!"

That is wisdom worth remembering. We all need individually to discover, think about, and store up gospel doctrines in our own way and in our own time. To do so, we may need to get up a littler earlier, stay up a little later, or consistently sneak a few precious moments for study during the day. Whatever price we have to pay, it will be worth the effort.

APPLYING THE DOCTRINE

When we learn and begin to internalize the doctrines of the gospel—in Jeremiah's words, to put them in our "inward parts, and write [them] in [our] hearts" (Jeremiah 31:33)—it will not be long before we and those around us begin to notice changes in our behavior.

A controlling parent who comes to understand the doctrine of agency will cease that control.

A selfish and self-centered spouse who is touched by the power of the doctrine of charity will no longer seek his or her own (see Moroni 7:45).

An honest investigator who comes to fully understand the doctrine and blessings of baptism, as taught by the missionaries, will not only accept their invitation to be baptized but will eagerly await performance of the ordinance.

All of us who truly come to comprehend the matchless doctrine of the Atonement will appreciate our enormous debt to the Savior and will seek diligently to repay that debt with offerings of repentance and Christian service.

As we personally study and apply the doctrines of the gospel in our lives, we will come to understand them in their relationship and necessary balance to each other. We will learn, for instance, that justice cannot be respected without a knowledge of the limitations of mercy; that agency operates best in a climate of unfeigned love; and that "repentance could not come unto men except there were a punishment" (Alma 42:16).

A determined effort to study gospel doctrine will also have the benefit of immersing us in the best source of that doctrine—the scriptures. As we study the "Good Books" consistently, we will eventually come to see a striking harmony in the doctrines of the gospel as they have been revealed through the ages to the prophets. We will come to know with certainty that the Spirit truly is "the same, yesterday, today, and forever" (2 Nephi 2:4).

TEACHING THE DOCTRINE

Perhaps the best measurement of how well we understand the doctrines of the gospel is how clearly and simply we can teach them. And teach them we must! "And again, inasmuch as parents have children in Zion, or in any of her stakes which are organized, that teach them not to understand the doctrine of repentance, faith in Christ the Son of the living God, and of baptism and the gift of the Holy Ghost by the laying on of hands, when eight years old, the sin be upon the heads of the parents" (D&C 68:25).

Can the sin spoken of in this passage, which will be upon the heads of the parents, be anything other than the failure to teach the saving doctrines of faith, repentance, baptism, and the gift of the Holy Ghost to our eight-year-olds? And if that omission is a sin, how about our failure to teach the law of chastity to our fourteen-year-olds? Or the doctrine of eternal marriage to our sixteen-year-olds? Or the plan of salvation to our friends and neighbors not yet of our faith?

Because we all love our families dearly, is there a better way tangibly to express that love than by teaching them the saving doctrines of the gospel? This certainly seems to be what Nephi says good parents do. "Having been born of goodly parents, therefore I was taught somewhat in all the learning of my father" (1 Nephi 1:1). Doctrinal teachings transferred by parents from one generation to the next have unusual longevity.

THE POWER OF DOCTRINE

The teaching of doctrine is accompanied by a special spirit and power that aren't usually present when the more mundane aspects of life are discussed. At the April 1991 general conference, Elder Carlos E. Asay talked about the Prophet Joseph Smith. For some reason his talk tugged at my heartstrings in an unusually forceful way. When I encountered Elder Asay a few days after conference and expressed my feelings about the power his words had seemed to carry, he taught me a valuable lesson: "Haven't you learned," he asked, "that there are certain gospel topics about which one can never give a poor talk?" (His question really caught my attention because I have managed to give quite a few substandard talks in my life!) He continued, "You can never give a poor talk about Joseph Smith."

I have come to know that what Elder Asay taught me about Joseph Smith is true of every doctrine of the gospel. When we teach doctrine, there will be an accompanying power and spirit that will carry our teachings deep into the hearts of those we teach and will also bring those teachings to their remembrance at appropriate and critical times.

Examples of this truth in scripture are numerous. I cite my favorite, which is young Alma's recounting of his conversion in Alma 36. He gives us a vivid description of the depth of his torment related to past transgressions and then says, "And it came to pass that as I was thus racked with torment, while I was harrowed up by the memory of my many sins, behold, I remembered also to have heard my father prophesy unto the people concerning the coming of one Jesus Christ, a Son of God, to atone for the sins of the world" (v. 17).

Whenever I read this passage and realize that in his moment of extreme need young Alma remembered his father's teachings concerning the Atonement, I wonder what, if anything, our children will remember of the doctrines Kathy and I have attempted to teach them. Wouldn't it be a wonderful thing to be remembered and quoted in this way by our children?

But the truly noteworthy element in Alma's story isn't just that he remembered his father's doctrinal teachings; it's the behavioral change that followed: "And from that time [meaning the time he remembered his father's teachings on the Atonement] even until now, I have labored without ceasing, that I might bring souls unto repentance; that I might bring them to taste of the exceeding joy of which I did taste; that they might also be born of God, and be filled with the Holy Ghost." (Alma 36:24.)

Alma's experience also illustrates the important fact that so much of the behavior we hope for in our own life and in the lives of others is related to our personal convictions and understanding regarding Christ's atonement.

A HOME TEACHING EXPERIENCE

I have recently had a very confirming experience of my own concerning the transforming power of doctrine. It involves a so-called less-active family I have home taught for many years. (By the way, I have long felt that there are two main weaknesses with both home and visiting teaching—the first is that we sometimes fail to go, and the second is that when we get there, we fail to teach.) In the case of this family, I had been going to their home quite regularly for many years and usually shared a "warm and fuzzy" message of some description but never really taught them the doctrines of the kingdom. All the while this good couple was working on the challenges of a second marriage for each of them and the resulting financial and family stresses such arrangements inevitably bring. They were good, honest people with no real background in the gospel and a social life that centered on a bowling league, western dancing, and the out-of-doors.

When Kathy and I returned home from a two-year mission in Rochester, New York, and I had gained a better understanding of what I am discussing now, I asked this family if my young companion and I could teach them the doctrines of the gospel. The reply of the wife still haunts me: "We always hoped you would do that," she said.

Because I was a recently returned mission president, I determined we would teach them the six basic missionary discussions. I'll never forget the first night we really taught them the doctrines of the kingdom. We had a brief prayer, and then I began with the first principle of the first missionary discussion, the one given perhaps thousands of times a day all over the world by the full-time missionaries. "You should know," I said, "that God is our Father; that we are His children; that He loves us, and because of that love has created a plan for our lives."

In that moment, as I for the first time taught that eager couple the doctrines of the kingdom, a spirit and power came into their home which in all my years of trying I had never been able to create. To make a very heartwarming story short, it wasn't long before this couple began coming to church—doctrine does change behavior! There they were directed to a terrific Gospel Essentials class and more doctrine, and exposed in sacrament meeting to even more gospel teachings. Two irrepressible sister missionaries were invited to teach them the six new-member discussions and more doctrine. A perceptive bishop extended a call to them to become our ward food storage coordinators. They accepted the call and became so enamored of our local cannery and the good people there that they agreed to serve a one-year welfare services mission, giving about twenty hours of service each week. They spoke recently of their mission in sacrament meeting and have a date scheduled on their anniversary to seal their marriage in the Salt Lake Temple. They are now attempting by precept and example to teach their children and grandchildren the doctrines of the kingdom. The husband, by the way, recently became one of our family's home teachers!

My message is plain and simple. An understanding of gospel doctrine changes behavior. Therefore, we must learn doctrine and teach it. If we do that, we will increasingly be found in our homes and elsewhere, as Nephi observed, talking of Christ, preaching of Christ, prophesying of Christ, and writing "according to our prophecies, that our children may know to what source they may look for a remission of their sins" (2 Nephi 25:26). That is the greatest favor we could ever do our families or anyone and the surest anchor to all our souls.

NOTES

1. Spencer W. Kimball, *The Miracle of Forgiveness* (Salt Lake City: Bookcraft, 1969), xii.
2. Boyd K. Packer, *Ensign*, November 1986, 17.

Index

223; in divorce, 278; and isolation, 331. *See also* Adversary

Satir, Virginia, 264

Saturday's Warriors, 79

Savings, 234

Savior, 280: relationship with, 48; witness of divinity of, 189; arms of the, 211, 231; and gospel principles, 281; road of the, 284

Schachter-Shalomi, Rabbi Zalman, 177

School with No Name, 153–54

Scriptures, 2, 350; study of the, 15, 20, 76, 168, 198, 207; and relationships, 46; and grace, 53–54; of the Restoration, 54; searching the, 66; appreciation for, 122; and the love of God, 129; as source of strength, 192; and choices, 224; reading, as families, 257; as a tool, 280

Second Coming, 333

Self-assurance, 55, 57

Self-confidence, 56

Self-control, 67, 224

Self-esteem, 191

Self-forgivenss, 282

Self-image, 278

Self-indulgence, 83

Selfishness, 83, 126, 221

Self-reliance, 56, 349

Service, 5–6, 24–25, 303, 356; to the Lord, 81; to Bosnia, 146–49; temple, 168, 329

Setting apart, 295

Sex, 268; affection and, 273

Sexuality, intimacy and, 273

Sharing, 226

Shelters, 163

Sills, Judith, 271

Sin, 83; results of, 4; of certainty, 49; forgiveness of, 54; confessing, 58; against God, 354

Sinatra, Stephen, 177

Sisterhood, 122

Slavery, 140

Smith, Amanda Barnes, 90

Smith, Bathsheba, 83, 102

Smith, David Hyrum, 90

Smith, Emma, 88–89, 309; and Relief Society, 89

Smith, Hyrum G., 18

Smith, Joseph, Jr., 322; on adversity, 27–28; on mercy, 36; on will of God, 60; on purpose of Relief Society, 74; and organization of Relief Society, 79, 94; and Eliza R. Snow, 88–90; and gift of Holy Ghost, 122; on spirit of Elijah, 133; First Vision of, 188, 350; and repentance, 309; on attributes of God, 310; on rebirth, 317; on Eve, 318; on thankfulness, 327; on fellowship, 328; on ancestors, 330; on hereafter, 336

Smith, Joseph F., 35, 64; on the immortal soul, 186; and salvation, 220; on Eliza R. Snow, 204; on revelation, 343

Smith, Joseph Fielding, 323

Smoot, Mary Ellen, 78

Snow, Amanda, 91

Snow, Celestia Armeda, 92

Snow, Eliza R., 79, 298, 304, 333–34, 336–37; on friendship, 87; importance to women of, 88; and Relief Society, 89; and Joseph Smith, 90; and emotions, 102–3; on will of God, 204

Snow, Erastus, 100

Snow, Leonora, 88

Snow, Lorenzo, 88, 97–98, 333

Snow, Rosetta, 91

Solace, 56

Solitary confinement, 127

Sorrow, 27, 176, 306–8

Speaking, public, 244

Spirit, Holy: following the, 23; gifts of the, 43; purification by the, 43; control of the, 56; promptings of the, 81, 144–45, 174, 299; killing the, 297–98; counseling with the, 303–4; whisperings of the, 320

Spiritual, the, 6–7

Stachowiak, James, 264

Standards, undefinable, 190

Stealing, 161

Steinem, Gloria, 346

Step-parents, 285–86

Stevens, Chris, 30–31